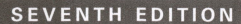

SEVENTH EDITION

D0713722

Instruction
A MODELS APPROACH

Thomas H. Estes
University of Virginia

Susan L. Mintz
University of Virginia

PEARSON

Boston   Columbus   Indianapolis   New York   San Francisco   Upper Saddle River
Amsterdam   Cape Town   Dubai   London   Madrid   Milan   Munich   Paris   Montréal   Toronto
Delhi   Mexico City   São Paulo   Sydney   Hong Kong   Seoul   Singapore   Taipei   Tokyo

Vice President, Editor in Chief: Jeff Johnston
Executive Editor: Meredith Fossel
Editorial Assistant: Maria Feliberty
Senior Marketing Manager: Chris Barry
Program Manager: Maren Beckman
Project Manager: Karen Mason
Project Coordination and Editorial Services: MPS North America LLC
Formatting and Production: Jouve North America
Manufacturing Buyer: Deidra Skahill
Cover Designer: Diane Ernsberger
Interior Design: MPS North America LLC

19 2022

ISBN 10: 0-13-398558-X
ISBN 13: 978-0-13-398558-0

Thomas H. Estes, professor emeritus of the Curry School of Education at the University of Virginia, is president of Dynamic Literacy, a company specializing in vocabulary development products based in Latin and Greek underpinnings of academic English. He received his PhD in reading education from Syracuse University. Dr. Estes taught in the McGuffey Reading Center of the Curry School of Education and in the Curriculum, Learning, and Teaching program for 31 years.

Susan L. Mintz, associate professor at the Curry School of Education at the University of Virginia, is the graduate program coordinator of Curriculum and Instruction. She received her PhD in teacher education from Syracuse University. Dr. Mintz teaches classes in curriculum theory, design, and pedagogy. She is an author of the CLASS-S observation manual, developed at the University of Virginia's Center for the Advanced Study of Teaching and Learning.

Contents

5   The Concept Development Model   78

PART THREE   TEACHING WITH ADVANCED INSTRUCTIONAL MODELS   135

8   The Integrative Model   137

11 | Inquiry Models   205

Teachers today are under pressure from all sides. Everyone, it seems, is an expert on teaching and on what to teach. Advice, mandates, and legislation speak with authority, telling teachers what to do in classrooms. In a sense, everyone *is* an expert on teaching. After all, didn't everyone go to school for many years and leave with the full knowledge of how school should have been? What has changed is that the cacophony of voices has become louder and more distracting to individual teachers.

Over the last several years, schools have changed. The student population is more diverse, the curriculum is more standardized, there is increased emphasis on teacher and school accountability, and the importance of prior knowledge and experience in learning is more apparent. In addition, budgets at the local and state level are tight and resources are thin. This seventh edition has responded to these changes by providing the newest research on student learning, access to linked video and Web resources for each model, and easier access to specific knowledge for teaching with instructional models through the identification of basic and advanced models and a glossary. Since the first edition of this text, many experienced teachers and teachers in training have found it to be useful. In fact, many teachers have told us that this book has become part of their permanent professional collections. We have reorganized the text to provide targeted support for novice and experienced teachers by organizing the models into basic and advanced sections. Readers can determine their own needs and chart their own progress as they master the specific models that are described in the text. Whenever possible, we have incorporated into this edition the excellent ideas and valuable corrections we have received from classroom teachers who use the models daily. These changes and those detailed in the New to This Edition list allow more opportunities to construct new concepts and principles of instruction.

New to This Edition

The seventh edition includes a number of noteworthy changes:

- Infusion of recent literature on student learning and teacher behaviors
- Implementation charts detailing teacher behaviors and student responses
- Linked videos* and Web resources with all presented instructional models
- A new elementary case study that demonstrates the use of instructional models in a mathematics teaching unit
- Detailed explanation of the connections between instructional strategies and instructional models
- Correlations to the Common Core State Standards
- Addition of the 5E Learning Cycle approach to Chapter Twelve's coverage of the problem-based inquiry model
- Updated references throughout the text and a comprehensive list of references at the end of the text representing the most relevant new literature and research
- A major revision of the Chapter Two information on planning for instruction
- A stronger focus on moving from standards to classroom objectives, and directions for how to accomplish this
- Invigorate learning with the Enhanced Pearson eText

- The Enhanced Pearson eText provides a rich, interactive learning environment designed to improve student mastery of content with embedded videos. The Enhanced Pearson eText is also available without a print version of the textbook.

- Instructors, visit pearsonhighered.com/etextbooks to register for your digital examination copy.

*Video clips are accessible in the Enhanced Pearson eText only, and not other third-party eTexts such as CourseSmart and Kindle.

Instruction

There is a sense in which everyone is a teacher. The root meaning of the word *teach* is "to show, to tell, to point out." Everyone teaches others, and so everyone is a teacher, at least in the amateur sense. This doesn't mean that everyone can be an *effective* teacher, however. If we look at the word *teach* in its professional sense, in relation to the word *instruction,* a more complex picture emerges. The meaning of the word *instruct* derives from "to build" or "to structure." Professional teachers not only *teach* in the usual sense of the word, they also instruct. They *structure* classroom environments and *build* experiences for a diverse group of students. Whereas parents, doctors, and others usually teach spontaneously by telling, pointing out, or showing, professional educators must carefully design and plan for their teaching. In fact, in our opinion, you are not teaching unless your instruction is helping students learn. There is a natural analogy between instruction and building based on the process of structuring environments. The teacher, as an instructor, is comparable to the builder in three ways:

1. *Planning for a specific audience.* Both builders and teachers must first figure out the needs of their clients or students. The house required for a single person with a large collection of automobiles should be different from that of a family of six with four dogs, three cats, two hamsters, and a rabbit. Similarly, the instructional design for a freshman conceptual physics class will be different from the design of the AP physics class. The background knowledge of the students and the challenge of the content require different approaches. Both the builder and the teacher must consider their clients, and they need to know how to formulate a plan that will be sound, original, and functional.

A good design for teaching grows out of a clear understanding of the needs of learners and the goals of education. Each design that a professional teacher creates is unique because different groups of learners have individual needs, and different types of learning require specific instructional approaches.

2. *Formulating objectives and evaluation procedures.* Both the builder and the teacher specify the intended outcome of their work as clearly as possible. No builder would think of starting a construction project without having a clear picture of how the final product should look. To get halfway through the project only to realize that what was emerging was not what the client wanted or needed would be professionally embarrassing and costly. The teacher who works without a careful design also leaves too much to chance, not providing appropriate supports that help students learn. As a professional, the teacher must plan how to achieve specific, intended learning outcomes. Otherwise, valuable instructional time can go to waste, and students will not have the appropriate experiences for success on the assessments for which they are accountable.

An essential part of setting objectives is determining effective assessment procedures to make certain that what was intended is taking place. Like the builder who must constantly check on the construction, the teacher must determine whether students are reaching the intended results. It would be foolish to wait until a building has been completed to check on the quality of the work and to determine whether all is proceeding as planned. Likewise, a teacher must use effective formative and summative assessment procedures throughout the teaching process.

Evaluation is continual, forming the basis of all decisions at every step: determining needs, formulating objectives, designing aligned assessments and instructional methods, and selecting materials. Evaluation is the process of continually asking questions: Where are we going? How do we get there? How far along are we? The teacher must continually collect information from students to determine whether the instruction is appropriate and effective. Thus, evaluation showing the intermediate and ultimate effects of instruction (formative and summative assessment) must be used to reform the process of teaching. Continual evaluation makes this possible.

3. *Selecting materials and procedures.* The builder has available a variety of materials and techniques from which to choose and must decide which combination will produce the structure most nearly like the one intended. Each project must be analyzed to determine the appropriate combinations; for instance, not every house is built only of wood or brick. Likewise, each student is an individual with his or her own needs, strengths, and interests. Moreover, each class is unique in terms of the dynamics of a particular group. Therefore, the teacher needs to have at hand a variety of approaches and techniques to accomplish specific instructional objectives and to manage problems as they arise. Unfortunately, there are classrooms in which there is no instructional variety, leading to monotony and boredom. The teacher who uses the same instructional technique is like the builder who will build only one type of house. The builder may become expert at building that house, but the house will not meet the needs of a wide variety of clients. A repertoire of instructional and management strategies is necessary to meet the varied needs of learners.

A Models Approach

We believe that the process of instruction unites all teachers as professional educators. Our intended audience includes teachers of any subject who teach or plan to teach learners of any age. Teaching is challenging and complex. Models of instruction can help teachers deal with the demanding environment of the classroom.

This text is not a rule or recipe book but an invitation to consider the opportunities for professional educators as instructional decisions are made. Progress toward mastery teaching is a continuous process of learning and adapting, modifying, and changing. With each group of students, teachers must make different instructional decisions, solve different problems, and meet different needs. We offer information that will help teachers make more appropriate and effective choices as they plan and implement instruction.

We have divided this text into four parts. Part One, Planning for Instruction, describes the process of integrating standards into written objectives, assessment, and instruction. A teacher must first decide what is to be learned in the classroom before considering how to present the material through the instruction. A thorough discussion of moving from standards to focused objectives is presented in this section. Once objectives are identified and aligned, a variety of instructional models can be considered.

Part Two, Basic Instructional Models, presents a selected group of what we have termed basic instructional models along with illustrations of how they can be used in the design process. These basic instructional models are aligned with the types of objectives and assessments that are frequently used in classrooms and are supported by a preponderance of evidence as to their effectiveness. Direct instruction, concept attainment, concept development, cause and effect, and vocabulary acquisition meet a variety of content and skill needs in all classrooms and provide basic instructional skills to teachers on which they can build and integrate a number of instructional patterns.

Part Three, Teaching with Advanced Instructional Models, extends the models approach. These models (the integrative model, Socratic seminar, cooperative learning, inquiry, and synectics) provide a structure for student learning and help teachers meet many content and skill goals, but they also require a more sophisticated understanding of classroom processes. When implemented, these models make a larger ripple in the classroom—there are more ramifications and possible difficulties involved, so their use requires more practice and attention.

Part Four, Putting It All Together, contains four chapters. Three are case studies that describe how teachers match objectives, assessments, and instruction in the design process and use a variety of models in service of an instructional unit. Part Four concludes with a chapter that suggests ways of creating a positive environment for learning in the classroom.

The content of this text reflects a process of learning by doing. Thus, ample opportunity must be provided for practice and feedback, ideally including peers reviewing videos of practice sequences. No one can learn these models simply from reading about them or memorizing the steps, just as no one can learn to drive a car simply by reading an owner's manual.

We have each had the opportunity to interact with both preservice teachers and experienced teachers who are discovering the possibilities of growing professionally through the use of instructional models. We have seen how the models approach provides tools for professional decisions about instruction that can be shared among professional instructors through a common body of knowledge.

Retained Features

The following features of previous editions are retained:

- A comprehensive approach to organizing content and skills and developing aligned instruction in planning
- Specific instruction in developing classroom objectives from state standards
- In-depth discussion of the steps and benefits of more than 10 different instructional models
- Attention to how the models can be used to meet individual needs
- Suggestions as to how models can be used to assess student learning
- Associated instructional strategies that can be used within and across different instructional models

Acknowledgments

We wish to thank the many students and teachers who have shared their experiences of instructional models with us to help us understand the challenges and opportunities involved in teaching with instructional models. The current and past graduate students in the University of Virginia Teacher Education program and the Curriculum and Instruction program have been particularly helpful.

Thanks also go to the reviewers who provided guidance for this new edition, including Dr. Marjorie S. Anderson, Cumberland University; Dr. Penny Finley, Florida Gulf Coast University; and Angelia Reid-Griffin, UNC Wilmington.

We wish once again to acknowledge that the manuscript of this edition would not have been completed without the help of Dr. Julie Estes; her knowledge, skills, and good humor have been invaluable.

PART ONE

Planning for Instruction

An old farmer was asked how his family happened to settle in a remote section of Arkansas. He replied, "Well, we were heading for California when Pap took a wrong turn at the Mississippi River."

Pity these travelers, crossing a continent with no map and only a vague notion of their destination. Likewise, many students and teachers traveling across unfamiliar intellectual terrain experience wrong turns in the classroom. Too often, students and teachers work without a map in the form of specific plans and without clearly defined objectives for their travels. At the end of a poorly planned lesson or unit, students are often let down, not having the support to reach the teacher's intended destination. In the classroom, careful planning is essential if students are to enjoy a successful journey toward knowledge and understanding.

The planning process we describe in the following chapters will guide both teacher and student behavior in ways that will provide students the opportunity to succeed in the classroom. Aligning objectives, assessments, and instruction gives students the chance to process new information and skills and relate them to prior knowledge. Aligned instruction also allows teachers to plan a variety of instructional and assessment opportunities. Although there is no exact formula or recipe for good instruction, it is known that good instruction depends on good planning.

Based on what is known about student learning, we recommend the following approach to instructional planning:

1. Study state and national standards.
2. Collect and reflect on individual and collective needs of students.
3. Define and state objectives in the form of what you want students to understand, know, and be able to do.
4. Construct assessments that allow students to demonstrate that they have reached the stated objectives and will be able to perform important transfer tasks at the end of the unit.
5. Create lessons and units that support students as they learn the necessary knowledge and skills to be successful on the assessments.
6. Use a variety of instructional models in lessons to meet a variety of learner needs.

These steps are discussed thoroughly in the next two chapters. We examine broad educational goals; the organization of instruction; and how to align objectives, assessment, and instruction in planning. Planning for instruction is a continual process, and the steps of planning overlap—based on the experience and background knowledge of the teacher and the needs and prior learning of the student. Some procedures for instructional design that can help in this process are covered in Part One. It is each reader's responsibility to determine the ways in which he or she will implement these procedures. What is not optional is the incorporation of a serious planning process into every teacher's approach to instruction.

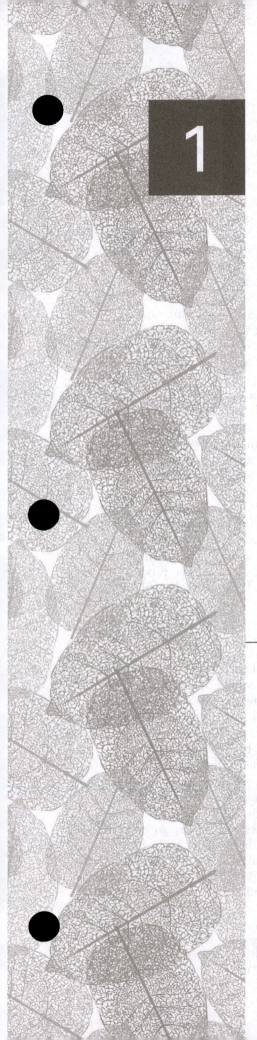

1

Standards and Content in Schools

Chapter Objectives

You Will Know

- The importance of planning
- How learning happens
- Student characteristics that affect learning
- The relationship between standards and academic content
- How to analyze content
- How to order content
- The elements of instructional planning

You Will Understand That

- Standards are the basis of instructional decisions that result in student learning
- Planning increases the likelihood of student learning

You Will Be Able To

- Explain the role of standards in determining school content
- Describe what we know about how learners learn
- Discuss the relationship between unit and lesson planning and the need for instructional alignment

Teaching is challenging and difficult. Learners come into classrooms with unique knowledge and experiences, interests, and learning preferences, making each classroom diverse and increasing the difficulties and complexities of determining appropriate decisions in planning for student learning. All students deserve the opportunity to learn and be successful in school. This chapter will provide information that will serve as the foundation for designing good instruction in your classroom.

Josh Anderson, the 2011 Chief State School Officers Teacher of the Year, shares his views regarding the challenges of teaching, his reasons for being a teacher, and his vision for schools. This is an inspiring video, not to be missed.

The Importance of Planning

We begin with the story of Anna, a girl in her sophomore year of high school. This young woman's parents were concerned about her academic achievement. Life at home was marked by dinnertime discussions of wide-ranging topics, though Anna did not participate much in those conversations. She had little interest in current

events or anything that was even vaguely academic. This left Anna feeling like an outsider in her own family. She made up for this by having more friends than she could count, a fact that kept her in school for the sake of close personal associations. This is not uncommon. "Liking for school is aligned with social and emotional factors such as personality and social factors such as the number of friends the individual student has at the specific location" (Hattie & Yates, 2014, p. 4). School can be important to students beyond academics. Anna was strong in what Gardner termed "interpersonal intelligence" (Gardner, 2006). But where does this quality fit in the curriculum of school? How could a teacher capitalize on this capacity in teaching Anna anything? This is a question worth thinking about.

Seeking the help of the high school guidance counselor, Anna's parents visited the school. They discussed Anna's constant need to use her smart phone and how much time she spent fixing her hair. They wondered how these skills would help her be successful. The counselor's response came as a surprise to the parents. For one thing, the counselor told them they were probably underestimating the skills that Anna possessed. She could be a beautician if she wished, but, if that were her choice, she would probably own the shop where she worked and would run a thriving business!

A few years later, after graduating from college with no particular aim in sight, Anna applied for a job in a large mortgage company. This job, in mortgage origination—a type of job Anna had never heard of—required talking to strangers about how they could save money on their house payments by refinancing at a lower interest rate. It also required a great deal of study and test taking to obtain licensure, but neither problem proved the slightest barrier. Anna worked hard at her job, studied, and passed every test. A few years later, she decided that she could do this mortgage origination thing on her own rather than work for someone else. The process was simple in her mind: All she had to do was identify potential customers through public records, fill out some paperwork, and make "new friends" with the real promise of saving them a lot of money. Two years later, she ran her own mortgage brokerage business. She was qualified at the highest levels and suddenly making a lot of money doing something she loved to do.

So how did a mediocre student become such a great success? Here is one possibility we might want to pay attention to: Instruction in school often tends to focus narrowly on knowledge transmission—on teaching content without apparent purpose. Thus, too often the reason to learn is opaque to the learner, resulting in isolated knowledge and superficial understanding and very little transfer outside of school—the true purpose of schooling. When the reason to learn became clear to Anna, her study and instruction resulted in contextualized knowledge and deeper understanding. When Anna and countless others like her cannot see the point of learning what teachers are attempting to teach, learning is *not* visible but exists only in the abstract. Students are unlikely to engage in the work required of them if they see no reason to learn, and they often have little confidence they *can* learn even if they try. By contrast, when students and their teachers visualize and discuss the point of what they are asked to learn and they are engaged in thinking together about the possible effects or consequences of what occurs in school, the outcomes are likely to be much more positive (Hattie, 2012). When Anna finally got to the time and place in her life in which she could see the point of what she was required to learn, her learning problems disappeared. This may not be the answer for all students, but for many of our disengaged and struggling students, showing them the reasons for learning will be helpful. And for many others, there are several concrete and empirically supported strategies that will result in greater school success (Hattie & Yates, 2014).

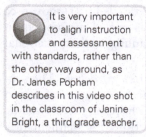

It is very important to align instruction and assessment with standards, rather than the other way around, as Dr. James Popham describes in this video shot in the classroom of Janine Bright, a third grade teacher.

The planning process we describe will guide both teacher and student behavior in ways that provide students the opportunity to succeed in the classroom. When teachers and students collaborate continuously to align objectives, assessments, and instruction, students have many chances to process new information and skills and relate them to prior knowledge and future goals. Aligned instruction also allows teachers to plan a variety of instructional and assessment opportunities. Although there is no exact formula or recipe for good instruction, we do know that good instruction depends on good planning to ensure that learning is relevant and visible to students. It is unlikely that students will be successful in school without visible learning—understanding why they are learning, how it relates to what they know, and how it may be useful.

To ground our discussion in the larger picture of education in our society, this introductory chapter examines broad educational goals; the need for quality education for students from all income levels; the organization of instruction; and the alignment of objectives, assessment, and instruction in planning. Planning for instruction is a continual process, and the steps of planning overlap. It is each reader's responsibility to determine the ways in which he or she will implement these procedures. What is not optional is the incorporation of a serious planning process related to instruction aimed at ensuring students' learning. Keep in mind that you are likely to have many students like Anna in your classes. You will also have students who come to school with large gaps in knowledge, physical ailments, and hunger. Many will come from homes where English is not spoken and money is tight. All students' intelligences, skills, interests, and needs will determine their learning. The key to success is to keep students engaged in the process of learning and committed to its outcome; this cannot be done without careful, intentional, and skillful planning.

How Learning Happens

Much is known about how people learn and how the brain works to organize experiences. All teachers must understand these processes in order to design effective instruction. The following points summarize a few of the principles of how people learn.

1. *Learning changes the structure of intelligence.* Academic achievement at any level of schooling by learners at any level of verbal and quantitative ability will have the effect of improving thinking. But abilities of learners are not limited to the verbal and quantitative. Neuroscientists have yet to untangle all the intricacies of how we learn and what teachers can do to enhance classroom learning. We do know, however, that we are all capable of learning and that when we learn, our brains change. Because the brain's structure changes with new knowledge, we should be able to enhance academic outcomes for all students by providing them with opportunities for learning (Wilson & Conyers, 2013). Many of our students are living difficult lives. Tough (2012) has identified several qualities that make a difference in school *and* in life. These include persistence, self-control, curiosity, conscientiousness, grit, and self-confidence. Anna has demonstrated these character traits throughout her training and career, as have many successful people. Interestingly, it is believed that these non-cognitive skills can be taught explicitly.

2. *The brains of learners are continually being organized and reorganized.* Learning improves thinking so as to make future learning all the easier. How does this happen? Primarily, it is because changes occur in patterns of cognition as new understandings are woven into the fabric of prior knowledge. David Ausubel said this most clearly and directly (Ausubel, Novak, & Hanesian, 1968, p. 168): "If we had to reduce all of educational psychology to just one principle, we would say this: The most important single factor influencing new learning is what the learner already knows. Ascertain this and teach him accordingly." Teachers need to be skilled in helping students gain

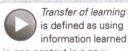

This amazing video looks at how synapses and neural pathways are the basis of learning by comparing synapse connections to crossing a ravine. www.youtube.com/watch?v=BEwg8TeipfQ

access to new information that is logically linked to prior knowledge (Donovan & Bransford, 2005). Helping students make this connection is one of the most difficult professional tasks of teachers, but with appropriate planning and instructional options, knowledge gaps can be diminished.

3. *The typical pattern of brain development is one of starts and delays.* The synapses of the brain work at processing information from a variety of experiences, and synaptic connections develop at diverse rates. A student may have very rich synaptic connections for literature and more impoverished connections for mathematics. Teaching must reflect that there is not one growth rate for all parts of students' brains and abilities. One facet will inevitably be more developed than another. The result is that a child may be good at one part of the curriculum while struggling with a different discipline, at least for a time, until the weaker "muscles" of learning can be exercised to become stronger. Thus, teachers may need to scaffold learning more for some content and learners than for others.

4. *Memory has different functions.* Sensory memory is temporary and sends information to working memory. Sensory memory may be fleeting and unconscious; working memory requires constant attention. Learners process information in working memory. If that processing includes repetition, details, application, and elaboration, the information is more likely to move into permanent memory. Teachers must keep in mind that students need repetition of skills and information and that knowledge and skills must be detailed and related to other, more familiar skills and information (Willingham, 2009).

5. *Learning must be transferred beyond the narrow contexts of initial learning if it is to be useful.* The purpose of school is to help learners use the knowledge that they acquire in the real world (Bransford, Brown, & Cocking, 2000). Learners often perform well in the context of instruction but fail to evidence this knowledge in practice outside of a particular classroom or in the real world. Other learners may come to understand what they are learning only when they see it in practice. To guard against such disparities, teaching must be explicit, skills must be practiced, the use of the skills must be determined, and understandings must be applied. Most importantly, students must see what it is to be skilled and must be conversant in new knowledge across multiple contexts. Transfer of new learning must occur at a deep level of knowledge—beyond recall. Teachers need to help students see the way new knowledge and skills can be used to solve problems similar to those practiced in the instructional context. What finds no application is soon forgotten by learners (Marzano, 2003). This knowledge of "how to do" will be revisited in Chapter Two. It is the linchpin of knowledge. The importance of applying knowledge—particularly procedural knowledge—cannot be overstated.

Transfer of learning is defined as using information learned in one context in a new context. This video emphasizes the importance of bridging academic content with everyday life. www.youtube.com/watch?v=GAscBEDDiXg

6. *Conceptual knowledge is based on facts and helps learners transfer information and skills.* To become a competent learner in any discipline, students must have a deep foundation of information, which is then organized into concepts and generalizations. They must understand the conceptual framework in which facts and examples fit and be able to organize this information so that it can be retrieved when applicable (Willingham, 2009). Individual facts will likely be lost, but generalizations will have more staying power. At least a basic threshold of knowledge must be achieved to support transfer. It takes time and practice to understand complex subject matter, and a satisfactory level of understanding basic elements is essential for successful transfer of information and skills (Bransford et al., 2000).

7. *Students who monitor their own learning are more successful in academic environments.* Learning is enhanced by *metacognition*—a big word describing the act of thinking about thinking and about oneself as information processor and learner. Metacognitive strategies help students become responsible for their own learning and help them learn beyond recall. Metacognitive strategies (using mnemonics,

In this video, a distinction is made between instructional and learning strategies. Metacognitive strategies are classified as learning strategies, and specific examples are provided.

summarizing, etc.) are learned and can be explicitly taught in classrooms. To be metacognitive, students need to know the goals toward which they are working, and they must receive feedback on how they are progressing toward these goals. This feedback most often stems from diagnostic evaluation and formative evaluation. Formative evaluation should be woven into the process of teaching. Formative assessments are designed to monitor instruction so that students and the teacher receive feedback on how the lesson is going and on whether students are moving toward the lesson's objectives. These assessments help students identify their strengths and weaknesses and target areas that need work, and they help teachers recognize where students are struggling and address problems immediately. With formative information, students can become aware of which behaviors lead to success and which are not as effective for them.

8. *Learning is enhanced by challenge and inhibited by threat.* Although challenge is always accompanied by risk to one's self-esteem or success, the learner will thrive in what Caine and Caine (1994) call "relaxed alertness." Students should perceive no risk in what they are asked to learn. Errors are natural in the early stages of learning, and learners need to feel comfortable about making mistakes. Hattie summarizes this idea cogently:

> Expert teachers create classroom climates that welcome admission of errors; they achieve this by developing a climate of trust between teacher and student, and between student and student. The climate is one in which "learning is cool" and worth engaging in, and everyone—teacher and students—is involved in the process of learning. It is a climate in which it is okay to acknowledge that the process of learning is rarely linear, requires commitment and investment of effort, and has many ups and downs in knowing, not knowing, and in building confidence that we can know. It is a climate in which error is welcomed, in which student questioning is high, in which engagement is the norm, and in which students can gain reputations as effective learners. (Hattie, 2012, p. 26)

9. *Each brain is unique.* Though virtually all children are born with the capacity to learn, the experiences they encounter actually shape and alter their brains as learning occurs (Bransford et al., 2000). "The single most powerful statement to come out of brain research in the last twenty-five years is this: We are as different from one another on the inside of our heads as we appear to be from one another on the outside of our heads" (Fulghum, 1989, p. 39). Teachers need to be completely open to infinite possibilities in learners; that is to say, they should expect that there will be great diversity in understandings of what they teach. There is reason to doubt the notion that everyone will have the same answer or that there is only one answer worth having. Teaching and learning activities should be varied, and learners should have multiple opportunities to learn whatever they are taught. The models in Part Two will provide many teaching options to accomplish these goals.

Taken together, these principles reaffirm that there is no one best way to teach, but there are principles of learning that good teaching must adhere to. The most important thing we know about learning is that teachers must use professional knowledge and adapt instruction to the needs of learners.

Student Characteristics That Affect Learning

In every classroom there are children with a variety of needs, including students with physical, mental, and emotional challenges; English language learners; students living in poverty; and gifted students. Some of these needs may shift and change daily. Teachers must respond to each of these students in a respectful and knowledgeable way, one that provides every child the opportunity for success. Our aim in this text is

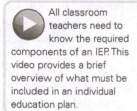

All classroom teachers need to know the required components of an IEP. This video provides a brief overview of what must be included in an individual education plan.

This video offers an introduction to the philosophy of Nel Noddings, who has written a great deal about the ethics of care both in and outside of school.
www.youtube.com/watch?v=sVIZ_mt9l3g

to provide an assortment of general instructional models for classroom use, each of which can help to accommodate learners with special characteristics.

Because classrooms include students with a variety of special challenges, you may work with a collaborative teacher in your classroom. Each identified special education student will have an individual education plan (IEP) that will help inform classroom decisions.

In addition, we are a diverse nation, and the population of English language learners (ELLs) is growing—in rural, suburban, and urban areas. Although English is the predominant language in America, Spanish is spoken by over 12 percent of the population (Gonzalez-Barrera & Hugo, 2013). This percentage varies greatly depending on the area of the country. English language learners can come from a wide range of ethnic backgrounds and many different background experiences. In all cases, however, schools and classroom teachers are responsible for teaching academic content and language skills alike.

All instruction is improved when there are respectful and caring relationships between students and teachers; when goals and directions are clear; when a variety of instructional strategies and models are used; and when teachers use students' prior experiences, culture, and, in the case of ELL students, language as a basis for presenting new knowledge and skills. Teachers of English language learners need to speak clearly, give attention to key vocabulary, scaffold through chunking and unpacking dense text, and be aware of the students' cultural heritage.

Poverty can also affect instruction. Poor children often have fewer positive academic experiences and thus arrive at school with a diminished set of references they can link with new knowledge. The more we learn, the greater our capacity is to learn, so it is important to enhance the experiences of children from poverty. Poor neighborhoods are often chaotic and unsafe, so children arrive at school fearful, which can make learning more difficult. Poor children may also lack sufficient food and health care, increasing the risk of school difficulties. A cooperative and safe classroom community in which good instruction is common can help children who are stressed by a lack of basic resources.

In addition, boys and girls of the same age have different patterns of development. In a sixth grade classroom, most males still look like little boys, while about half of the females look like young women. In their early teens, girls are usually taller, stronger, and more verbal than boys. As teachers set goals for teaching and learning, they need to be conscious of the many ways in which children differ from one another.

Standards and Academic Content

Standards have become a large part of the educational experience in the United States. All teachers must learn to use the standards to design instruction that meets the needs of diverse learners. Most states have accepted the Common Core State Standards (CCSS) and have developed (or are developing) aligned curriculum frameworks. New assessments that are aligned with the CCSS are in the process of being created as we write this text. It is important that you be familiar with either your

┌─ **WEB RESOURCE** ──────────────────────────────

Common Core

Explore the Common Core State Initiative website at corestandards.org and learn more about the Common Core initiative and the standards that are being used in several states.

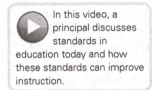

In this video, a principal discusses standards in education today and how these standards can improve instruction.

state's standards or the CCSS. As you read through those standards, ask yourself the following questions:

1. What would the behavior of a student who had accomplished this standard look like?
2. What are the specific activities and behaviors one might engage in to practice the standard?
3. What specific information and skills does each standard imply?
4. What are the skills and knowledge that should precede this standard?
5. What are the skills and knowledge that will come after students meet this standard?

Standards provide the basis for the instructional decisions you will make in your classroom. To begin unpacking standards for your own use, look carefully at the verbs that describe the standards of learning for each content area you are teaching. You will probably not see many verbs like *remember* or *recall*. On the contrary, you are very likely to see verbs such as *clarify, explain, use knowledge, question, describe, distinguish, evaluate,* and *compare and contrast.* The tests, especially the new assessments aligned with the CCSS, may include questions such as these: "What would happen if . . . ?" "What factors were most important?" "Which statement is best supported by the information given?"

To ensure students are not surprised by being asked to utilize this thinking, the instruction they receive needs to emphasize the same kind of reasoning. If your state's department of education provides sample tests or released test items, examine them carefully to see exactly what a student might need to know or be able to do in order to perform well on the test items. Think of these test items as discrete tasks, each of which can be practiced and mastered. Compare these items with the curriculum guides provided by your school district. With sufficient practice and eventual mastery of the knowledge required by the test, students can perform well on the tests precisely because they do understand what is being asked of them. That will require they be taught in the same way they are to be tested. This is not an appeal to teach to the tests. It is an appeal to teach what you know will be tested. This is referred to as "instructional design with the end in mind." Of course, the tests are only one end. Your district and school will have additional goals that will guide your planning and instruction.

Grant Wiggins, president of Grant Wiggins and Associates, offers a succinct description of "backward design" in this brief video.

Analyzing Content

The connections between standards and instructional design may not always be apparent, but classroom instruction must be aligned with the state's standards, district curriculum, and associated high-stakes tests in order to provide students the opportunity to be successful. This does not imply that instructional decisions should be geared toward drilling students on anticipated content of the test. Each of the instructional models in this text is designed to help students build connections between what they know and what they are learning. Think of understandings as a complex network of concepts that instruction continuously builds on and reinforces. For example, young children can develop an understanding of city, state, and national governments and the responsibilities of community members by looking at the parallels in how their classroom and their school are organized; but they need the opportunity to reflect on their own role, their classroom, and their school before they can make the connections regarding these concepts. Always start with the known and most obvious, and then move incrementally to the new.

Willingham (2009) makes the case that factual knowledge precedes skill (also known as *procedural knowledge*) and is required for reading and memory has to support the development of skills. However, having students memorize lists of unrelated facts in hopes of passing a high-stakes test is not a reasonable strategy. Unrelated facts are difficult to remember. Facts that are woven together into a rich, meaningful conceptual network of generalizations (statements of relationships) and principles will increase student performance. For example, knowing the names of the elements of the periodic table alone will not help in developing a deep understanding of the ways chemicals behave or the logic of the periodic table. It is the relationship of the elements that allows for deep understanding. Knowledge of the famous table is built on knowing the characteristics of the elements, pictured as "periods" and "groups" in the table's rows and columns. All of the instructional models in this text support the development of generalizations in all disciplines and with students at all grade levels. How content should be analyzed will be discussed in greater detail in the next chapter.

Ordering Content

▶ Prior knowledge is often the key to comprehension. In this video, you see a fourth grade teacher, Debra Jongebloed, coach her students in using what they already know to infer the likely meaning of a word with which they are not familiar.

As we have mentioned previously, educators owe a great debt to David Ausubel, a founder of cognitive psychology. Modern ideas about ordering and presenting content are based on his work. Ausubel's approach is rooted in two fundamental principles of the psychology of learning: (1) the single most important factor influencing new learning is what the learner already knows, and (2) any concept is explainable at many different levels of generality, with the highest or most general level most easily understood and the lowest or most specialized level the most difficult (Ausubel, 1968). These principles have had a major impact on both curriculum development and instructional practice (Marzano, 2001; Wiggins & McTighe, 2005) and must be guideposts in our instructional planning.

▶ Donna Ogle, professor of reading at National Louis University, first conceived and named the KWL strategy. Watch this video to meet her and hear her describe the strategy.

Prior learning is the foundation for all instruction. Every child comes to school with knowledge and experiences that must be acknowledged and respected as new understandings, information, and skills are taught. All teachers must develop procedures for identifying and using the knowledge that students bring with them to the classroom. Sometimes prior knowledge is academic content; other times teachers need to make purposeful connections to the cultural knowledge with which students are intimately familiar. If a student lacks academic knowledge of a concept, that does not mean he or she has no prior knowledge on which to base new learning. Students can be helped to organize their thinking about a topic or reading through the KWL strategy, as described in the Strategy Alert.

The implication of Ausubel's second principle is that *any stage of learning and understanding builds on previous, more general levels.* It is useful to think of teaching in terms of what has been called the "given-new" strategy of successful communication (Haviland & Clark, 1974): In speaking or writing, people must assume that the

STRATEGY ALERT   KWL

KWL, designed as a reading comprehension strategy (Ogle, 1986), can be used with a particular reading or as a strategy to engage students at the beginning of a unit of instruction. Students are asked what they know about the topic or skill (K), what they want to learn about the topic or skill (W), and, at the end of the instructional episode, what they learned about the topic or skill (L). The content may be narrow or broad— a short text excerpt or an entire text. The process may be done individually, in small groups, or in a whole class setting. The power of the strategy lies in its elasticity. The KWL strategy is student centered because it encourages engagement and metacognition; students develop a purpose for instruction and a way to monitor instruction. Teachers have information to use in their instructional decision making. The strategy is flexible. It can be extended to additional columns and can be shared in small groups or with the whole class.

listener or reader is aware of certain information (the "given") and that what he or she is communicating (the "new") is logically attachable to what is already known. The logic of this strategy applies equally well to teaching and learning. Successful teaching of anything depends on the right balance between what the learner already knows and what the teacher wants that learner to learn.

Elements of Instructional Planning

Monica Sahlmark narrates this video, which demonstrates how to chunk content in defining a personal health plan. Watch the video, and think about how these ideas might apply to the content you will be teaching. www.youtube.com/watch?v=84UKDHyQz1Q

Instructional planning can involve different periods of time and different amounts of instructional content. *Lesson planning* and *unit planning* are terms used to describe the chunking or grouping process teachers and curriculum developers go through. Chunking mainly takes place before instruction, because there is too much information at any grade level or in any content area to cover, and there has to be a way to organize these collected facts and data into bite-sized pieces. Chunking organizes large pieces of information into digestible chunks—a smaller number of information-rich items. Small chunks or parts allow for increased comprehension and help learners retrieve information quickly. Teachers determine what a meaningful unit of information is for their specific content and students. The specificity of these decisions is key—how information for lessons is organized and how long to spend on each lesson are important instructional decisions that are dependent on the classroom context. Chunking will usually be different from one group of students to another, even if they are learning the same material.

Chunking occurs within instructional periods. There are no absolute rules for how long a lesson should take. Although school days are divided into periods, a lesson may occur over any length of time. We know that planning is related to student achievement, but the amount of time for which you plan instruction may vary from short lessons to units that include several weeks of daily plans. Wiggins and McTighe (2005) have isolated important decisions about unit and lesson design, represented by the following questions:

- What is worthy of being taught?
- How will students demonstrate that they have learned what has been taught?
- What learning experiences will students need to have so that they can demonstrate this learning?

Thus, planning requires a look at the scope, focus, and sequence of what is going to be taught. Scope refers to the knowledge that is presented to the students, focus considers how the learning will be demonstrated, and sequence discusses the ways that instruction is organized.

SCOPE

There is too much information to cover in any single course, so teachers must make decisions about the breadth and depth of the content that will be addressed in the classroom. Some direction for deciding what to teach comes from standards. Kendall and Marzano (1997) reviewed national and state content standards and calculated that in order to meet these benchmarks, more than 15,000 hours of additional instruction would be required—an unattainable goal. Of course, no standard should be taught in isolation, and standards and benchmarks are not a curriculum. It is up to the teacher to decide on the scope of what is taught, and the choices should rest on two considerations:

1. The relative importance of factual, conceptual, procedural, and metacognitive knowledge that might be taught in terms of the continuum of the overall curriculum

2. The relative importance of the content to be taught with respect to the age, interests, and abilities of specific learners

Often, scope decisions are influenced by state or district pacing guides.

WEB RESOURCE

Pacing Guide

Go to any school district website and search for a pacing guide at the grade level or content area in which you want to teach. Examine the guide carefully and list any questions you may have about teaching using the guide. Discuss your questions with practicing teachers. The Mansfield, Ohio, school district has several pacing guides for you to study. Go to tygerpride.com/PacingGuides.aspx.

FOCUS

Units of instruction are blocks of lessons that are related by a concept or a big idea—they have a focus. Sometimes units are focused on a concept, like migration, change, or nutrition. The content of the unit is designed to explain the concept. Often, a question or set of questions is the focus of a unit. These essential questions require open-ended, messy, and divergent responses. Divergent questions may have many responses that are dependent on thinking about big ideas. They are frequently used in units to engage students and encourage study and reflection. What makes the United States great? What would happen if our country ran out of oil? Other unit questions may be more specific and more convergent—questions that have a right answer based on the content read or discussed in class. What can be done to help correct the problem of obesity in the United States? What are the differences between jazz and rock? Table 1.1 shows the difference between broad, essential questions and lesson-based questions whose answers can be found in the classroom lesson or text. The questions or concepts that frame the unit are intended to help students understand that knowledge is made up of answers. Too often, students leave school never realizing that knowledge is made up of answers to someone's prior questions, produced and refined in response to puzzles, inquiry, testing, argument, and revision. Knowledge comes from curiosity.

The scope and focus of units are determined, in part, by standards and standards-based assessments. Teachers must be intimately familiar with standards and related assessments so that units of instruction that will help students build strong neural networks for new learning can be developed.

In addition to analyzing the district curriculum, common benchmarks, and high-stakes tests so that they can design lessons and units to ensure student success,

---

TABLE 1.1   Essential and Lesson-Based Questions

Essential Questions	Lesson-Based Questions
Why do revolutions occur?	What were the direct causes of the American Revolution?
What makes a person revolutionary?	Who were the heroes of the Revolutionary War?
What does it mean to be brave?	What were the beliefs that the leaders of the American
From where do new ideas come?	Revolution espoused?

teachers must also take into account what is known about student learning. During the last two decades, there have been changes in our understanding of learning that also demand changes in teaching. Information about how students learn requires teachers to look at unit and lesson planning in a new way. Classrooms must be tailored to the needs of students through acknowledgment of students as learners, the standards and content that need to be taught, and how learning will be communicated, demonstrated, and evaluated—all aspects of unit planning. Since we know that new learning occurs when neural networks become more sophisticated—when there are more connections—units should be planned to take advantage of students' prior knowledge. A unit on weather taught in the Gulf Coast region, for example, would have references to Hurricane Katrina or a geography unit might begin with where the school is located and what other areas students have visited.

SEQUENCE

Chronology/Thematically

A third set of decisions to be made concerns the order of subject matter. Subjects may be ordered chronologically or thematically. In a unit on the American Revolution, for example, important events may be presented chronologically, from the prior events such as the Tea Act and the Boston Tea Party, to Patrick Henry's "Give me liberty or give me death" speech in March 1775, to April 1775, when war broke out. The stories of specific events may be shared in the order in which they happened. On the other hand, a unit on the same topic may include the theme of bravery, consisting of similar information from a different conceptual lens. Specific stories about the bravery of well known and lesser known people might be shared. For example, the well known ride of Paul Revere can be discussed in conjunction with the story of the ride of a lesser known hero, Jack Jouett, who saved Thomas Jefferson and other Virginia legislators from capture by the British.

Complexity

Basic skills, such as the fundamentals of reading or arithmetic, usually require that the sequence of skills proceeds from the simpler to the more complex. Learning trajectories are implied in both state standards and the Common Core State Standards, and most new curricula address these progressions. District pacing guides may dictate the order, but you can revisit themes and topics according to the interests of your students. In the unit on the American Revolution, the sequence of information might be ordered based on historical competencies. The unit might begin, for example, with the first historical thinking skill—making an historical argument from evidence—then move on to analyzing and evaluating the patterns that can be found in a chronological study of the Revolutionary War. Following that the teacher can prepare activities and information that allow students to compare and evaluate multiple perspectives of a specific Revolutionary experience. The unit can end with supporting the students in developing interpretations and synthesis of the information that was presented.

Prior Knowledge

Because new learning is based on previous learning, it is important to provide connections to help the learner identify how the new learning fits into what is already known. In short, there should be a logical order for the sequence and there must be obvious connections between the information to be learned and that already known by the students. The breadth and depth of content and how it is focused and sequenced are significant teacher decisions that directly affect instructional planning.

CHUNKING INSTRUCTION: UNITS AND LESSONS

Units are collections of lessons that have similar goals leading to broad understandings. They help teachers plan for large pieces of content and skills, and they help students make connections between individual teaching episodes. Units contain lessons that hang together and form an entity. Both units and lessons contain objectives addressing what students should understand, know, and be able to do (see Chapter Two). The unit objectives will be more general; the lesson objectives will be more specific. Individual lessons that comprise the unit will help students reach the detailed unit objectives.

DEVELOPING LESSON PLANS

Lesson plans are the component parts of a unit design. Just as a course is divided into units, units are divided into lessons. A lesson may span several days, or it may take only one day. The time a lesson takes is not determined by the school's bell schedule. It is determined by the best way to chunk information for a specific group of students.

In deciding how many lessons are necessary to accomplish the unit objectives, it is necessary to be flexible. You may need to rethink and modify the unit objectives because they may prove too ambitious or too limited. The design process is always circular in that prior decisions may be modified as the teaching progresses. Each lesson should be a logical part of the unit plan. Once there is a clear chart of the main factual, conceptual, procedural, and metacognitive knowledge to be studied, lesson planning flows easily.

Here are four guidelines for the development of effective lessons:

1. Limit the concepts and content to be covered in a lesson to allow time for the students to review, practice, and get feedback on what they have learned. This is formative assessment that occurs during instruction and allows both the teacher and student to make mid-lesson correction toward student learning.
2. Be sure that new material is connected to what has been learned previously and that the connections are clear.
3. Check frequently with students to ensure that they are acquiring the intended knowledge, attitudes, and skills. Continue to gather formative information; be prepared to alter your plans or reteach if the learning is not taking place or if the students seem to be disengaged.
4. Never accept students' failure to learn as inevitable or unavoidable. Keep in mind that error is inevitable in learning and merely points the way in teaching.

Remember that good lesson plans have common emphases—appropriate objectives, opportunity for practice and feedback, and flexibility.

SUMMARY

It is essential to understand the standards governing the content of what students are expected to learn, but it is equally important to have a firm grasp on how students learn anything as a consequence of teaching. Students and teachers must share a commitment to specific learning outcomes and have a clear sense of why knowing what is taught might make a difference to one who learns it. Learning needs to be relevant and visible to students; part of the art of teaching is to ensure that happens. Teachers must understand learners as well as they understand what is to be learned.

EXTENSIONS

ACTIVITIES

1. Many states post standards documents on their department of education websites. Look at the standards on your state's department of education website. Review the standards and the supporting materials available to you.

2. If you will be using a textbook in your teaching, compare the text with the state standards you have examined. What are the similarities and differences?

3. Ask a variety of people who they think should determine what is taught in schools. Probe by asking who should determine what knowledge is worthy of being taught. Think about the answers you receive. Did any of the responses clarify your thinking?

4. Look at a textbook you might be using in the near future. Identify some essential questions you might use in one of the units designed from the text.

5. Look carefully at a state standard in a content area that you will be teaching. What are the transferable big ideas in the standard? How are these big ideas related to other disciplines? Did you uncover any personal misconceptions as you read the standard and thought about your own thinking? Are there common misconceptions associated with this standard? How might you help students become more interested and excited about learning the knowledge presented in the standard?

6. For links to a variety of examples of formative assessments, search the Web with the terms *formative assessment examples, formative assessments,* and *instructional assessments.*

7. For an elaborated discussion of KWL, along with downloadable materials, see readingquest.org.

REFLECTIVE QUESTIONS

1. With what ideas presented in this chapter did you disagree? Why?

2. How will the idea of metacognition affect you as a learner and as a teacher?

3. Which content that you will be teaching is the subject with which you are least familiar? How will you go about becoming more familiar with the content? How will the lack of knowledge affect your teaching?

4. Did any of the principles of learning discussed in this chapter change your thinking about your own educational experiences? Which of the principles do you believe will be the most difficult to apply to your classroom?

5. What are your beliefs about how intelligence affects how students learn? What do you still want to know about theories of intelligence?

6. Think about the context in which you are teaching or will teach. What can you do as a teacher to decrease barriers to student learning in this context?

7. How can you organize your classroom to maximize student learning? What would your ideal classroom look like?

2 Objectives, Assessment, and Instruction

 Chapter Objectives

You Will Know

- The purpose of instructional objectives
- The KUD format for instructional objectives
- How to move from standards to objectives
- The importance of instructional alignment
- How to assess instructional objectives

You Will Understand That

- Effective instructional decisions are planned and intentional

You Will Be Able To

- Explain the role of standards in determining school content
- Describe the planning process for aligned instruction
- Distinguish between types of school knowledge
- Design aligned KUD objectives
- Vary the cognitive impact of *able to do* objectives
- Discuss the relationship between unit and lesson planning and the need for instructional alignment

Let us introduce Emily and Jeremy. Jeremy is a third grade teacher in an urban school, and Emily is a 10th grade English teacher in a suburban school. Both are certified teachers in their first year of teaching. Novice teachers are frequently unsure of where to begin planning for teaching. Jeremy and Emily are no exception. Should they simply follow the textbook, stick to the pacing guide, or use the methods that were practiced in their teacher education program? Remembering that one of her field instructors told her that instructional objectives are a waste of time, Emily is totally confused about how and why to plan. Jeremy isn't far behind. We have some advice to share with these new teachers.

This chapter addresses instructional objectives—their purpose and design. Instructional objectives are vibrant goals required for good teaching and student learning. Without clearly articulated targets, teachers and students will have difficulty traversing the road to student learning. The instructional objectives must represent the culmination of a process for the teacher—a process that includes prioritizing subject matter content and skills. Good instructional objectives cannot be legislated. Although they can and should be derived and adapted from state and district curriculum standards, they must be determined by careful consideration of disciplinary content, student prior knowledge, what is known about how people learn, and available materials and resources. Good instructional objectives illustrate an understanding of pedagogy. They allow teachers to adhere purposefully to the principles of learning that all good teaching must reflect.

The Purpose of Instructional Objectives

Instructional objectives represent key decision points in teaching in which goals are articulated and shared. Clearly defined intentions allow lessons to be focused and challenging rather than haphazard and shallow. Teachers and students alike require targets toward which to progress. Why are we learning about the Civil War? Can I just learn what interests me? Are there any ideas about the Civil War that will help me understand other conflicts? What is it my teacher wants me to learn? What do historians know and understand about the Civil War? What will be on the test? Questions like these, asked or implicit, should be reflected in instructional objectives.

Instructional objectives can be stated as what students will *know, understand,* and be able to *do* (KUD), a format that provides a foundation for all curricular, instructional, and assessment decisions made in classrooms. This approach to designing instructional objectives helps ensure the alignment of instructional objectives with assessment and teaching strategies. Clearly articulated instructional objectives are easier to assess, and they provide boundaries for what will occur in a lesson or unit. Thus, instructional objectives imply what will happen in classrooms. A list of instructional objectives also gives a preview of the subsequent instruction and assessments whose content will follow directly from the objectives. This approach to curriculum is called backward design (Wiggins & McTighe, 2005). Beginning with the end in mind, instructional objectives detail what we want students to know, understand, and be able to do at the end of an instructional period.

Research shows that students need learning experiences that are well organized, related to prior knowledge, and assessment focused. Because instructional objectives guide teacher and student behaviors, they allow teachers to present information in ways that are congruent with student needs while simultaneously meeting state curriculum standards (Hattie, 2012; Hattie & Yates, 2014). Figure 2.1 shows the relationship between the three different forms of instructional objectives or learning targets. The broad *understanding* target is the most abstract, the *able to do* objectives are the most concrete. Figures 2.2 and 2.3 show the relationships between the three types of objectives in two different content areas.

Backward design is not a new concept. As early as 1962, Gilbert suggested that instruction should begin with the end in mind (Cohen, 1987). Mastery learning, an educational reform popular in the early 1970s and currently seeing some resurgence, supports instructional alignment and backward design in that the assessments are planned before the instruction occurs, allowing teachers and students to focus on specific goals, rather than face uncertainty about tests or quizzes. The importance of this approach to instructional planning is supported by recent research on learning

Kristine Kershaw in this **video** (www.youtube.com/ watch?v=3Xzi2cm9WTg) provides a humorous illustration of the importance of backward design. Grant Wiggins, an author of *Understanding by Design,* explains backward design in this **video** (www.youtube .com/watch?v=4isSHf3SBuQ) and this **video** (www.youtube.com/ watch?v=vgNODvvsgxM).

FIGURE 2.1   Instructional Objectives

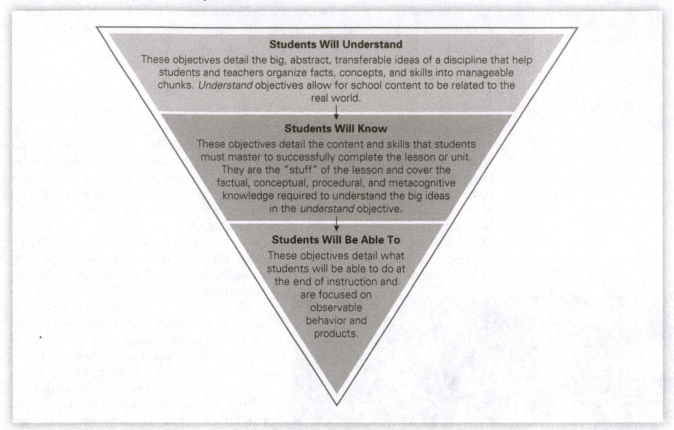

and by the current accountability movement that mandates end-of-course high-stakes testing (Bloom, 1983; Bransford, Brow, & Cockling, 2000; Hattie, 2012). Figure 2.4 shows the steps involved in backward design related to *know, understand,* and *do* instructional objectives.

FIGURE 2.2   KUD Objectives for a Lesson on Changes in Painting during the Renaissance

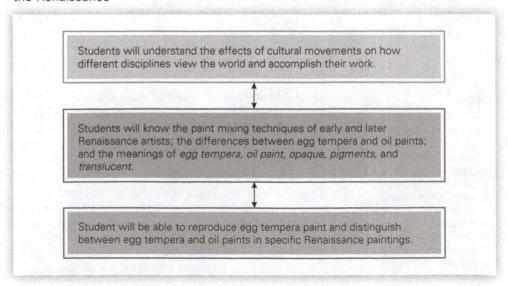

FIGURE 2.3   KUD Objectives for a Lesson on the Costs and Benefits
of Physical Activity

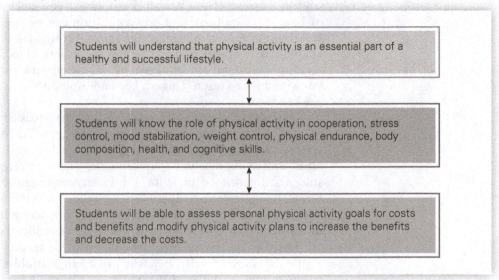

Teaching comprises many decisions made in the complex, multidimensional, fast-paced world of the classroom. Teachers may not be consciously aware of all of the decisions that are made and the impact that these decisions have on teaching and student learning. Careful planning makes allowances for the unforeseen—such things as snow days, fire drills, and various interruptions that must be accommodated within the "routine" of instruction.

FIGURE 2.4   Backward Design

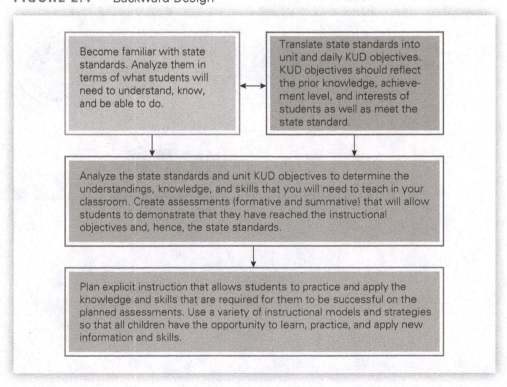

Successful teaching implies student learning. Research on teaching and learning indicates that there are clear paths to better instruction—a road to follow to increase student learning. Thus, not all decisions are equal. Those based on the knowledge of how students learn and how education can be organized to promote learning will result in greater student achievement. Writing good instructional objectives and aligning assessments and instruction with these objectives can increase the likelihood of successful student learning. Knowing how to nurture student learning is knowing how to teach. This is a key understanding on which both Emily and Jeremy need to focus.

Instruction can be designed to address the needs of learners if teachers are purposeful in constructing instructional objectives. For example, in considering the learner need for meaningful engagement, teachers can identify the knowledge, big ideas, and skills that will be meaningful and motivating to a particular group of students. Intentional planning helps teachers organize student experiences along a reasonable trajectory of student learning. Knowing what students should know, understand, and be able to do at the end of instruction means that teachers can continually monitor a student's progress toward specific objectives.

Lucid instructional objectives also provide targets for scaffolding instruction. Figure 2.5 shows teacher behaviors that can scaffold student learning. Scaffolding provides support for students as they are learning new and challenging materials. Scaffolding is not possible without clear learning targets, because the scaffold must help the student or students reach specific goals. Unambiguous instructional targets also provide a framework for the remediation of student learning. Instructional objectives will help in the selection of different, supporting instructional models for reteaching. Without these predetermined ends, student progress is difficult to ascertain, explain, and support, and thus opportunity is wasted. Remember that instructional objectives provide a focus for teaching and learning that allows for assessments and instructional strategies to follow. The alignment of objectives, assessments, and instruction improves the chances for successful student learning.

FIGURE 2.5   Scaffolding

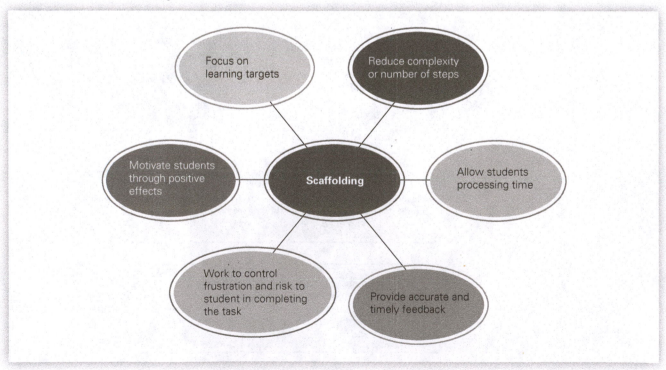

For Jeremy and Emily to develop aligned instruction, they will need to develop clear *know, understand,* and *able to do* objectives.

The KUD Format for Instructional Objectives

KNOW OBJECTIVES

Instructional objectives can be written in many forms (Gronlund & Brookhart, 2008; Marzano, 2009). We prefer the KUD format—*students will know, students will understand,* and *students will be able to do.* This format allows for the articulation of specific understandings, knowledge, skills, and performances that can help guide teaching behaviors and make teaching transparent and equitable. Each of the chapters in this text has objectives that follow the KUD format.

The decision of where to begin planning for instruction is somewhat arbitrary. Instructional objectives that define what teachers want students to know *(students will know)* is as good a place as any to start. However, in other circumstances, there may be reasons to begin with an *understand* or an *able to do* objective. It depends on the teacher, the context, the standards, and the pupils with whom a teacher is working. Writing instructional objectives is not a linear process; it is possible to begin anywhere and move around as the exact targets of a unit or a lesson emerge.

Know instructional objectives detail the content and skills a student must master to complete the lesson or unit successfully. The "stuff" of the lesson is listed in the *know* instructional objectives and is determined by the teacher from standards, pacing guides, curriculum blueprints, past experiences, and personal knowledge. With the glut of information available, teachers must be careful to prioritize and organize what is taught. With an approach that ranks and chunks information, students can have the opportunity to learn the important knowledge and skills. As a consequence, they will be able to transfer this critical knowledge to novel situations both in and beyond school. The *students will know* objective forces teachers to choose and focus on particular types of knowledge during instruction. Again, the knowledge and skills that students need to know are articulated in state standards, and an analysis of each will provide information for the specific content needs to be conveyed to students. To analyze each standard, it is important to understand the different kinds of content and skills that are represented in standards.

Know instructional objectives remind teachers of the essential disciplinary information worthy of teaching. These instructional objectives insure against digressions and help keep a healthy flow to classroom discourse. If the teaching target is for students to remember the characteristics of each of the geologic time eras, the lesson will focus on this information but not on, for example, the accuracy of the movie *Jurassic Park.*

Factual Knowledge

Facts are discrete bits of information that provide building blocks for concepts and generalizations. A fact can be a definition or a verifiable observation. It is often singular in occurrence. Here is a fact that students can determine: "On Wednesday of last week, we had half an inch of rain." (See Figure 2.6 for additional examples of facts.) Facts can also be defined as the elements that students must know in a discipline to understand concepts or to solve problems. For example, students learning to read music must be able to identify or *know* musical symbols; students studying current events must *know* the names of political figures, events, and geographical features of different places in the world. Anderson and Krathwohl (2001) posit that factual knowledge encompasses knowledge of vocabulary and knowledge of specific details. This sense of facts is useful to the classroom teacher and is the definition on

FIGURE 2.6   Examples of Facts, Concepts, and Generalizations: Impressionism

Facts	• In the middle of the 19th century, photography was becoming more popular, and the Romantic movement was ebbing.
	• Monet, Renoir, Sisley, Bazille, Cezanne, Pissarro, and Guillaumin became friends and often painted together.
	• They and others used a different approach to painting than was seen at the Salon de Paris.
	• Their paintings were of outside scenes, used visible short and thick brushstrokes, and had an emphasis on light and the reflection of color while often focusing on movement.
	• In 1863, the Salon de Paris rejected a painting by Manet.
	• The artists using these new techniques organized their own art shows.
Concepts	Impressionism
	Art of spontaneity
	Collective
	Art techniques
Generalizations	Impressionism was a reaction to more formal art techniques.
	Art is influenced by and influences the context in which it is created.

which we will base our discussion of instructional models. All of the models presented in this text rely on academic content and the foundation of academic content is facts. Many facts can be linked into an understanding of concepts and many concepts can be linked together to form generalizations.

It is the teacher who chooses the facts that support the predetermined concepts and generalizations. This choice comes from the teacher's understanding of the standards, students, and resources, and from the teacher's experiences. There are many facts from which to choose to make a lesson meaningful to a class of learners. In Emily's classroom, she teaches many skills that are dependent on factual building blocks. In one case, she wants her students to know that word origins can help them read unfamiliar words. Emily needs to make certain that the examples she uses to support this understanding are accurate and familiar to her students through past experiences or prior knowledge. So, the factual examples that she uses may be specific loan words from other languages with which students are familiar (taco, kayak, liberty) or with blended words (brunch, smog, simulcast).

Conceptual Knowledge

Concepts are the names given to categories formed as a result of classifying factual data. To make sense of stimuli in the world, learners of all ages form concepts and give them names. Imagine the cognitive overload if all things in the world were seen as separate and unrelated entities. To form concepts, learners pay attention to likenesses, ignore differences, and place similar objects in the same category. A pussycat asleep by the fire and a tiger in the jungle have many differences, but by attending to similarities and ignoring those differences, young people form the concept of *cat*.

Statements that link two or more concepts are generalizations. Unlike facts, generalizations are predictive. Consider the following. "Pat has just finished two novels that are on the current best seller list. Her brother, Owen, has completed a long, nonfiction work about World War I. In the evening, the siblings and their parents spend time in the living room reading." These are factual statements formed on the basis of observation. They do not tell us whether the books were enjoyable or whether Pat and Owen would recommend the books. They are simply statements of what was observed. "The Smith family buys a lot of books." This is a generalization based on the observation and on our understanding of concepts such as "books," "novels," "nonfiction," and "living room." We have inferred from our observations that the Smith family reads a lot, and we may predict that they buy a lot of books to read. Of course, this statement is not necessarily true. The family may use the public library and borrow books for free, or they may be in a cooperative that shares books, or they may borrow ebooks online. However, based on our observations, we formed a generalization and made a prediction. Only data from additional observations would determine the accuracy of the generalization. Conceptual knowledge subsumes and organizes discrete bits of information as these bits are related to one another and function together. For conceptual knowledge, students must have bits of factual information to categorize and classify. In Parts Two and Parts Three, we will delve into the issues of concepts and their relationships to facts and generalizations. Figure 2.6 shows an example of academic facts, concepts, and generalizations.

Procedural Knowledge

Not all knowledge is factual or conceptual. Procedural knowledge is the knowledge of how and when to do something—it is what we need to know in order to perform various tasks. Learning how to do something requires that we know (1) the steps for completing the task (*know that*), (2) how to complete the steps (*know how*), and (3) when to implement the procedure (*know when*). For example, a student in Jeremy's class learns that single-syllable words ending in a silent *e* often have the long sound of the vowel. The student learns *how* to make the long vowel sound. Then by examining exceptions to the rule in words such as *circle, since,* and *house,* the student learns when the rule does or does not apply. Thus, Jeremy's lesson about single-syllable words requires a procedural *know* objective.

Procedural knowledge includes methods of inquiry and the criteria for using subject-specific skills that are explicitly taught in classrooms through demonstrations and definitions. By defining and demonstrating a skill and its importance, students can learn to determine when it is appropriate to implement the skill. Skills such as summarizing, identifying similarities and differences, and brainstorming are a few of the skills discussed in this text. These strategies represent general procedural knowledge and are supplemented with subject-specific skills such as identifying word origins by examining prefixes, roots, and suffixes.

Metacognitive Knowledge

Metacognitive knowledge is the ability of learners to analyze, reflect, and understand their own cognitive and learning processes. Students who identify appropriate learning strategies in the right context are using metacognition. For example, a student may know that she has trouble picking out the main idea in a reading passage. If she has been taught to use a simple graphic organizer to identify a main idea, and then chooses on her own to map out a passage in a web, then that student has used metacognition to complete the task. Procedural knowledge is the knowledge that is accumulated about how to do something and when to use specific strategies and procedures; metacognitive knowledge encompasses information about learning, in general, and awareness of one's own learning, in particular.

Each of these four knowledge types is critical in learning a discipline. Each offers the "stuff" of what we teach—the focus of *students will know* instructional objectives. Table 2.1 demonstrates the different types of knowledge as taught in a science class (with content based on Common Core English/language arts standard RST 6-8.1 [corestandards .org]). It also demonstrates related *students will know* examples.

TABLE 2.1   Examples of Knowledge for Use in Geologic Time

Type of Knowledge	Example of *Students Will Know* Instructional Objectives
Factual	
Geologic time is the age of earth according to the record of rock strata.	Students will know the definition of *geologic time*.
Conceptual	
Geologists have divided earth's history into eras—spans of time that are based on the general characteristics of living things during that time. The time periods are relative and not absolute.	Students will know the critical attributes of fossils.
Procedural	
Geologists are able to determine the age of a rock through the natural radioactivity of chemical elements.	Students will know the procedures used for determining the age of rocks.
Metacognitive	
Students studying geologic time must remember the various divisions of relative geologic time in chronological order.	Students will know a variety of mnemonics for relative geologic time.

UNDERSTAND OBJECTIVES

Students will know instructional objectives can be seen as the foundation of lesson and unit content. *Students will understand* instructional objectives, on the other hand, move beyond bits of "stuff." *Understand* objectives are the pinnacle toward which all information and tasks in school are aimed—abstract, big ideas that students may remember over a long period of time.

The *students will understand* instructional objectives help teachers and students make sense of the knowledge on which lessons are based by forming big ideas or generalizations that serve as umbrellas for the *know* objectives. These big ideas are critical in getting the meaning of the discrete pieces of information represented in the *students will know* instructional objectives. Because there are simply too many bits of material to learn, *understand* instructional objectives help teachers to organize facts, concepts, and skills into manageable chunks. The developmental level of the learner, available resources, and the teacher's background dictate the level of content specificity in lessons and in determining objectives. Knowing the "stuff" of a discipline is not enough. "Stuff" needs to be interwoven into abstract, transferable ideas. Global goals for schooling demand that school content translate into real-world ideas and skills. Wiggins and McTighe (2005) call these transferable ideas "big ideas." Helping learners prioritize and frame important knowledge, big ideas are the linchpins or central, cohesive elements of a discipline and are essential for understanding a subject area. Big ideas answer the important questions in a field of study. Lynn Erickson (2007) defines big ideas as statements that are broad and abstract, universally applied, and represented by different examples that share common characteristics. They are the ideas toward which we teach. Because knowledge is constantly accumulating and changing, big ideas must be continually validated by contemporary factual examples. New information may change the emphasis of a strong generalization, and a big idea is a generalization. Thus, the relationship between *students will know* instructional objectives and *students will understand* instructional objectives takes on importance.

TABLE 2.2   Characteristics of a Key Generalization (Big Idea)

- Ties concepts together
- Organizes facts into broader understandings
- Requires instruction because the idea is not always obvious
- Represents persistent challenges in a discipline or in life
- Can help us understand new ideas in the future
- Transfers to different settings, times, and cultural traditions
- Is insightful, beyond vague notions familiar to students

Without the demarcation of a broad, abstract understanding, teachers and curriculum developers may choose less important, insignificant bits of information to support a big idea; without an interrelated set of factual, conceptual, procedural, and metacognitive information, it is difficult to understand the abstractions toward which teaching is directed. Jeremy and Emily must think about the big transferable ideas that are supported by the identified instructional strategies and assessments in their units.

We know that big ideas are important generalizations that require guided instruction for student attainment. Table 2.2 identifies the critical characteristics of these important understandings. Whether they are called *big ideas* (Erickson & Lanning, 2014; Wiggins & McTighe, 2005), *main ideas* (Taba, 1962), or *key generalizations,* the critical characteristic of a big idea is that it has "pedagogical power"—it provides for understanding the core foundation of a discipline by making sense of the discrete facts and skills that are important to those who practice the discipline. Students need to move beyond pieces of information to understand the important ideas of a discipline. Content knowledge is only a means to an end. Deep understanding of the discipline is the goal, and big understandings help to get there. With deep understanding, students are more likely to apply knowledge to new problems and situations. Transferring to new settings, to different times, or to different cultures requires conceptual understanding (Erickson & Lanning, 2014). Big ideas can extend beyond specific disciplines.

Students will understand instructional objectives are broad and abstract; they work to tie together a number of conceptually linked lessons. Consider an instructional objective like the following: "Students will understand that many individual decisions and behaviors contribute to a healthy life." Several lessons may need to be taught using this *understand* goal to help students gain information and skills necessary for demonstrating understanding of this big idea. For example, one lesson in the unit may focus on how to determine a healthy diet while another lesson may provide steps in conflict resolution. Each of these skills is supported by facts (calorie counts, how to manage emotions, etc.) and can be connected to the big idea of the unit.

Understand instructional objectives aid in the articulation of what teachers and curriculum designers mean when they say they want students to "understand." What does it mean to understand? Wiggins and McTighe (2005) believe that when students understand, they can explain, interpret, apply, identify critical perspectives, and empathize. A *students will understand* instructional objective can also indicate, more generally, that students are able to construct meaning from instruction—to think about the concepts and generalizations that are important for the discipline they are studying. In any case, *understand* objectives are assessed through student performance, which requires knowledge and skill. Therefore, the *students will understand* objective is clearly associated with what we want students to *know* (the *understand* instructional objective is an abstraction of the *know* instructional objectives) and what we want students to be *able to do* (the performance aspect).

TABLE 2.3   Examples of *Students Will Know* and *Students Will Understand* Instructional Objectives

Students Will Know	Students Will Understand That
The definitions of *beginning, middle,* and *end* (of a story)	Reading helps us to write well
How to plan and write a story	
English derivatives of Latin	Languages evolve over time
The definition of *perspective*	Multiple perspectives deepen understanding of a story
How to identify multiple perspectives in a story	
A circle can be described by an equation	Curved shapes can model objects and events
The definition of *main idea* and *supporting details*	Texts convey important ideas

The relationship between *know, understand,* and *able to do* instructional objectives is critical. The three are closely linked, and a change in one may shift emphasis on one of the others. This connection allows teachers to organize instruction for individual classes while still teaching to the important and transferable ideas in each discipline. KUD objectives provide clear and robust learning targets that are specific, and they provide design boundaries for teachers in planning lessons.

Examples of *students will understand* instructional objectives, and the *students will know* instructional objectives to which they are related, can be found in Table 2.3. Notice that *understand* instructional objectives are written in the form "*Students will understand that.*" By using this sentence stem, a generalization rather than a topic will follow. The statement will be a better signpost than one or two words. "*Students will understand that* all organisms need energy and matter to live and grow" provides more guidance to teachers as they plan instruction (and to students as they learn) than would "*students will understand* basic principles of life science." *Understand* objectives constitute what students remember years after the discrete facts and skills have faded from memory. The *students will understand* instructional objective makes sense of the articulated content in the *students will know* instructional objective. The *understand* statement opens the file drawer of facts and skills that are needed to make sense of the big ideas.

ABLE TO DO OBJECTIVES

Students will be able to instructional objectives are statements of the learning that will occur as the result of instruction. Both of our young teachers, Jeremy and Emily, are comfortable with these types of objectives although, as we discuss later on, they often make the common error of writing learning activity goals rather than instructional goals that focus on student behaviors. Goals focused on student behaviors are observable and measurable and can involve cognitive, affective, and psychomotor instructional objectives (Airasian, 2005; Anderson & Krathwohl, 2001). This text focuses on the cognitive skills that are the foundation of classroom instruction because the authors are devoted to cognitive instructional strategies and models that are based on what is known about how people learn. There are other types of objectives—affective (feelings, attitudes, and emotions) and psychomotor (physical and manipulative skills). These are also important classroom considerations.Discussions of the relationship between affective (social and emotional) and psychomotor objectives and academic achievement can be found in other resources (Elias, 2005).

Students will be able to instructional strategies have also been called *behavioral objectives* because they focus on student behaviors. Some instructional objectives only use the *students will be able to* format. The focus on objectives has seen several iterations in the last 50 years, always with a focus on clearly articulated targets for student learning (Anderson & Krathwohl, 2001).

Able to do instructional objectives can be written at different levels of specificity. Instructional objectives for a course are stated in more general terms than instructional objectives for a unit of study, which are more general than instructional objectives for a lesson to be completed in a class period. But whatever the level of generality, *students will be able to* instructional objectives must be in agreement with *students will know* and *students will understand* instructional objectives, and together all of the instructional objectives must allow for the congruence of objectives, assessment, and instruction.

Bloom's taxonomy is often used to identify the behaviors that teachers are targeting in their lessons (Bloom, 1956). Bloom's taxonomy is a classification system of the cognitive, affective, and psychomotor domains. The cognitive domain is used frequently in the development of classroom learning objectives. The processes identified in *A Taxonomy for Learning, Teaching, and Assessing* (also known as *Bloom's revised taxonomy* [Anderson & Krathwohl, 2001]) allow for careful construction of instructional objectives that target specific student thinking behaviors. Objectives should not be confused with activities—a common error new teachers frequently make. Instructional objectives are not activities. They do not describe how students will spend their time. It is necessary to clearly identify the behaviors that students will demonstrate after successful instruction and not to confuse these end performances with classroom pursuits. The construction "students will be able to" is important for the distinction between activities and instructional objectives, because the objectives detail the behaviors that are expected as a result of teaching. Instructional objectives define the purposes of instruction and help to limit the kinds of assessments and instructional strategies that will be used to help students reach the instructional targets.

Bloom's revised taxonomy (Anderson & Krathwohl, 2001) provides six categories of student behavior that describe student learning. These distinct cognitive processes form one basis for developing *students will be able to* instructional objectives.

- Remembering
- Understanding
- Applying
- Analyzing
- Evaluating
- Creating

Note that *understanding* in this list refers to comprehension, not to understanding big ideas.

This video introduces the elements of Bloom's revised taxonomy of cognitive objectives. www.youtube.com/watch?v=g1lc-GWtGII

WEB RESOURCE

Bloom's Taxonomy

The Vanderbilt University Center for Teaching has a web page on Bloom's taxonomy that provides information on the background of the taxonomy, the original and revised versions, reasons for using it, and additional resources. Go to cft.vanderbilt.edu.

Webb's depth of knowledge (DOK) (Webb, 2011) is another tool that can help teachers design *able to do* instructional objectives. DOK focuses on the outcome measure that is determined by a standard. The DOK framework is frequently linked with the Common Core State Standards (CCSS). The ultimate goal of the DOK is to ensure that instruction matches the intent of the academic standard. The DOK does not use a verb as the focus of objective design as Bloom's taxonomy does—it examines the cognitive demand of the task described in the standard and the associated assessment. For example, DOK level 2 requires students to summarize, estimate, organize, classify, and infer. The focus, however, is not on these verbs, but on the complex tasks students are asked to perform to demonstrate their depth of knowledge. For level 2, students may be asked to classify a series of procedural steps, explain the meaning of a concept or how to perform a task, or make a map. The intended learning outcome determines the complexity of the task.

Learners need repetition and elaboration in lessons so that information can be readily stored in permanent memory. *Students will be able to* instructional objectives allow teachers to specify the knowledge and skills that must make up instruction. Specifically articulating the types of cognition students will be developing and practicing ensures specific opportunities for student learning. When we combine the types of cognition with academic concepts and generalizations, we can be very clear about what our instructional objectives are. For example, "students will identify the characteristics of rational numbers" is a target toward which students can progress. We know that the cognitive behavior is at the lower level of Bloom's revised taxonomy. We can then design instruction to meet this goal. Table 2.4 describes each of the cognitive behaviors that students can exhibit, as defined and adapted from Anderson and Krathwohl's revised taxonomy (Anderson & Krathwohl, 2001). The table also includes a definition of the behavior and associated verbs that can be used to describe the behavior.

Able to do instructional objectives should incorporate core disciplinary tasks (as well as the core disciplinary processes referred to in Table 2.4), which are the

TABLE 2.4   Possible Student Cognitive Behaviors

Behavior	Definition	Associated Verbs
Remembering	Retrieve relevant knowledge from long-term memory	Identify, recognize, recall, retrieve
Understanding	Construct meaning from instructional materials	Interpret, paraphrase, illustrate, classify, categorize, summarize, generalize, infer, conclude, predict, compare, explain
Applying	Carry out or use a procedure in a novel situation	Execute, implement
Analyzing	Break material into parts and determine how parts relate to one another and to whole	Discriminate, select, organize, integrate, outline, structure, attribute
Evaluating	Make judgments based on criteria and standards	Check, critique, judge
Creating	Put elements together to form a coherent whole or new structure	Hypothesize, design, construct

realistic tasks accomplished in a subject area—experiments in science, analysis of historical documents in social studies, critique of peer work in language arts, and the like. It is important that learning outcomes—the lesson's instructional objectives—be worthwhile and representative of important disciplinary knowledge and skills. Time in school is short. It must be used wisely.

Moving from Standards to Objectives

Standards are written at many different levels of specificity and clarity. Once you become familiar with the standards in your state, you will need to mold the standards for which you are responsible to align with instructional objectives. Standards are the mandated curriculum framework, but standards are not an instructional curriculum. They are the foundation for the development of a curriculum that can be enacted in instruction. Standards cannot be swallowed whole for classroom use. Nor can textbook objectives be used unchanged. It is a teacher's professional responsibility to design objectives specific to each class based on state standards. Each classroom context brings different background information, achievement levels, resources, and interests to bear on the standards.

Excellent classroom teachers take all of these responsibilities into consideration when developing KUD objectives. Two skills are required for designing good instructional objectives from standards. First, you will need to be able to construct *know, understand,* and *do* objectives from the given standards by reading them carefully and deconstructing them. Sometimes standards are written as *understand* objectives. They are abstract and broad. From the standard, you will need to identify the aligned *know* and *able to do* objectives. If the standard is written as a student behavior (an *able to* objective), you will need to construct an aligned *understand* objective and a list of items students will need to know in order to do successfully what the standard requires. Second, you will need to write the standard into student-friendly language—language that reflects the developmental level of the students with whom you are working. This allows students the opportunity to take responsibility for their progress toward the targets you have set. Table 2.5 shows aligned *know, understand,* and *able to do* objectives that are derived from standards. For standards written to align more closely to one of the three forms of objectives, teachers must be able to move from one form to another in order to provide quality instruction.

Instructional Alignment

Instructional alignment represents more than congruence between the three types of instructional objectives; it also reflects unity in the lesson or unit objectives, assessments, and instruction. This alignment allows for efficient and effective student learning.

Instruction is the building of knowledge and the teaching of skills. Teachers instruct in the classroom—they teach. But the decisions they make about what and how to teach are also part of instruction. To complicate matters, instruction is often linked with the word *curriculum.* Curriculum is what is taught, and what is taught is associated with standardized testing. If a high-stakes test is curricularly aligned, it tests what students have had the opportunity to learn. Providing the opportunity to learn involves more than presenting information to pupils. It requires that students have had the scaffolding and extensions necessary to process the knowledge and skills they are acquiring. This is an important distinction. Students must have the opportunity to prepare for high-stakes assessments; it is not enough to tell students what they have to know. You can see that effective teaching is a complex and demanding endeavor.

TABLE 2.5 Examples of Aligned *Understand, Know,* and *Able to Do* Instructional Objectives

Standard	Students Will Know	Students Will Understand	Students Will Be Able To
CCSS English/Language Arts W.1.3: Write narratives in which they recount two or more appropriately sequenced events, include some details regarding what happened, use temporal words to signal event order, and provide some sense of closure.	The definitions of *beginning, middle,* and *end* How to plan and write a story	Reading can help us to write well	Plan and write a short story about elephants
Students compare the language being studied with their own language.	English derivations of Latin	Languages evolve over time	Analyze their own vocabulary for derivatives of Latin
CCSS English/Language Arts RL.6.6: Explain how an author develops the point of view of the narrator or speaker in a text.	The definition of *perspective* How to identify multiple perspectives in a story	Multiple perspectives deepen understanding of a story	Describe and provide examples of perspective in a children's book
CCSS Math HSG.GPE.B.4: Use coordinates to prove simple geometric theorems algebraically.	A circle can be described by an equation	Curved shapes can model objects and events	Rearrange an equation in order to determine whether it describes a circle
CCSS English/Language Arts RI.5.2: Determine two or more main ideas of a text and explain how they are supported by key details; summarize the text.	The definitions of *main idea* and *supporting details*	Texts convey important ideas	Identify the main idea and supporting details in a speech

Instructional alignment in the classroom is similar to curricular alignment, but it does not focus on decisions based on high-stakes tests. Instead, the emphasis centers on the opportunity for student learning on a day-to-day basis. Decisions at the classroom level focus on how to translate state standards into instructional objectives and, in this manner, describe what students need to know, understand, and be able to do. This alignment of the three elements of teaching—objectives, assessments, and instructional strategies—increases student learning. When instruction is not representative of the established targets or the assessments on which the targets will be demonstrated, the likelihood of success will diminish. This means that Jeremy and Emily will need to make certain that their *understand* objectives are supported by aligned instruction and assessment and that *able to do* objectives are represented in assessments.

Let's look at two world history standards: "Understands civilizations around the Aegean Sea and how they emerged." and "How various geographic areas developed relationships during the Bronze Age." The standards provide guidance for instruction and, consequently, instruction must include the knowledge and skills that support the standards. The curriculum can be supported with the following knowledge:

1. There was assimilation, conquest, migration, and trade among the Aegean world, the Near East, and Egypt, but each citizenry kept its own cultural identity.

2. Military conquests supported cultural benefits as well as cost.
3. Cultural mixing and exchanges to all of the geographic areas were extensive.

An *understand* objective associated with these standards might read, "Students will understand that cultural diffusion is a consequence of assimilation, conquest, migration, and trade." The supporting *know* objectives would provide specific details about conquests (especially those of Alexander), their impact on other cultures, and the consequences that followed. Taking students' interest, achievement levels, and prior knowledge into consideration, *students will be able to* objectives can be written for a particular class. For this standard, there are many options for *able to do* objectives, such as the following. "Students will be able to draw a map of Alexander's conquests and subsequent trade routes." "Students will be able to write a journal of an immigrant to Greece from Egypt during this time." Instructional objectives form the intersection between the curriculum (the state standards) and what happens in classrooms.

Moving from the standards to actual classroom instruction, teachers deconstruct or pull apart the mandated standards; the knowledge, understandings, and skills that compose the standard; the prior experiences of their students; the way people learn; and the available resources in the school and the community. From this mix of content knowledge, pedagogical knowledge, and knowledge of student learning, classroom instructional objectives and assessments are determined and instruction is designed. The big idea of instructional alignment is the congruence between objectives, assessment, and instruction. This strategy promotes effective and efficient student learning.

Assessing Instructional Objectives

As you can see in Figure 2.4, which describes the backward design process, once instructional objectives have been written—but before instructional procedures have been considered—assessments are designed. These assessments will provide information about whether students have attained the objectives. This is the key to backward design. Making certain that your instructional objectives and assessments clearly align provides an equitable way to prepare students for both formative and summative assessments. Instead of deciding on assessments during and after instruction, assessments are planned as soon as the instructional objectives are identified, thus allowing instruction to be designed so that students will get the support they need to show they have reached the objectives. Knowing the instructional targets and how these targets will be assessed focuses teacher and student behaviors during instruction. A clear path makes the ride more comfortable and successful.

Assessments are the basis for making judgments. Most decisions teachers make in the classroom reflect judgments, and many of these judgments are based on assessments. Some assessments lead to judgments about student learning in the form of grades. Other assessments provide information to students and teachers about what has been learned and what knowledge and skills still need to be addressed and practiced so that learning targets can be achieved.

FORMATIVE ASSESSMENTS

Assessments are designed in relation to instructional objectives that have been planned by the classroom teacher, the curriculum developer, the school district, and/or the state. Assessments can be either formative or summative. Both types of assessments should be used to support student learning. Formative assessments provide students and teachers with information about how students are progressing toward stated goals, but they are typically not for the purposes of grading. They take place during instruction. Formative assessments allow both the students and the teacher to make mid-lesson or mid-unit corrections so that they can meet objectives. Formative assessments use instructional objectives to provide feedback on practice that is clear, accurate, and aimed at informing students of their progress. Black and Wiliam (2009) state:

> Practice in a classroom is formative to the extent that evidence about student achievement is elicited, interpreted, and used by teachers, learners, or their peers to make decisions about the next steps in instruction that are likely to be better founded than the decisions they would have taken in the absence of the evidence that was elicited. (p. 9)

Thus, formative assessment informs a teacher's instructional decision making and allows learners to adjust their behaviors toward explicit learning targets.

The feedback that students receive on formative assessments allows the teacher and student to close the gap between the instructional objectives and the understandings and performances that the student has demonstrated. Black, Harrison, Lee, Marshall, and Wiliam (2003) have shown that formative assessment information increases achievement for all students, with the largest gains for lower-achieving students and students with learning disabilities. Formative assessments work best when teachers and students act on the information provided to adjust teaching and learning—to help students move closer to the targets. A formative assessment quiz helps students only if the items are clearly related to instructional goals, if the feedback on student performance is clear and timely, and if both students and teachers have the opportunity to change instruction and learning opportunities in ways that help ensure future success in meeting the instructional targets. Formative assessments, because of the power they give students over their own learning, have been shown to increase student motivation and efficacy (Stiggins, 2005). Jeremy and Emily will need to carefully consider when to use formative assessments and will need to make certain that the formative assessments are congruent with instructional goals.

WEB RESOURCE

Formative Assessment Techniques

Go to wvde.state.wv.us for more information about specific formative assessment techniques.

SUMMATIVE ASSESSMENTS

Summative assessments are designed to occur at the end of a chunk of instruction in which students have had the opportunity for formative assessment feedback. Summative assessments provide information about student learning that is frequently translated into a grade. Formative and summative assessments must be clearly coupled. It is unfair to students to assign practice tasks during class that are substantially different from the upcoming summative assessment. All students should have the opportunity to practice and receive feedback (formative assessment) before they are tested and graded (summative assessment). This does not mean that the summative assessment and the instructional activities leading to the assessment must be identical, but the instruction preceding the assessment should be similar and contain all the important elements of the assessment. How similar will depend on the instructional objectives. If the goal is for students to recognize and identify specific bits of content, the assessment will be very familiar. If the assessment is designed to evaluate understanding, there will be some novelty in the assigned tasks to ensure practice in knowledge transfer.

Each of the instructional models in Parts Two and Three of this text incorporates assessment strategies and instructional objectives that are a good fit—they are congruent and form a coherent whole. For example, constructed response assessments (short-answer, essay) work well with instructional objectives that ask students to apply, analyze, and evaluate knowledge. The cause-and-effect instructional model is congruent with these instructional objectives. Parts Two and Three will describe several instructional models in terms of objectives, procedures, assessments, and ways to personalize instruction.

SUMMARY

This chapter has examined instructional objectives and instructional alignment. Good teaching is built on clearly articulated instructional objectives that provide a clear road to student success. Formative assessments furnish information to students and teachers during instruction while there is still time to adapt and scaffold student learning. Summative assessments evaluate student learning at the end of an instructional episode, frequently for a grade. Instructional objectives and assessments determine the kinds of instructional strategies a teacher will use to help students reach learning targets.

EXTENSIONS

ACTIVITIES

1. Read the following health standard and the associated benchmarks carefully and list as many factual, conceptual, procedural, and metacognitive pieces of knowledge as you can, using the matrix that follows.

The student knows positive personal health habits.

Benchmarks: The student
- Understands the influence of healthy habits on a person's well-being and what the risks are for not having healthy habits
- Knows signs of common health problems and understands the differences between being proactive and reactive
- Sets a personal health goal and can chart progress toward its achievement.
- Knows the structure and functions of human body systems

What types of knowledge are represented in the standard and benchmarks? Fill in at least two examples for each knowledge type.

Factual Knowledge	
Conceptual Knowledge	
Procedural Knowledge	
Metacognitive Knowledge	

2. Write an *able to do* objective for each of the provided *know* and *understand* objectives.

   Students will understand that political, economic, and religious interests contributed to the resistance of colonials to English rule.

   Students will know the significance of the First and Second Continental Congresses.

   Students will know the moral and political ideas of the Great Awakening and how these ideas are associated with the American Revolution.

   Students will know the views and impact of key individuals from the revolutionary time period.

3. Read the following short case and determine whether the instructional objectives, assessment, and instructional strategies are aligned.

   Case: Mrs. Jones teaches sixth grade world history. She has just finished a unit on ancient Mesopotamia, Egypt, and Kush based on the following instructional objectives:

   - *Students will understand* that civilizations develop in a particular place to meet the physical needs of a society and that there is a strong relationship between religion and social and political order in Ancient Egypt and Mesopotamia.
   - *Students will know* the geography of the early civilizations in the Near East and Africa, Hammurabi's Code, features of Egyptian art and architecture, Egyptian trade routes, and the political, commercial, and cultural ties between Kush and Egypt.
   - *Students will be able to* analyze the geographic, political, economic, religious, and social structures of the early civilizations of Mesopotamia, Egypt, and Kush.

   Mrs. Jones used cooperative learning, lecture, and discussion as her primary instructional strategies.

   The formative assessment she used was individual student conferences in which one two-part question was asked: "In which civilization would you have liked to live? Why?"

   Her summative assessment required students to make a diorama for each of the three civilizations.

   Is Mrs. Jones's instruction aligned? Explain.

REFLECTIVE QUESTIONS

1. How would you explain the purpose of instructional objectives to someone interested in becoming a teacher?
2. What role do factual, procedural, conceptual, and metacognitive knowledge play in the construction and implementation of instructional objectives?
3. What are the difficulties in implementing formative assessments into instruction?

PART ONE SUMMARY

The two chapters in Part One have looked broadly at student learning, standards, and instruction. The first chapter, "Standards and Content in Schools," examined what we know about student learning and the role that standards play in organizing content in schools. Generalizations about the role of standards in organizing classrooms were considered. The chapter continued with a focus on the relationship between unit and lesson planning and the need for instructional alignment to support student learning.

The second chapter, "Objectives, Assessment, and Instruction," parsed the role of instructional planning and organization in making learning visible in classrooms (Hattie, 2012). The purpose of the KUD format and how to use standards to develop these aligned objectives were introduced. These skills are foundational for student learning in the classroom. Aligning instruction, developing strong and demanding learning objectives, and planning intentionally with student learning in mind contributes to your readiness to learn about the instructional models presented in the next sections of the text. With a strong understanding of the role of instruction, you will be able to develop the knowledge and skills to vary instruction to meet the learning needs of your diverse students.

Basic Instructional Models

A MODELS APPROACH

Remember what it was like to make something from a pattern for the first time, such as a model airplane or a cake? The task seemed difficult, if not impossible, in the beginning. You made some mistakes and needed some advice and coaching from more experienced hands. Gradually, you acquired the skills and techniques necessary for making many model airplanes and cakes even without following a pattern. In fact, you could even design models or special recipes of your own that others could follow.

Instructional models are also a pattern, and this text provides a series of instructional patterns that are available to you as you plan instruction. Like recipes or blueprints, instructional models present very detailed steps necessary to reach desired student learning outcomes. The selection of which instructional model to use depends on the learning objectives that the targeted students are expected to reach as a result of instruction.

When planning to make a chocolate cake, it is necessary to select a recipe for a chocolate cake, not lasagna or a burrito. A blueprint for a birdhouse will not produce a model airplane. Likewise, a model of instruction designed to help students define a concept will not result in the development of map reading skills. Teaching students how to make generalizations requires a different instructional approach than the instruction required to teach students how to drive a car. *An instructional model is a step-by-step procedure that leads to specific learning outcomes.* The best models are based on what we know about students and how people learn; they have been used extensively and are supported by empirical research. This text examines several of the best instructional models that have the following characteristics:

- They reflect research about how people learn.
- They can be used in backward design planning.
- They encourage active student participation in the learning process.
- They take students through specific, sequential, and predictable steps.
- They are adaptable for a wide diversity of students, grade levels, and content areas.
- They support the development of critical thinking skills as well as academic content and skills.
- They are sophisticated professional tools that require time and attention to learn.

Why Models of Instruction?

The models approach emphasizes the need for instructional variety in the classroom. This variety can only be accomplished by developing a teacher's repertoire of instructional approaches to support a wide variety of students and to meet a range of objectives. Today's classrooms are increasingly diverse—culturally, academically, and economically—and instructional models can help teachers meet the needs of many different students. These children and adolescents come to school with a variety of learning orientations. Some students learn well in a highly structured environment; others need a more open setting with many choices. Some learn more comfortably using inductive thinking; others favor a deductive approach. Some students prefer individual, competitive work; some work better collaboratively. These preferences are not the only way that students can learn, but if a teacher only uses one approach, there are students who may be marginalized and even left out.

If the instructional environment of the classroom is monotone—the same instructional approach is used consistently—students who do well with that type of instruction have an advantage over other students. The teacher who appropriately uses a variety of instructional models and strategies is more likely to reach all students in the classroom; moreover, students will be able to expand a preferred mode of learning by being encouraged to learn in a variety of ways.

There is no one correct manner in which to instruct all of the students all of the time. Even special populations such as learners with severe learning challenges can benefit from a variety of approaches. No group or stratum of society needs to be relegated to one approach for all school learning, although it may be reasonable, at times, to use certain approaches more than others.

In Part One, we discussed the design of aligned instruction and identified the types of objectives that should be represented in an instructional plan. Some objectives focus on broad understandings and generalizations, some on content knowledge, and some on academic, social, and emotional skills.

A careful instructional design takes into account the ages and interests of the learners, the knowledge that they bring with them to instruction, and the conditions under which instruction will occur. Additionally, the design must be grounded in content standards and classroom environments that promote learning.

Basic Instructional Models

In Part Two, we present five basic instructional models, selected from an array of sources that provide a solid repertoire for the beginning teacher. We define a basic instructional model as a model that (1) is accessible and can be readily practiced in a standards-based classroom, (2) can easily be combined with other basic strategies and models, and (3) has fewer moving parts. Of the 10 instructional models (and their associated versions, in some cases), we have chosen 5 that meet our criteria. As in all instruction, these models require teachers to manage classrooms well, build a strong learning community, and have high expectations for all students. But some of these pedagogical requirements are infused in the steps of the basic models. For example, direct instruction provides a gradual release of responsibility from teacher to students; it engages students in clear and attainable activities that decrease management problems, places students together in small groups to practice targeted skills, and promotes high expectations. The basic instructional models are a strong foundation for pedagogical excellence.

The basic models of instruction are direct instruction, concept attainment, concept development, cause-and-effect, and vocabulary acquisition. Taken together, these models will provide the novice teacher with basic pedagogical skills that will meet the needs of all content areas and grade levels, especially in a classroom that is standards based. The classroom organizational requirements for these models are straight-forward, and students will be able to learn the steps of the models relatively quickly.

Chapter Organization

Each chapter presents one model (and, in some cases, variations on the model). We provide a research base for each model, describe the steps, and discuss instructional situations in which the model might be used. The discussion of each model opens with two classroom scenarios, one in an elementary classroom and the other in a middle or secondary classroom. Thus before the model is described and its steps detailed, you will see what it looks like via a brief glance at student–teacher interactions around a topic that might be taught in any school at the particular level you are looking in on. Steps of the model are detailed to make it easy to adapt the model to your teaching. At several points, you will also encounter what are called Strategy Alerts, descriptions of instructional strategies that would easily find a place nested in the model. To close each chapter, we look again at the scenarios that opened the chapter, this time looking at the lesson plans that are tied to Common Core State Standards and that underlay the instruction that formed the basis of the scenarios.

- *Chapter Three: The Direct Instruction Model.* Direct instruction is a highly structured model that is helpful in teaching skills and discrete bits of information that can be broken down into small, distinct segments. The teacher models what is to be learned and, through guided and independent practice, there is a gradual release of responsibility from the teacher to the student.

- *Chapter Four: The Concept Attainment Model.* This model helps students comprehend and analyze the meaning of a particular concept. Through a series of positive and negative examples of the concept, students define the concept and determine its essential attributes. The concept attainment model is particularly effective in meeting objectives related to comprehension, comparison, discrimination, and recall.

- *Chapter Five: The Concept Development Model.* Originated by Hilda Taba, the concept development model encourages students to group data based on perceived similarities and differences and then to form categories and labels for the data, effectively producing a conceptual system. In the process, students learn to think about the conceptual relationships they are manipulating, the ideas that these concepts represent, and their own thinking. This model helps students understand how concepts originate and is effective with objectives related to contrasting, applying, categorizing, and analyzing data.

- *Chapter Six: The Cause-and-Effect Model.* This model leads students through an investigation of a significant action, situation, condition, or conflict. Through inference, students hypothesize about causes and effects, consider prior causes and subsequent effects, and generalize about human behavior in similar situations. The cause-and-effect model is particularly effective for those objectives related to analysis, generating hypotheses, and making generalizations.

- *Chapter Seven: The Vocabulary Acquisition Model.* The vocabulary model was developed for this text by one of the authors, Tom Estes, a recognized expert in the teaching of reading and vocabulary acquisition. This model presents the exciting possibility of teaching vocabulary through the history of language and word derivation rather than through the memorization of lists.

3

The Direct Instruction Model

TEACHING SKILLS, FACTS, AND KNOWLEDGE EXPLICITLY

 Chapter Objectives

You Will Know

- What the direct instruction model looks like in both elementary and secondary classrooms
- The basis for the direct instruction model
- The steps in the direct instruction model, including steps in the lecture-presentation model and demonstrations
- How to evaluate learning in the direct instruction model
- How to meet individual needs in the direct instruction model
- The benefits of the direct instruction model

You Will Understand That

- The direct instruction model provides an effective and efficient framework for instruction

You Will Be Able To

- Identify the direct instruction model in K–12 classrooms
- Design, implement, and reflect on a direct instruction lesson

In the Elementary Classroom

Ms. Davis is using nursery rhymes to help her kindergarten students identify and generate rhyming words. She begins the lesson by reading some of the rhymes from a Mother Goose book.

> **Ms. Davis:** Why do you like me to read Mother Goose to you?
> **Anika:** They are funny.
> **Micah:** I like the sound.
> **Ms. Davis:** What do you like about the sound?
> **Sophia:** It has rhyming words.

Ms. Davis points out the rhyming words in several of the Mother Goose rhymes. Students enthusiastically point out rhyming words.

> **Ms. Davis:** Today we are going to look at and hear rhymes and point out the rhyming words. We are also going to try to think of rhyming words. Let's begin by looking at this poster.

She directs the students' attention to a big poster with the nursery rhyme "Tom, Tom, the Piper's Son" written on it. Ms. Davis reads the poem, pointing to each word.

> **Anika:** What is a piper?
> **Ms. Davis:** Does anyone know what a piper is?
> **Macy:** I think it's someone who plays a pipe.

Ms. Davis also defines the word *beat* and tells students that rhyming words are words that end with the same sounds, giving them some examples (*cow* and *wow*, *hat* and *rat*, *ham* and *ram*, *man* and *pan*). Some of the students share rhyming words. Ms. Davis reads "Tom, Tom" again and asks students to raise their hands when they hear two rhyming words. She puts colored circles around the words that rhyme.

> **Ms. Davis:** You've done a good job of identifying rhyming words. Are these words rhyming words? *Son* and *eat*? *Stole* and *piper*? *Crying* and *street*?

The students know that the words are not rhyming words because they do not sound alike. Together the class makes a list of rhyming words in "Tom, Tom." For guided practice, Ms. Davis reads a poster of the nursery rhyme "Little Miss Muffet." She defines the unfamiliar words and asks individual students to come up to the poster and show her the rhyming words. Ms. Davis circles the rhyming words in matching colors.

> **Ms. Davis:** Here are some rhyming words that we found today. Let's see if we can add to the list. What other words can you think of that rhyme with *beat* and *eat*?
>
> **Daniel:** Heat.
>
> **Ava:** Seat.
>
> **Anika:** Meat.

Ms. Davis provides students with more rhyming words and asks students to explain why they rhyme. After several rounds, she takes out a felt bag that is labeled "Rhyming Words." Inside are small cards with a variety of words. Students are given the opportunity to pull out a card and say a rhyming word. Each student has a chance to play the game while the rest of the class gives a thumbs up when the word rhymes or a thumbs down when it doesn't.

> **Ms. Davis:** You each have a big sheet of paper. On the paper, you will draw a picture of three things that rhyme with the word *hat*. Ms. Smith and I will come around to help you write the correct rhyming word under each picture. When you finish, you can draw three pictures of words that do not rhyme with the word *hat*. ∎

In the Middle/Secondary Classroom

The eighth graders were just settling into their fourth-period English class. Mr. Bennett, their teacher, began the lesson by discussing some of the nature poems that they had read earlier in the school year.

> **Mr. Bennett:** Is anyone familiar with the term *haiku?*
>
> **Emma:** Hey guys, do you remember, we wrote haikus in sixth grade with Ms. Figgins?
>
> **Chris:** I remember. They're short.
>
> **Mr. Bennett:** Yes, they are short. Let me show you some examples of haiku, and you might remember the specific rules for writing them. Today's big idea is that poetic forms vary. We are going to look at one form of poetry—haiku.

By the end of class you will be able to compare haiku with other poetry, specify the rules for writing haiku, and compose your own haiku. That's a lot to cover in a one class period, but I believe each one of you will walk out of class with a perfect haiku and will understand that this is just one form of poetry.

Mr. Bennett proceeds to share several examples of haiku with the class. He projects the poems and reads them orally. Through discussion, he helps students recognize that haiku are (1) very short—only three lines, (2) descriptive—usually about nature, (3) personal, and (4) are divided into two parts. In addition, Mr. Bennett points out the 5 syllable–7 syllable–5 syllable pattern.

Mr. Bennett: Now we will work in our base groups. The recorder for each group will be the person whose birthday is closest to today. Raise your hand when you know you are a recorder. I am giving each group a sheet with four poems that are about nature. Choose which of the poems are haiku and write a short explanation of why you have classified it as a haiku poem. You have five minutes to complete the sheet.

Five minutes pass, and Mr. Bennett has group 5 report. He then asks whether the other groups agree or disagree with group 5's findings and asks students to put the list of rules for constructing a haiku in their English notebook. The class continues.

Mr. Bennett: You can see that haiku use descriptive language about something that is important to the poet. Let's brainstorm some ideas for a haiku. First, we can think about something that happens during a particular season, and then we can come up with a list of words to describe the event. Let's think about winter. What might happen in the winter, and what words would describe this best? We'll keep track of our word bank on the chalkboard. What might happen in the winter?

Barbara: A blizzard.

Eileen: When I think of a blizzard, I think of white.

Mr. Bennett: What other descriptive words remind you of a winter blizzard?

Sandi: Icy, snow piles, snowballs!

Etan: Cold, cozy, still.

Mr. Bennett: Cozy?

Etan: Cozy in my house with a fire in the fireplace!

Paul: Frozen and quiet.

After several more students share their ideas, Mr. Bennett follows the same format for spring, summer, and then fall. With four lists on the board, students are asked to vote on a season on which to focus for their first class haiku. After the vote, the whole class writes a haiku about a blizzard in winter. Mr. Bennett then asks the base groups to choose a different season on which to focus and to write a haiku about something seen or done during that season. Mr. Bennett circulates to each group, providing feedback based on the rules for constructing a haiku.

> **Mr. Bennett:** Your groups have done a good job of writing haiku. Now, I would like you to write your own haiku. You can choose to write about any season or any other aspect of nature. Try to use at least one of the words on the board. Once you have written your haiku, share it with your partner and, using the rules we have discussed and that are in your notebook, critique each other's haiku. ■

Basis for the Direct Instruction Model

Direct instruction is an instructional model used to explicitly teach targeted knowledge, skills, or both. At the beginning of direct instruction, the teacher models what is to be learned. Then, through clear, timely, and accurate feedback during guided and independent practice sessions, students are gradually able to demonstrate successfully the targeted knowledge and skills. The theoretical and research foundation of the direct instruction model is varied—it is based on what we know about student learning, and it benefits from findings in behavioral psychology, social learning theory, and cognitive learning theory. Behavioral psychology contributes the principles of conditioning behavior: (1) clear targets; (2) diagnostic testing to see how much of the target behavior the learner already possesses; (3) realistic goals; (4) a task that is broken into small, interrelated segments that are introduced a single step at a time; (5) use of positive reinforcement principles; and (6) good records to ensure a reasonable reinforcement schedule.

Social learning theory purports that people learn by observing others and that learning may or may not result in a change of observable behavior. In contrast to behavioral psychologists, social learning theorists posit that reinforcement and punishment have indirect effects on learning. Teacher modeling is an essential component of the direct instruction model, and students are encouraged to attend to the teacher's behavior. Students will learn the modeled behavior when they pay attention to the model, remember the behavior, replicate the behavior, and demonstrate what they have learned—all aspects of the direct instruction model and fixtures in social learning theory.

Cognitive learning theory also contributes to the research base of the direct instruction model. As students construct their own knowledge from previous experiences, direct instruction carefully relates new knowledge and skills to the background knowledge students bring to the classroom. The model also allows students to develop proficiency by providing specific, timely feedback—a necessary requirement for students to accurately construct new capacities. There is ample evidence that direct instruction is associated with increased student achievement (Archer & Hughes, 2011; Rosenshine, 1986).

The direct instruction model uses explicit steps to help students reach the lesson's objectives. The steps move from the teacher having all the responsibility to students' taking on the responsibility of successful demonstration of knowledge and skills. This follows an "I do, we do, you do" pattern.

Steps in the Direct Instructional Model

There are six basic steps in the direct instruction model. They are organized so that the teacher and students can concentrate on the targeted knowledge and skills through a logical and public sequence, using small instructional moves.

STEP 1: REVIEW PREVIOUSLY LEARNED MATERIAL

In direct instruction, the students must clearly understand what they are expected to learn, the steps they will follow in that learning, and how the new learning connects to what has been learned previously. Read how the following teachers conduct a review:

1. Mrs. Benito is preparing to teach a lesson on alphabetizing. She begins by reviewing with the class what they learned the day before: "Yesterday we grouped words according to their first letters. On the table are the word stacks we made, each beginning with the same letter. Today we are going to order these stacks by the second letter's place in the alphabet, starting with the A stack. First, let us review the names of the first letters in each of the stacks we made yesterday."

2. In the gym, Mr. Terry instructs his swimming class: "Let's talk about what we did last week. How did you feel when you were in the water? Last week, you learned how to float. Now, get in the water and practice floating for about five minutes so I can see if everyone remembers that skill. Then you will learn how to move your hands to propel yourself in the water."

3. In math class, Miss Tomlin says, "Yesterday we learned about using X to represent an unknown. Sara, will you please put the first homework problem on the board; Jesse, will you put up the second; and, Frank, will you please put up the third? Let's all look at these problems and determine their accuracy. I will ask you to explain why the problems are or are not correct. When we are sure that we understand how to use the unknown X, which you practiced for homework, we will learn how to use the X in an equation."

Each of these teachers is practicing an essential technique of the direct instruction model: Begin with a short review of previous learning that is necessary to anchor the new learning. Homework that is checked and discussed can be used as a review. Before proceeding to a new skill, make certain students have mastered the learned material. If necessary, the previous lesson should be retaught before going on, particularly when the new skill is dependent on mastery of the preceding one. In the long run, reteaching saves instructional time by allowing students to be prepared for new information and skills.

Pretesting the class to determine skill levels is essential before teaching a new skill. Analyzing students' abilities to learn the skill helps the teacher determine the pace at which to proceed and allows the teacher to prepare for individual differences in the class. In earlier chapters, formative and summative assessments were discussed. Good instruction also demands diagnostic assessment—determining where students are in relation to the goals of the lesson or unit. Diagnostic assessments can be informal (as in the case of discussions, recitations, or individual interviews) or formal (as when a teacher utilizes a paper-and-pencil pretest). Diagnostics and reviews are aligned to unit objectives and assessments.

This video demonstrates review through the use of a sponge activity in a science classroom. The teacher also links the review to a forthcoming performance task as together the class designs a rubric for the summative assessment.

STEP 2: STATE OBJECTIVES FOR THE LESSON

Lesson objectives should be stated clearly and perhaps written on the board in language the students can understand. We visited one second grade classroom during a writing lesson and saw this "objective" written on the board: "The students will practice holding the pencil in the proper position to form the numbers 0–9." Do you see the problem here? The language is not appropriate for the age of the students or even

David Ausubel (1960) argued that teachers can promote student learning by making explicit connections between what the students know and what they will be learning. Generally, when using an advance organizer, the teacher prepares a brief talk before the lesson begins, or graphic organizers or outlines can be used. The key is to make explicit connections between old and new knowledge that will help the learner transfer and apply what is known to what will be learned. This is called "connecting the new to the known." Advance organizers are not summaries; they are constructed at a high level of generality. For example, the concept of independence could serve as an organizer for a lesson on the Revolutionary War, nutrition for a lesson on the basic food groups, and punctuation for a lesson on the comma. Teachers must do more than explain the meaning of something. Good teaching compares things by connecting new learning to previously learned material or to experiences that are familiar to students via analogy and comparison. For instance, a lesson on the Industrial Revolution could begin with a discussion of the transformation from manual to mechanical production, and how that transformation continues to the present day.

In constructing advance organizers, keep the following in mind:

1. Review the lesson objectives and present the objectives in student-friendly language to the class.
2. Organize the content. Present general information first with specific examples and more detail later.
3. Remind students of the bigger picture—where the information or procedures fit in an organized body of knowledge.
4. Potentially include a variety of viewpoints or a critical approach to the subject matter.
5. Clarify important points by rephrasing previous information as you add new information.
6. Share what successful learning will look like at the end of the lesson (Hattie & Yates, 2014).

for the instructional objective—that is, practice in forming hand-written numbers. The objective describes not an objective but an activity—practice—that the students will do rather than what students will be able to do at the end of an instructional period. The more appropriate wording for this objective would be "Students will be able to form accurate numbers from 0–9." But even that is not stated in student-friendly language; instead, it should read, "You will be able to write the numbers 0–9 correctly." The purpose of stating objectives is to tell the learners clearly and simply what the purpose of the instruction is and what outcomes they should expect. Lesson objectives should be connected to previous learning and should be within the reach of all the students. Advance organizers can be a helpful strategy during the beginning steps of direct instruction because they link prior knowledge and lesson objectives to support students in learning new information and skills.

STEP 3: PRESENT NEW MATERIAL

Teachers must prepare to present new material to students. It is not sufficient to know the content or the procedure; you must also be able to teach it in a manner that promotes student learning. Many subject experts are unable to convey their expertise to others. They have become so familiar with the content that they do not remember what it feels like to be a novice learner in their area or the kinds of support that a novice learner might need. In fact, teachers need a variety of knowledge to be successful in classrooms. Pedagogical content knowledge is made up of the specialized skills that are required to teach effectively the specialized content and procedures of a discipline. Along with content knowledge and pedagogical content knowledge, teachers also must know general principles and methods of instruction and classroom management that are essential for pupil learning. Instructional models are an example of general pedagogical knowledge. They can be used across any content area and age level. Therefore, both pedagogical content knowledge and general pedagogical knowledge must be tapped as teachers prepare to present new material.

Good presentations should have the following characteristics:

- Are clear and detailed
- Include instructions and explanations
- Are punctuated with questions and corrective feedback
- Focus learners on the material
- Allow for the systematic evaluation of student understanding

This step of the model is the "I do" step. The teacher models what the students should be able to do at the end of the lesson. Talking through the process of doing the task—think-alouds—can be helpful because successful presentations combine effective verbal techniques with media, questions, demonstrations, and student participation. The information that is presented should be interesting, highly structured, well organized, and limited in scope. The content to be learned must be selected and then analyzed according to the learners' needs. Presenting material that is too difficult or presenting too much material at one time hinders learning and defeats the purpose of the presentation. Presenting a few significant points accompanied by many illustrations and questions is generally more effective than covering many points. When introducing a new skill, the procedures should be broken into small segments that can be introduced in a sequence.

New information and skills can be presented to students in many ways. Many of the instructional models discussed in this text may be used to present new material to students. The presentation step of direct instruction can be either inductive or deductive; it can range from a lecture or a concept attainment activity to a demonstration. An inductive lesson begins with many examples of a generalization and a principle, and, by induction, students are guided to the principle. Most of the instructional models in this text are inductive. Common deductive forms of presenting new information and skills are lectures and demonstrations.

Brief lecture presentations are often an essential part of classroom instruction and one way in which new material is efficiently delivered to students. Such conveyance of information, used sparingly, can be inserted into step 3 of the direct instruction model. The steps of using a lecture presentation or a demonstration to present information are as follows:

1. Analyze the content to be presented according to the needs of the learners.
2. Chart the content from the most general to the most specific material to be presented.
3. Break all skills into small segments to be presented in a logical order.
4. Develop an advance organizer for the lesson that will provide a reference point for the new material.
5. Select the main points or steps to be presented and limit these to a reasonable number, depending on the learners.
6. Select examples to illustrate each main point and connect each point or step to the one preceding and to the advance organizer.
7. Ask questions to check for understanding and watch for signals from the class that indicate lack of attention.
8. Summarize the main points and connect them to the next phase of the lesson.

To prepare for all presentations, the main points to be covered must be identified. This is important, as lecture presentations must be short and concise; digressions will make it more difficult for students to engage and comprehend. Most adults can listen to a lecture for only about 20 minutes without becoming inattentive (Middendorf & Kalish, 1996). Children have an even shorter attention span. Many speakers adhere to a rule of no more than five and no fewer than three points to be covered in a single lecture. For younger children, three points may be too many. Depending on the amount of material to be covered in the lesson and the background knowledge of the learner, several brief lectures over a period of days may be desirable.

An advance organizer can help with conveying the main points of the lesson concisely. Keep in mind the importance of selecting an idea that is more general than the new material and that can provide the learner with a context within which to relate the new learning. Hattie's metaphor for an advance organizer is a coat hanger—something on which we can hang our new learning (Hattie & Yates, 2014, p. 115). For instance, a lecture on baking a cake might begin with an advance organizer tracing the development of cakes from simple patties prepared by native tribes to the complex confections available in modern bakeries.

Use examples to illustrate each important point. Examples serve as memory hooks for the listener. Sometimes speakers do not use visual aids; they rely on stories and anecdotes to illustrate their main points. The same technique is effective in the classroom in helping the students remember main points. Anecdotes remain in memory and assist in the recall of the points made in the lecture. In the classroom, the teacher can also use many audio or visual materials to illustrate the points made in the lecture.

Repetition can be used to reinforce main points. Repeat all the points previously made when each new point is made, and ask questions to monitor interest and understanding. At the end of the lecture presentation, summarize the main points and conclude with a reference to the advance organizer. This helps to wrap up the presentation for the students.

If the lesson is to include a demonstration, prepare the material to be exhibited and learned in small segments; check for understanding at the end of each segment. One of the most difficult tasks of the expert is to anticipate the learning steps of the beginner, particularly one who may not have the same aptitude or enthusiasm for the skill that the teacher has. The content and skills of the lesson must be carefully considered not only as objectives are written for the lesson, but as the instructional moves are designed for the demonstration. Organize the material in a logical order.

Visual and real examples work particularly well in the presentation stage of direct instruction. Too often, teachers depend on telling, despite the fact that pictures or a live demonstration can be more effective and can provide learners with a memory hook for new information. Imagine a lesson on baking a cake without a demonstration phase. Many teachers forget that one picture (activity, experiment, or demonstration) can be worth a thousand words.

STEP 4: GUIDE PRACTICE, ASSESS PERFORMANCE, AND PROVIDE CORRECTIVE FEEDBACK

Once the teacher has modeled the knowledge and skills—the "I do" phase of the lesson—there is a gradual release of responsibility from the teacher to the student. Students will practice the knowledge and skills that were modeled—the "we do" part of the process. Practice, both guided and independent, is an essential part of direct instruction. New material is presented in small steps, with ample opportunity for practice following each step of the process. In the following examples, the teacher controls the process and monitors the practice of both the group and individuals within the group. The teacher provides direction and feedback, but students are actively engaged in modeling the process. Here are some examples of guided practice:

- "To tie our shoes, we start with holding a lace in each hand. Now take the lace on the model shoe in front of you and hold a lace in each hand. Good. The next step is to cross the lace in the right hand over the one in the left hand. [Note: be sure to plan for children who are left-handed.] Let us all practice putting the right lace over the left lace like this. Tommy, hold up your right hand. Good. Now cross the lace in that hand over the one in your left hand, like this. Very good."

- "To operate a tablet, we must first turn it on. Please locate the on/off button and push it to the *on* position."

- "We have just seen a presentation on the four chambers of the heart. Let us review each of these four chambers as we fill in this diagram on the board together. Who can name one of the chambers?"

Teacher questions are an important part of guided practice and should be prepared before the lesson. Teachers frequently feel that the class will become bored if too many questions are asked during instruction; however, in learning new material, repetition and review are essential. Guided practice questions are diagnostic; they are used to see where students are in relation to the lesson's objectives. As students take on more responsibility for learning during the lesson, teachers need to evaluate the accuracy and depth of understanding that students exhibit. When direct instruction is used to teach basic skills, questions should ask students to recall specific information and demonstrate comprehension of the lesson's objectives. These questions are typically convergent, requiring a short one- or two-word answer. Wait time, the time a teacher allows for a student to answer a question, is also an essential component of the process. A wait of approximately three seconds seems to produce the best results, along with following up with students who do not respond individually (Slavin, 2000). To monitor participation during guided practice, the teacher can maintain a checklist of students responding to questions. If the same students answer most of the questions, the teacher should evaluate the questions asked and determine whether the rest of the class is comprehending the material.

Effective teachers set up situations in which those who need further explanation or help can get it. They ask students to repeat the directions or the information. They ask students to summarize for each other and share those summaries. They call on students for additional examples and applications of information. As students practice their new learning and teachers observe and diagnose problems, there are several instructional moves that can help keep students engaged in the guided practice. Lemov (2010) suggests using cold calls (calling on students even when they have not raised their hands) and call and response in which the whole class answers a question. In both cases, there must be a positive climate in which both wrong and right answers are normal as we learn in school.

For efficient and effective learning, students must have correct and adequate information about their performance. The feedback must be clear and be related to detailed objectives or targets. Feedback is value neutral and tells students what happened, the result of their actions, and information about distance between their performance and the target goal. Good instruction allows students to self-assess by providing detailed feedback. Guided practice allows both teachers and students to see how close they are to the lesson's objectives.

If the students have not learned the material, don't blame them and don't go on. A swimming coach does not allow students to drown if they are in the deep end of the pool and cannot tread water. He or she goes back to a more basic step. The same approach is needed in learning any skill or new content. If students do not meet the instructional objectives, the teacher should evaluate and analyze the original presentation, determine the problem, and then find a way to reach the entire class. The success rate for the learning of directly taught skills should be as close to 100 percent as possible. Students who understand the first presentation will benefit from any reteaching, particularly if the later presentation is different from the first. Better yet is to have early learners help others by putting their understandings into their own words for others to follow. The guided practice step allows for reteaching.

Providing feedback during guided practice is an important teacher behavior. We know that achievement is enhanced by asking students to work until accuracy is achieved. To achieve success, feedback must be timely, specific to the task, and detailed. A student teacher using the direct instruction model for the first time might hear the following feedback:

- "Your presentation included an analogy that helped students make sense of the new material."

- "You did not provide feedback to students during guided practice."
- "The presentation did not have any audio or visual displays and continued for most of the period. There was little time for your students to practice the skill in either guided or independent practice."

STEP 5: ASSIGN INDEPENDENT PRACTICE, ASSESS PERFORMANCE, AND PROVIDE CORRECTIVE FEEDBACK

Once students have had practice in performing the lesson's objectives and receiving feedback on their work, they take on even more responsibility for learning. They work on the new knowledge and skill without the support of the teacher or peers. This is the "you do" part of the lesson. Independent practice requires careful monitoring of students' practicing a new skill on their own or in small groups. Before students are assigned independent work, however, sufficient time must be spent in guided practice to ensure that they are prepared to work on their own. Observations during guided practice will indicate when students are ready to move to independent practice.

The teacher should circulate during independent practice, checking that no student is repeating a mistake or is actually practicing error. In addition, there should be some way for students to check their results as they proceed independently. Sometimes, the answers in the back of the textbook are an excellent resource. Some teachers provide checkpoints, or stations, in the classroom where students can go periodically to check their work.

Independent practice provides students the opportunity to process and rehearse the new information or skills that were presented in the earlier steps of the direct instruction model. The goal of this step is to help students "own" the new information or skill by moving from the guided practice phase—where slow and deliberate effort results in only a few errors—to the automaticity of being able to work quickly and respond automatically without having to think through each step of the process. Think about learning a new computer program or application for your cell phone. At first, we are somewhat tentative as we learn the new procedures, but eventually our use becomes automatic and we spend more time thinking about why we are using the tool rather than how we are using the tool. Effective independent practice occurs when students are making only a few errors in the guided practice phase and before they get to the automaticity stage.

Most independent practice uses a product such as a worksheet, a writing task, or oral responses to questions. Of course, there are many other ways for students to practice new information and skills that students find more engaging. Teachers may embed the practice into a meaningful context, motivating students to complete the work. Possible independent practice products include the following:

- Creating and solving problems or situations
- Designing a game, poster, or demonstration
- Writing a poem, story, book, or brochure
- Doing a role play or puppet show
- Drawing a map, picture, cartoon, or diagram

These products can be assigned as classroom independent seatwork, in learning centers, or as homework. In all cases, the task objectives must be congruent with those rehearsed in guided practice. The direct instruction model is designed to scaffold student learning by breaking knowledge and skills into small steps, modeling, and practicing. By following the steps of the model, you are scaffolding student learning. The evaluation of independent practice products in the direct instruction model is discussed in the "Evaluating Learning in the Direct Instruction Model" section later in this chapter.

 Scaffolding is a learning process in which students are supported as they work toward deeper understanding or greater automaticity in skills. Scaffolding is used at the beginning of a learning cycle and may include coaching, specific feedback, templates, outlines, study guides, notes, and additional resources. As students practice and develop greater facility with the new information and skills, the scaffolding is gradually removed. Scaffolding is based on several psychological theories that describe the supports that novice learners need as they attempt to master knowledge and skills. Figure 2.5 provides some examples of scaffolding. Scaffolding fifth and sixth graders during a reading comprehension lesson can be viewed in this video. The "I do, we do, you do" structure is evident throughout the lesson. www.youtube.com/watch?v=gleNo8dqHb8

STEP 6: REVIEW PERIODICALLY, OFFERING CORRECTIVE FEEDBACK IF NECESSARY

Periodic review of new and recently acquired material should be built into every instructional plan. Overlearning is essential to mastering a new skill, particularly when each skill is necessary to learning the next. While students are in the process of learning a new skill, review of skills learned previously is essential for automaticity.

Homework can provide periodic review and should be checked before proceeding to new information and skills. If homework is worth assigning, it is worth checking, yet many teachers neglect this important part of the review process. If the students have not understood the assignment, do not go on to the next step. Reteach the material and analyze the reasons for failure to learn. If a weekly review indicates that a skill has not been retained, then reteaching is necessary. Students often forget skills and information during the summer, so it is particularly important to test for retention at the beginning of a new school year or semester. Although pacing guides may make reteaching more difficult to plan, reteaching will save you time in the long run by making certain that students have a foundation on which to learn new skills.

Teachers should demand a high success rate for their students. If students are not learning, there must be a reason. Answers to the following questions can help teachers understand any lack of success.

- Did the students have the required background to learn the new set of skills or material?
- Were the steps in the learning process broken into sufficiently small steps?
- Was each step learned before a new step was introduced?
- Were the learning objectives and the directions stated clearly?
- Was the content organized logically, and were the examples, lectures, and demonstrations effective?
- Were sufficient questions asked to determine whether the class understood what was being taught?
- Was there enough guided practice? Were all the students involved in the practice, and were errors corrected quickly?
- Was there independent practice of the skill or learning? Was this independent practice checked carefully to determine whether the students were performing without error?
- Were there periodic review and opportunities for practice of the new learning?

SUMMARY OF STEPS IN THE DIRECT INSTRUCTION MODEL

1. *Review previously learned material.* Make certain that students have mastered the material taught previously and that they understand the connections to the new learning.
2. *State objectives for the lesson.* The objectives should be presented to the students at the beginning of the lesson in student-friendly language.
3. *Present new material.* New material should be well organized and presented in an interesting manner. Frequent checks should be used to determine whether the students are comprehending the information.
4. *Guide practice, assess performance, and provide corrective feedback.* Guide the students through practice sessions, making certain they are performing correctly.
5. *Assign independent practice, assess performance, and provide corrective feedback.* Continue to supervise the students as they work independently, checking for error.

Homework should be assigned for independent practice only when the teacher feels certain that the students can perform the work correctly.

6. *Review periodically, offering corrective feedback if necessary.* Homework is checked before new instruction is given, and reteaching is conducted if necessary. The teacher conducts periodic checks to make certain that the new learning has been retained.

The preceding list does not completely convey the generative and dynamic nature of the direct model of instruction. Direct instruction entails a complex dance of reciprocal responsibility from the teacher to the student. This complexity, of course, is difficult to capture in text. Therefore, we examine the possible behaviors of teachers and students working within the direct instruction framework. This approach allows for the consideration of what is needed to master the model and include it in your professional toolbox. In addition, Table 3.1 is a guide to help you consider what student behaviors are associated with student learning, allowing you to mold your teaching behaviors.

Case studies showing how to use direct instruction in context can be seen in Chapters Thirteen, Fourteen, and Fifteen.

Evaluating Learning in the Direct Instruction Model

The purpose of the direct instruction model is to promote knowledge and skills that are readily definable, easily illustrated, and reliably improved with practice. Evaluating student learning occurs throughout the model in each of the steps. For example, guided practice can serve as a formative assessment because it provides students and teachers with information about prior knowledge and skill acquisition. Formative assessments collect information to inform instructional decisions and student behavior. Both teachers and students gain information that can guide their next instructional steps. Teachers can use checklists or notes during guided practice to document the problems and accomplishments students exhibit so that, if necessary, reteaching can occur, ensuring that independent practice will produce automaticity. Guided practice tasks must be designed to provide meaningful clues to student knowledge and understanding and should be as identical to the task in the presentation step as possible. Students should be able to practice what they have seen modeled.

Independent practice can also provide data about student learning. If paper-and-pencil tasks (worksheets, question responses, graphic organizers, problem sets, etc.) have been used throughout the lesson, they can also be used for the independent practice step. Assessment tasks must be congruent with the objectives and the instruction of the lesson. Instructional models offer an aligned blueprint, but the tasks that are used within the steps of the model must have internal alignment—all of the steps must be designed to help students reach identified targets. This becomes particularly important if grades are being assigned to independent practice products. The replication of tasks can be less similar in independent practice than that in guided practice as you prepare students to transfer the skills to unfamiliar settings. But all assessments, especially graded assessments, must contain only the elements students have had the opportunity to practice during previous instruction.

Independent practice products can be evaluated using rubrics, which are guides for assessing student learning. They make scoring criteria clear and focus feedback for students, peers, and teachers. Good rubrics specify the characteristics of an outstanding assignment. These characteristics are developed by analyzing the assigned task, the purpose of the task, and the evaluation criteria embedded in the task. Differentiating between excellent, good, adequate, and poor examples of an assignment allows for the articulation of criteria. Independent practice product rubrics should be task specific. Although there are many examples of rubrics on the Internet, be sure

TABLE 3.1 Potential Teacher and Student Behaviors in the Direct Instruction Model

Step	Teacher	Student
1. Review	• Reviews previously learned material necessary for new learning • Designs and administers diagnostic assessment	• Participates in review using metacognitive strategies • Reviews diagnostic assessment; identifies gaps in knowledge
2. State objectives	• Presents objectives in student-friendly language • Relates content of lesson to prior student knowledge/experience (advance organizer) • Provides lesson overview	• Demonstrates understanding of objectives • Makes connections between what will be learned and what is known • Describes what he or she should be doing during lesson
3. Present new material	• Presents new material in clear and detailed fashion orally and visually • Provides specific instruction and explanations • Uses engaging voice • Focuses on learners • Identifies all steps of new skill • Identifies all essential attributes of new concept • Checks for student understanding	• Follows teacher's presentation • Asks for clarification when necessary • Makes explicit connections to prior knowledge • Rehearses steps when appropriate • Identifies essential attributes when appropriate • Responds to formative assessments • Thinks about the personal challenges in learning the new material
4. Guide practice, assess Performance, provide Feedback	• Reviews new material in small steps • Scaffolds practice • Circulates, monitors, and assesses student learning through observation and questioning • Provides appropriate feedback (timely, detailed, specific) • Determines when to begin independent practice	• Identifies and supplies examples of new concept when appropriate • Practices each step of the new skill when appropriate • Answers questions from teacher and peers • Asks clarifying questions • Acts on feedback • Reflects on own learning
5. Independent practice, assess performance, corrective feedback	• Monitors student performance based on objectives • Provides feedback after the task is completed	• Processes and rehearses new information • Works toward automaticity
6. Periodic review with feedback	• Monitors automaticity of student learning through homework, scripted questions, and activities • Provides feedback when necessary	• Demonstrates automaticity of knowledge and skills • Responds to reteaching, when necessary • Reflects on own learning

that you are capturing the essential elements of quality for the direct instruction (or other model) lesson that you have taught. An example of a rubric for a haiku writing assignment is shown in Figure 3.1. This rubric would be helpful to Mr. Bennett as he evaluates the student work described in the scenario at the beginning of this chapter.

FIGURE 3.1   A Rubric for Evaluating Haiku

	Excellent	Satisfactory	Poor
Focus	Clear focus on nature; words support focus in an original way	Clear focus on nature; words used are commonly associated with topic	Focus on nature doesn't exist or is not clear.
Voice	Strong personal voice; appeals to reader	Clear personal voice; only somewhat engaging	Personal voice is not apparent to reader
Word choice	Vivid words leave picture in reader's mind	Words used that communicate clearly, but lack variety	Limited vocabulary that does not capture reader
Structure	5 syllable–7 syllable–5 syllable format followed; no spelling errors	5 syllable–7 syllable–5 syllable format followed; a few spelling errors	Format incorrectly applied; includes some spelling errors

Meeting Individual Needs in Direct Instruction

By using a variety of instructional models and strategies, teachers differentiate instruction. Differentiation strategies are responsive to individuals and groups of students; using a variety of processes is one way of differentiating instruction. All instructional models provide opportunities for differentiation. It is not possible to describe all of these opportunities in this text. However, there are strategies that are a good fit for specific models. In the case of the direct instruction model, there are two important differentiation techniques that are closely tied to the purpose, basis, and processes of the model—flexible grouping and varying questions.

FLEXIBLE GROUPING

All differentiation opportunities are based on clear objectives and an understanding of student background knowledge and achievements in relation to these targets. Both of these requirements (clear objectives and acknowledgment of students' prior knowledge) are met by the structure of the direct instruction model.

Practice is also a critical attribute of direct instruction. Flexible grouping allows students to practice new knowledge and skills with a group of peers of similar interests, skills, or background knowledge or with a mixed-achievement group so that peers can share insights and skills. Students learn in a social context, and groups need to be fluid to provide many opportunities to learn. The key here is flexibility—groups should never be stagnant during guided practice; they shift to meet the needs of individual students. Although much direct instruction is done with the whole class, continued guided practice can be completed in groups. It is important, however, that before group work is implemented, clear guidelines are taught and practiced.

VARYING QUESTIONS

Variations in questions can be used as a differentiation technique within all of the steps of direct instruction. In fact, varying or adjusting questions is an important strategy within all of the models presented in this text. Questions can be adjusted based on learner readiness, experiences, interests, and preferred approaches to learning. By knowing where your students are in relation to your goals and their individual learning profiles, you can target questions to specific learners during the review, presentation, and guided practice steps of the direct instruction model. There are many ways to categorize questions. One way is to use Bloom's revised taxonomy, discussed in Chapter Two, to vary the cognitive demand on your students. For those students with a low readiness level in relation to your specific objectives, you can focus your questioning on "remember" and "understand" levels. "Apply" questions can be used with learners who have demonstrated some foundational skill in the content with which you are working; for those students with high readiness levels, you can focus on the "analyze," "evaluate," and "create" categories. Student background knowledge can also be used. For example, during a lesson on Gothic architecture, the teacher might ask a student who has traveled in Europe and is interested in architecture a question about the gargoyles she saw. Other students may be asked questions about how they might decorate a building and why. The purpose of varying questions is to help individual learners make connections with the content and develop the understandings, knowledge, and skills of the lesson. All students are held accountable for learning the lesson's objectives, but their road to the objectives through teacher questioning may vary.

Benefits of the Direct Instruction Model

The direct instruction model has been clearly related to student achievement (Rosenshine, 1986) and provides the opportunity for students to learn clearly defined skills and knowledge. The model is a generative model that can be used as a frame or template for a number of instructional models, strategies, and approaches. Once the teacher has provided the lesson objectives and reviewed the necessary background knowledge, the next step is the presentation of content or skills. This step can be carried out with an inductive approach (examples are presented first, and then students inductively derive the broad principle or rule from the examples) or a deductive approach (the teacher provides the broad principle or rule, and then students deduce examples that illustrate the principle or rule). How the material is presented is not a critical attribute of the direct instruction model. What is critical in this model, and what is essential in all good teaching, are the links to background knowledge, the small chunks of information, and guided and independent practice, all with corrective feedback. These should be part of every instructional approach. The direct instruction model is inherently aligned—another important characteristic for instructional models. The goals of the model allow lesson objectives to be clearly articulated, and all steps of the model are geared toward helping students be successful at demonstrating lesson objectives.

ELEMENTARY GRADES LESSON

DIRECT INSTRUCTION: Rhyming with Mother Goose	
OBJECTIVES	**Common Core State Standards—English/Language Arts R.F.K.2** Demonstrate understanding of spoken words, syllables, and sounds (phonemes). Recognize and produce rhyming words. **Students Will Know** • Rhymes are heard when two or more words have similar ending sounds • How to identify rhyming words in Mother Goose rhymes by listening for similar sounds

Students Will Understand That

- We can hear rhymes when people talk, sing, or recite

Students Will Be Able To

- Identify rhyming and nonrhyming words in a Mother Goose rhyme
- Generate a rhyming word when given a spoken word

ASSESSMENTS

- *Diagnostic.* Ask students to define a rhyme. Ask students whether particular words rhyme.
- *Formative.* During guided and independent practice, students identify and generate rhyming words.

PROCEDURES

1. *Review previously learned material.* Show students the Mother Goose book that you have read before. Talk to the students about why we like Mother Goose rhymes. Highlight rhyming words and how they sound.
2. *State the objectives of the lesson.* Tell the children that we frequently see and hear rhymes and that today we will identify rhyming words.
3. *Present new material.* Show students the Tom, Tom poster.

> Tom, Tom, the piper's son,
> Stole a pig, and away he run,
> The pig was eat,
> And Tom was beat,
> And Tom ran crying down the street.

   Read "Tom, Tom the Piper's Son" from the prepared poster. Point to each word as you read. Define the words *piper* and *beat*. Read the poem again with one of the students tracking the words. Explain that rhyming words are words that end with the same sound; give examples—*cow* and *wow*, *hat* and *rat*, *ham* and *ram*, *man* and *pan*. Read "Tom, Tom" slowly and ask students to raise their hands when they hear two rhyming words. Then ask volunteers to identify the rhyming words in the text. Circle the rhyming words on the "Tom, Tom" poster in the same color. Ask students whether the following words are rhymes: *son* and *eat*, *stole* and *piper*, *crying* and *street*. Ask how we can tell that they are not rhyming words. Make a list on the board of rhyming and nonrhyming words in "Tom, Tom."

4. *Guided practice.* Show the poster of "Little Miss Muffet." Define unfamiliar words. Ask students to circle the rhyming words in the same color. Provide corrective feedback. Continue with additional Mother Goose rhymes, if necessary.

> Little Miss Muffet sat on a tuffet
> Eating her curds and whey.
> There came a big spider,
> He sat down beside her,
> And frightened Miss Muffet away.

5. *Presentation II.* Give students two rhyming words and ask them to provide a different rhyming word. Begin with the rhymes identified in "Tom, Tom" and "Little Miss Muffet."
6. *Guided practice.* Have students reach into the rhyming word bag (a bag filled with index cards on which simple rhyming words are written) and pull out a word. Read the word and ask the student to provide a rhyming word.
7. *Independent practice.* Students are asked to list three words that rhyme with a given word and three words that do not rhyme.

MIDDLE/SECONDARY GRADES LESSON

DIRECT INSTRUCTION: Writing Haiku

OBJECTIVES

CCSS English/Language Arts W.7.3.D
Use precise words and phrases, relevant descriptive details, and sensory language to capture the action and convey experiences and events.

Students Will Know

- Haiku is a simple and sophisticated poetic form that sharpens language, observation, and expression
- The defining characteristics of haiku (very short, descriptive, personal, and divided into two parts)
- The rules for constructing haiku:
  - 5 syllable–7 syllable–5 syllable form
  - Two parts; break after first or second line
  - Clue to season in one word (*kigo*)
  - Snapshot of everyday experience in nature or human life

Students Will Understand That

- Poetic forms vary and serve different purposes

Students Will Be Able To

- Use the list of rules and conventions of haiku to distinguish between haiku and other forms of poetry
- Develop a list of words that might be used in writing a haiku
- Compose a haiku poem based on personal experience

ASSESSMENT

Students may choose to do one of the following:

- Submit a haiku to the school literary magazine
- Make a poster with a haiku and illustrations
- Create their own haiku anthology
- Teach haiku writing to other classes or groups of students

PROCEDURES

1. Review previously learned material related to the study of haiku. Ask students what they know about haiku.
2. State lesson objectives.
3. Provide examples of haiku. Include both classic and contemporary examples. Have students read each poem aloud and ask students to comment on the similarities they see between the poems. Through this discussion, help students recognize that haiku are very short, descriptive, personal, and divided into two parts.
4. Based on reported similarities, provide an outline of the main rules for writing haiku.
5. Have students distinguish between several short poems dealing with nature by identifying the haiku and defending their choice by using the list of rules.
6. Have students brainstorm a glossary of words they might use, based on the rules and conventions of this form of poetry. Then, for each season, have students choose an occurrence that might be the subject of a haiku

and brainstorm descriptive language that would help a reader visualize that scene. List their suggestions on the chalkboard; use the list to have students generate ideas for a haiku, encouraging them to see the range of possibilities beyond a description of nature. Write two or three haiku with the class. This may be done as a whole-group or small-group activity.

7. Have students write a haiku based on a personal experience, using at least one of the words they have brainstormed in class. Pair students to edit and suggest improvements to one another's work.

8. For independent practice, students may choose one of the assessment options.

SUMMARY

It is important to repeat a statement made in the beginning of this chapter: The direct instruction model is a necessary, but not a sufficient, instructional tool. To be without this effective tool is a handicap, because the steps in this model provide a framework for instructional design. However, to use this model exclusively is deadening.

The direct instruction model can be used to teach many knowledge-level objectives and skills. It begins with a review of previously learned material, often in the form of an advance organizer. After connections to what is known are made explicit, the teacher presents clear objectives for the lesson. Presentations of new material may come in many forms and employ a variety of materials. Once the teacher has modeled the new information or skills, students practice while receiving corrective feedback. Ideally, once students can demonstrate that the task can be completed with only a few errors, independent practice can be assigned to develop automaticity. Feedback and periodic review ensures that students have reached and continue to maintain the lesson's objectives.

EXTENSIONS

ACTIVITIES

1. Interview a teacher about the types of instructional models that are used in his or her classroom and the reasons why instructional models are or are not helpful.

2. Design a direct instruction lesson for a foundational skill in a content area you are or will be teaching. Be sure to include KUD objectives, all of the steps of the lesson, and a formative assessment.

3. Prepare a one-page handout summarizing the direct instruction model.

4. Find examples of direct instruction videos on the Internet. Analyze any differences that might exist between the model that is presented in this chapter and what you notice in the video.

REFLECTIVE QUESTIONS

1. Learning centers can be used for independent practice in the direct instruction model. What questions do you have about setting up learning centers in a classroom? How will you find the answers?

2. Rubrics are helpful to both teachers and students. What are the problems with using rubrics? How can teachers overcome these problems?

3. What knowledge or skill do you teach, or will you be teaching, that could be used successfully in a direct instruction lesson? Why do you believe this knowledge or skill is congruent with the direct instruction model?

4. Think about how frequently you will be using direct instruction in your classroom and why you might be using this model with this frequency.

4 The Concept Attainment Model

DEFINING CONCEPTS INDUCTIVELY

Chapter Objectives

You Will Know

- The basis of the concept attainment model
- The steps of the concept attainment model
- Variations in the concept attainment model
- How to evaluate learning in the concept attainment model
- How to meet individual needs with the concept attainment model
- Benefits of the concept attainment model

You Will Understand That

- An inductive instructional approach builds on innate ways of learning

You Will Be Able To

- Argue for the use of inductive teaching to support student learning
- Design, implement, and reflect on a concept attainment lesson

In the Elementary Classroom

During a unit on animal adaptations, Ms. Sarembock teaches the concept of hibernation. She wants her students to understand that hibernation is an animal behavior in which the animal appears to be sleeping while its bodily functions are dormant. At the beginning of class, Ms. Sarembock reminds her students of the rules of the concept attainment "game" that they have played before.

"Class, now that we have reviewed the way you will raise your hand and work together to solve the concept attainment mystery, let me tell you that our mystery has something to do with animal behaviors. Here are pictures of our first two examples." Ms. Sarembock shows pictures of a groundhog and a gopher and puts the pictures on the board under "Examples." "Is anyone ready to hypothesize as to what animal behavior the gopher and the groundhog have in common?"

The children begin to share ideas and the teacher writes each on the board under the "Hypotheses" column.

> They hunt for food.
> They stand watch.
> They burrow.
> They make tunnels.
> They live underground.
> They use their teeth.

Ms. Sarembock tells the children that they have a good list. She reminds them what to do with the list as she shows them a nonexample of the animal behavior they are looking for. "Look at the picture of the animal that does not have the behavior we are looking for." She shows them a picture of a dog and puts the picture on the board under "Nonexamples."

"What are the things that a dog has in common with our examples? Because the dog is not an example, whatever they have in common is not our mystery behavior." The discussion that follows results in a new hypothesis list as Ms. Sarembock crosses out the behaviors that don't fit. Only one behavior is left.

They make burrows.

After several more rounds of examples (frogs, garter snakes, bears, salamanders, and bats) and nonexamples (house cat, parrot, rats, kangaroos, camels, elephants), the class has this hypothesis list.

~~They hunt for food.~~
~~They stand watch.~~
~~They burrow.~~
~~They make tunnels.~~
~~They live underground.~~
~~They use their teeth to kill their enemies.~~
~~They have feet to run with.~~
~~They have fur.~~
We don't see them in the cold weather.

Ms. Sarembock asks the students to hypothesize what animal behavior occurs that would mean that we would not see the animals in the winter. With the help of her class, she defines the word *hibernate*. She then presents the students with some test examples of different animals, discusses the process with the students, and asks them to write a paragraph about why animals hibernate. ∎

In the Middle/Secondary Classroom

Mrs. Gonzales is teaching the concept of metaphor to her eighth grade class. She explains that they are going to learn the meaning of a new concept, and that the name of the concept will be a mystery until they have identified what makes the concept different from other ideas or concepts. She adds, "We will find the concept by looking at examples and contrasting nonexamples. The examples will have all of the essential parts of the concept; they will represent the essence of the concept. I will show you some negative examples that may contain some of, but not all, the essential qualities of this concept. You will solve the mystery by comparing the examples and identifying the criterial or critical elements of the positive examples." She puts three columns on the board—"Examples," "Nonexamples," and "Hypotheses."

The first example is put on the board under "Examples": "The moon is a silver ship sailing in the night sky." The students come up with the following hypotheses, which Mrs. Gonzales writes in the appropriate column on the board.

Descriptions of ships
Sentence
Poetry
Quotation
Comparison of different things

Mrs. Gonzales provides another example: "Superman—the Man of Steel." She asks students to review their list of hypotheses and asks them to remove any that do not fit with this new example. The students are able to eliminate (with explanations) all but the *comparison* entry.

With student input, the hypothesis list looks like this:

~~Descriptions of ships~~
~~Sentence~~
~~Poetry~~
~~Quotation~~
Comparison of different things

Next, the students are provided a negative example: "He had a heart like a lion."

Mrs. Gonzales: What about this example is different from the others?

Kanye: Not much, there is still a comparison of different things, but the word *like* is there.

Mrs. Gonzales: Would you like a positive or a negative example?

Class: A negative example.

The teacher writes "frightened as a mouse" under the appropriate column.

Kanye: It's still a comparison, but instead of *like* the word *as* is there.

Chad: Can we see another positive example?

The teacher writes "a recipe for disaster."

Ben (yelling from the back of the room): All of the examples are comparisons that don't use *like* or *as*.

Mrs. Gonzales: Here is a sentence. Tell me if it is an example or nonexample. "The father was a tower of strength."

Helen: That is an example because it is a comparison without using *like* or *as*.

Mrs. Gonzales: Is there anything you can add about the things that are compared?

Helen: Well, they are very different—comparing ships to moons and people and steel.

Mrs. Gonzales: Here is another example. "The ship plows the sea." What is being compared here?

Yolanda: The ship is being compared to a plow that is used in the ground at a farm.

Savanna: The ship is the plow in the example.

Mrs. Gonzales: Are you ready to label and state the definition of this concept?

Rebecca: I don't know the name, but the definition is a comparison of things that are different.

Tommy: A comparison of things that doesn't use *like* or *as*.

Ben: One object in the comparison actually becomes another, like the ship plowing the ocean. The ship becomes a plow.

Brian: How about putting together some of what you are saying—a comparison that joins two different things to make a new image or idea without using *like* or *as*?

Mrs. Gonzales: That is an excellent definition. We call this a *metaphor*. How did you figure out what the main attributes of a metaphor are?

Rebecca: By comparing what was similar in the different examples and what was different between the examples and nonexamples.

Mrs. Gonzales: Here is a selection of figurative language examples. Identify the metaphors. ■

Basis for the Concept Attainment Model

The concept attainment model is based on the research of Jerome Bruner, Jacqueline Goodnow, and George Austin, which was reported in the landmark work *A Study of Thinking* (1986). Bruner and his associates were concerned primarily with the process through which individuals categorize data and attain concepts. Educators have been particularly interested in the use of this research in teaching concepts to learners. According to Bruner and his associates, categorizing reduces the world's complexity, allowing us to label the objects of the world. Because we establish categories or concepts based on defining characteristics, there is reduced demand for constant learning. Knowing the broad category *dog*, for example, helps us to identify a wide variety of dogs. We do not have to relearn the essential qualities of dogs each time we see one.

The common features that define a concept may be concrete or abstract. It is easier to learn tangible concepts that have only a few criterial characteristics than it is to learn a more abstract concept that has numerous fuzzy essential attributes. So it is easier to learn the concepts *maps* or *bicycles* than it is to understand the idea concepts of *freedom*, *justice*, or *honesty*. All concepts have (1) a name and definition, (2) examples of items that are included in the concept class, and (3) critical attributes that define the concept. We teach concepts to ease the cognitive pressure of learning too many discrete bits of information or facts.

Teaching concepts is congruent with the ways in which we process new information. Concepts help us to develop patterns and schemata to make sense of the world. A concept is both a summary of what we already know and an organizing device to help us make sense of the new information with which we are bombarded: "concept attainment requires a student to figure out the attributes of a category that is already formed in another person's mind by comparing and contrasting examples (called exemplars) that contain the characteristics (called attributes) of the concept with the examples that do not contain those attributes" (Joyce, Calhoun, & Hopkins, 2009, p. 34).

Concepts are different from facts and generalizations. Facts are discrete bits of information that typically are an outcome of observation and have no predictive value without other facts. Knowing that Hurricane Katrina hit the Gulf Coast on August 29, 2005, doesn't predict when or if another devastating hurricane will hit the area in the next few years. "Hurricanes frequently hit the Gulf Coast" is a generalization. Generalizations are statements that show a relationship between two or more concepts. In our example, the concepts are *hurricanes* and *Gulf Coast*. Hurricanes can be used in a concept attainment lesson by using a data set of recent hurricanes as exemplars versus other natural disasters such as mudslides, earthquakes, and tornadoes.

To make sense of all the various stimuli in the world, learners of all ages form concepts and give them names. Imagine the cognitive overload if every single thing in the world were seen as a separate and unrelated entity. To form concepts, learners pay attention to likenesses rather than differences and place similar objects in the same category. Apples come in many sizes, shapes, and colors, but by attending to their similarities and ignoring their differences, we form an initial concept of *apple*.

Many concepts used in the classroom are abstract and have different interpretations; they frequently are used, however, as though every student shared the same definition. Consider the word *democracy*. If you asked a class of university students to write their own definitions of the term, you would get many different answers. Yet we often expect that learners in elementary school have a shared definition of concepts like democracy in their vocabulary. Concept attainment can help us sharpen our definitions to the shared criterial attributes of what makes a democracy. Students can learn the important distinctions between examples and nonexamples—allowing for the development of more sophisticated ideas and generalizations.

Teaching students to understand the meaning of the concepts taught in the classroom is one of the most important challenges of teaching. Concepts have names as well as definitions that contain essential attributes that place them in a particular category. For instance, for the concept *table*, one definition is "a piece of furniture consisting of a smooth, flat slab fixed on legs." The essential attributes of *table* are (1) piece of furniture; (2) smooth, flat slab; and (3) fixed on legs. The students are more apt to understand the meaning of the concept and be able to recognize the essential attributes if they arrive at a definition through numerous examples instead of through memorizing the concept name and definition.

In the concept attainment model, the emphasis is on the learners' determining the essential attributes of the concept that have been preselected and organized by the teacher. The final step of this model encourages learners to explore how concepts are formed through a process of attending to similarities and ignoring differences. The model serves both to teach a meaning of a particular concept and to teach students how the thinking process occurs. In preparing to use the concept attainment model, one must determine ahead of time the following basic elements of the concept to be learned:

1. The name of the concept
2. The concept definition or rule
3. Conceptual attributes
4. Examples of the concept
5. The relationship between the concept and other concepts (concept hierarchy)

Steps in the Concept Attainment Model

STEP 1: SELECT AND DEFINE A CONCEPT THROUGH THE CONCEPT'S ESSENTIAL CHARACTERISTICS

The concept attainment model is an inductive model—it begins with examples and asks students to induce a definition. Inductive reasoning supports the move from observations to hypotheses to a general theory. In a deductive approach to teaching, the teacher presents the broad generalizations, and students then progress to specific examples. The direct instruction model, in contrast, is a deductive teaching model because it relies on deductive reasoning. Concept attainment and concept development (Chapter Five) use the inductive approach. The concept attainment process is most appropriate for teaching concepts that have clear criterial attributes so that students can observe what all of the concept examples have in common and think logically about a definition. For example, the parts of speech can be taught as concepts with clear attributes. The classification system in biology is very suitable for concept attainment, as are the concepts of maps and types of government, triangles and other shapes in geometry, different artistic styles in fine arts, and each of the types of sentences (simple, compound, etc.). When using concept attainment, choose concepts that can be defined by features that clearly distinguish them from other similar concepts.

Concept Hierarchies

The relationships between concepts are important. Concept hierarchies are tree structures that move from the general large concept to more subordinate specific concepts. A hierarchy helps teachers choose examples and nonexamples and helps students check their concept definition at the end of the concept attainment process. It can be used as a reminder and study aid for students as they rehearse their concept definition. In fact, concept hierarchies can demonstrate how teachers frame their understanding of the curriculum—it makes familiarity of the curriculum visible to learners and to other professionals (Hattie, 2012). Figure 4.1 depicts a concept hierarchy for apples. In teaching the concept *apple,* students can see that the superordinate concept, the larger category, is *fruit.* The age and readiness of students determines how you will relate the concepts. The concept hierarchy in Figure 4.1 works well for young children, whereas a botany class may divide fruit into true berry, pepo, hesperidium, epigynous, aggregate, multiple, and accessory fruits. The simple fruit hierarchy shows the relationships between the superordinate, coordinate, and subordinate concepts. Fruit is the concept that is superordinate to apples; apples fit into the fruit category, as do the coordinate concepts of pears and oranges. Coordinate concepts, such as pears and oranges, supply the nonexamples of a concept attainment lesson. They are fruit but do not have the essential characteristics of an apple—they are a different kind of fruit. The types of apples—McIntosh, Gala, and Winesap—are the positive examples of the lesson. They are all apples and have all of the critical attributes that make an apple an apple. They have appleness!

Once you have identified a concept that is aligned with the concept attainment model, you need to construct a definition that includes the superordinate concept and all of the essential features of the concept. From our knowledge of apples and through observation, we know that apples are colorful (red, green, yellow), tasty (sweet to tart), and crispy, and they grow on trees. The definition of an apple could be a tasty, crispy fruit that is red, green, or yellow and grows on trees. The students may define the word *apple* somewhat differently by the end of the lesson, but you will need a working definition to help you choose positive and negative examples.

Rectangles are a concept that lends itself to a concept attainment lesson. Their essential defining attributes are clear—four sides, all right angles, and opposite sides that are parallel and equal. Therefore, the definition of *rectangle* is a geometric figure

FIGURE 4.1 Concept Hierarchy for the Concept *Apple*

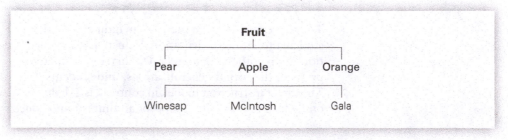

(superordinate concept) that is four-sided, contains all right angles, and has opposite sides that are parallel and equal. A clear concept definition follows this form: concept name, superordinate concept, and criterial attributes.

The point is not merely to find a definition that will, in turn, be given to the students. Instead, it is important that the teacher formulate the definitions to be used in the design of the concept attainment lesson and select the appropriate examples. The major purpose of the lesson is to allow students the chance to author their own definition in order to create their own understanding. In any event, the outstanding function of the concept attainment model is to provide an alternative to telling learners what to understand, instead allowing them to participate in constructing their understandings. The support that the model supplies is invaluable for helping the student construct a lesson. This support includes both a concept hierarchy and a definition. A concept hierarchy does not include the definition—it includes the specific examples of the concept. Thus, at the end of a concept attainment lesson, students will be able to construct both a definition and a hierarchy.

STEP 2: DEVELOP POSITIVE AND NEGATIVE EXAMPLES

Create as many examples of the concept as possible. Each positive example must contain *all* the essential attributes. If rectangle is the targeted concept, some examples can be drawn on the chalkboard, some can be made of cardboard, some can be projected on a screen, and others can be cut out of construction paper; however, each example must contain all the essential attributes: four sides that meet at four right angles, and each pair of sides parallel and of equal length (see Figure 4.2).

Prepare some negative examples that do not contain all the attributes. For instance, a triangle is a geometric figure, but it does not contain all the attributes of a rectangle—it does not have four sides that meet at four right angles. These negative examples will help students focus on the essential attributes of the targeted concept.

Positive examples of apples—fruits that contain all of the essential attributes of apples—include McIntosh, Granny Smith, and Stayman. All of the positive examples come from subordinate concepts of apple. Subordinate concepts are concepts that "fill" the apple category. The negative examples come from the coordinate concepts—those concepts that come from the same superordinate concept pool but do not contain all of the criterial attributes. There are many swimmers in the fruit pool, but not all of them are wearing the same bathing suit!

Concept hierarchies are one type of concept map—they show the relationships of concepts in an organized and hierarchical fashion. This video shows students mapping concepts in small groups to show relationships.

FIGURE 4.2   Positive and Negative Examples of Rectangles for a Concept Attainment Lesson

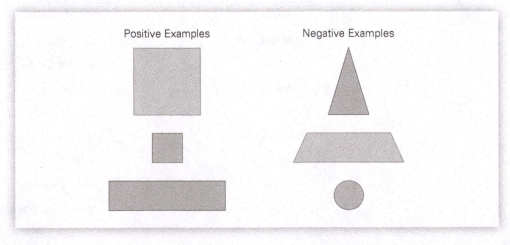

STEP 3: REVIEW THE CONCEPT ATTAINMENT PROCESS WITH THE CLASS

Explain carefully to the students that the goal of the activity is to define the mystery concept by finding out what all of the examples have in common that the non-examples do not have. You may want to practice the process of identifying similarities and differences between examples and nonexamples of a concept as you describe the steps of the model. By helping students gradually construct an understanding of the concept, they will be able to define the concept in their own words.

Put three columns on the board. The first two, "Yes" and "No," are to keep track of the examples and nonexamples that you will present to the class. Even if you use pictures, realia (real-life objects), or projected slides for your examples, use words to describe the examples and nonexamples on these lists so that students can continue to refer to what has been presented as they are hypothesizing the concept label and characteristics. The third column, "Hypotheses," is where they will list, defend, and eliminate their suppositions. Keep a running list of all of the hypotheses that students generate. As new examples or nonexamples eliminate the categories or concept names, cross them out, rather than erasing them, so that the list can be examined throughout the process and be reviewed once a definition has been determined. The ability to see what has already been "disproved" is very important as individual students work toward resolving the mystery of the targeted concept.

STEP 4: PRESENT THE EXAMPLES

The way in which you sequence the examples and nonexamples during the concept attainment lesson controls the difficulty of generating an accurate hypothesis. Table 4.1 demonstrates two different sequences for presenting examples during a lesson on whole grains. Each sequence leads students toward different hypotheses. In sequence one, the teacher first presents two example (y)–nonexample (n) pairs, gently guiding students to the hypothesis that the concept name is "breakfast food." When students realize that "corn flakes" is a negative example, they will need to change their breakfast food hypothesis. In the second sequence, the teacher presents four yes examples, leading the class to a hypothesis of "side dishes." By the time "white rice"

TABLE 4.1   Whole Grain Examples

Sequence One	Sequence Two
oatmeal (y)	brown rice (y)
spaghetti (n)	quinoa (y)
muesli (y)	bulghur (y)
macaroni (n)	buckwheat (y)
popcorn (y)	white rice (n)
corn flakes (n)	noodles (n)
bulghur (y)	grits (n)
grits (n)	white bread (n)
wild rice (y)	whole wheat bread (y)

comes along as a nonexample, students will have to revisit the list and come up with a different concept name. The difficulty of the lesson is determined by the teacher and is based on the students' background knowledge, the lesson's objectives, and the content of the lessons that will follow.

STEP 5: GENERATE HYPOTHESES AND CONTINUE THE EXAMPLE/HYPOTHESIS CYCLE

As examples and nonexamples are presented and students contrast the positive and negative examples, hypotheses will be generated. The hypotheses are categories that include all of the positive examples. Remind students that a hypothesis is a decision that is based on information. The examples and nonexamples are the information from which hypotheses are developed. And for a hypothesis to be viable, all of the positive examples must fit.

Every student hypothesis should be recorded; it should be crossed out if it is found that the evidence does not support the supposition. By crossing out the hypothesis rather than erasing it, students can return to the list to check and extend their own thinking. During this step, teachers must explicitly ask students to explain why the hypothesis is still supported, given new information or examples, or why it needs to be crossed out. The cycle of presenting positive and negative examples and checking the hypothesis list may continue for several rounds, depending on the specificity of student responses and the timeliness of the convergence on a hypothesis. Generating and testing hypotheses through concept attainment allows students to practice the important skill of making inferences. By examining the examples and nonexamples, students make inferences—hypotheses that are clearly associated with student achievement gains (Marzano, 2007).

STEP 6: DEVELOP A CONCEPT LABEL AND DEFINITION

Once a reasonable list of hypotheses has been generated, the teacher can ask the students to try to develop a label and a definition of their new concept that incorporates all of the remaining hypotheses. At times, students will be able to come up with a definition and not a label. In other situations, they will be able to articulate a label or word describing a category quickly. Be patient with this part of the process; students are not accustomed to stating definitions in their own words. You may need to encourage one student to make an initial effort so that others can add to or change the definition. With experience, the class will gradually become more adept at this part of the process. A concept hierarchy can be shared with the students to aid in their definition construction and to show the relationships between

STRATEGY ALERT   Generating and Testing Hypotheses

When students sort through data and make inferences, they are generating and testing hypotheses, which are examined further and refined. Teachers need to help students establish a hypothesis, collect evidence to support or refute the hypothesis, and refine the hypothesis based on collected evidence and information. Generating and testing hypotheses are part of the principles of inference lessons postulated by Silver, Dewing, and Perini (2012). These principles include (1) identifying what needs to be figured out, (2) helping students identify information sources and search for information among these sources, (3) helping the class formulate and refine hypotheses (including having students explain and defend ideas), and (4) reflecting on the process. Generating and testing hypotheses have been shown to increase student learning. ■

the broader categories in which the concept fits. It is important to remember that the main purpose of a concept attainment lesson is not the development of the definition. The major objective is to engage students in the process of defining and forming concepts.

STEP 7: PROVIDE TEST EXAMPLES TO SOLIDIFY THE DEFINITION

Once students have developed an initial definition of the concept they are learning, show them a few more positive and negative examples to test whether they can identify examples of the concept. Ask the students to provide their own examples and then to explain why their examples fit the concept definition.

STEP 8: DISCUSS THE PROCESS WITH THE CLASS

The discussion step is essential to ensure that the students understand how they reached the definition and are able to link this process to the natural process of their own thinking. Attention to likenesses and differences is essential to any type of research or analysis, in both formal and informal thinking; the more conscious a learner is of his or her own thinking process, the sharper that thinking will be. As previously mentioned, identifying similarities and differences is associated with increased student achievement (Marzano, Pickering, & Pollock, 2001). Therefore, as you use concept attainment in teaching, have students identify the point at which they understood the essential attributes and tell which examples were the most helpful.

SUMMARY OF STEPS IN THE CONCEPT ATTAINMENT MODEL

Steps 1 and 2 are done prior to instruction.

1. *Select and define a concept through the concept's essential characteristics.* Determine whether the concept is appropriate and teachable according to this model. The definition should be clear, and the attributes should be identifiable. Determine those qualities that are essential to the concept.
2. *Develop positive and negative examples.* This is the key step, because the positive examples must contain all the essential attributes, yet they may contain some nonessential attributes that are gradually eliminated. Negative examples may have some of, but not all, the essential attributes.
3. *Review the concept attainment process with the class.* It is important to take the time to explain clearly what you will be doing and what each step will entail.
4. *Present the examples.* Think about the order in which positive and negative examples will be introduced. Keep a list of both positive and negative examples.
5. *Generate hypotheses and continue the example/hypothesis cycle.* Be certain to ask why hypotheses are retained or eliminated.
6. *Develop a concept label and definition.* Focusing on the positive examples, students articulate a definition of the concept. Students may need help in producing a concept label.
7. *Provide test examples to solidify the definition.* Test examples will help you ascertain whether the class understands the concept. Some of the students will arrive at the definition more quickly than others. Test examples will provide more time to students who are still working on the concept meaning and will provide reinforcement for those who know the label and definition.

8. *Discuss the process with the class.* Help students understand how they arrived at the definition. This shows students how we form concepts.

Variations on the Concept Attainment Model

The concept attainment model is flexible and can be adapted in a variety of ways and with a variety of materials, as shown by the following suggestions.

1. Present all of the positive and negative examples, labeled accordingly, to the students at one time. Have them look for the essential attributes of the positive examples so that hypotheses about the concept label can be made.

2. Present all of the positive and negative examples without labeling any as positive or negative. The students group the examples into positive and negative categories and then hypothesize a concept label for those they determine to be positive.

3. Students develop positive and negative examples for a concept already studied in class. The object of the lesson would be to define the concept succinctly, to identify the essential characteristics of examples of the concept, and then to choose examples and nonexamples. This can be done by individuals or groups and can be used as a formative assessment.

Figure 4.3 is a set of pictures given to groups with the instructions to determine the essential attributes and then to define the concept *chair*. In each of the positive

FIGURE 4.3   Positive and Negative Examples of Chairs for a Group Concept Attainment Lesson

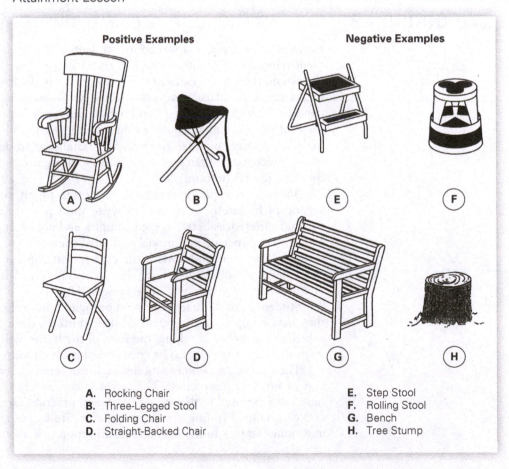

Positive Examples   **Negative Examples**

A   B   E   F

C   D   G   H

A. Rocking Chair		**E.** Step Stool	
B. Three-Legged Stool		**F.** Rolling Stool	
C. Folding Chair		**G.** Bench	
D. Straight-Backed Chair		**H.** Tree Stump	

examples in Figure 4.3—A, B, C, and D—all three essential attributes implied by the illustrations are present:

1. They are seats.
2. They were designed by someone.
3. They hold one person.

In the negative examples, a person could sit on E, F, and H, but those were not *designed* for seating. Example G was designed for seating, but it is for more than one person. Other negative examples are a bed and a low table; those were not designed for our specific purpose. A negative example from nature, such as a flat rock or a log on which a person might sit, emphasizes that chairs are intentionally designed. When these examples have been presented to a class, students may produce a variety of definitions, such as the following:

- An object that is manufactured for the purpose of providing a seat for one person
- A piece of furniture intended for the seating of one person
- A seat designed to hold one person in an upright position

All three of these definitions contain the essential attributes, even though they are stated in slightly different terms. The class may decide to vote on the definition that most clearly states the essential attributes. Students may have their own twist on the definition, but it is important for the class to converge on the essential attributes of the concept so that it can be used to enhance future learning.

Evaluating Learning in the Concept Attainment Model

Concept attainment is designed for students to learn the definition of a concept by identifying the concept's name, the larger category or superordinate concept, and the essential characteristics of the concept that make it what it is. Formative assessments can take place at several points in this process. Can students identify the concept label? Can they explain how the concept is related to larger concepts? Can they list the criterial attributes of the concepts—the collection of characteristics that make the concept unique? You might also challenge students to expand the definition of the concept and then provide positive and negative examples that would support the expanded definition.

Short-answer questions can ask students to supply an accurate definition or draw a concept hierarchy. Students can write short paragraphs identifying the similarities and differences between the examples and nonexamples. They can illustrate the concept on paper or in a model and label each of the critical characteristics. Once students are comfortable with the concept attainment process, they can generate examples and nonexamples of related concepts, explaining why they were chosen and in what order they would be presented.

Students can evaluate their own participation in the process after the lesson, or they may complete a flow chart of their thinking during the lesson. If students are asked to track their thinking, the pace of the lesson will need to be adapted. Metacognitive thinking can also be encouraged through journaling.

The concept attainment model itself can serve as a review at the beginning and end of units of instruction. The targeted concept can be something that students have been exposed to that needs additional practice. Or the concept attainment process can be used to link instructional units. Students can be asked to sort examples and nonexamples individually, in small groups, or as a class. Students can identify which is the nonexample in a set of examples or identify the example in a set of non-examples. Students may be asked to develop concept hierarchies with the targeted concept and other concepts that have been studied to see whether the connections and relationships can be identified. In all cases, the student is practicing important skills. Concept attainment can be sliced, diced, and marinated in a variety of combinations to assess student learning both after a concept attainment model lesson or after a lesson using a different instructional approach.

Meeting Individual Needs with the Concept Attainment Model

All differentiation decisions must begin with knowledge about the learners' readiness, interests, and learning profiles. For the concept attainment model, differentiation opportunities occur before, during, and after the implementation of the model. As decisions are made about the concept to be used, attention should be paid to the level of complexity of the concept and the readiness level of students in terms of both the method and the content being studied.

Early exposures to concept attainment require experience with concrete concepts—concepts with limited attribute descriptions that use familiar vocabulary. Once students become knowledgeable about the method (after several experiences), teachers can scaffold student hypothesis generation by linking to previous concept attainment lessons. "Yes, Jamie, you are using the same observation skills that the class used when we learned the concept *rhythm*." For the students who need this scaffolding, you provide a specific reminder of how to be successful. Students can also relate the new concept to previously learned concepts through concept hierarchies and other graphic organizers. There will be students in each concept attainment lesson who will be able to intuit criterial elements of the concept readily. Others will need cues and support. Teachers can manipulate the complexity, abstraction, and accessibility of examples and nonexamples to meet the individual needs of students. In some cases, students can provide their own positive and negative illustrations of the concept and develop detailed concept hierarchies to show concept relationships.

Participation rules and the role of competition in the classroom can be designed to meet student needs. Some students are more comfortable with a competitive approach to concept attainment, although the model promotes collaborative construction of concept definitions. Differentiation opportunities are abundant once the model of instruction is complete and students are applying the new conceptual knowledge they have acquired.

Learning or interest centers can be developed to allow for student choice. The activities at these centers can be tiered to help all students use their knowledge in sophisticated ways. Tiered activities are designed around common objectives—all students are expected to reach the same objectives. The activities themselves may vary in terms of complexity, amount of structure provided, pacing, number of steps, form of expression, and so on. Some teachers try to have three different ways of meeting the same objectives and allow students to choose the challenge—either a gentle walk, an uphill climb, or mountainous terrain. Readiness can also be used as a guide. One activity can be focused on supporting students struggling with a particular concept, another can be designed for students who appear to have learned the concept but need extra reinforcement, and yet another can challenge those students who have already mastered the concept. Tiered groups should be specific to a lesson, and the groups should be flexible.

Benefits of the Concept Attainment Model

The concept attainment model mirrors the way that we learn concepts in the real world, allowing students to develop even greater concept analysis tools. The model is structured around two important academic skills: (1) identifying similarities and differences and (2) generating and testing hypotheses; both have been associated with increased student learning (Marzano, 2007). Because hypothesis testing is not often seen outside of science classes, concept attainment gives students the opportunity to practice this skill in different settings.

In addition, the concept attainment model requires clear definitions with identified essential attributes that help students construct a personal understanding of a concept. Students are active participants in the lesson and are encouraged to develop conceptual flexibility, inductive reasoning skills, and a tolerance for ambiguity (Joyce, Weil, & Calhoun, 2009).

ELEMENTARY GRADES LESSON

CONCEPT ATTAINMENT: Hibernation

OBJECTIVES

Science Standard

Animals adapt to their environment to improve their chance of survival.

Students Will Know

- The definition and essential characteristics of hibernation

Students Will Understand That

- There are cycles of environmental change that affect all of earth's living creatures

Students Will Be Able To

- Generate and evaluate hypotheses
- Identify the essential characteristics of hibernation
- Define the concept of hibernation

ASSESSMENT

Ask students to draw a six-slide storyboard that shows a bear hibernating and explains why the bear hibernates.

PROCEDURES

1. *Select and define a concept by its essential characteristics.* Select examples of the concept that contain all essential and critical attributes and nonexamples that do not contain all of the essential attributes. The development of a hierarchy is also helpful. Here is a possible hierarchy for this lesson:

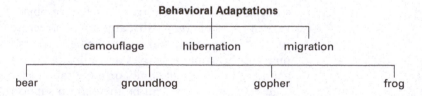

2. *Develop a list of positive and negative examples.*

Examples	Nonexamples
groundhogs	house cats
gophers	parrots
frogs	rats
garter snakes	kangaroos
fish	camels
salamanders	elephants
insects	monarch butterflies
bats	swallows

3. *Review the concept attainment process with the class.* Explain to the students that they are going to explore an important concept by comparing some examples of the concept with some nonexamples. Students will share observations and compare the attributes in positive and negative examples while generating hypotheses about the concept label and definition.

4. *Present the positive and negative examples.* Choose an appropriate order for presenting the examples and nonexamples. This will vary for different groups of students.

5. *Generate hypotheses and continue the example/hypothesis cycle.* Ask students to examine the positive examples and to ascertain the essential characteristics that are evident in all of the positive examples but are not collectively evident in the negative examples. Students are asked to hypothesize possible categories that would include the positive examples. The whole group works together to infer hypothesis from their observations. You can provide cues for student observations. Cycle through the example/hypothesis phases until students eliminate all but one hypothesis.

6. *Develop a concept label and definition.* Ask students to identify the critical characteristics of the concept (these characteristics will be part of the definition) and determine the category name and definition.

7. *Provide test examples to solidify the definition.* Ask students to classify additional examples as positive or negative or generate additional unique examples of their own. The teacher can confirm the hypothesis, name the concept, and restate the concept definition. A concept hierarchy may be shared at this point.

8. *Evaluate the process with the class.* Students are asked their thoughts during the concept attainment process. Where did you have difficulty? When did you "attain" the concept? What helped you figure out the concept label and definition? In what order would you have put the positive and negative examples?

MIDDLE/SECONDARY GRADES LESSON

CONCEPT ATTAINMENT: Metaphors

OBJECTIVES	**Common Core State Standards—English/Language Arts W.2.d** Use precise language, domain-specific vocabulary, and techniques such as metaphor, simile, and analogy to manage the complexity of a topic.

continued

Students Will Know
- The definition and essential characteristics of metaphors

Students Will Understand That
- Figurative language enhances the power of texts

Students Will Be Able To
- Generate and evaluate hypotheses
- Identify the essential characteristics of metaphors
- Define the concept of metaphor

ASSESSMENT   Provide students with examples of metaphors, personification, hyperbole, and similes and ask students to identify metaphors and explain why each example is a metaphor.

PROCEDURES
1. *Select and define a concept by its essential characteristics.* Select examples of the concept that contain all essential and critical attributes and nonexamples that do not contain all of the essential attributes. The development of a hierarchy is also helpful. Here is a possible hierarchy:

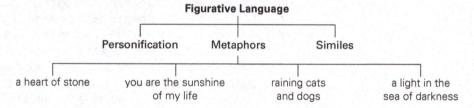

Figurative Language

Personification   Metaphors   Similes

a heart of stone   you are the sunshine of my life   raining cats and dogs   a light in the sea of darkness

2. *Develop a list of positive and negative examples.*

Examples	Nonexamples
The moon is a silver ship sailing in the night sky.	She is as cold as ice.
Superman—the man of steel	The stars smiled down on us.
A recipe for disaster	He had a heart like a lion.
The father was a tower of strength.	Frightened as a mouse
The ship plows the sea.	Jill is blind as a bat.
Jumping for joy	An angry wind is blowing.
It is raining cats and dogs.	Lend me your ears.
Heart of stone	His heart is as hard as stone.
A light in the sea of darkness	He's a thousand years old.

3. *Review the concept attainment process with the class.* Explain to the students that they are going to explore an important concept by comparing some examples of the concept with some nonexamples. Students will share observations and compare the attributes in positive and negative examples while generating hypotheses about the concept label and definition.
4. *Present the positive and negative examples.* Choose an appropriate order for presenting the examples and nonexamples. This will vary for different groups of students.
5. *Generate hypotheses and continue the example/hypothesis cycle.* Ask students to examine the positive examples and to ascertain the essential characteristics that are evident in all of the positive examples but are not collectively evident in the negative examples. Students are asked to

hypothesize possible categories that would include the positive examples. The whole class works together to infer hypotheses from their observations. You can provide cues for student observations. Cycle through the example/hypothesis phases until students eliminate all but one hypothesis.

6. *Develop a concept label and definition.* Ask students to identify the critical characteristics of the concept (these characteristics will be part of the definition) and determine the category name and definition.

7. *Provide test examples to solidify the definition.* Ask students to classify additional examples as positive or negative or generate additional unique examples of their own. The teacher can confirm the hypothesis, name concept, and restate the concept definition. A concept hierarchy may be shared at this point.

8. *Evaluate the process with the class.* Students are asked their thoughts during the concept attainment process. Where did you have difficulty? When did you "attain" the concept? What helped you figure out the concept label and definition? In what order would you have put the positive and negative examples?

SUMMARY

The concept attainment model is an instructional model that supports student inductive thinking. Positive and negative examples are presented to the class until the students can identify the essential attributes and state a concept definition. In addition, this model helps students understand the process through which concepts are defined. The teacher may present a new concept to the class or focus on one particular aspect of a familiar concept. Because the understanding of concepts is so essential to learning in the classroom, the time taken to identify and clarify these concepts is time well spent. In addition, teachers find that in preparing to teach this model, they clarify their own understanding of essential concepts.

The concept attainment model is a series of steps: (1) select and define a concept, (2) develop positive and negative examples, (3) remind the class of the concept attainment process, (4) present positive and negative illustrations of the concept and identify essential attributes, (5) develop and refine hypotheses, (6) construct a concept label and definition, (7) provide test examples, and (8) reflect on the process with the class.

The preceding list does not capture the dynamic nature of instruction that occurs in the complex environment of the concept attainment model. Concept attainment is highly engaging to students, and, after one or two experiences, the energy in the classroom increases. To help this to happen in your classroom, we have taken the steps of the model and examined what concept attainment has to offer in terms of potential behaviors for both students and teachers. This approach allows you to consider what is needed to master the concept attainment process and include it in your professional toolbox. Table 4.2 is a guide to help you consider what students need to do to benefit from the model, allowing you to mold your teaching behaviors toward student learning. It takes time and patience to make a model of instruction part of your instructional repertoire. We hope the table will be helpful to you on this journey.

Case studies demonstrating how to use concept attainment in context can be seen in Chapters Thirteen, Fourteen, and Fifteen.

TABLE 4.2 Potential Teacher and Student Behaviors in the Concept Attainment Model

Step	Teacher	Student
1. Select and define concept.	• Selects an appropriate concept • Defines concept • Constructs concept hierarchy based on student prior knowledge	
2. Develop positive and negative examples.	• Creates 15–20 positive examples with all essential attributes • Creates 15–20 negative examples with none or only some of the essential attributes • Determines possible sequences of example/nonexample presentations	
3. Review process.	• Explains and reviews concept attainment process • If students are new to models, provides short example using common concept • Monitors student understanding of process • Reteaches process, when necessary	• Asks clarification questions about process • Participates in example • Asks for definitions of unfamiliar words (concept, concept hierarchy, attributes, etc.) • Monitors own understanding or process
4. Present examples.	• Presents labeled examples in intentional sequence • Follows identified process • Monitors challenge to students and makes adjustments when necessary	• Compares similarities and differences in positive and negative examples • Asks questions to clarify personal understanding • Attends to peer comments
5. Generate hypotheses and continue cycle.	• Continues to present examples/nonexamples • Lists hypotheses • Monitors students responses, providings scaffolding when necessary • Crosses out unsupported hypotheses as determined by students • Asks for explanation of hypotheses • Asks students to review hypothesis list and provide support items	• Compares positive and negative examples • Looks for commonalities in positive examples • Generates and test hypotheses working with peers • Explains reasoning behind hypotheses • Asks clarifying questions to peers and teacher • Monitors personal understanding
6. Develop label and definition.	• Asks students to examine list and label the concept • Asks students to define concept • Provides concept hierarchy if appropriate • Monitors student understanding • Provides scaffolding when necessary	• Works with peers to construct a label and definition • States definition based on essential attributes • Extends concept hierarchy if appropriate • Monitors personal definition and compares to that of teacher and peers

EXTENSIONS

ACTIVITIES

1. Review resources that you are or might be using in your teaching. Look for clear, understandable concept definitions that have explicit essential attributes identified. How many can you find? Is there a pattern of clear definitions? What is the pattern in the resource for helping students learn concept definitions?
2. Interview a classroom teachers about the concepts they usually teach and the methods they use to convey the concepts.
3. Design a concept attainment model lesson for the students you are teaching or plan to teach. Keep a list of the questions you have about designing this lesson. What do you notice about these questions? What problems do you anticipate in implementing the lesson?
4. Choose a concept that you may be teaching in the near future. Identify positive and negative examples of the concept using a variety of mediums—words, pictures, and realia.

REFLECTIVE QUESTIONS

1. Concept attainment lessons take time and imagination to plan. Is it worth using our limited time to teach with this model? How can we maximize the time that we spend organizing a concept attainment lesson?
2. What kinds of behavior management problems will you need to plan for as you think about implementing the concept attainment model? Does the model always have to be used with the whole class? How can you adapt the model to ensure that there will be few or no behavior problems?
3. How can you use the concept attainment process to help prepare your students for standardized tests?
4. What concepts in your discipline or in your curriculum would you choose not to teach using concept attainment? Why?

5

The Concept Development Model

ANALYZING THE RELATIONSHIPS BETWEEN PARTS OF A CONCEPT

Chapter Objectives

You Will Know

- The basis for the concept development model
- The steps of the concept development model
- How to evaluate learning in the concept development model
- How to meet individual needs in the concept development model
- The benefits of using the concept development model

You Will Understand That

- Thinking is dependent on the process of attaining and developing concepts

You Will Be Able To

- Identify the concept development model in K–12 classrooms
- Design, implement, and reflect on a concept development lesson

In the Elementary Classroom

Ms. Fowler's second graders have made a list of all of the items they saw on a walk around the school's courtyard. This is the list that they put together:

Coke can	basketball net	mushrooms
stones	cars	flowers
snail	school bus	doors
trading card	people	grass
candy wrappers	spider	coffee cup
worm	baseball cap	pine cones
leaves	cigarette butts	birds
plastic bag	bleachers	insects
sticks	frog	book
tennis ball	playground equipment	pencil

Ms. Fowler puts each word or phrase on a card and makes five sets of cards. After putting the students into five groups, she hands each group a set of cards, and the lesson continues:

Ms. Fowler: We made a list of all of the things we saw on our walk. I made a set of cards for our list. Each group has a set of cards with all of the words. We are going to group words that have something in common. There are many ways that the words can be grouped. For example, we could put books, bleachers, birds, baseball cap, and basketball net together. Can you tell me what they have in common?

Charquea: They all begin with the letter *b*.

Ms. Fowler: Yes, they do. That is one way that we could organize the cards. In your groups, see if you can find other ways to group the words. Think of characteristics that the things have in common. Make certain that each card has a group.

The students work together for a few minutes.

Ms. Fowler: Give each of your groups a name. You can use one of the blank cards to write down the name of the group. Put the name of the group at the top of the pile.

The students work for several more minutes.

Sarah: Ms. Fowler, my group is finished. When we did a lesson like this before, we mixed up the cards again and made a new set of groups. Should we do that?

Ms. Fowler: Yes, we'll do that later. Let's let the others finish up.

The other groups finish.

Ms. Fowler: Let's make a list on the board of all of the category names that you made.

The second graders enthusiastically respond and produce the following list:

litter	things that move	useful things
dead things	outside things	things that grow
sports things	happy things	scary things

Ms. Fowler looks at the list and points out two of the categories: things that move and things that grow.

Ms. Fowler: I notice that these two categories apply to living things. Living things grow and living things can move or change.

Students are then asked whether they can put groups together or put different cards into more than one group. By asking students for examples and combining two groups, the list of two category names becomes things that move and things that are useful. Ms. Fowler helps her students see that they can also divide the list into two categories and call the categories living things and nonliving things. Once the students have agreed that the two category names are acceptable, they check to make certain that each item on the original list fits into one of the categories.

The list of living and nonliving things is put on the board.

Ms. Fowler: When you look at this list, what do you notice?

Wendy: Some living things are insects and some are plants.

Rodney: The nonliving things don't grow.

Janine: Some living things are very small like a spider and some are very big like a tree.

Students continue to provide generalizations and Ms. Fowler points out the characteristics of living things as they share their ideas. Once everyone has had a chance to share, Ms. Fowler shows the class some pictures and asks them to tell her whether each picture represents something that is living or nonliving. ■

In the Middle/Secondary Classroom

A ninth grade class is exploring the concept *grudge* before they read a story in which a grudge is the cause of the conflict. The teacher, Mr. Irani, has reviewed the important ideas that the class has already covered in their characterization unit, highlighting the ways in which readers make inferences from a character's speech, actions, and responses from other characters. Today they are going to discuss how a specific feeling can communicate information about a character.

> **Mr. Irani:** What sort of things does the word *grudge* bring to mind?

The class produces the following list:

hurt	binge	friends
mean	evil eye	enemies
fight	stare	stiff
cruel	hold	hard
fudge	hate	cold
yell	deep	whisper
stomach	dark	secrets
empty	not talking	argue
silent	talk behind back	faces
silly	eyes	childish
cloud	mist	embarrassed
burden	anger	feelings
cut off	people	heavy
ground	children	black
gossip	fat	misunderstandings

> **Mr. Irani:** Which of these items are alike in some way? Which of these items do you think belong together? Once you have figured out which go

together, think about why they go together and give the group a name. Try not to use a name to group the words; come up with a name *after* you have made the groups.

After several minutes, students begin to share some of their examples.

Paul: We have a group and a name!

Feelings Caused by a Grudge

hurt	hate	hard	black
mean	empty	cold	heavy
cruel	silly	cut off	burden

Sandi: Our group had something similar. We also had the word *embarrassed* in our group.

Mr. Irani: Let's have another example from your group work.

Marisa: OK, we had a category called "things people do when they hold a grudge."

Mr. Irani: What words did your group contain, Marisa?

Marisa: *Whisper, not talking, embarrassed, secrets, fight, hold, cut off, evil eye, yell, hate, hurt, stare, argue, childish, mean, talking, talk behind back, cold, binge.*

Mr. Irani: What other categories did you find?

Students share other category labels and Mr. Irani repeatedly asks for examples of words that fit into that category. Complimenting the class on their grouping and labeling, Mr. Irani asks the class to go back to the original list and regroup the items.

Mr. Irani: Are there other groups that could be made? Any ways that we can mix up the words and make new categories that are not listed on the board?

Marisa: I'm always confused at this part.

Mr. Irani: Look at the list of categories on the board and try not to use any of them. Rely on your base group to help you and I'll come by to offer support. Are there other groups having trouble with this step? [There is no response.] Any new categories?

Sandi: We made a list of things that cause a grudge—*anger, friends, gossip, enemies, fights, misunderstandings.*

Marisa: We came up with one! Things associated with food: *binge, people, fudge, stomach, heavy, silly, fat.*

Mr. Irani encourages other groups to share their new categories, and a few new ones are shared. The students in this class have used the concept development model before, so as soon as all of the new categories are shared, they quickly move into synthesizing the activity by summarizing their discussion. Here are some of the students' statements about grudges.

Madison: Holding a grudge is not good for you.

Arnold: Holding a grudge can make you do things you will be sorry for later.

Stu: A grudge can grow from something little to something very destructive.

Marisa: Fighting is just another way of acting when you feel bad because someone has hurt you. You hold a grudge. I eat. Some people fight. None of these helps to solve the problem.

Mr. Irani: You have made some important observations about holding a grudge. How might a character who is holding a grudge in a story behave? What might we see the character saying or doing?

The discussion continues with examples and predictions conveyed by students. At the conclusion of the lesson, Mr. Irani reflects on the positive aspects of the experience.

One benefit of using this model is the growing trust among class members as they share the contents of their "mental files." As this trust grows, their constraints about revealing thoughts and feelings diminish. These ninth grade students were more open and frank in this discussion about grudges than they had been in the past. As one student's idea triggered another student's idea, they became excited. They showed a growth in creativity that they had not exhibited before. I think that as I get more comfortable using the model, so do the students. ∎

Basis for the Concept Development Model

The concept development model is the result of work described by Hilda Taba in the 1960s (Joyce, Weil, & Calhoun, 2009). Much of Taba's work is out of print, but her ideas have had a major impact on inductive teaching strategies. She developed specific teaching moves that shift students toward inductive thought (see Table 5.1). At the same time, Bruner, Goodnow, and Austin (1986) were articulating the attainment of concepts, which is congruent with Taba's teaching ideas. Bruner et. al. (1986)

TABLE 5.1   Concept Development Sequence

Reason for Question	Examples of Questions	Possible Student Response
Generate list of items	What do you notice? What do you see? Are there any patterns?	Observes prompt and lists items that are noticed
Group items by various characteristics	Do any of these items have things in common that would make them a group? Do some items seem to belong together?	Finds similar characteristics to form groups
Label groups by specific characteristics	Why did you group some items together? What do they have in common? What name might you give these groups?	Discusses and identifies the common characteristics in each group. Names the groups based on the identified characteristic
Group items in more than one place. Re-label items	Could any of the items belong in more than one group? Can any of the same items fit into different groups? Explain why you would regroup these items.	Identifies new item characteristics and relationships
Summarize and synthesize information	What can you say about all of the groups that we have identified and labeled? Can we say something about what we learned in one or two sentences?	Summarizes learning

provided the reason for examining thinking at a time when behavioral psychology was the popular approach.

> We begin with what seems a paradox. The world of experience of any normal man is composed of a tremendous array of discriminably different objects, events, people, impressions. There are estimated to be more than seven million discriminable colors alone, and in the course of a week or two we come in contact with a fair proportion of them. No two people we see have an identical appearance and even objects that we judge to be the same object over a period of time change appearance from moment to moment with alterations in light or in the position of the viewer. All of these differences we are capable of seeing, for human beings have an exquisite capacity for making distinctions (p. 1).

The authors believed that examining how we acquire and develop particular categories helps us gain insight into "one of the most elementary and general forms of cognition by which man adjusts to his environment" (p. 2). The goal of this series of studies was to find out how we learn concepts. In the end, the studies resulted in both the concept attainment model and the foundations of the concept development models. Even more than 50 years ago, psychologists and educators believed that thinking can be taught and that good thinking should not be separated from content acquisition—a very current educational belief. Taba developed a series of steps that replicate the way that we make sense of our world (Gallagher, 2013). Table 5.1 shows the basic ideas of inductive thinking—noticing, grouping, listing, regrouping, and generalizing from a specific data set. These thinking moves can be used with all grade levels and content areas, as can most of the instructional models found in this text.

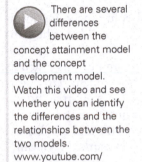
There are several differences between the concept attainment model and the concept development model. Watch this video and see whether you can identify the differences and the relationships between the two models. www.youtube.com/watch?v=xxiajb5zloc

The constructivist theory of learning is congruent with both concept attainment and concept development. We know that learning is an active process and that students must make connections between prior knowledge and new information. A model of instruction can help students make those links more readily and with richer associations. Both concept attainment and concept development help students develop rich conceptual schemata—the organizational structure of the human mind. And this rich conceptual schema can be developed using a small set of examples and information.

Concept development goes beyond concept attainment. Simply put, the early research described in *A Study of Thinking* indicates that we attain concepts by identifying their criterial attributes. In extension, more recent theories demonstrate that ideas can also be represented by a prototype (a typical instance of a class) or an exemplar (a typical prototype) and that these are also useful in learning concepts (Klausmeier, 1990). In all cases, it is necessary to see the concepts to be taught in terms of their relation to other concepts and to possible misconceptions. Concept attainment (Chapter Four) helps students label and identify a class of things (e.g., a banana is a fruit that is long and slightly curved, has skin that changes from green to yellow, and has a soft inside). Concept development moves beyond the definition to inferences that are not observable. You may accurately identify a banana and its criterial attributes in a concept attainment lesson; in a concept development lesson, you can then develop the concept of banana further by inferring other things (e.g., bananas rot quickly when the skin turns yellow, they are often used in muffins, etc.). Bruner and his colleagues (1986) state that the "working definition of a concept is the network of inferences that are or may be set into play by an act of categorization." We categorize; we infer; we develop a concept. Thus, concept development is a strategy that extends and refines our knowledge by providing an opportunity to extend and refine our personal concepts—concrete or abstract. We need both concept attainment and concept development to learn and be able to transfer our knowledge of concepts.

Conceptual Thinking Is Learned

A child will not approach his or her intellectual potential without guidance and practice in the process of thinking. And much possible critical thinking will never take place if a curriculum is so strongly content oriented that processes of learning and thinking are left to chance. On the other hand, we know that a strong content foundation is necessary for the application of learning skills (Willingham, 2009). We need content to teach thinking skills, and we need thinking skills to use content well. To develop thinking skills is to develop an increasingly complex mental organization with which to view the world and to solve problems. Cognitive skills are seen as products of a dynamic interaction between the individual and the stimulation he or she receives. Thus, students and teachers must follow a series of structured questions to support deeper levels of thinking (Gallagher, 2013).

Lev Vygotsky, the founder of modern constructivist theories of developmental psychology; Bruner; and others assert that concept development and deep understanding are the essential goals of instruction. The students are learning to integrate new ideas and approaches to learning with prior views and experience, thus constructing new knowledge from within. The teacher acts as a guide and facilitator who provides the opportunity for students to link main concepts throughout the learning process.

Concepts Are Creative Ways of Structuring Reality

Concepts provide easy access as learners classify and thus simplify incoming information in a meaningful and retrievable form. Concepts make it possible for humans to process data mentally. Scientists tell us that our senses are constantly being bombarded by thousands of stimuli simultaneously. Our ability to simplify, as much as our ability to absorb complexity, allows us to act on our environment. Driving is an activity that would be impossible if we were attuned to every sign, tree, house, vehicle, or person we passed. Safety and the dictates of driving demand that we screen data and assimilate only certain relevant noises, landmarks, and conditions. Subconsciously, as we drive, we put incoming data into categories marked "relevant" or "irrelevant."

As young children, we learn to pick and choose and to assimilate only stimuli that we determine have meaning or, more accurately, to which we can assign meaning. When children come to school, the process does not change; what they can learn is what they can accommodate. Teaching is helping children in their natural process of learning new information and assigning meaning to that information.

Concepts Are the Building Blocks of Patterns

The process of creating conceptual frameworks is quite natural and forms the basis of our understanding of the world. Touching a hot stove leads to an understanding of heat. *Hot* becomes a category into which we place many things (see Figure 5.1), including the idea of caution. Experiments with falling objects (including one's own self) lead to an understanding of gravity. We impose order in our world by observing and creating patterns. We divide time into hours, minutes, and seconds. We divide space into miles, feet, inches—all manageable, bite-sized pieces. We attempt to predict the future by observing patterns in the present and recalling patterns from the past.

Concepts are the building blocks from which generalizations spring. In Chapter Four, we described a model that helps students acquire specific definitions of a concept by identifying the critical attributes of the concept, allowing for the discrimination of one concept from another. In this chapter, students take those identified concepts and share what they know about the concepts and, together with their peers, form ideas and identify relationships between a variety of concepts. By opening

FIGURE 5.1   Building a Concept

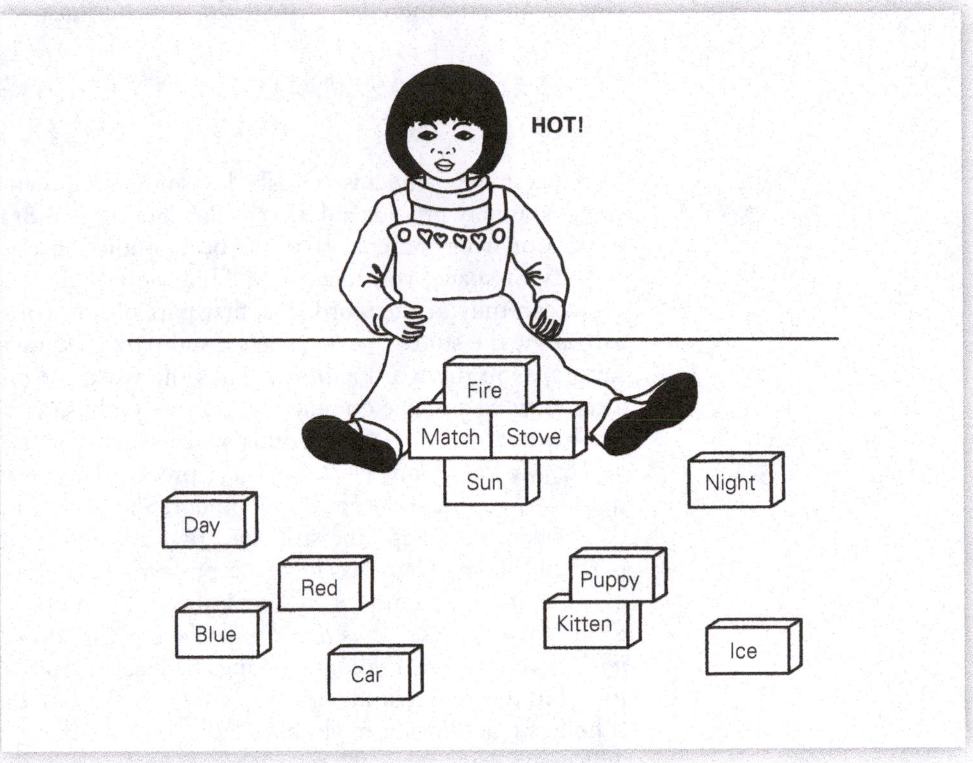

the contents of our personal mental files to others and by hearing about the contents of theirs, we refine and extend our understanding of concepts, and we refine and extend the precision of our generalizations. In the concept development model, a ministructure that mirrors how the human mind works is created. The focusing question produces data—not miscellaneous, indiscriminate data, but data relevant to an idea contained in the focusing question. From the data come comparisons, contrasts, and finally a theory that makes sense of myriad data. This theory constitutes one's present view of the concept under scrutiny. The purpose of the concept development model is to form generalizations from concrete data.

Steps in the Concept Development Model

When performed consecutively, the steps of the concept development model mirror a process humans employ individually as they marshal their thoughts on a particular subject, as they organize and reorganize these thoughts, as they seek out new relationships and new meanings, and as they make their way through the uncharted terrains of cognition. This model may be used in kindergarten through grade 12 and beyond to explore basic concepts in different disciplines. In social studies, it may be used to explore concepts such as *capitalism, imperialism,* and *expansionism;* in mathematics, to explore concepts such as *velocity, expansion,* and *relativity;* in science, to explore concepts such as *adaptation, evolution,* and *interdependence;* and in English, to explore concepts such as *character, theme,* and *point of view.* World language classes may focus on family, clothing, tenses, and literary themes. These same concepts may be expressed in simpler terms for younger students.

Using this model to explore a central idea from any discipline allows all teachers to assess students' prior understandings, enables students to broaden and enrich their previous understandings, and serves as an excellent review. Students enjoy the process because the ingredients are their contributions, and the product is their product.

STEP 1: LIST AS MANY ITEMS AS POSSIBLE THAT ARE ASSOCIATED WITH THE SUBJECT

In the first step, students are asked to enumerate items related to a subject. In some cases, you may provide a data set. The data may be drawn from students' own experiences or from material that has been studied in the classroom. Before beginning a study of space, you might say, "Tell me everything you know about astronauts. Look carefully at the word. The first part of the word refers to star, as in the word *astrology,* the study of stars; the second part of the word refers to sailing ships and sailors, as in the word *nautical.* Thus the word *astronaut* refers to 'star sailor.'" Or after viewing a movie on outer space, you might say, "Let's name everything that you just learned about existing in outer space as an astronaut." Taba (Taba, Durkin, Fraenkel, & McNaughton, 1971) was very precise in the way she ordered and worded the questions guiding concept development. She believed that helping students develop concepts required specific strategies that are widely applicable but that maintain a particular form. Her ideas for concept development are summarized in Table 5.1.

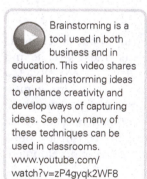

Brainstorming is a tool used in both business and in education. This video shares several brainstorming ideas to enhance creativity and develop ways of capturing ideas. See how many of these techniques can be used in classrooms. www.youtube.com/ watch?v=zP4gyqk2WF8

The items or data set in step 1 should be written somewhere visibly accessible to all participants. *Items listed must be specific; otherwise the next step, grouping, will be confusing.* If you are asking the class to enumerate items about Halloween, for example, and a student says "scary things," ask the student to be more specific. If he has trouble, you might ask, "What sort of things are scary?" You hope that he will name some scary things, such as a beckoning finger or a rattling skeleton. The problem with writing down *scary things* is that it does not name, it groups, and that gets you one step ahead in the process. Alternatively, a data set of items on cards may be provided to students during this step. This approach is particularly helpful in large classes or when the model has not been used before. Small groups can manipulate the cards readily and, for some students, the later steps are easier to follow.

It is important to have a comprehensive list from which student generalizations can emerge, because generalizations have far more validity when they are based on a variety of data. Encourage students to continue listing, even after they appear to have run out of information. The ideas that follow the first pause are the less obvious ones, frequently derived from greater insight and more thought. Make certain that students are adding more concrete data than abstract categories. Gallagher (2013) recommends that the list should be capped at about 25 items.

When the subject under scrutiny is already familiar to the participants, such as *football* or *grudge* or *school,* step 1 is similar to brainstorming. Here are a few items generated by a high school class exploring the topic *football: school colors, jostling, ball, pom-poms, muscle, strutting, blitz, striped shirts, hot dogs, whistles.* They generated more than 140 items in five minutes.

STRATEGY ALERT   Brainstorming

Brainstorming is the rapid, noncritical, noncensored listing of any and all ideas or associations on a given topic. Brainstorming focuses student attention on generating a number of ideas and encourages sharing and building on the ideas of others. Brainstorming taps into our emotions, imaginations, memories, in short, our whole creative selves. Students list everything they can think of about a particular subject and the leader lists each item—a word or a phrase. Connections may be obvious to all or personal to the contributor. All contributions are accepted. In brainstorming, students share their individual files with others. Be sure to encourage full participation by calling on students, if necessary.

STEP 2: GROUP THE ITEMS BECAUSE THEY ARE ALIKE IN SOME WAY

When you believe that sufficient items have been listed, it is time to move to the other half of the board or screen and ask, "Which of the items we have listed go together because they are alike in some way?" In this step, students begin to examine the relationships between items. Students are asked to recognize things that have shared attributes and then to form groups based on these characteristics. Try to elicit several groups. The first groups may be put together for the most obvious reasons. The groups mentioned after some thought are usually put together for more unusual reasons.

An example of one group is *helmets cracking, flying tackles, collisions, bone crunching,* and *injuries.* The teacher had assumed that all the items related to injuries, until a student added injuries to the group. The students later labeled the group as the *might makes right* aspect of football. By using individual cards or sticky notes, steps 2 and 3 can be completed in small groups.

STEP 3: LABEL THE GROUPS BY DEFINING THE REASONS FOR GROUPING

In this step, students give labels (one to three words) to the newly formed groups. In a discussion of Halloween, for example, the items *beckoning fingers* and *rattling skeletons* and *leering pumpkins* might be labeled *scary things.* The sophistication of the labels depends on the age and background of the group. Older students, for instance, might use a label such as *habitat,* whereas younger students might label the group *places where animals live.*

It is important in this step to ask students to explain the reasons for their choices. Their explanations are often surprising! Even if the reasons for grouping seem obvious, ask students to articulate their reasons. Having to explain the label they gave a particular group of items forces them to articulate and defend their reasoning processes, frequently expressing connections they have sensed but have not precisely verbalized, allowing for what is known to be connected to new information.

Your role at this stage is basically that of recorder. You may ask what other students think, but the students need to feel that their judgments are valued by the teacher and the rest of the class. It is important to develop the students' skills in drawing inferences and in making generalizations. The students should question one another and decide among themselves. You may also insert particular inferences or generalizations that are found in the curriculum but that students have not acknowledged. Teachers should explain their thinking about why they made these statements.

Examples of group labels from the high school class analyzing football were *stadium, parking lot, commercialism, rules, might makes right, emotions, microcosm, costumes, food,* and *atmosphere.* This step helps students learn to generalize.

STEP 4: REGROUP OR SUBSUME INDIVIDUAL ITEMS OR WHOLE GROUPS UNDER OTHER GROUPS

Step 4 centers on the questions "Are there items now in one group that you could put in another group?" and, later, "Are there whole groups that could be placed under one of the other labels?" Again, ask for the learner's reasoning here: "Why do you think _____ belongs under _____?"

For example, when regrouping on the topic of Halloween, a student might want to add *witches on broomsticks,* which had been under *decorations,* to the *scary things* group. If you believe the groupings were done for rather shallow or superficial reasons and that the students can go further, erase the second half of the board, leaving the initial items clearly visible, and ask the students whether they can generate some new groups. Obvious groups such as *treats* or *decorations* are fine, but perhaps students will begin to see more obscure connections such as *feelings* or *masks* or *facades*. Also, no list of items is final; new items may be added at any time.

In step 3, the more obvious items are thought of first; with grouping, the more obvious relationships are pointed out first. Also, the connections seen when the model is first used are much less complex than those recognized after practice. As time goes on, students will find out for themselves that every person, object, or idea has many characteristics and may be grouped in many different ways. For example, when a ninth grade student observed that the item *leering pumpkin* could be labeled *decorations* or *food* or *scary things,* depending on how you thought about it, she showed her understanding that the same object may be viewed from different perspectives. We all tend to put constraints on our thinking. If A is B, it cannot be C. In this model, students discover that one item can be viewed from several vantage points and can, therefore, appear in several groups. In this way, students are building a series of hierarchies of ideas.

Whole groups may be included with other groups. One group under *football* included *strutting, pushing, shoving, beefy, cocky,* and *butting heads.* One student had commented that these types of behaviors reminded him of bulls, so they had labeled the group *bulls.* In step 4, the students put this entire group under another group labeled *macho.*

The first steps of the concept development or concept formation model can be seen in this video. Look at the adaptations made in this lesson from the model just described. www.youtube.com/watch?v=acKWJUcq0Mo

STEP 5: SYNTHESIZE THE INFORMATION BY SUMMARIZING THE DATA AND FORMING GENERALIZATIONS

In step 5, ask the class to look over the entire chalkboard, consider all the groups and labels, and try to make a general statement about the topic in one sentence. Then ask the students to create a generalization that represents the ideas discussed in the earlier steps. Thus, students must try to pick out trends. Young children tend to think in terms of either/or. Either Halloween is a "good" holiday or a "bad" one. They do not see that Halloween can have two faces. Scary situations need not be dangerous if controlled, and they can even be fun. A private Halloween party can offer some thrilling and terrifying moments that pose no danger. If not supervised, however, trick-or-treaters can be in danger from traffic, overzealous pranksters, or the occasional sick mind. By looking at all the conflicting data at once, students begin to realize that Halloween is complex, fraught with pleasures and dangers. Even older students tend to think in terms of either/or. Football is either "good" or "bad," usually depending on whether they enjoy the sport (playing it or watching it). They need to realize that football is an exciting and popular sport that can also be dangerous. This step offers an opportunity for students to begin to appreciate the richness and complexity of ideas.

You will need to give students several examples of generalizations the first few times this model is used. Examples of generalizations from the analysis of football are as follows:

- The game of football is fun but dangerous.
- Many boys and men define themselves by their degree of success in football, which can be both helpful and harmful to their self-images.
- A football game is a microcosm of the major elements in our society, both good and bad.

SUMMARY OF STEPS IN THE CONCEPT DEVELOPMENT MODEL

1. *List as many items as possible that are associated with the subject.* Ask the students to name as many ideas, objects, associations, memories, concepts, or attributes related to the subject under scrutiny as possible. In doing so, what the learners already know is identified. The information may be based on general knowledge that students have of a subject or on what they know or think they know already. It may come from a personal experience they have had, such as school-related field trips, a preparatory reading, or a film.

2. *Group the items because they are alike in some way.* Ask the students to group the items by finding ways in which they are similar or related. Thus what learners know is qualified. Similar ideas, or ideas related to a common concept, bear similar qualities. An important part of learning consists of identifying these qualities.

3. *Label the groups by defining the reasons for grouping.* Ask the students to articulate the relationships between the items. Thus, what learners know is defined. Qualities that are shared form the basis of the categories into which those ideas fit. Often, different labels are possible.

4. *Regroup or subsume individual items or whole groups under other groups.* Ask the students to look at the board and see whether they can find items or whole groups that they could put somewhere else. This step involves looking at a single item from different perspectives. It also involves analyzing through regrouping and subsuming additional items under already established labels or subsuming labels under other labels according to relative inclusiveness. For example, under the heading *democracy,* the category *campaign*—containing items such as *shaking hands* and *making speeches*—might be subsumed under another category, *elections.* The most creative connections occur in this step.

5. *Synthesize the information by summarizing the data and forming generalizations.* Ask the students to look over the board and see whether they can make a general statement or generalization about the subject under scrutiny that summarizes the information in the briefest terms possible. To generalize, the students must put the parts together or synthesize the information. For example, if they were studying Halloween, they might say that Halloween is both fun and dangerous.

The preceding list describes the process of using the concept development model, but it does not detail the behaviors that the teacher and students may use to be successful in reaching the goals of the model. By examining the potential behaviors of teachers and students working within the concept development framework, you can consider what is needed to master the model and include it in your professional toolbox. Table 5.2 is a guide to help you consider what student behaviors are needed for making sense of concepts successfully, providing you with a roadmap for molding your teaching behaviors to students. It takes time and patience to make a model of instruction part of your instructional repertoire. Concept development is an important basic model and worth your time and effort.

Case studies showing how to use concept development in context can be seen in Chapters Fourteen and Fifteen.

Evaluating Learning in the Concept Development Model

One of the purposes of the concept development model is to help students generate original ideas. Practice in brainstorming helps students become more creative and willing to share. Using a timer during step 1, students can try to generate as many items as possible in a short period of time. Both the teacher or facilitator and students

TABLE 5.2   Potential Teacher and Student Behaviors in the Concept Development Model

Step	Teacher	Student
1. List data set.	• Identifies concept to be analyzed based on academic standard • Provides or elicits list of items related to subject (data set) and prior student knowledge • Organizes data set using text, realia, pictures, etc.	• Asks for clarification of process if necessary • Participates, if appropriate, in generating data set • Reviews prior knowledge and experience concerning the topic • Checks for unknown words in data set and asks for definitions
2. Group like items.	• Asks students to group like items from data set • Requests that students try not to label groups immediately	• Searches data set for like items • Groups items based on identified attributes • Works with small group if appropriate
3. Label and explain.	• Directs students to label groups • Requires students to provide explanation for groups • Records group names	• Labels groupings individually or with small group • Provides explanation for group label • Identifies and seeks help for difficulties with process
4. Subsume and regroup.	• Directs students to identify items that can belong in more than one group • Asks students to identify new ways to group items on list • Monitors student understanding of content and process	• Reclassifies data set • Explains reasoning for moving items from one group to another • Identifies relationships between items in data set
5. Synthesize.	• Invites students to make generalizations (summary statements) based on categories developed by class • Provides an example of generalization if necessary • Reminds students that generalizations are conclusions based on information • Asks students to support generalizations • Monitors student understanding	• Looks at data and infers summary statements • Discusses possible generalizations with peers if applicable • Writes possible generalizations and support for generalizations before sharing with the class, when appropriate • Assesses the accuracy of presented generalizations and shares conclusions with class • Considers what was learned in the lesson and how it was learned

can keep track of the number of ideas shared over several concept development lessons. Facility with brainstorming can help beyond generating lists; it can aid in creative problem solving, for example.

Along with the number of items shared, teachers and students can evaluate the originality of the group labels. There will be an increase in the number of and the originality of the connections over time and with experience with this model. You can evaluate individual student thinking by asking each student to come up with a different group and asking him or her to write a paragraph about why the items in the group belong together. In addition, students can be asked to add new items or ideas to the groups that evolved from the class discussion.

The concept development process itself can be used as an evaluation tool. Paper-and-pencil tasks can be designed in which data sets are provided and students must group, label, regroup, relabel, and make generalizations. This work can be assessed for accuracy, originality, and the number of groups generated. In addition, students can be asked to create short essays explaining how and why items were grouped as they were and how these groups support specific generalizations.

Meeting Individual Needs with the Concept Development Model

The concept development model is inherently differentiated—it meets a variety of student needs in the way it is structured and implemented. For example, student interests can be met by allowing students to generate data sets. Student readiness can be addressed by dividing students into groups and varying the information database or prompts. In the lesson on Halloween, for example, you can provide different data sets to particular groups of students. If one group is challenged by abstract concepts, you might provide a data set that includes such words as *terrifying, horrifying, apprehension, anticipation, greed, profit, creativity, partners,* and *darkness.* These words represent less tangible and more symbolic concepts related to Halloween. Learning preferences can be addressed by modifying the directions of the concept development task. Students who need more structure will receive detailed, specific directions that are clearly modeled and offer little choice, whereas students who are comfortable with a more open approach will receive directions that are somewhat vague, have no modeling, and include more choice. Of course, all students should eventually have access to both approaches.

Data sets can be lists of words, realia, pictures, or symbols so that student learning access can be addressed in more than one way. Some students will find grouping and regrouping an easier task if they hold the items in their hands and actually place the items in groups. Teachers can also vary the pace of the lesson and provide more time and practice to students as necessary.

Each of the steps in the concept development model is an opportunity to meet individual needs. Step 1 can cater to students' interests and misconceptions as teachers manipulate data sets to reach specific objectives. The scaffolding provided to students as they group like items together allows step 2 to work as a differentiation tool. Students can also be supported when they provide the reasons for grouping. Probing questions and a think-pair-share strategy can be helpful here. The questions and prompts can vary by readiness or interest. Regrouping and relabeling can be a difficult task for students and should be modeled. In fact, in some cases, it might make sense to eliminate this step, especially if students are new to the model. Once students have worked through the model several times, regrouping becomes less confusing. The last step, summarizing, can occur as discussion or recitation, or it can be a structured activity. For example, you can pair students and ask one of the pair to talk about the lesson for 30 seconds while the other student listens carefully. Roles are reversed, and the first student listens while the second student reflects on the lesson for 30 seconds; but that student cannot repeat anything that the first student said. After the activity, students share a one-sentence summary.

Benefits of Using the Concept Development Model

The academic purpose of concept development is to extend and refine students' knowledge and to develop specific thinking skills—generalizing and explaining generalizations from a set of data. Because we look at the world through the lens of our own personal experiences, recognizing our limitations and sharing our knowledge increase our grasp of the complexities of perception and open us to additional points of view. The concept development process also encourages the generation of original ideas because all subjects can be analyzed through listing, brainstorming, grouping, labeling, and generalizing—all of which promote creative thinking. In fact, the concept development process also promotes new avenues for extracting meaning from reading, methods for problem solving, and development of writing skills (particularly paragraph unity). While participating in a concept development lesson, students have the opportunity to summarize and examine the accuracy of their ideas.

The concept development approach also supports affective skills. Brainstorming requires seeking and listening to the ideas of others and describing personal feelings when appropriate. Students must also exhibit self-regulation as they listen to the ideas of peers without comment. They must be able to acknowledge the saliency of the ideas of peers. It is obvious that there are strong academic and social benefits for students when the concept development model is used in the classroom.

ELEMENTARY GRADES LESSON

CONCEPT DEVELOPMENT: Living and Nonliving Things

OBJECTIVES	**Science Standard** There are living things on land and in the water. **Students Will Know** • Living things need food, air, and water, and produce young **Students Will Understand That** • Living things have particular characteristics that make them different from nonliving things **Students Will Be Able To** • Sort living and nonliving things and provide reasons for the choices
ASSESSMENT	Given a set of pictures, children will accurately distinguish between living and nonliving things and give reasons for categorizing a picture as a living thing.
PROCEDURES	1. If possible, take the children for a walk around the school and have them make a list of what they see. 2. Return to class and make a list that includes everyone's observations. 3. Ask students which things on the list belong together. Using a piece of colored chalk, circle the items that the children identify as belonging together. Use a different color for each group. Have students explain each grouping. Keep in mind your objectives (especially your *know* objective) and try to infuse the characteristics of living things into the discussion as much as possible. 4. Once the groups have been identified, ask students to label or name each group. Put the names on the board using the same color as the group's circles. 5. Ask students whether some of the items in the groups might fit into more than one group. Which items should go into which groups? Record the responses. 6. Ask whether there are any other ways that the original list of items can be organized into a group. (This can be an optional step and will depend on the teacher's determination of student engagement at this point.) 7. Ask the students to tell you something about the groups and the discussion that the class had about the groups. Repeat each statement and ask students why or how they came up with their conclusion. Add any statements that promote the objectives. Provide cues and scaffolding for helping students summarize and synthesize.

MIDDLE/SECONDARY GRADES LESSON

CONCEPT DEVELOPMENT: Grudge

OBJECTIVES	**Students Will Know**
	• How we can infer the feelings of a character
	Students Will Understand That
	• Characterization is the basis for reality in a story
	Students Will Be Able To
	• Examine and expand on the concept of *grudge*

ASSESSMENT After reading the assigned text, students will identify the speech and actions of the character holding a grudge, as well as responses from other characters. The product in which students make the identifications can be written, drawn, or performed and may be accomplished in pairs or individually.

PROCEDURES For this lesson, students are divided into reading circle groups.

1. Review previous lessons in the characterization unit.
2. List as many items as possible that are associated with the subject. After making certain that everyone knows the word *grudge*, ask students to generate a data set of words associated with holding a grudge.
3. List words on the chalkboard or a SmartBoard, or project them from a computer or a transparency.
4. Group the items because they are alike in some way. Students put together like words from the list.
5. Label the groups by defining the reasons for grouping. Students are asked to label the groups and to share the category names with the whole class. Students provide explanations for their groupings and category labels.
6. Regroup or subsume individual items or whole groups under other groups. Students are asked to look at the original list and make different groups with new names. Students share the groupings, labels, and reasons for sorting in this way.
7. Synthesize the information by summarizing the data and forming generalizations. Students summarize what they have learned about the word *grudge* in the lesson by making a one-sentence statement.
8. Students identify actions and words of literary characters who are holding a grudge.

SUMMARY

There are several benefits to using the concept development model regularly (once a month or more frequently). From this model, students learn much from one another about the concept, object, event, or person studied. They absorb a great deal of the accumulated knowledge and ideas of the whole group. They expand and refine their own concepts of the topic being studied; concomitantly, they expand and refine their ability to perform these mental processes.

Concepts are the building blocks of intellectual activity. Knowledge is not static. Knowledge of even a simple object can grow and take on new dimensions, or it can recede and grow hazy with lack of exposure. It might be helpful to think of growth in knowledge as a series of overlays projected on a screen. We add to and change an already existing impression, much as one makes an addition to a basic drawing. The concept development model is helpful to teachers because it not only allows them to enrich the original impression but also affords a glimpse of that original impression on which to build.

The concept development model is organized as a series of steps.

1. List or present a list of items associated with a particular subject.
2. Group like items together.
3. Label the groups and provide a reason for the label.
4. Regroup or subsume individual items or whole groups under other groups.
5. Synthesize the information by summarizing and forming generalizations.

All of these steps encourage important cognitive and social skills and provide the opportunity for students to become more metacognitive about their learning.

EXTENSIONS

ACTIVITIES

1. Choose a concept that you teach or will be teaching. List as many items as you can that are related to the concept. Label each of the groups. Now regroup the items and relabel. Remember to be flexible. You should use each item only once, and you may omit items if necessary. This exercise will remind you of what the students will experience as they move through the steps of a concept development lesson.
2. All teaching is related to concept development. Choose a concept that you will teach in the future and review the steps in the concept development model. Script at least one question that you might ask your students at each step of the concept development process: listing, grouping, labeling, analyzing, and synthesizing.
3. Find a teacher's edition of a textbook that includes the concept you used for activity 2. Compare your questions with those suggested in the text. How would you evaluate the text in supporting the acquisition and development of the concept? Do the authors assist students in the concept development process?
4. List the three or four most important concepts in a particular instructional unit. Draw a concept hierarchy to show the relationships between the concepts and determine which of the concepts would best be suited for a concept development lesson.

REFLECTIVE QUESTIONS

1. Are there concepts that you will be teaching that are not a good fit with the concept development model?
2. How might the use of concept development in your classroom contribute to your classroom management concerns?
3. How might you distinguish the concept attainment model from the concept development model?

6

The Cause-and-Effect Model
ANALYZING CAUSALITY BY NOTING EFFECTS

 Chapter Objectives

You Will Know

- The basis for the cause-and-effect model
- The steps in the cause-and-effect model
- How to evaluate learning in the cause-and-effect model
- How to meet individual needs in the cause-and-effect model
- Benefits of the cause-and-effect model

You Will Understand That

- Cause-and-effect relationships are central to all disciplines

You Will Be Able To

- Identify when the cause-and-effect model would benefit the curriculum and students in varying contexts
- Design, implement, and evaluate a cause-and-effect lesson

In the Elementary Classroom

Over the last several weeks, Mr. Fisher has noticed his fourth grade students had some difficulty with identifying causes and effects. As they review their science unit on the water cycle, Mr. Fisher sees an opportunity to practice cause-and-effect relationships and extend what students know about the water cycle of precipitation, infiltration, evaporation, and condensation. Each of these describes effects with certain causes, so they are good examples of cause-and-effect relationships. To review, he displayed a poster from the U.S. Geological Survey that pictures the water cycle.

This provided background information for a lesson on a fascinating book about one particularly extreme weather condition in American history: Mr. Fisher begins the lesson by reading an excerpt from *The Long Winter*. The book tells the story of the difficult winter of 1800–1801 on the Dakota prairie.

Mr. Fisher: What do we know about the winter of 1800–1801?

Rebecca: There was a lot of snow and blizzards.

Laura: They didn't have the Internet to check the weather!

Mr. Fisher: What causes snowstorms and blizzards? How is what we know about the water cycle involved in snowstorms and blizzards?

Julie: The water cycle explains how precipitation happens, and snow is precipitation.

Randy: A blizzard is more than snow, though. It gets really windy and blows the snow around. Sometimes you can't see in a blizzard—everything is white.

Mr. Fisher discusses the role of warm and cold winds in winter storms and some of the characteristics of blizzards. He asks students in a think-pair-share exercise

Source: U.S. Geological Survey. Retrieved from pubs.usgs.gov/gip/146/pdf/gip_146_poster.pdf

FIGURE 6.1   Cause-and-Effect Organizer for *The Long Winter*

Prior Causes	Causes	The Long Winter of 1800–01	Effects	Later Effects
		• Cold • Lots of snow • Blizzards • Railway closed down trains • 7 months of bad weather		

to compare rain, snowstorms, and blizzards and explain how precipitation occurs, making sure that they use the words *evaporation* and *condensation*. After the students share their comparisons, Mr. Fisher reviews the cause-and-effect organizer in Figure 6.1.

Beginning with the center of the organizer, Mr. Fisher asks students to share what they know about the long winter of 1800–1801. Several students volunteer information about the winter, which is then listed on the organizer.

Mr. Fisher: What are the causes of blizzards?

Ruth: It's cold enough to make snow.

Tina: There is a lot of water in the air, and clouds form.

Robert: Isn't there something about warm and cold air together in the air?

Mr. Fisher provides additional information on the warm and cold air interactions and helps students fill out the "Causes" section of the organizer.

Mr. Fisher: What was the immediate effect of the two-day blizzard in the story? What happened right after the storm stopped?

Ruth: Families had to go and find the children or other people who were missing.

Karen: They had to figure out whether to stay on their homestead or move into town.

Tina: They had to take care of the people who were sick or didn't have enough food.

Laura: They had to fix any damage.

After several other contributions, the class fills in the "Effects" section. Mr. Fisher leads a short discussion about prior causes, and the class settles on the fact that although this was an unusually harsh winter, people did the best they could to survive.

ReNita: What do we put down in the last column?

Karen: Weather prediction got better.

Laura: People were better prepared.

Tina: Some people moved away. ∎

In the Middle/Secondary Classroom

Mrs. Coffey's advanced senior class has just finished studying *Hamlet*. She feels there were certain issues they had not grappled with sufficiently. She decides to use the cause-and-effect model with one of the play's central issues: why Hamlet continued to hesitate to act against Claudius. This hesitation led to the death of all of the royalty at Elsinore Castle.

The emphasis will be on causes and prior causes, because the effects and subsequent effects are obvious. Mrs. Coffey writes, "Hamlet continues to hesitate to take action against Claudius" under the heading *Topic* in the center of the chalkboard. She begins by asking for causes:

Jerome: Hamlet was squeamish; he couldn't kill in cold blood. He couldn't even kill Claudius after the play, when he had proof.

Judy: But remember Hamlet's previous reputation for bravery and his military success against the older Fortinbras.

José: Hamlet wasn't sure about the ghost. It could have been a trick. People in those days believed ghosts could be real or could be messengers of the devil.

Maria: Hamlet was sort of in shock. Everyone at the castle was acting strangely—not like they had always acted. So he hesitated until he could figure out what was going on.

Phil: Like the suddenness of the queen's second marriage.

Jane: Hamlet didn't know whom to trust, except for Horatio.

Andy: He was afraid of death. That's what he says in his soliloquy.

Anne: But he seems more afraid of not setting his father's ghost free.

Phil: But if he takes action, everyone else might think he just wanted to be king.

Maria: No one else suspects the king. It's really odd.

Andy: Hamlet overanalyzes everything.

Maria: Well, what do you think he should have done?

Andy: He should have killed Claudius after the play.

Phil: And be thought of as a power-hungry murderer?

Andy: Couldn't Horatio have defended him?

Phil: But it's only Horatio, and he didn't even hear what the ghost said.

Caneka: He wants others to see what he sees: Claudius's guilt.

Maria: He hesitates because he hates Claudius so much.

Everybody: But that's a reason to kill him.

Maria: No, you don't understand. Hamlet has this sense of justice. If he's wrong, and he kills him, then he's worse than Claudius. That's why he has to expose him first. (The others began to see Maria's point. Some agreed.)

Mrs. Coffey: Where should I put his sense of justice?

Maria: I guess that's a prior cause. (They moved to prior causes.)

Phil: I guess the main prior cause is his father's death or murder.

Rashad: The ghost's request for revenge.

Caneka: He's got to be careful. These are all people who cared about him and those whom he cared about: his mother, Ophelia, Horatio, Laertes, even Polonius.

Jerome: And Yorick, and Fortinbras admired him.

Jane: You know, I don't think all these people would have been fooled. I think Maria's right. If Hamlet had been evil or overly ambitious, they would not have cared for him quite so much. I think he does feel some princely responsibilities, and he does have a sense of justice. He isn't afraid for himself. He wants to be sure; he wants to do the right thing. It's ironic that people keep getting hurt because Hamlet is trying to do what is right. (They all began to agree with this perspective.)

Mrs. Coffey felt they had reached a depth of understanding of the play and of its main character that they might not have reached without this model.

Conclusions

1. Hamlet's hatred of Claudius caused him to be especially careful in trying to find proof of his guilt.
2. Hamlet understands that he must prove conclusively that Claudius is guilty or people will think Hamlet simply wanted to be king.
3. Hamlet realizes that if he takes action against Claudius, and Claudius is innocent, Hamlet will be judged far more guilty than will Claudius.

Generalizations

1. In trying to find proof of guilt, we must attempt to be objective, or the proof may be suspect.
2. Guilt must be proved convincingly, or justice will not have been served.
3. If we wrongly convict an innocent man, we are guilty of the injustice we have accused him of. ■

The Basis of the Cause-and-Effect Model

Cause-and-effect relationships thread throughout the curriculum of school at every grade level. In this video, the teacher uses the relationship of causes and effects to teach middle school students the important principle of geography and economy.

The model presented in this chapter leads students through the study of significant facts, actions, situations, conditions, or conflicts. In history, anything from a single action to a war to the passing of a bill to the election of a candidate can lead to fruitful discussion. Almost any experiment or condition in science will lend itself to this model, as will particular problem-solving strategies in mathematics. When a class has finished a piece of literature in English, a significant action or a climax or a pivotal moment makes a stimulating topic. Newspaper articles, particularly advice columns, can lead to exciting discussions, especially if the subject is important to the students. Using situations such as students coming late to class or disrupting class as the topic will enable students to understand the reasons behind certain rules. There are many opportunities for using the cause-and-effect model in a classroom. Sometimes cause and effect will be identified in the standards and learning objectives with which you are planning. Other times, the available resources and materials will direct you in the direction of cause and effect. Look for cues as to when this model will benefit your students.

By inferring, students hypothesize about causes and effects, prior causes, and subsequent effects. They draw conclusions and arrive at generalizations about how causes and effects are related, noting that often effects become causes for subsequent effects. During this process, the teacher is a facilitator, asking set questions, not contributing to or commenting on the contributions except to ask follow-up questions or to correct gross errors.

The value of group explorations of cause-and-effect relationship cannot be overestimated. Hearing the ideas of others opens up possibilities that students say would never have occurred to them on their own. They become more flexible thinkers and they can more readily construct individual knowledge from prior experiences. Once students have used this model several times, they can perform it alone. It can become an extremely valuable metacognitive tool in that an individual's repertoire of techniques for problem solving, generating ideas, making decisions, and analyzing data.

The cause-and-effect model begins by examining a specific situation and ends by generalizing about courses of action in similar situations. Students have an opportunity to study a situation in detail, to put names to mental activities they have used in their own thinking, and to hear the thinking of others. They also have an opportunity to speculate

The understanding of causes and effects is one of the most basic reading comprehension skills. It can be taught directly to students in early elementary grades, as you see in this video. Notice how the teacher draws the ideas of cause and effect, including use of a graphic organizer, into this multilayered discussion of a story that the students have read.

about different courses of action and their consequences. This is an inductive approach to teaching that also draws on an intellectual community to help students determine cause and effect.

Generalizations show the relationships between concepts. These relationships help direct student thinking in all discipline areas. Students need to construct their own generalizations in a community of learners that provides for feedback and correction, if necessary. Generalizations help students in transferring new knowledge; because they are approximations, gaining new information and perspectives about these broad ideas may change the focus or content of thinking. The practice of constructing generalizations through the use of making inferences and comparing similarities and differences is a critical thinking skill (Bransford, Brow, & Cockling, 2000) and is an element in the Common Core State Standards for English/language arts. To see the CCSS wording on this topic, simply Google "CCSS cause and effect."

—WEB RESOURCE————————————————

Cause-and-Effect Model Lesson

You can find a model lesson on the basics of cause and effect, focusing on the key words of this relationship at the website studyzone.org. This lesson is fairly elementary but offers hints of how one can read to distinguish "why" from "what."

Steps in the Cause-and-Effect Model

The discussion of the steps of the cause-and-effect model will relate to teaching a topic in science that combines geology, geography, and life science. The topic is "Reasons for the Seasons." The reason, in this case, is somewhat complex and even counterintuitive—the "obvious" reason (the earth is closer to the sun in summer, farther away in winter) seems logical but is false.

Figure 6.2 can be used to structure the discussion within each of the model's steps. The order of steps of the cause-and-effect model are listed by number on the organizer.

FIGURE 6.2   Steps of the Cause-and-Effect Model

4 Prior Causes	2 Causes	1 Topic	3 Effects	5 Later Effects
6. Conclusions				
7. Generalizations				

FIGURE 6.3   Example Chart for "Reasons for the Seasons"

Prior Causes	Causes	Earth's Changing Seasons	Effects	Subsequent Effects
Soon after Earth formed, it was struck by a huge meteor that knocked it askew.	Earth rotates the sun on a 23½ degree tilt to the orbit.	Temperature and weather patterns change across the year. The northern and southern halves of earth experience the same climatic features at opposite times of the year.	The light of the sun strikes earth at a slightly different angle each day, more directly in summer months, less directly in winter months.	Weather varies throughout the year in both hemispheres.

STEP 1: CHOOSE THE DATA OR TOPIC, ACTION, OR PROBLEM TO BE ANALYZED

The topic or problem may be a significant action, event, condition, or conflict. It may be fictional, hypothetical, or real. It may come from any discipline in the curriculum. Write the topic in the center of the chalkboard or on a large tablet. In this example, write "Reasons for the Seasons." Figure 6.3 is an example of the chart you will be building.

STEP 2: ASK FOR CAUSES AND SUPPORT FOR THOSE CAUSES

In step 2, the students look for how the situation comes about. If no one knows about the fact that the earth rotates around the sun yearly and on a tilt to its axis, use a classroom globe to show the tilt and a flashlight to demonstrate the light of the sun as it strikes the earth.

STEP 3: ASK FOR EFFECTS AND SUPPORT

Moving to the right side of the topic column, ask for effects. Students may be able to see the angles at which the sun's rays must strike earth differently each day throughout the year.

STEP 4: ASK FOR PRIOR CAUSES AND SUPPORT

Moving to the far left side of the chart, ask for prior causes. For this "Reasons for the Seasons" topic, you will probably need to provide the information that will be filled in for column 1, "Prior Causes." Prior causes can also be seen as distal or underlying causes. An example is: Scientists now believe that shortly after its formation, earth was struck by a huge meteor, which had the effect of knocking it off its north-to-south alignment with its poles (and, incidentally, knocked off a piece large enough that it became earth's moon). Reference to these facts can be found in *Geology for Dummies* and at space.about.com.

STEP 5: ASK FOR SUBSEQUENT EFFECTS AND SUPPORT

After repeating the request for prior causes several times, and when students seem to be completely out of ideas, move to the far right of the organizer and ask for

STRATEGY ALERT   Flow Charts

A flow chart is a type of graphic organizer that shows the series and order of steps in a complex process. Flow charts are used in many fields and can often represent mathematical or computer processes. In the classroom, however, flow charts are frequently used to simplify and illustrate a complicated situation or series of events. Flow charts can be linear, forked, or cyclical and can make a variety of cognitive demands on both the teacher and the learner. There are many websites that provide examples and templates of graphic organizers, including flow charts. A linear flow chart can be used to plot a chain of cause and effect by showing a logical ordering of information and allowing students to see that a chain of events is a process in which there are decision points that can lead to different outcomes. Flow charts can be used as a summary before the cause-and-effect model begins and as a scaffold during the discussion of causes and effects. Figure 6.4 is an example of a flow chart that could be used in connection with a lesson on Wilder's *The Long Winter*.

FIGURE 6.4   Flow Chart Example for *The Long Winter*

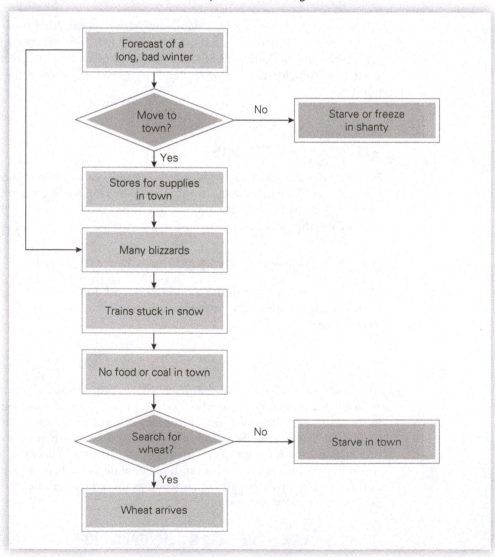

FIGURE 6.5   Cause-and-Effect Flow Chart for "Reasons for the Seasons"

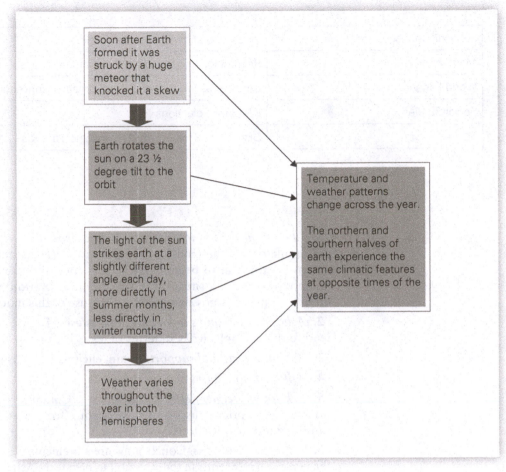

subsequent effects. Take each effect separately. Figure 6.5 illustrates how all this work might look in that form.

STEP 6: ASK FOR CONCLUSIONS

Conclusions are statements we infer about the causes and effects that have been listed and discussed. Conclusions can come from reading related items on the board from left to right or top to bottom.

Step 6 is the most difficult because it involves the most abstract thinking. You will initially have to give the students several examples of conclusions drawn from the circumstances being discussed. Performing the model as a class and then in small groups will allow students to see numerous examples of conclusions—yours and those of other students—and, frequently, many catch on to how one thinks abstractly. Thinking abstractly seems to be one of those "lightbulb" experiences in which examples suddenly clarify the necessary thought processes.

STEP 7: ASK FOR GENERALIZATIONS

Generalizations are conclusions expressed in general terms—that is, terms not specific to the topic or the people involved. Students should simply replace the specific names in the conclusions with general names such as *people* or *one*.

FIGURE 6.6   Possible Topics for Cause and Effect in Classrooms

English/Language Arts	Plot, word origins, motives
Mathematics	Renaming, compounding, order of operations
World Languages	Differences in translations, grammatical conventions, dialects
Social Studies	War, laws, elections
Science	Disease control, gravity, technological access

SUMMARY OF STEPS IN THE CAUSE-AND-EFFECT MODEL

1. *Choose the data or topic, action, or problem to be analyzed.* When your students are familiar with the model, you may want to ask students to choose the critical action or situation to be analyzed in a chapter in history; a novel, short story, or poem in literature; a situation in science; an operation or process in mathematics. Figure 6.6 presents possible topics for the use of this model in classrooms.

2. *Ask for causes and support for those causes.* Try to elicit as many as possible. We tend to think simplistically in terms of a single cause as opposed to multiple causes.

3. *Ask for effects and support.* Again, elicit as many as possible.

4. *Ask for prior causes and support.*

5. *Ask for subsequent effects and support.* Comment occasionally on the connections between prior causes and subsequent effects. Seemingly unimportant actions can build into major effects.

6. *Ask for conclusions.* Conclusions are statements we infer about the behavior of the persons or elements in the situation under study. Ask the students to support their conclusions.

7. *Ask for generalizations.* Generalizations are statements of inference about how people in general or events behave in situations similar to those under study.

Evaluating Learning in the Cause-and-Effect Model

The cause-and-effect model allows students to infer causes and effects, and any evaluation should focus on this relationship. Students may demonstrate their understanding of cause and effect by writing a story based on a single text (picture, graph, piece of music, etc.) and then expanding the text through prior causes and subsequent effects. This allows students to move beyond chronology to the patterns of relationships. The model's graphic organizer can serve as a blueprint for a persuasive essay. The conclusions are potential theses, and the listed actions are supporting evidence.

Flow charts can also be used as an assessment. Students can design their own flow charts or fill out a template to demonstrate their understandings and knowledge about an event or process. Flow charts can be particularly helpful in evaluating student knowledge of specific algorithms or processes in mathematics and science.

The ultimate goal of the cause-and-effect model is to help students predict future events in a systematic way. Students can be asked to predict future events and provide support for their predictions in many ways. Written work, skits, diagrams, and case study analyses are a few of the ways an evaluation can be structured. Individual or small-group conferences can be held, with the teacher asking for clarification of the relationships discussed in class. Students can also be assessed on the generalizations that were constructed at the end of the lesson. Or the assessment may ask students to make additional generalizations.

Meeting Individual Needs with the Cause-and-Effect Model

Although there are many opportunities for differentiation in the cause-and-effect model, the most important is the problem or situation under analysis and the text or situation from which the problem comes. The selection of the situation and text must be centered in the required curriculum, the needs and interests of the students in the class, and the available resources and materials. Specific questions should be framed with individual student knowledge and experiences in mind. It is critical that teachers choose a problem for which explicit connections can be made to students' prior knowledge and past experiences. Discussions can accommodate individual students' needs through varying the complexity of questions and through the teacher's paying attention to individual student misconceptions. Teachers may also scaffold individual students by providing examples of conclusions and generalizations. This is especially important when the model is unfamiliar.

The graphic organizer presented in this chapter (or another chronological or relational organizer) supports both visual learners and those students who are analytic. According to Sternberg and Grigorenko (2004), in order to meet the needs of all learners, teachers must focus their teaching on more than analytic skills. Creative and practical intelligences must also be addressed. The cause-and-effect model can be used to foster both of the approaches. For example, when constructing conclusions and generalizations, students can be asked to apply those to real-life situations.

Creative intelligence tasks ask students to create, invent, discover, imagine, and predict. In the cause-and-effect model, students can create alternate problems to be analyzed, invent examples of conclusions and generalizations in other situations, discover new and different connections between the causes and the effect, imagine scenarios in which the generalizations play out, and predict what might happen if any of the causes or effects are changed. By using these three aspects of intelligence, teachers can widen the net so that all students have an increased chance to demonstrate what they have learned.

To assess the transfer of knowledge, students can be asked to analyze a new situation or problem. Students can complete a graphic organizer, develop a new organizer for demonstrating relationships, write a narrative that describes the cause and effect and the generalizations that can be made, or demonstrate these relationships in another way.

Performance assessments can be a useful tool. Tasks can be developed that ask students to apply their new cause-and-effect analysis skills. Students can be asked to provide an explanation for or a defense of a recent decision—their own or someone else's. A critique of a decision-making process can be made as a dramatic work, a letter to the editor, or a persuasive essay. Students may also create a display of the cause-and-effect relationships under study. In all cases, the performance task must be carefully constructed so that students are asked to share both content and critical thinking skills and not just performance abilities.

Student choice can be incorporated into the model as students develop familiarity and flexibility in its use. Once the phases of the model become routine, students can choose the problem or situation to which the steps should be applied. And they can choose how to present the information—through the graphic organizer, a narrative, a storyboard, or a multimedia presentation, for example.

Flexible grouping can become a way of differentiating instruction once students can use the model independently. Groups can be formed by choice, background knowledge and experience, readiness, and learning profile. For creative students, teachers can encourage students to vary the way the analysis is organized and presented. Students who are comfortable focusing on the practical applications of the problem can focus on the applications of the analysis.

Benefits of the Cause-and-Effect Model

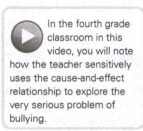

In the fourth grade classroom in this video, you will note how the teacher sensitively uses the cause-and-effect relationship to explore the very serious problem of bullying.

The cause-and-effect model allows students to explore why things happened or are happening, even if there is an unexpectedness about the causes or the effects. The model allows students to understand that causes are more than special occurrences that lead to specific events. Rather, causes may help to explain an effect, and both effects and causes are usually complex and interrelated. Once students construct causal models, they can build patterns of explanation about a series of events. This model takes on one event or problem at a time, but its use over time with similar problems can allow for pattern recognition of similar causes or effects.

The model promotes student engagement and student construction of critical thinking skills as well as curriculum content. Cause and effect are part of everyday life and are represented in every discipline area and virtually every human concern. The relationship between the two is basic to human understanding. An understanding of how the cause-and-effect relationship works in varied settings with varied materials and knowledge helps to increase student learning and efficacy. Once the model is internalized by students, it becomes a metacognitive tool that will help them analyze specific situations.

ELEMENTARY GRADES LESSON

CAUSE AND EFFECT: Water Cycle, Blizzards, and *The Long Winter*

OBJECTIVES	**Common Core State Standards—English/Language Arts RI.4.7**
	Interpret information presented visually, orally, or quantitatively and explain how the information contributes to an understanding of the text in which it appears.

Students Will Know

- The three states of matter
- The definition of evaporation, condensation, and precipitation
- The causes and effects of blizzards

Students Will Understand That

- There is a relationship between the water cycle and weather

Students Will Be Able To

- Explain and diagram the water cycle
- Complete a cause-and-effect organizer about the long winter

---

ASSESSMENT	Students will complete the following cause-and-effect graphic organizer about the Ingalls living through the long winter.

Prior Causes	Causes	The Long Winter of 1800–1801	Effects	Later Effects

PROCEDURES	1. Read an excerpt from Laura Ingalls Wilder's *The Long Winter*.
	2. Discuss the winter of 1800–1801 on the prairie.
	3. Review the water cycle and how blizzards happen. Make certain that students can define evaporation, condensation, and precipitation.
	4. Ask the following questions and guide students to the appropriate responses. Together fill out a sample cause-and-effect organizer
	a. What do we know about that winter from our reading?
	b. What causes snowstorms and blizzards? (Highlight the water cycle and the role of cold and warm winds.) How do you know?
	c. What was the immediate effect of the blizzards of 1800–1801? How do you know? What would the effects be of a blizzard today?
	d. We know that blizzards are caused by specific weather conditions. How does the earth's water cycle contribute to weather conditions? (Have students support their answers. Explain the term "prior causes.")
	e. What might the later effects of the long winter be? What might the later or subsequent effects be of a blizzard today?
	5. What did we learn about the winter of 1800–1801 on the Dakota prairie?
	6. What do you think that the people who survived the blizzard learned? How might their behavior have changed because of the experience?
	7. If we had a blizzard today, how might our behavior differ from the behavior of those who survived the long winter of 1800–1801?

SECONDARY GRADES LESSON

CAUSE AND EFFECT: Hamlet and Claudius	
OBJECTIVES	**Common Core State Standards—English/Language Arts RI.9-10.3**
	Analyze how complex characters develop over the course of a text, interact with other characters, and advance the plot or develop the theme.
	Students Will Know
	• The plot and characters in *Hamlet*
	Students Will Understand That
	• Guilt must be proven before action is taken
	Students Will Be Able To
	• Discuss the causes and prior causes of Hamlet's hesitation to take action against Claudius
ASSESSMENT	Students will summarize the class discussion in two written paragraphs that focus on the following generalization: "A civilized nation assumes that a person is innocent until proven guilty."
PROCEDURES	1. Provide students with the following question for discussion: "Why did Hamlet continue to hesitate to take action against Claudius?"
	2. Record all answers on the board.
	3. Probe student responses if necessary.
	4. Monitor the discussion to distinguish between causes and prior causes. For example, if someone says that Hamlet's sense of justice or lack of a need for revenge is a cause, explain why it is a prior cause.

continued

5. Make certain that students support their statements.
6. Ask for conclusions. Remind students that conclusions are statements we infer about the behavior of the persons in the situation. Ask students to support their conclusions.
7. Ask for generalizations—statements that go beyond Hamlet's situation and are instead about people in general. Ask students to support their generalizations.

SUMMARY

The cause-and-effect model allows students to explore a problem situation to determine the relationships between actions and subsequent events. Active engagement is essential to the model as students identify prior causes and subsequent effects. The model can be used in both elementary and secondary classrooms and in all curriculum areas. The graphic organizer associated with the model helps students to visualize the chronology of the quandary (e.g., getting through a long winter or why a character behaved in a particular way) under discussion. Going from causes to effects and then from prior causes to subsequent effects may reveal the connections between these events more effectively. However, you may feel that establishing the cause-to-prior-cause relationship or effect-to-subsequent-effect relationship is easier for students to grasp initially. In addition to the examples described in this chapter, the model can be used to review content. Using their textbooks or other informational sources, students can use critical events as their data. This may be done as a whole class or with individual groups. Figure 6.7 shows a science example.

Before class, decide on the topic or data to be analyzed. Just before the discussion, provide the organizer. The steps of the model include (1) choosing the topic, (2) asking for causes and support for the causes, (3) asking for effects and support for the effects, (4) asking for prior causes and support for the prior causes, (5) asking

FIGURE 6.7   Cause and Effect as Content Review in Biology

Data	High blood glucose levels
Causes	Beta cells of pancreas undersecrete the hormone insulin; diabetes mellitus, body doesn't respond to insulin
Prior Causes	heredity, age, obesity, destructive or infectious condition of pancreas
Effects	Glucose not absorbed into cells; glucose accumulates in plasma; excess sugar is excreted in urine; less water absorbed into blood by kidney tubules; because glucose not available, a shift in cellular metabolism to fats and proteins for energy production
Subsequent Effects	Extreme thirst; some fats may be deposited in blood vessels, causing a variety of vascular problems (e.g., if retinal vessels are affected, blindness can result, or when limbs and feet are affected, gangrene can result); many fats completely oxidized producing acidosis, which can result in diabetic coma
Conclusion	When glucose accumulates in plasma, excess sugar is excreted into urine
Generalization	What happens in one part of the body affects other parts of the body

TABLE 6.1   Potential Teacher and Student Behaviors in the Cause-and-Effect Model

Step	Teacher	Student
1. Choose topic or problem	• Chooses data, topic, or action to be analyzed • Checks for alignment with standards, objectives, and assessments • Considers what students know about the topic • Defines cause and effect • Reviews model process with students, including graphic organizer	• Connects topic to what is known • Recognizes and knows how to use cause-and-effect organizer • Asks questions about the process if necessary • Defines cause and effect
2. Causes and support for causes	• Asks for identification of proximal causes of topic or problem • Elicits reasons for the identification • Monitors student understanding of the situation, particularly cause and effect • Uses graphic organizer	• Identifies proximal causes • Points out multiple reasons for the proximal causes of the situation • Explains why these reasons make sense • Uses graphic organizer • Requests help if there is confusion
3. Effects and support for effects	• Asks for identification of effects associated with the cause • Elicits reasons for identification • Monitors student understanding of immediate effects • Fills in graphic organizer	• Identifies immediate effects • Points out multiple reasons for the immediate effects • Contributes to graphic organizer • Monitors personal comprehension of discussion
4. Prior causes and support	• Asks for identification of prior (more long-term) causes • Elicits reasons for the identification • Monitors student understanding of the situation, particularly cause and effect • Fills in graphic organizer	• Identifies prior causes • Points out multiple reasons for the prior causes of the situation • Explains why these reasons make sense • Contributes to graphic organizer • Requests help if there is confusion
5. Subsequent effects and support	• Asks for identification of subsequent or later effects associated with the problem or situation • Elicits reasons for identification • Monitors student understanding of immediate effects • Fills in graphic organizer	• Identifies subsequent or later effects • Points out multiple reasons for the subsequent effects • Contributes to graphic organizer • Monitors personal comprehension of discussion
6. Conclusions about this problem	• Asks students to consider the graphic organizer and draw conclusions about this situation or problem • Elicits reasons for conclusions • Provides feedback on logic and utility of conclusions	• Examines graphic organizer • Provides several examples of conclusions based on discussion • Shares thinking about conclusions • Monitors understanding of conclusions
7. Generalizations	• Explains difference between conclusions and generalizations • Elicits generalizations that move beyond this specific problem or situation • Monitors student understanding	• Explains difference between conclusions and generalizations • Contributes generalization or generalizations to discussion • Monitors personal understanding

for subsequent effects and support for the subsequent effects, (6) asking for conclusions, and (7) asking for generalizations.

The preceding list describes the process of using the cause-and-effect model, but the detail in specific teacher and student behaviors is lacking. By examining the potential behaviors of teachers and students working within the cause-and-effect framework, you can consider what is needed to master the model and include it in your professional toolbox. Table 6.1 is a guide to help you consider what student behaviors are needed for successful understanding of cause and effect, providing you with a roadmap for molding your teaching behaviors to students. Analyzing cause and effect is an essential skill for students and teachers, and the time and energy you put into mastering this model will contribute to your professional success.

A case study showing how to use the cause-and-effect model in context can be seen in Chapter Fifteen.

EXTENSIONS

ACTIVITIES

1. If you were appointed principal of a school where you had either studied or taught, think of a change of policy that you would initiate. Now list three effects and three subsequent effects that you think would occur after the policy was implemented.
2. Choose a piece of curriculum that you currently teach or will be teaching. Write a cause-and-effect content review for each of the steps of the model, as in Figure 6.1.
3. Ask a practicing teacher what problems students have with identifying cause and effect. Explain the model to the teacher and explore the possibility that the steps of the model may help students understand these complex relationships. Probe the teacher for suggestions about implementing the model or making adjustments to the model.
4. Google the phrase "cause and effect teaching" for a great list of articles and discussions of cause-and-effect instruction. Be sure to click on "Images" to find dozens of teacher-made worksheets and posters related to teaching cause-and-effect relationships.

REFLECTIVE QUESTIONS

1. Why do you think it is important to help students identify cause-and-effect relationships? Do you think this is a skill that will help students be successful in your classroom? Why or why not?
2. How does the cause-and-effect model relate to other instructional models? In what ways is the model similar to concept attainment, concept development, and cooperative learning? In what ways is it different?
3. How might becoming proficient in using the cause-and-effect model contribute to your professional development?
4. It might be fun to engage your students in discussion of the fact that in January 2014, 200 linguists at the American Dialect Society met and voted on the "Word of the Year" for 2013. They decided on an old word now used in a new way: *because*. The word now need not be followed by *of* or by an other object or clause. For example, we can expect to see and hear sentences like "We know a lot about nature because science" or "Need to take a nap now because tired." The reason for this new use of an old word may relate to the origin of the word itself. *Because* came into English from the two-word prepositional phrase *by cause*.

7

The Vocabulary Acquisition Model

LEARNING THE SPELLINGS AND MEANINGS OF WORDS

Chapter Objectives

You Will Know

- The basis of the vocabulary acquisition model
- Principles underlying the vocabulary acquisition model
- How vocabulary is acquired
- Steps in the vocabulary acquisition model
- How to evaluate learning in the vocabulary acquisition model
- How to meet individual needs with the vocabulary acquisition model
- Applications of the vocabulary acquisition model
- Benefits of the vocabulary acquisition model

You Will Understand That

- Words reflect disciplinary content

You Will Be Able To

- Identify the purpose and steps of the vocabulary acquisition model
- Plan content lessons using the vocabulary acquisition model

In the Elementary Classroom

Mrs. Schafer designed an introductory lesson to teach her third grade class the basic units of measure—volume, mass, and length. Her goal was that students would learn to measure volume to the nearest milliliter, mass to the nearest kilogram, and length to the nearest millimeter. The prefixes associated with these units, *milli-* (one thousandth), *kilo-* (thousand), and *centi-* (one hundredth), were particularly important for the students to learn in association with these measures. She began by detailing her instructional objectives:

A Lesson on Units of Measurement

Objectives

Common Core State Standards—Mathematics 2.MD
Measure and estimate lengths in standard units

Students Will Know

- The prefixes used in measurement
- The measurements used for volume, mass, and length

Students Will Understand That

- Prefixes signal a change in the scale of measurement

Students Will Be Able To

- Identify the correct prefix for different measurements
- Measure objects using the correct units and prefixes

To put various measures in concrete form that the students could understand, Mrs. Schafer brought to class a bag of wooden blocks of various sizes for students to manipulate. As a pretest, she asked the students to define in their own words the ideas of volume, mass, and length and to match each with its typical unit of measurement: cubic millimeter, kilogram, and millimeter. The students' answers varied, but the class decided that volume means "the amount of space" occupied by something, mass means "how much of something," and length means "how long" something is. These definitions were written on the chalkboard. Next to *volume* was written *milliliter,* next to *mass* was written *kilogram,* and next to *length* was written *millimeter.*

> **Mrs. Schafer:** We are going to study the basic units of measure today by measuring some things. Using the wooden blocks you have at your desks, your task will be to make measures of volume, mass, and length of each one.
>
> **Baker:** How are we going to measure these things?
>
> **Mrs. Schafer:** You have a ruler at your desk and I have a scale here that will give you mass in metric terms. You should also check the values in the table of metric system units (Table 7.1) that I have provided. Remember, the metric system is simple because it is a system of units of ten, or tens, hundreds, and thousands.
>
> **Marcia:** But we don't measure that way. We use feet and inches.
>
> **Mrs. Schafer:** That is generally true, but around the world and in all the sciences, the metric system is the choice. Think of it as learning two languages, one that you use in some places, the other in other places. You might find you like your new language of measurement, once you get the hang of it. Many rulers have both scales so you can have a choice.

TABLE 7.1   Table of Metric System Units

Quantity Measured	Unit	Symbol	Relationship
Length	millimeter	mm	10 mm = 1 cm
	centimeter	cm	100 cm = 1 m
	meter	m	1 km = 1000 m
	kilometer	km	
Mass	milligram	mg	1000 mg = 1 g
	gram	g	1 kg = 1000 g
	kilogram	kg	1 t = 1000 kg
	metric ton	t	
Volume	milliliter	mL	1000 mL = 1L
	cubic centimeter	cm^3	$1 cm^3 = 1mL$
	liter	L	$1000 L = 1 m^3$
	cubic meter	m^3	

Preston: Wow. I never noticed that on my ruler.

Mrs. Schafer: Here are three hints to make it easy for you. I've also written these on the board:

1. To measure length, find the number in millimeters with the rulers you have at your desks. Be sure to use the scale labeled *mm*.
2. To measure mass, assign a number in fractions of a kilogram, which you get by weighing the blocks on the metric scale.
3. The measure of volume will be a number in cubic centimeters. To get this, measure the height, length, and width of a block in centimeters and multiply these three values together. A cube has three sides, so "cubic" or "cubed" means the product of three different measures, each the same length. For example, 4 cubed is $4 \times 4 \times 4$.

You may work together in small groups to discuss these procedures as you complete your measures. If you run into difficulty, raise your hand and I will come help you. ∎

In the Middle/Secondary Classroom

The eighth grade social studies class is just beginning a unit on the Middle Ages. Their teacher, Mr. Torres, is concerned about the sophisticated vocabulary in the text and decides to begin the unit with a vocabulary acquisition lesson.

A Lesson on the Middle Ages

Objectives

Common Core State Standards—English/Language Arts RH.6-8.4
Determine the meaning of words and phrases as they are used in a text, including vocabulary specific to domains related to history/social studies.

Students Will Know
- The Catholic Church shaped the Middle Ages
- The origin and historical development of the words *Middle Ages* and *Crusades*

Students Will Understand That
- Religions have shaped history

Students Will Be Able To
- Apply their knowledge of word origins to historical themes
- Identify their current knowledge of the Middle Ages
- Generate personal questions about the Middle Ages

The standards on which Mr. Torres is basing his unit indicate that students should know the sequence of events and the influence of the Catholic Church throughout Europe during the years 500 to about 1000 AD. Because the Crusades occurred just after this period, Mr. Torres decided to begin with these two terms, *Middle Ages* and *Crusades*. He asks the students to spell and to write down anything they associate with each of the words.

He notices that most of the students spell *middle* correctly, but the associations vary. The most common idea that comes up in the ensuing discussion is the concept of "between." The word *crusade* was spelled in several different ways and defined in reference to war, religion, and Robin Hood.

Mr. Torres: Look first at the word *middle* in the phrase Middle Ages. Middle of what? What does it mean to say of anything that it's in the middle?

Karen: It's between two other things. Between two ages.

Mr. Torres: Like middle school is between elementary and high school and a middle child is between an older and younger sibling.

Marcus: But is Middle Ages between old age and young age? Like some people are middle aged.

Karen: Sort of. It's more between ancient times and modern times, right?

Omar: But we are only supposed to be studying 500 to 1000 AD, and there is nothing modern about the year 1000.

Mr. Torres: Karen is correct and so is Omar. The Middle Ages occurred between the end of the Roman Empire and the beginning of the Crusades—it was the middle of these two historical periods, when the Church served the social, political, and religious needs of the people. Let's look more closely at the idea of middle. Sometimes in English, the idea gets spelled *med.* Like in medium. How are middle and medium related?

Ivy: Medium is in between two extremes—big and little, hot and cold, and things like that.

Mr. Torres: Yes, and can you think of other words in which *med* occurs? We can see if they have anything to do with middle.

Jason: Median, like in a road.

Dominique: Mediate, but what does mediate have to do with anything in the middle?

Jason: It's like finding the middle of an argument so both sides will be happy.

Susan: I've heard of medieval. Is that the same thing?

Mr. Torres: That's an adjective describing something from the Middle Ages. "Chivalry was a medieval custom," for example. You could say that instead of saying "Middle Ages custom." But you see how the idea of middle is in all of these words?

Marcus: How about Mediterranean?

Rachel: Or medical?

Mr. Torres: Let's look at the map and see where the Mediterranean Sea is.

Jason: Like between Africa and Europe?

Marcus: But in the middle of what?

Susan: All that land. It's almost all surrounded by land.

Mr. Torres: Let's think about the word "medical" that Rachel mentioned before. And perhaps the word "mediate" that Dominique and Jason suggested. Can you think of any connection between "median" and these words?

Rachel: Looking at these maps, I was thinking that *med* might also be related to the idea of measure. Doctors measure—they take your temperature and weight.

Jason: Doctors seem to mediate, don't they? Like finding middle ground between when you're well and when you're sick. Does that make sense?

Mr. Torres: You're definitely onto something there. Good thinking. But I know also that some words look like they may belong to the same family when actually they don't. Like people who look alike but are not related. Often when I get to this point in thinking about a word, I turn to my dictionary for help in tracing the history of a root. Let's do that now. I'm sure we are on the right track, thanks to your good thinking, but let's confirm, sort of like checking our GPS, our global positioning system, when we're traveling.

Note that the teacher here is another learner, as good teachers always are. He's modeling the behavior he wants students to adopt by demonstrating with an online dictionary (for example, dictionary.com). Projecting the dictionary entry onto a screen to look at the etymology (the history of the word), he and the students find that the word *medical* is built of three parts—a suffix *ic*, meaning "having the quality of"; a second suffix *al*, which makes the word an adjective meaning "related to"; and the root *med*, meaning "heal" and "to take measures, tend to, see about, intervene."

> **Mr. Torres:** Good work, all of you. Now, to get back to the Middle Ages, let's investigate the word *crusade*. Remember what we know about the Crusades— they had a profound impact on social, political, and economic factors in Western Europe.

The conversation about *crusade* begins with *ade,* which Mr. Torres points out means "furnished with." The students think of lemonade, Kool-Aid, and orangeade. All are flavored drinks "furnished" with sweeteners. Mr. Torres provides the information that the word element *crus* means "cross." Those who marched on the Crusades were furnished with a cross and sent to the Middle East to furnish the cross to the "barbarians" who were occupying the territory after the fall of the Roman Empire. That, naturally, led to a lively discussion! ∎

This videotaped discussion and teaching in two different science classes suggests a basic principle of teaching vocabulary in content areas: Only if students come to the reading with a working sense of the key vocabulary will they comprehend what we want them to learn.

The Basis of the Vocabulary Acquisition Model

THE SPELLING–MEANING CONNECTION

Unfortunately, the connection between spelling and meaning is ignored in most spelling and vocabulary instruction. This is one of a number of peculiarities about how words are taught in school, mainly owing to the fact that words are often presented to learners in lists, with the words more or less arbitrarily grouped together and assigned weekly. The accompanying instructions generally require activities such as "Look the words up in a dictionary, use each one in a sentence, and learn their correct spellings and definitions for a test on Friday." But dictionary definitions are notoriously unhelpful, typically circular rather than descriptive. As Robert Marzano, an expert in vocabulary development, cautions, "Effective vocabulary instruction does not rely on definitions" (Marzano, 2004, p. 70). To see why this is so, pick any word you think might be critical to understanding a topic you will soon teach. Look it up in your classroom dictionary, pretending that you really do not know the word. For example, you will find the word "gravity" defined in the typical dictionary as "the quality or state of being grave." The etymology of the word is likely more helpful since that may point out that the word derives from Latin *gravis,* meaning "heavy." In actual use, this word refers to "the force that causes things to fall to the ground if not impeded" or "the seriousness of a statement or circumstance." To understand the meaning of a word, students need to explore how the word is used, along with the derivation of the word and its meaningful parts, rather than to memorize its definition. These are important keys to effective vocabulary instruction. What readers most need is descriptions of how words are used in ordinary language where they will see the words in print and use them in their speech and writing.

Sometimes, of course, students are required merely to memorize the spellings and definitions of the words by looking at each word to get an image of its spelling, copying the word in their own handwriting, and writing the word and its definition 10 times without looking at the correct spelling. Endless hours are spent in activities like this every week of the school year! One has to wonder how many Thursday evenings find parents "calling words" to their children, not just for language arts or English class but, at one time or another, for every subject in school.

Despite all this effort, the cost-effectiveness of this approach is extremely meager because of two major problems with trying to learn lists of words: (1) the students learn practically nothing about the *system* of English spelling and word meaning and

(2) lists of words are de-contextualized so that the chance at understanding how words are used to mean something is lost. The experience of many people who have studied words in the traditional ways just described illustrates each of these two shortcomings.

The major shortcomings of much vocabulary and spelling instruction are predictable in light of what is known about characteristics of the brain, the organ of learning. It would be no exaggeration to say that requirements to "look the words up in a dictionary, use each one in a sentence, and memorize their correct spellings and definitions for a test on Friday" are contrary to the way the human brain works. The brain is a pattern-seeking machine, an organ designed specifically to look for pattern and meaning and to ignore what it judges to be random or meaningless information. Fortunately, the vocabulary of English is neither random nor meaningless. In fact, it is systematic and meaningful. This can guide the study of the spellings and definitions of words *precisely because the human brain thrives on pattern and meaning* and, as Caine, Caine, McClintic, and Klimek (2009, pp. 74–91) explain, "the search for meaning is innate." The vocabulary acquisition model described here honors this insight.

Principles Underlying the Vocabulary Acquisition Model

The model for vocabulary acquisition described here rests on the following three principles:

1. *The principle of system.* Language is nonarbitrary and metaphoric; it is fundamentally a tool for communicating about unfamiliar things in terms related to familiar things. The study of any subject, in school or otherwise, is an exploration of a way of knowing and thinking about the topics that constitute the subject as well as the language in which that knowing and thinking are expressed. Background knowledge, so essential for comprehension, is closely tied to word knowledge. Much successful teaching hinges on the relationship between concepts and vocabulary, between ideas and the language in which those ideas are expressed. Words do not arbitrarily label ideas, concepts, or things. To the contrary, words in English make up a system that mirrors the connections between ideas, concepts, and things.

2. *The principle of incidence.* You have probably had the experience of learning a "new" word that you then begin to hear and see frequently, as if now that you know it, the word is everywhere! This happens because vocabulary is naturally and incidentally acquired as a means for expression of understandings that they already have. People generally acquire only those words that are important and necessary to the expression of ideas they understand and care about. They usually do this incidentally, as in conversation with someone else who cares about the same thing or in reading about something in which they are interested. One might say that with newly acquired vocabulary, "use it or lose it" is the rule. Vocabulary instruction must include opportunities to see new words in use and to use those words to express new understandings. Words are labels associated with packets of knowledge stored in memory (Marzano, 2004, p. 32). Thus, study of any subject should be aimed at the simultaneous acquisition of ideas and labels for those ideas.

3. *The principle of conceptualization.* Teaching vocabulary is a matter of helping learners move simultaneously to greater sophistication in their understanding of concepts and their understanding of language.

What would these three principles look like in teaching? How might these principles change the way teachers interact with students regarding the various topics of the curriculum? Certainly the instructional conversation should include discussion

In this video, two reading experts discuss the idea of intentional vocabulary instruction, or as one of them puts it "indirect intentional" instruction. What they are driving at is that vocabulary instruction should be seamlessly woven into teaching of any subject in school.

about the language in which ideas and information are expressed as well as discussion of ideas and information *in* the language of the topic.

Part of the answer to the oft-repeated question "What should schools teach?" is "Teach students to participate in the great conversations that have defined what it means to be educated." Teach them the joys of language in which distinctions of thought are reflected. Conduct their way into the particular conversations that have contributed to humankind's knowledge. Use the language of the discipline, and, more importantly, invite the students to adopt key vocabulary as their own as they come to see how the language they are acquiring ties together the concepts they are studying. Retention is highest for ideas the learner truly understands and can accurately put into language; the rate of forgetting newly learned material is high for ideas the learner cannot verbalize. This helps explain why meaningful words, those tied to well understood concepts, are retained so well by most learners. It seems unlikely that someone could understand a subject such as geometry or a topic within that subject such as right triangles and lack the language with which to express their understanding. Likewise, it is difficult to imagine how one might understand social studies or a topic within social studies such as forms of government and yet have no technical language to discuss those forms. Every subject and every topic in the curriculum is couched in a language peculiar to its expression. Words are best learned and retained when they are embedded in a subject domain rather than studied in arbitrary lists.

Think, for example, of the words and phrases associated with the topic of right triangles: *right angle, hypotenuse, square,* and *square root.* Likewise, the terms associated with forms of government are essential to expression of what one understands about governments in general. Among these terms are the words *represent, govern,* and the root *archy* in its many forms. Also in that group is *polis,* meaning "city," the common root of words such as *politic, police, polish, cosmopolitan,* and *polite.*

WEB RESOURCE

More Words

When you need to find words that share a common prefix, root, or suffix, you and your students can access the website "More Words" at morewords.com. Here you can enter any string of letters and ask for a list of words that have those letters in that order. Follow the directions and try this with the letters *poli.* You will get a list of over 200 words, most of which (though not all) have to do with citizenship or government.

Think of teaching as a conversation, a special conversation in which comments of the teacher and texts lead students toward inquiry and curiosity about the concepts under study and about the language in which those concepts are expressed. This conversation, teaching, is extraordinary in several ways. One conversational participant usually knows a great deal more than the others about the point of the conversation, and that one—the teacher or author—usually talks more than the others. The purpose of that talk, though, is to engage the other participants in thinking that leads to insights and understandings. Such conversation might accurately be seen as a shared inquiry, an inquiry in which the teacher and students are equally engaged. The major goal of education is to introduce learners to the conversation that has created the concepts they are trying to learn, extending to them an invitation to contribute to the creation itself.

The special conversation that is teaching is conducted in language particular to the topic under discussion. Concepts and ideas new to the learners are initially framed in language familiar to them, as this helps to activate prior knowledge. As understandings emerge in the learner, the teacher and text may introduce language that expands the thinking and the range of such understandings. Students participate in that conversation to become conversant with the curriculum topics.

The success of students' learning requires that they learn two things simultaneously. First, learners must understand what they are taught well enough to put their understandings in their own words. Second, they must own the language in which the understandings they have acquired are typically expressed by experts. Learners need to see experts' vocabulary as both a way of labeling concepts and a way of tying those concepts into the structure of human knowledge.

There are other ways to be expert in a topic besides firsthand experience. Much that we know, that we claim to be expert in, we gain from conversation. In instructional conversation, ideas and experiences are gained vicariously, and the learner is free to take risks, to be wrong, or to be right in unique ways. Imagine classroom conversations marked by the qualities associated with expertise, and you begin to get an idea of an aim that is possible in teaching: learners who are virtual experts in their studies.

This aim will be realized when teachers see themselves as more than conveyors of information—when they define themselves as conductors of and participants in a conversation to which students also are invited to participate. This conversation is about more than the topic under study, however. It is a conversation simultaneously about a topic and about the words in which the topic has come to be expressed. The guide to that conversation is as follows:

1. Teach the topics of the curriculum as bodies of knowledge, information, and concepts that are born in language, live in language, and expand in language. Human understanding typically happens in words—we observe, we collect information, and then attempt to label what we see in words we think best describe it.
2. Teach as if everything to be taught and everything to be learned existed and were understandable in language created precisely for its expression. As students learn, they must encode their new insights and understanding in words they can remember.
3. Teach the topics of the curriculum *as* language. Learning new ideas and information is similar to learning new ways of expressing those ideas and information.

How Vocabulary Is Acquired

Learners, young and old alike, all acquire vocabulary in fundamentally the same way: from the conversations they engage in, first with intimate caretakers and later with teachers and with authors of texts removed in space and time. *Vocabulary* shares a common root with *vocation*: *voc,* meaning "to call." So vocabulary is the lexicon, or glossary, of a calling and the means by which experts express their callings. In formal study, vocabulary is the language particular to a subject, created as a means of expression for understandings and ideas gained from both personal experiences and the experiences of others. When learners acquire understandings and words to express those understandings, they replicate, in microcosm, the evolution of the information they are gaining. Put another way, as learners become experts, their understandings evolve through the stages in which those understandings originally evolved. The differences lie in efficiency and timeliness. The teacher saves the learner the trouble of re-creating knowledge, all the while realizing that learners in this conversation must create their own knowledge. Seen as conversation, teaching requires of the teacher two kinds of expertise: expertise in the subject to be taught and expertise in the language of the subject.

Steps in the Vocabulary Acquisition Model

STEP 1: PRETEST KNOWLEDGE OF WORDS CRITICAL TO CONTENT

At the beginning of any unit of study or new topic, a formative pretest of knowledge of a few words critical to the content under study can serve several purposes. The *unannounced* pretest (actually, an informal diagnostic assessment) is an opportunity for students to show what they know and can be a place to begin learning more. As you call out each word, ask students to spell and define the words the best they can. Emphasize that this is not a test to find out what they *do not* know but rather a test to find out what they *do* know. Teaching and learning must proceed from the known to the new, so the first step in learning is to identify the known.

To generate the list of words to be pretested and systematically taught, carefully examine the information to be taught—the textbook or other sources of information—and identify the basic vocabulary in which that information is expressed. Textbook chapters often begin with lists of this vocabulary, or there may be a few words italicized in each chapter for special attention. The glossary of the text may be of help, and there is even a handbook for identifying words to emphasize, entitled *Building Academic Vocabulary: Teacher's Manual,* by Marzano and Pickering (2005). The words selected in this first step need not be technical words, but they should be words that express the basic concepts underlying the information under study. Keep the list short, as the goal is to teach a few words so well that the understandings will form a major part of the prior knowledge necessary to comprehension. As an example, consider a science lesson we taught at the fifth grade level on the topic of changing forms of energy. Perusing the textbook chapter carefully, we identified and pretested the following five words: *energy, potential, kinetic, conservation,* and *transformation.* As we expected, our fifth grade students gave us quite a number of spellings and a great variety of definitions for each word. This particular pretest and the conversation that followed are used in the following sections to illustrate the steps in this model.

STEP 2: ELABORATE AND DISCUSS SPELLINGS AND MEANINGS

Students usually come to believe that school is a place that honors being right, without error. The basic idea of the informal pretest is to acknowledge that "error" is a judgment of what is more or less conventional, such as whether a spelling attempt matches its correct form. John Hattie (2012, p. 26) points out that the optimal classroom climate for learning is one "in which error is welcomed, in which student questioning is high." Being right or wrong is only one possible judgment. "State of knowledge" is an alternative, potentially more useful judgment. It opens up a greater range of possibilities for the teacher and admits a greater range of thought on the part of the learner. Certainly it is more respectful in conveying to the learner that every person's knowledge is incomplete. Knowledge of language in any aspect (spelling and word meaning in speaking, listening, reading, and writing) is never an all-or-nothing affair.

If possible, display various spellings and meanings given for each word for all to see. Emphasize that each attempted spelling and each meaning given reflects some knowledge of the ideas and words that represent them. Many misspellings are phonetically derived; they are attempts to represent sound with print. But English spelling is based on meaning as well as sound. (Thus "spelling demons" such as the words *debt, sign, hasten,* and *mortgage,* with their confusing silent letters, are easy to spell once one sees the connection to *debit, signal, haste,* and *mortality.*) The think-pair-share strategy can apply as a follow-up to the invented spellings and hypothesized meanings of vocabulary study. Ask students to work in pairs to discuss the various spellings of the pretested words, all the while assuming that no misspelling is random. For each word, students will individually think of reasons for the various spellings offered, followed by paired discussion of reasons for the spellings and hypothesized meanings, and concluding with an opportunity to share ideas with the whole class. Keep the pace lively by allowing only a couple of minutes for each step in the process and quickly moving on to the next word to be discussed.

Marzano and Pickering (2005, pp. 14–15) detail a six-step process for teaching new terms. Their description of this process is well worth examining in detail, but to summarize, we will abbreviate the first four steps here:

1. Give students a description, explanation, or example of each key word you want them to understand. Use each word in a general context and point out each in the textbook passage to be read.
2. Ask students to restate the description, explanation, or example in their own words, as if they were trying to explain each word to a person who might never have seen or heard it.
3. Ask students to create a drawing to represent each word, as if they were playing charades with the word.
4. Have students enter each word in a notebook to create a personal glossary of words related to the topics they are studying.

STEP 3: DIRECTLY TEACH WORDS ON WHICH COMPREHENSION WILL HINGE

Marzano (2004, p. 69) strongly argues for direct teaching of key vocabulary when he says, citing a meta-analysis of research on the topic, "students' comprehension will increase by 33% when vocabulary instruction focuses on specific words important to the content they are reading . . . . In summary, the case for direct vocabulary instruction is strong." The reason for this is likely that by teaching a few words critical to understanding what they are reading, a teacher is building students' background knowledge on which their comprehension will ultimately depend. The problem with teaching vocabulary is that, although the finding may be intuitively contradictory, research has repeatedly demonstrated that having students look up the meanings of words in a list and then use the words in sentences is a particularly ineffective way to teach vocabulary. Instead, the vocabulary of a reader will improve as he or she acquires strategies for learning word meanings independently and as he or she keeps notes on newly acquired words. Here, in one sentence, is a summary of what years of research into vocabulary development has taught us: *All vocabulary instruction should aim at skills and strategies that help students become independent word learners who are able to figure out the meanings of unfamiliar words they encounter in frequent, wide reading.*

There are no known shortcuts to vocabulary instruction; vocabulary development is continuous. Many teachers have found the following graphic helpful as a guide to vocabulary discussion and a record of evolving understandings their students are experiencing.

In addition, linking is a powerful tool for vocabulary recall. Information that can be linked to or associated with already familiar data and ideas is most likely to be recalled. For example, think of helping students to understand and remember lines of longitude and latitude. Longitude is marked by the "long" up and down lines on the globe; latitude is marked by the "lateral" lines that run across the globe. Think of the lines of longitude as running longwise between the north and south poles; think of the lines of latitude as being similar in direction to a lateral to another player in football. For another example of using linking in instruction, the continents "contain" countries or vast sections of land, as a box of puzzle pieces

We remember everything by associating what we are trying to remember with something that we already know. This can be done intentionally and with purpose; other times, we are not aware that our brain is making these connections. By helping students attach new information to what they already know, they are likely to remember the information and thus be able to apply the information to new settings. Remembering is the basis of application, and teachers can design instruction so that students consciously make associations from new to prior knowledge. A number of linking strategies can be used in classrooms—visual imagery, mnemonic key words, and making associations with unusual information are a few. The basic idea is to connect each event or fact with something familiar—a person, place, thing, event, or feeling.

might contain pieces that are the shape of the countries "contained" by Africa, Europe, Asia, and North and South America. This linking from larger to smaller pieces of land will help students make distinctions between these five continents and the countries they include.

Some teachers have found it helpful to have each student use copies of the graphic organizer shown in Figure 7.1. These pages provide a way for students to take notes on words they are learning. The target word, correctly spelled, is written in the center of the graphic by the teacher and copied by the students. They compare their spellings and begin to discuss differences. Then the teacher writes the prime dictionary definition in the appropriate space on the graphic. Again, the students compare their definitions. They discuss similarities between spellings and definitions, with emphasis on why the word is spelled as it is and why it means what it means. Often, the students are very close in their spellings and definitions. Because learning what a thing is not can be very helpful in understanding what it is, the discussion of differences between the conventional and unconventional spellings and definitions helps everyone get closer to actually knowing the word.

Next, the sentences proposed by students are examined in the same spirit as the spellings and definitions. The teacher and students create an example sentence using the target word, based on what they have found together to that point. The teacher refers the students to the actual spelling and definition as the context of the discussion requires. This keeps the focus on the actual target of the lesson.

Next, students are asked to think of words that might be synonyms or antonyms of the target word. These brainstormed words are examined to see which ones share an etymology, which are synonyms, and which are antonyms. At this point, students can offer additional words to be included on the chart. Etymologically related words are words with the same root—words that share their lineage like family members. Synonyms are words of similar meaning, regardless of whether they are members of the same family. By contrast, antonyms are words of opposite meaning. Knowing a

Proposed by Frank Lyman in 1981, the think-pair-share strategy is a cooperative learning strategy that supports and provides time for individual student thinking while acknowledging that we all learn from others. Think-pair-share allows students to (1) spend some time thinking on their own, (2) share their thoughts and ideas with a partner, and then (3) share their discussion with the large group. This strategy can be used with all grade levels and content areas and serves a variety of academic goals (generating hypotheses, applying new information) and behavioral goals (limiting off-task behavior). Think-pair-share is responsive to individuals and can function as a common classroom interaction structure.

FIGURE 7.1   Graphic Organizer for Vocabulary Acquisition

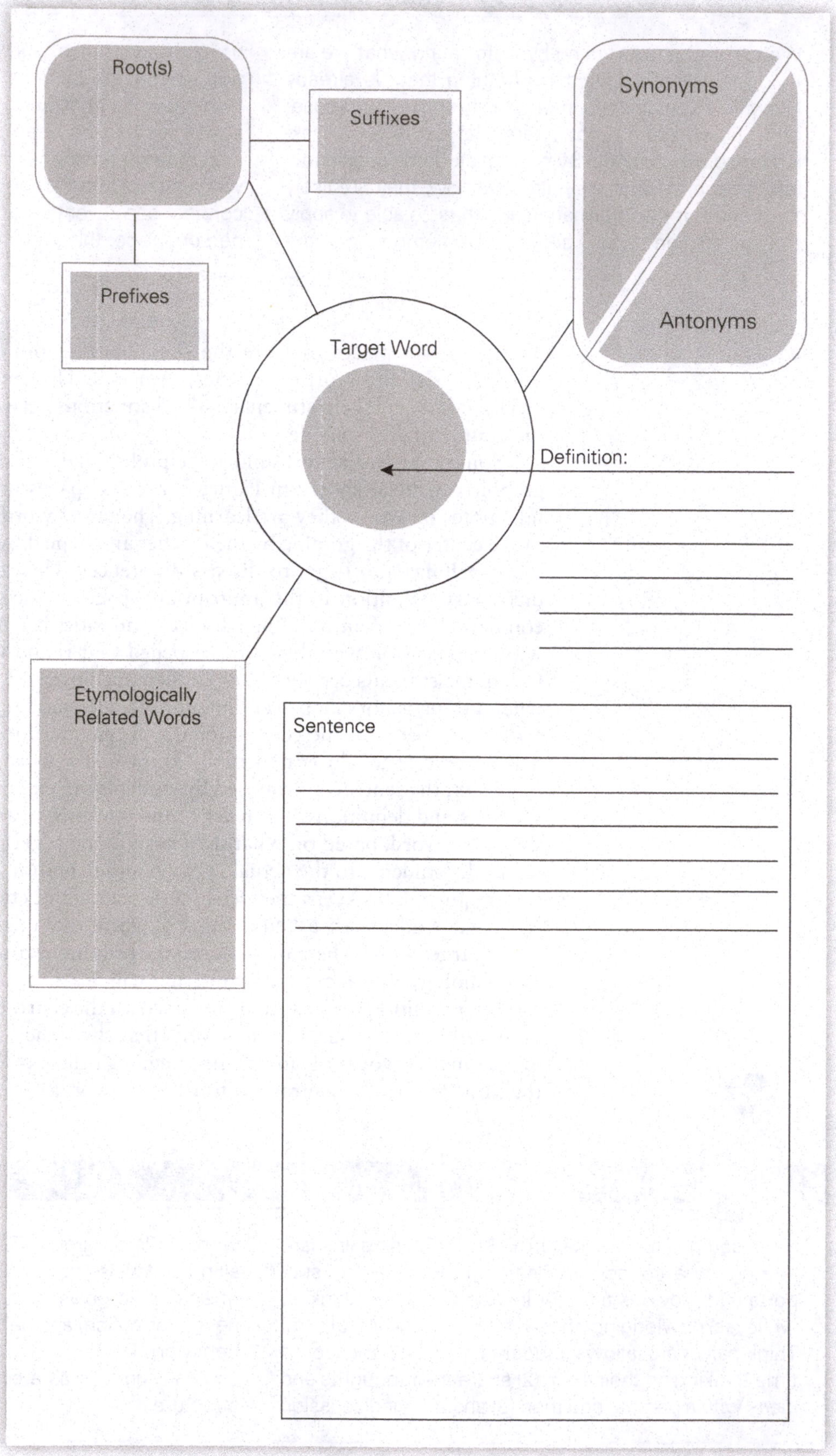

Root(s)

Suffixes

Synonyms

Prefixes

Antonyms

Target Word

Definition:

_____

_____

_____

_____

_____

Etymologically
Related Words

Sentence

_____

_____

_____

_____

_____

word often involves knowing words it is like and words it is not like; acquiring this knowledge is the point of the exercise, similar to the concept attainment processes introduced in Chapter Four.

As the class is discussing etymologically related words, synonyms, and antonyms, possible prefixes, roots, and suffixes can be brought to light. English is a system of combinations. Young readers need to learn to combine, or blend, sounds into words as they decode print to speech. But beyond the basic phonics patterns, readers need to see the patterns of meaning that are also encoded in print and need to be "blended" to make sense. Why is there a silent g in *sign,* for example? The answer is that the g is needed to maintain the meaning connection between *sign* and *signal* and any number of other words of the same meaning family. Why do we say *rented, walked,* and *roused,* in each case spelling the *-ed* part the same but pronouncing it differently? We spell this part of each word the same to maintain the similar function of the word part in each word. We pronounce the endings differently because we gravitate, over time, to the easiest way to say words—a fact that often has led to a mismatch between sound and spelling. There are thousands of similar examples. Bearing in mind that English is a combinatorial system that works to encode both meaning and sound can help readers enormously in their quest for meaning, which is, after all, the point of reading.

The key to independence in word learning and the ability to figure out the meaning of an unfamiliar word lies in a simple precept of language: Just as sentences and phrases are built out of words combined by the rules of syntax, words themselves are built out of smaller bits, called morphemes, combined by another set of rules, the rules of morphology (Pinker, 1994). Language users are hardly aware of these latter rules and procedures, because the processes are virtually automatic at the simplest levels, such as the formation of a plural noun. But at some point, language becomes much more complex, and the similarity of morphemes becomes obscured by variations in spelling and pronunciation. Consider words like *congratulate, grateful,* and *ingratiate,* all of which are built from the same root. Students, as well as most of their teachers, are unable to see most of the morphemic building blocks that compose words in English. But as they become explicitly conscious of what was before only implicit about how words encode their meanings, they begin to recognize meanings of words they have never seen before. Maturing readers become increasingly aware of the meanings of the parts from which words are built.

Building Vocabulary through Classroom Conversation

The most important feature of vocabulary development in the classroom lies in daily conversation about words. The essential facts, concepts, and generalizations of every content area of study live in the core vocabulary of those subjects. What builds vocabulary is curiosity and fascination with language. The basic goal of vocabulary instruction is to engage students throughout the day in figuring out how words have come to mean what they mean. Focus not so much on *what* words mean as on *how* they mean. The answer to that question will lie in the etymology of the words. It is noteworthy that 65 percent of English words are made up partly or entirely of prefixes, roots, and suffixes derived from Latin and Greek. There is a morphological formula that students need to learn to look for and use: (prefix)(es) + root(s) + (suffix)(es) = WORD. This formula means that every word in English is a combination of one or more roots plus, usually, one or more prefixes and suffixes. (Everything in parentheses is optional. All a word absolutely requires is a root.) Understanding how words are built from these units of meaning is the foundation of reading for meaning. Many words are simply roots that stand alone as words without an affix. For example, *act* is a root that can stand alone as a word. Most words, however, are built out of several morphemes, each of which contributes to part of the meaning of the word—for example, *acts, acting, active, action, actively, react, reactor,* and so on. A root such as *anim,* by contrast, is not a word; it must combine with at least one prefix or suffix to make a word. For example, *animal, unanimous,* and *inanimate* all share the same root, meaning "mind" or "spirit." Understanding that words are built of units of meaning, as a house is built of bricks and pieces of wood, opens up a whole new perspective on language. For younger students, this can be illustrated with pop beads of various colors that snap together in the same way units of meaning go together to form words. As students move from sounding out words to understanding what words mean, they will be able to see meaning in words that are new to them. Why? Because they are not completely new if the reader already understands the parts from which words are built. English is composed of over a million words, built of a few hundred meaningful parts. Once a core of these parts is mastered, there remain relatively few truly "unfamiliar" words one is likely to encounter in reading.

Using Vocabulary to Tie the Curriculum Together

Vocabulary has the power to tie together many pieces of the curriculum. Interdisciplinary study requires a common vocabulary. Because a major goal of schooling is the transferability of knowledge and skills, this common vocabulary is critical. Encourage students to hunt for words in content area textbooks, newspapers, fiction, and other texts, looking for words that are in the family of the root they are studying this week or have studied previously. Once students begin to explore the cross-curricular connections that lie in language, what they will discover is that many words of a single root family can be found in multiple subject areas of the curriculum. For example, the root *fract,* referring to "break," can be seen in math *(fractions)*; in science *(refraction)*; in social studies *(fractious)*; in health *(fracture)*; and even in English class, where its spelling changes slightly but the meaning connection remains *(fragment)*. Students may hear or see the word *fracking* in the news. There are dozens of cross-curricular connections that can serve to expand and deepen understandings of essential concepts.

Instruction in the Most Basic Meaningful Parts of Words

Do not automatically assume that students know much about prefixes and suffixes. Begin with simple affixes, those that attach to roots without changing their own spelling or the spelling of the root. A good starting point for teaching prefixes is to teach the prefixes that are the most common in English; 58 percent of all prefixed words have one of the following three prefixes: *un-,* meaning "not," as in *unfair* or *unequal; in-* (also spelled *ig-, il-, im-,* or *ir-*), meaning "not," as in *insane, illegal, irregular,* or *immortal;* and *dis-* (also spelled *di-* or *dif-*), meaning "apart" or "not," as in *disrupt, disgrace, divert,* or *diffuse.*

The common suffixes are also easy to identify and teach, because *-s, -es, -ing,* and *-ed* account for 65 percent of all suffixed words in English. Concentrate initially on suffixes that alter the grammatical form but do not alter the meaning of a root. The most elementary suffixes are *-s, -ing, -ed,* and *-ly.* You will teach more than these few, certainly, but do not assume students necessarily know these basics. The suffix *-s* changes a noun from its singular form to its plural form *or* marks a verb as third-person singular. Thus *act + -s = acts,* more than one act. But *acts* is also the third person of the verb *to act:* "She acts." The syntax of a sentence will determine the difference between these two forms. The suffix *-ing* indicates the present participle (progressive or adjectival form) of a verb or its gerund form. This is how we distinguish "I run" from constructions like "I am running," "Running deer are dangerous to traffic," or "Running is good exercise." The suffix *-ed* marks the past tense of a regular verb, as in *act* + *-ed* = *acted*. The suffix *-ly* changes an adjective into an adverb, as in *act* + *ive* + *-ly* = *actively,* meaning "done in an active manner."

STEP 4: READ AND STUDY

Once the target ideas and vocabulary are introduced and discussed in the vocabulary acquisition model, reading and study may be guided by any companion model such as concept development, classroom discussion, or cooperative learning. Encourage the students to observe carefully how the words they have studied are used in the texts they will read. Seeing a new word used in an appropriate context is another step in vocabulary acquisition. In addition, the students can listen for uses of any of the words in conversation, on radio, or on television or watch for uses of the word in readings other than their textbook. Fiction and nonfiction alike will use all these words in many ways. Wide reading is a good (if sometimes overrated) way to improve one's vocabulary, but only if one is sensitive to the subtle distinctions that writers achieve by their careful choices of words.

STEP 5: EVALUATE AND POSTTEST

The effects of the vocabulary acquisition model are relatively easy to assess. The model begins with a pretest and ends with an informal summative posttest of the spellings and meanings of the same words. One can expect very large differences in the scores on these two tests, considering the intensity of vocabulary study. In this model, mastery is the goal, and nearly perfect scores are the intent.

Part of the evaluation of language is always informal. We all commonly make judgments about a person when we hear the person speak or see the person's writing. The conversation about the vocabulary that has been taught with the vocabulary acquisition model will continue across time; in that conversation, evaluation and encouragement to use more precise language will be inevitable. Keep an informal tally of how often the words taught in past lessons are used. Draw attention to places where a recently discussed word may express more precisely what the students mean. Such informal diagnostic attention to the words students use might be the best part of evaluation for the vocabulary acquisition model.

When testing learners about what they have been expected to learn from their study, include a spelling and meaning test covering the words and concepts targeted in the vocabulary acquisition lesson. The results will show marked improvement of understandings of spellings and meanings of words. The effect will be significantly higher grades, with the added benefit of reinforcing vocabulary study. Furthermore, teaching using this model will greatly enhance the chances that if last Friday's test is washed away in a weekend flood, the students will do just fine on Monday's retest.

SUMMARY OF STEPS IN THE VOCABULARY ACQUISITION MODEL

1. *Pretest knowledge of words critical to content.* This test will establish baseline information for the teacher and students alike: information on what students already know about the fundamental concepts of a topic to be taught. By spelling and defining words, students provide a window on their understandings and a starting point for the instruction.

2. *Elaborate on and discuss spellings and meanings.* Invention and hypothesis form the basis of instruction and growth in understanding. New understandings are built

on prior knowledge, and whatever students attempt in spelling and defining words can become the basis for growth in understanding.

3. *Directly teach words on which comprehension will hinge.* Discuss how words fit together with their synonyms, how words are used in the language, and how words came into existence in modern English. Spelling is more than speech represented in print. English is a morphophonemic system, which means that a word in print gives clues to its sound (i.e., its pronunciation) and to its meaning. Thus, how a word is spelled often has as much to do with what the word means as with how it sounds in speech.

4. *Read and study.* Exploring basic concepts before reading and studying creates a context in which students can confirm what they already know while they elaborate and refine their understandings.

5. *Evaluate and posttest.* The evaluation of learning makes the most sense when the teacher and students can examine an outcome measure—a test following instruction—against a preinstructional measure of the same information. The steps of the vocabulary acquisition model are set up to ensure marked growth in understandings and knowledge of words and their associated concepts.

WEB RESOURCE

Building a Better Vocabulary

The Internet is full of resources that can help in the teaching of vocabulary. A Google search on the topic will yield many sites to choose from. "Building a Better Vocabulary" at grammar.ccc.commnet.edu is one example to explore. Find what's useful to you here or do your own simple search for resources that suit you best.

Evaluating Learning in the Vocabulary Acquisition Model

There are many creative ways to assess students' understanding of vocabulary other than asking them to spell and define words they have studied. These methods may cut across content areas and instructional models and may occur in the midst of a variety of lessons with goals other than vocabulary acquisition.

- Call out different words of the same meaning family with different suffixes and have the students identify the part of speech of each word.
- Ask the students to identify synonyms and antonyms for words that they have studied.
- See whether the students can identify the meanings of new words that they haven't studied, using their knowledge of the meaning parts of words.
- Give the students a fill-in-the-blank exercise with sentences (accompanied by a bank of words at the bottom of the page) in which they must change or add prefixes or suffixes to words to make them fit the context.
- Have the students identify root parts of boldfaced words in sentences and then define the roots and the words.
- Give the students a set of incomplete sentences or a story that they must complete by using words that have a certain root.
- Rather than simply spell words on a test, ask the students to break them into their meaning parts.
- Occasionally ask the students to define nonsense words based on their knowledge of the meanings of word parts.

Meeting Individual Needs with the Vocabulary Acquisition Model

During class, demonstrate for students your own curiosity about the meaning elements of language by frequently calling attention to word elements that you come across in print. You might also hold a spelling bee in which students get one point for the correct spelling of a word and additional points for identifying the prefixes, roots, and suffixes of the word. Additional strategies include the following, offering a variety of opportunities for meeting individual needs.

- Display words on walls and bulletin boards. Use color coding to differentiate prefixes, roots, and suffixes so that these meaning parts are visible. This is particularly helpful for younger students and students with special needs who respond to aids such as color coding.

- Using index cards, write a word part on one side of each card and a key word illustrating the element on the other side. Allow students to play adaptations of games such as Memory or Go Fish in which they must put these elements together to form real words.

- Define words in ways that ensure the definition is in students' own words and contains the meaning of the root in the definition to illustrate the connection between the word and the root.

- Complete a word hunt for words with the same root, using students' textbooks. For example, have students look in the American history textbook chapter on civil rights to locate words with the roots *leg* and *legis,* meaning "law"; or *judic, judg,* and *jud,* meaning "fairness" or "rightness"; or *greg,* meaning "group" or "flock."

- Represent the meanings of roots or words through pictures. For example, have students find, cut, and paste pictures from magazines or draw pictures representing a root such as *gener,* meaning "family," "creation," "birth," or "sort."

- Create exercises in which students add on and take away prefixes and suffixes to make a variety of words in the same root family with different meanings or parts of speech.

For students whose reading skills are low, it will be very helpful to have them look for and build lists of words that begin or end with one of the common prefixes and suffixes. Many students are not aware of prefixes or suffixes and do not see the meaning connections between words that share these beginnings and endings.

Students whose first language is Spanish may have an advantage over students who know only English. This advantage can be shared with English-only students and can certainly work in favor of students who are struggling to learn English. In many cases, the spelling of a prefix or suffix in Spanish is close enough to the spelling in English words that the meaning connections are transparent and easy to grasp. Table 7.2 illustrates a few of these transparencies that can be of help to English learners with Spanish as a first language.

Benefits of the Vocabulary Acquisition Model

The vocabulary acquisition model benefits from being built on what we know about how students learn and how new concepts are learned. Fundamentally, the new is always tied to the known when learning is successful. The elements of the model provide scaffolding for students as they interact with new ideas and the words that accurately express them. This model also opens the door to disciplinary conversations in which students make cross-curricular connections.

TABLE 7.2 Equivalencies of Affixes in Spanish and English

Affix Meaning	English Form	Spanish Form	English Examples	Spanish Examples
genus, condition	-y	-ia/-ía	complacency anatomy	complacencia anatomía
state or quality	-ity	-idad	civility fidelity	civilidad fidelidad
state or process	-(t)ion	-(c)ión	information composition	información composición
agent	-or	-or	doctor actor	doctor actor
act or function	-ure	-ura	censure curvature	censura curvatura
down	cata-	cata-	(to) catalogue catastrophe	catalogar catástrofe
upon	epi-	epi-	epitaph epidemic	epitafio epidemia
below	hypo-	hipo-	hypothesis hypothermia	hipótesio hipotermia
together (Greek)	sym-	sim-	symmetry sympathy	simetría simpatía
together (Latin)	con-	con-	confection contiguous	confección contiguo
out	ex-	ex-	exclusive (to) expatriate	exclusivo expatriar

ELEMENTARY GRADES LESSON

VOCABULARY ACQUISITION: Units of Measurement

OBJECTIVES	**Students Will Know** • The prefixes used in units of measurement • The measurements used for volume, mass, and length **Students Will Understand That** • Prefixes provide keys to understanding words **Students Will Be Able To** • Measure objects using the correct units and prefixes
ASSESSMENTS	• *Diagnostic.* Use a pretest to determine existing knowledge. • *Formative.* Students will measure different objects using the correct units and prefixes.

PROCEDURES	1. Give the students a pretest on relevant units of measurement.
	2. Elaborate and discuss invented meanings. Ask the students what they think each of the beginnings and endings of these words on the diagnostic test means. Make certain that the following prefixes are mentioned: *deci-, deca-, centi-, milli-,* and *kilo-.* Make sure that the following base words are mentioned: *liter, gram,* and *meter.* Ask the students to justify their responses on the pretest.
	3. Explore patterns of meaning.
	• Provide definitions of the prefixes.
	• Explain what liters, meters, and grams are used to measure.
	• Ask students for examples of use of these units.
	• Explain the distinction between the Standard International (SI) and U.S. systems of measurement.
	• Explain the focus on the SI system in science class.
	4. Read and study. Have students measure a variety of objects in terms of volume, mass, and length. Put the units of measurement on the class matrix
	5. Evaluate and posttest. In groups of three, students will measure and record three different objects using the correct prefix and unit.

MIDDLE/SECONDARY GRADES LESSON

VOCABULARY ACQUISITION: The Middle Ages	
OBJECTIVES	**Students Will Know**
	• The origin and historical development of the terms *Middle Ages* and *Crusades*
	Students Will Understand That
	• Religion helps to shape history
	Students Will Be Able To
	• Apply their knowledge of word origins to historical themes
	• Identify their current knowledge of the Middle Ages
	• Generate personal questions about the Middle Ages
ASSESSMENT	Students will be asked to read a short text about the Middle Ages and define unfamiliar words by using the strategies identified in the model.
PROCEDURES	1. Pretest knowledge of words. Ask the students to define *medieval* and *crusade.*
	2. Have students share their responses in class.
	3. Elaborate on and discuss invented spellings and hypothesized meanings. Tell students about the words and then brainstorm synonyms. Have students create sentences from the list they generated.
	4. Have students use the words as often as possible as you review the major content understandings to follow in the next lessons:
	• The Roman Catholic Church grew in importance after Roman authority declined. During the medieval period, the Church served the social, political, and religious needs of the people.
	• The Crusades were expeditions to the Holy Land to demonstrate piety. They had a profound impact on social, political, and economic factors in Western Europe.

continued

5. Have students read the text on the Middle Ages and identify unfamiliar words.
6. Choose two or three words for study and, with students, use the graphic organizer for vocabulary acquisition (Figure 7.1) to analyze one word together and one word individually.

SUMMARY

Vocabulary is notoriously badly taught in schools, with endless memorization and subsequent forgetting. We have provided an alternative that fills in some of the missing pieces. Adoption of this model can result in lasting acquisition of the vocabulary learned in school, with the added benefit of improved comprehension of textbook reading and study.

Three principles underlie this model: (1) There is a system governing vocabulary, such that words are related to each other in ways reflected in their spellings and meanings; (2) words are acquired by learners as they acquire precise ways of expressing what they have come to understand; and (3) the learning of concepts and of the vocabulary that labels those concepts happen in support of one another.

Every subject taught in school is more than a body of arbitrary facts. You may think of everything taught in school as the result of a conversation that has been going on for a long time. The words of this conversation do not merely label things or ideas but are the ways we distinguish things and ideas one from another. Thus, each subject area of the curriculum represents a particular way of viewing, interpreting, and describing the world with words that reflect the distinctions that constitute the subject under study.

The vocabulary acquisition model is intended to create a conversation that begins with what students know about words essential to their study—the words that carry the brunt of the conceptual load of their school topics. Beginning with an unannounced pretest, this conversation would turn next to the place of these words in the English language: the synonyms of the words, various uses of the words, and the origin and historical development of the words. Following this part of the discussion, students turn to their reading and study, which should now be much more successful than they might have been otherwise. After all, students should be fairly familiar with the basic concepts of their study before reading begins. The model ends with a posttest. Scores on this test of spellings and definitions should be much higher than the pretest scores.

Implementation of the vocabulary acquisition model is described as a sequence of steps.

1. Pretest knowledge of words critical to the content to be taught with an *unannounced* informal test. Assure students that this is not a test to see what they don't know, but rather a test to see what they do know already about how these words are spelled and what they mean.
2. Discuss the invented spellings and hypothesized meanings of the words revealed by the pretest.
3. Use copies of the graphic organizer provided in this chapter to accumulate pages in personal vocabulary notebooks for students.
4. Explore the patterns of meaning in the words, using strategies like think-pair-share or linking.

5. Assign readings on the topic under study, not only from the textbook in use but a variety of texts selected from the library and other sources. This will ensure that more students get to see the concepts and vocabulary in contexts they can apprehend without frustration.

6. Evaluate student learning with a posttest that is identical to the pretest. The intent of the model is to have students achieve mastery of the topics of their study; thus their grades in school might soar. If that happens, we think the vocabulary development model is well worth the time and effort. If students catch a glimpse of the joy of language that can live with them from that point forward, they will leave school with a gift for language that will distinguish them from others.

The preceding list describes the process of using the vocabulary acquisition model, but does not detail all of the behaviors that the teacher and students should use to successfully reach the model's goals. By examining the potential behaviors of teachers and students working within the vocabulary acquisition framework, you can consider what is needed to master the instructional moves of the model and include the model in your professional toolbox. Table 7.3 will help you consider what student behaviors are needed for successful understanding of the process of learning new vocabulary, providing you with a roadmap for molding your teaching behaviors to students. It takes time and patience to make a specific model of instruction part of your instructional repertoire. Looking at the specific behaviors that comprise the model will be helpful.

Case studies demonstrating how to use the vocabulary acquisition model in context can be seen in Chapters Thirteen, Fourteen, and Fifteen.

EXTENSIONS

ACTIVITIES

1. In most textbooks, a list of words appears at the beginning of each chapter. These are sometimes called the "key words" for the chapter. Students also encounter boldfaced or otherwise highlighted words in their reading: words that are important to the topic under study and likely included in the glossary at the end of the text. Examine a textbook, perhaps the one you are using in teaching, to see how words' meanings are conveyed. Can you find any discussion of why the words mean what they do or why they are spelled as they are? Are the etymologies of the words mentioned?

2. Take a close look at the next lesson you are going to teach or a lesson you have taught. Pick out the key concepts—the three or four really big ideas—in that lesson. Now look at the words in which those ideas are expressed. Examine the words carefully to figure out why they mean what they mean. Look them up in a good dictionary, such as *American Heritage* or *Merriam-Webster*, to ascertain their etymology. How could you use this information to better teach these concepts?

3. For an amusing way to delve into the role of memory and word usage, do an Internet search for the blog "Dive into Language"; once there, click on the "June 2013 archive" link and read the article entitled "Don't Forget What You Just Learned—The Role of Memory in Vocabulary Acquisition."

REFLECTIVE QUESTIONS

1. Textbook chapters often begin with key vocabulary. Would it be helpful to use these words as the basis of vocabulary instruction, or should you look for additional words that are key to the major concepts being taught? Should students be invited to participate in this word search?

TABLE 7.3   Potential Teacher and Student Behaviors in the Vocabulary Acquisition Model

Step	Teacher	Student
1. Pretest	• Selects targeted vocabulary (aligned with objectives, assessment, and instruction) • Diagnoses student prior knowledge • Sets positive tone for assessment by showing benefits of error analysis	• Connects words on diagnostic pretest to prior knowledge • Responds to assessment • Notes gaps in personal knowledge
2. Elaboration	• Reviews assessment with students • Discusses relationships of words, sounds, meaning, and spelling • Analyzes student errors with class • Reminds students of relationship between words and concepts • Monitors student understanding	• Attends to assessment review • Uses discussion information to support new learning • Analyzes personal errors along with those of peers • Defines relationship between words and concepts • Monitors personal understanding
3. Explore patterns	• Discusses how words are related and used • Shares word history, when applicable • Invites students to share personal definitions • Brainstorms antonyms and synonyms of targeted words • Compares targeted words with brainstorm list • Monitors student use of words in writing and speech	• Seeks connections between prior knowledge and new vocabulary • Asks for clarification for new, confusing, and unusual words • Shares personal definitions with others • Participates in brainstorming and discussion • Monitors personal understanding of new vocabulary
4. Read and study	• Chooses an instructional model or strategy that allows students to apply new vocabulary knowledge • Scaffolds students as they encounter new vocabulary in context • Monitors student demonstrations of vocabulary knowledge • Provides corrective feedback as students read and use new vocabulary	• Participates in reading and word study • Asks clarifying questions when appropriate • Reflects on what is known and what still has to be learned • Responds to teacher and peer feedback • Monitors personal understanding by noting persistent challenges
5. Evaluate and posttest	• Designs assessment tasks aligned with objectives and instruction • Provides students opportunities to practice new vocabulary for assessment and beyond • Aligns posttest with diagnostic assessment • Reviews assessment results with class and individuals if necessary	• Participates in review activities • Notes difficulties with particular vocabulary words • Asks peers and teacher for help in learning difficult words • Takes assessment • Reviews assessment results with class and teacher • Monitors personal knowledge of vocabulary words and develops steps to relearn words if necessary

2. Too often, spelling is disregarded in classes other than English class. Would it be of value to students learning science, social studies, and math to know that words are spelled at least as much by how they mean as by how they sound?

3. Words are built of meaningful parts called *prefixes, roots,* and *suffixes.* Think seriously about the common word parts that frequently occur in the subject area you teach, whether it is one of the sciences, a branch of social studies, or an area of mathematics. Could your students build lists of these word parts and words in which they occur in their reading?

PART TWO SUMMARY

Part Two described five basic instructional models that can be used in K–12 classrooms. All of the models help students gain knowledge and develop skills. In addition, they help novice teachers develop foundational pedagogical knowledge and skills. Direct instruction, concept attainment, concept development, cause and effect, and vocabulary acquisition are instructional models that were discussed in this part of the text. Each chapter included scenarios, research support, steps of the model, possible adaptations, and specific ways to use the model in a standards-based classroom.

Classrooms are diverse settings. Students differ on many characteristics. The basic instructional models provide a way to vary access for students to access the required knowledge and skills. At the same time, novice teachers are able to develop an increasingly sophisticated set of instructional tools. The needs of both teachers and students are served with the use of different instructional models. Variety widens the net and helps meet the needs of both teacher and students while stretching the ability to use different ways of learning for both.

Teaching with Advanced Instructional Models

In Part Three, we present the advanced models of instruction towards which novice teachers can work after mastering the basic models in Part Two. Advanced models require complex planning and implementation skills for the teacher and students. These skills and the background knowledge to support these skills are described in each of the chapters. The format of the chapters in this section is the same as in Part Two—scenarios, background knowledge, how to apply the model through listed steps and tables, strategy alerts, and discussions about meeting individual needs and evaluating student learning.

We noted in the presentation of basic instructional models that it is important to follow the steps carefully as you are learning the ins and outs of the model's implementation. This is especially true of the more advanced models. These models will also require a bit more time to master and may be used less frequently in the classroom than direct instruction, concept attainment, concept development, cause and effect, and vocabulary acquisition. As in the basic and more frequently used models, these instructional patterns can meet a variety of objectives across all content areas and grade levels. Each model can be adapted to meet the context and needs of students in a classroom. However, the cognitive pressure on teachers and students will be high when the advanced models are first used in classrooms.

The models covered in this part of the text are as follows:

- *Chapter Eight: The Integrative Model.* This model helps students and teachers make generalizations from organized bodies of knowledge in all curriculum areas. Together students observe, describe, explain, generalize, and hypothesize from data sets—covering a wide range of academic and critical thinking objectives. Many different types of data can be used in this model—maps, matrices, charts, graphs, and photography, for example.

- *Chapter Nine: The Socratic Seminar Model.* The Socratic seminar model guides the planning, construction, and selection of questions to be used in the Socratic seminar. Both students and teachers are able to critically examine a text using sophisticated questions and supporting information. This model helps the teacher direct the process of classroom interactions for effective discussions. The Socratic seminar model is particularly effective for those objectives related to analysis, evaluation, and creation.

- *Chapter Ten: Cooperative Learning Models.* Cooperative learning models describe ways in which the teacher can encourage students to work with and help other students in the classroom while they are gaining depth in their content knowledge. The variations on cooperative learning are effective for creating a positive environment in the classroom and for meeting cognitive objectives. These models are useful in all content areas and with students of different ages and varying achievement.

• *Chapter Eleven: Inquiry Models.* In the inquiry model, learners take a puzzling situation and follow a process that leads to the generation and testing of a hypothesis. The emphasis here is on the need for careful, logical procedures in problem solving, on understanding the tentative nature of knowledge, and on the need for group endeavor in solving problems. Learners are encouraged to seek more than one answer to a question, to explain why they are moving toward a specific solution, and to share new information and ideas with peers. The inquiry model is effective in meeting the objectives related to problem solving, analyzing, hypothesizing, and evaluation. Group process, cooperation, and communication are also emphasized.

• *Chapter Twelve: The Synectics Model.* The three versions of the synectics model use group interaction to stimulate creative thought using metaphorical analogies. Creative thinking and expression become group activities in which each individual can participate. Through the model, students are able to use analogies and metaphors to extend ideas. The synectics model is particularly effective for those objectives related to exploration, comparison, identification, insight, and analogy.

All of the models of instruction are adaptable and appropriate for all elementary, middle, and secondary classrooms. The advanced models require more intricate and complex application. However, with desire and intent, all teachers can master these models and extend their instructional repertoire, helping to engage a wide variety of students in their instruction.

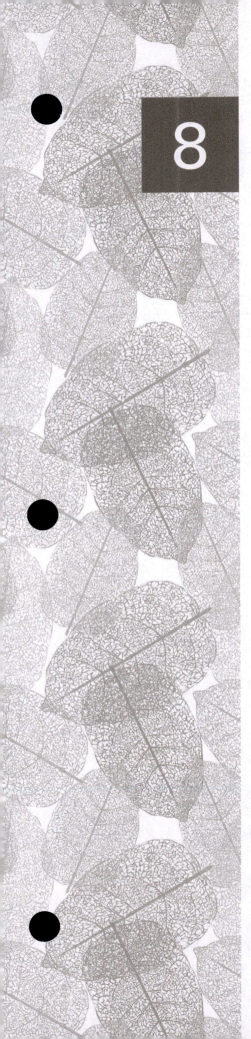

8 The Integrative Model
GENERALIZING FROM DATA

 Chapter Objectives

You Will Know

- What the integrative model looks like in both elementary and secondary classrooms
- The basis in research and theory for using the integrative model in the classroom
- The steps of the integrative model
- How to organize data for use in integrative lessons
- How to adapt the model to meet individual needs
- Ways to assess integrative lessons
- The benefits of the integrative model

You Will Understand That

- The amount of information presented in school is overwhelming and disjointed

You Will Be Able To

- Identify the integrative model in K–12 classrooms
- Design, implement, and reflect on an integrative lesson

In the Elementary Classroom

As Tom Baran works with his third graders on fractions, he decides that his students will benefit from using fraction strips to practice comparing the numerical values of fractions with the same numerator but different denominators. The standard guiding Tom's teaching focuses on understanding that the denominator tells the number of equal parts in a whole and the numerator tells how many equal-size parts are being considered. Tom has thought about his students' skill sets and has determined that they need to review how to compare fractions. He decides that the integrative model not only will allow him to review information about fractions but will also help his students in identifying patterns, hypothesizing, and generalizing. Using Table 8.1, Tom plans his integrative fraction lesson.

Mr. Baran: Look at the comparing fractions table. What do you notice? What is the table about?

TABLE 8.1 Comparing Fractions

1/2 > 1/5	1/4 > 1/6	1/8 > 1/10
1/5 < 1/3	1/10 < 1/5	1/10 < 1/3
1/5 > 1/8	1/6 > 1/10	1/5 = 1/5

Riko: There are a bunch of fractions with greater than or less than symbols.

Mr. Baran: Yes. Can you read each box on the matrix? Is the pair in each box correct?

Once Mr. Baran is confident that students can accurately and completely describe relationships between the pairs, he moves on to the second step of the model—the causal step. In this step, he reminds students that they can use their fraction bars (Figure 8.1) to help answer any of the questions.

Mr. Baran: Let's look at the first pair in the top row. It says that 1/2 is larger than 1/5. Explain to me why.

Marisa: If you compare the fifths fraction bar and the half fraction bar, 1/2 is bigger.

Nolan: And the bottom number, the denominator, is a smaller number.

Mr. Baran: Now, let's move down the first column to the next pair. Which is the larger number? Explain how you know this.

Pedro: The larger number is 1/3. The denominator is smaller, so the pieces are larger.

Mr. Baran: Riko, pick one of the pairs and tell me which is the smaller number and how you know it is smaller.

Riko answers the question and Mr. Baran continues to ask students to describe and explain the comparisons in Table 8.1. Mr. Baran continues working with this table until he is certain that students can explain why one fractional number is smaller or larger than the other. If necessary, he may include additional examples.

Mr. Baran: What if we made some changes to our comparing fractions table? What would happen to the first pair if 1/2 were changed to 1/3? Would 1/3 also be larger than 1/5? Raise your hand if you think so.

FIGURE 8.1   Fraction Bars

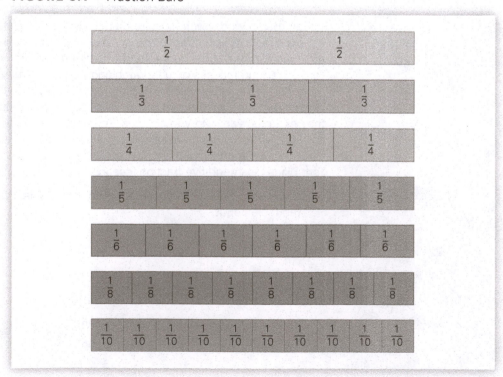

Everyone in the class has a hand raised. Mr. Baran continues to make changes until he feels comfortable that students can substitute numbers and still identify which fraction in the pair is smaller or larger. He even asks students to hypothesize different combinations. For example, if we substitute 1/8 for 1/2 in the first pair, would the relationship be the same or would you need to change the symbol? As students develop ease in predicting the effects of different combinations, Tom asks students to summarize their discussion by making a statement.

Riko: Like we learned last week, wholes can be broken into equal-sized parts.

Fatma: The bottom number tells how many equal parts there are in a whole.

Nolan: The smaller the number in the denominator, the fewer the parts of the whole.

Marisa: If the top number is one, small numbers are bigger than larger numbers in the denominator. ∎

In the Middle/Secondary Classroom

Using a family photograph taken in 1950, Iris Sterman leads a discussion in her middle school social studies class about chronology and changes over time—two critical social studies concepts. Mrs. Sterman's *understand* objectives are that students will understand American society has changed in many ways during the last 70 years and that they will recognize that these changes have had a major impact on American families. Her *know* objective is that students will be able to explain differences in clothing, homes, technology, educational opportunities, and attitudes toward women from 1950 to the present. Her *able to do* objectives are that students will make generalizations by examining an old photograph and that they will be able to hypothesize changes to family life in the next 70 years.

Mrs. Sterman begins class by asking students to work with their social studies partners and examine the photograph that she has distributed. She asks the pairs to

make a list of the things that they notice about the picture. After five minutes, Mrs. Sterman begins the discussion:

Mrs. Sterman: What did you notice in the picture?

Marcy: The picture is old, and the people in the picture are wearing funny-looking clothes.

Kenny: Are they all part of the same family? They look like they are getting ready to go to church or something. They are all dressed up, and that little girl even has a hat on, but it isn't cold outside.

Mrs. Sterman: Let's talk about the clothes in the picture. This picture was taken in 1950—that's almost 70 years ago. Do you think that clothes are different now? In what ways?

Jordan: Girls don't wear those kinds of dresses anymore, and they look like they are too small. The collar on the boy's shirt is also way big.

Mrs. Sterman: What else do you notice about what these children are wearing?

Randi: The shoes? No one is wearing flip-flops, and the girls are all wearing white socks. This picture looks like the ones my Nana has in her house.

Mrs. Sterman: You have noticed three important things. The children in the picture—who are cousins, by the way—are dressed up. The dresses and shirts they are wearing are different from what you would find in stores today. Likewise, the shoes the children are wearing are different from shoes children would be wearing today. Think about a family picture that was taken this year—a family picture of five cousins. How would the 21st-century picture differ from this 1950 picture? Think about the clothes that the cousins would be wearing in a picture taken last week.

Randi: Flip-flops!

Arnold: Everyone would be in jeans or shorts and T-shirts with the names of sports teams.

Brett: No one would be standing so still.

Mrs. Sterman: That is an interesting observation, Brett. Why do you think the children in the picture were standing "so still"?

Alyssa: Maybe it's because they didn't usually get their picture taken. We have an exchange student in our house, and he said that in his village, picture taking happens only on holidays and at graduations.

Mrs. Sterman: Do you think that there were a lot of family pictures taken in 1950?

Randi: My Nana has boxes and boxes of photographs that she always wants me to look at with her. It gets really boring, but she has pictures of my great-great-grandparents, and that was way before 1950.

Mrs. Sterman: So there have been family photographs for a long time. Do you remember the Civil War photographs we saw at the museum? How long before this photograph of the cousins was taken were those pictures taken?

The discussion continues, with students bringing up points about the changes in the technology of cameras and the differences in houses. Mrs. Sterman also asks her students what changes have occurred in society since their grandparents took family pictures of children. We return to the discussion as she is asking about some of these societal differences.

Mrs. Sterman: You mention that some of the differences between your grandparents' America and today is that there is more divorce and more mothers work, and I said that more people graduate from high school and go to college than they did 70 years ago. You also noticed that cameras and clothes have changed over the last 70 or so years. Can you tell me why some of these changes have happened?

Marcy: Did they have jeans in 1950?

Brett: Yeah, a Levi commercial I saw said that jeans were invented during the California Gold Rush, and that was before the 1900s!

Randi: So, how come kids didn't wear jeans?

Barbara: I think people in the old days dressed up more. When I look at pictures of my grandparents when they were little, they are always dressed up.

Nancy: My father says that clothes have changed a lot. He tells us that we are lucky that we don't have to iron our clothes the way he did. Maybe the clothes have changed because of what they are made of.

Mrs. Sterman: That's a really good point, Nancy. The way clothes are made has also changed.

Randi: Oh, oh. I know—there are better machines now and the machines can make more clothes faster. Maybe that's why we can buy so many clothes. Maybe the people in the picture didn't have as many choices. Maybe that's why those dresses look so small—they had to keep them a long time or they were handed down from somebody else.

Mrs. Sterman asks for other explanations and then moves the discussion to the hypothesis phase of the model. Notice that this has already begun when the children start to speak with the hypothetical "maybe."

Mrs. Sterman: The cousins in the picture look like they are taking care of the little girl. The older girl is looking at the baby in the picture and one of the other cousins has her hand on the baby's shoulder. I'd like you to think about how the picture might have changed if the littlest cousin were not in the picture.

The students comment on how everyone might be looking at the camera and that we might, then, be able to see more details of the clothes. Mrs. Sterman continues asking students to hypothesize by asking what might have happened to the cousins in the last 70 years.

Mrs. Sterman: If the boy cousin in the picture was 10 in 1950, what might have happened to him in terms of military service? When can a young man enter the military? Were we at war during the time that this young man was between the ages of 18 and 35? What do you think might have happened to this young man if he did serve in the military?

Many students responded to these questions, and there was some discussion about whether the young man could have been killed in the Vietnam War. Perhaps because he was older than the average infantry soldier, he might have been an officer. Mrs. Sterman then points the students to the young girls in the picture. She asks the students to choose one girl and, with their partners, write a story about what might have happened to her during the 70 years that followed the taking of the photograph. Mrs. Sterman told them that their stories had to reflect some of the themes that were previously discussed—technology, divorce, opportunity for education, and working mothers—and that their stories had to explain why they thought these events had occurred. Students then shared their stories with the class.

Mrs. Sterman: What interesting stories! What can we say about the changes that have occurred in our society since this picture was taken?

Here are some examples of the generalizations that students produced:

- The Vietnam War made a difference to families.
- Family pictures would look different today because we have better cameras and technology than they did in 1950.
- Children in 1950 had fewer choices than we do when it comes to getting dressed in the morning.
- Machines and different fabrics have made cheaper clothes available to families.
- More children finish high school today than in 1950. Finishing high school can make a difference to families because people can get better-paying jobs. ■

Basis for the Integrative Model

The integrative model is rooted in the inductive strategies of Hilda Taba (Taba, Durkin, Fraenkel, & McNaughton, 1971) and has been popularized by Eggen and Kauchak (2012). Basically, the model is a controlled discussion—a structured conversation that allows teachers to focus on helping students acquire academic information while practicing complex reasoning skills. In an integrative discussion, students have the opportunity to construct personal understandings of organized bodies of knowledge—information that includes intricate relationships between facts, concepts, and generalizations.

The integrative model is designed to help students see relationships between the components of a complex topic (for example, migration, animal classification, or branches of government). As students try to make sense of complicated webs of association, they build or revise the schemata that they have previously constructed to make sense of similar information. Schema theory supports the integrative model in that the instruction helps participants arrange information so that it is easily assimilated and subsequently retrieved. A schema is a structure that organizes large amounts of information into a retrievable system (Schunk, 2004). People's brains are active in storing information and making new connections as they are exposed

Schema theory, the ideas of how our brains process new information and move it into retrievable long-term memory, is complicated. This video provides a humorous explanation. www.youtube.com/watch?v=o4HHCgFmkcl

to novel experiences and information. Schemata are the configurations that organize these experiences by connecting prior and new knowledge. The integrative model presents content to students in an organized way, allowing connections to be built smoothly and effectively.

In addition, the integrative model allows for increased knowledge. Brain capacity benefits from experience, and experience that is well organized provides the best advantage. Through structured bodies of knowledge, students are able to prioritize information and link new data to existing schemata, increasing the opportunity for school success. Bransford and his colleagues (Bransford, Brow, & Cockling, 2000) acknowledge that not all instruction is equal, noting that:

> It is clear that there are qualitative differences among kinds of learning opportunities. In addition, the brain "creates" informational experiences through mental activities such as inferencing, category formation, and so forth. These are the types of learning opportunities that can be facilitated. (p. 127)

The structure of the integrative model allows students to develop and practice important critical thinking skills. The expectation underlying the model is that students will make logical inferences, identify similarities and differences, generate explanations and hypotheses, and synthesize information while they are learning academic content. These strategies are all associated with school achievement. When teachers identify similarities and differences or ask students independently to identify similarities and differences, students' understandings are enhanced. These identifications can be made through comparisons, classification, and the development of metaphors and analogies—the skills of saying one thing in terms of another or of drawing comparisons in order to clarify.

Patterns are crucial components of the integrative model. Schemata are the means by which learners impose patterns on complex information, the tools with which students deal with content and procedures. Schools cannot cover all of the bits of information that are available for curriculum development and instructional design. There is too much information to incorporate easily into long-term memory. The integrative model helps teachers and students organize discrete pieces of information into a more manageable whole so that deep understanding of topics and the relationships between topical elements can be developed. In fact, "the more complex and interconnected a schema is, the more places learners have to connect new knowledge and understanding" (Eggen & Kauchak, 2012, p. 212).

Steps in the Integrative Model

STEP 1: PLANNING FOR THE INTEGRATIVE MODEL

Organized bodies of knowledge are just that—organized. Integrative lessons are developed around data sets—bits and pieces of information that are ordered in matrices, graphs, maps, pictures, or other displays. First, a topic must be identified. Content standards, curriculum materials, and district scope and sequence charts are filled with topics rich in complexity and relationships. Second, teachers decide on the target generalizations toward which a lesson is built—the *understand* objectives and information that supports the big ideas. As objectives are being determined, it is helpful to construct a concept map showing the relationships between the focal elements under study. A corresponding matrix may then be developed by the teacher, by students independently or in small groups, or as part of a class discussion. Teachers or curriculum materials will determine the relationships that are highlighted—the categories that will organize the information. In fact, curriculum materials, newspapers, and magazines, as well as electronic resources such as the Internet, can offer a range of data sources that can serve as the basis of an integrative lesson.

Debbie Moss is planning a new geography unit on regions in the United States. Regions constitute a rich topic for information and connections. There are economic, cultural, and physical aspects of regions; these are connections that students need to understand. Checking the state standards, Debbie finds that students must be able to explain how regional landscapes reflect the cultural and economic characteristics of their inhabitants and how cultural characteristics can link or divide regions. By looking through the state's curriculum framework, reflecting on the prior knowledge and needs of her students, and examining available resources, Debbie highlights the big ideas and essential knowledge and skills that will compose her unit. (Note that these planning behaviors are similar across all of the instructional models in this text.)

The big idea of Debbie's unit is that regions have unifying characteristics, both physical and cultural, and that the characteristics of regions may change as people interact with their physical, cultural, and economic environment. Debbie believes her students will need to know that the concept of regions is used to simplify a complex world and that physical and cultural regions can change over time. Students will also need to know that regional "landscapes" include specific cultural characteristics (architecture, language, history, and religion). *Able to do* goals of this integrative instruction include being able to locate regions on maps, interpret regional patterns, compare and contrast information, draw conclusions and make generalizations about data, and explain cause-and-effect relationships. Based on a unit described in the text *Differentiation in Practice* (Tomlinson & Edison, 2003), Debbie has decided that the culminating assessment will be an independent project that asks students to view the course material through the lens of a physical, cultural, or economic geographer (see Table 8.2).

Feeling a sense of accomplishment as her planning continues, Debbie is now ready to think about the kinds of instruction that will help her students reach the unit objectives. Debbie considers lecturing, but she doesn't believe that she can help students see the connections between the different aspects of regions by merely talking about them. She also considers a cooperative learning jigsaw (see Chapter Ten) but determines that this too will not highlight the interconnections between the physical, cultural, and economic aspects of the regions. Finally, Debbie considers the benefits of the integrative model, an instructional model that uses rich, complexly organized bodies of knowledge or, in the words of the designers of the model, "topics that combine facts, concepts, generalizations, and the relationships among them" (Eggen & Kauchak, 2012, p. 213). Debbie determines that the model examined in this chapter is a good match for her objectives because regional differences and the historic, economic, and cultural consequences of those differences constitute an example of such a complex topic.

Effective data displays help in the development of generalizations; they include facts that are not too narrow to make connections. Also, effective data displays have enough information so that students have the chance to provide explanations for the relationships that they identify. Data displays can be prepared prior to the lesson by the teacher or filled in with the class before the integrative model begins. These displays must be accurate and highlight the information reflected in the lesson's objectives. There must be at least two comparisons and there should not be more than four or five. Make certain that there is alignment between the objectives and the data display—use the correct tool (matrix, pie chart, photograph, etc.) Try to keep the display as simple as possible. As the following description of the steps of the model illustrates, the data in Table 8.2 meet the basic requirements—opportunity for generalization and opportunity for explanation of relationships.

TABLE 8.2 U.S. Geographic Regions

Four Geographic Regions	Physical Characteristics	Cultural Characteristics	Economic Characteristics
Northeast States included: Connecticut, New Jersey, Maine, Massachusetts, New Hampshire, New York, Pennsylvania, Rhode Island, and Vermont	• Bordered by Canada, Midwest, South, and the Atlantic Ocean • Rocky coast to fertile farmland • Four major rivers: Delaware, Hudson, Connecticut, Kennebec • Berkshires, Adirondack, Green, White Mountains • Lake Champlain, Great Lakes of Ontario and Erie, Niagara Falls	• Education legacy (top-rated colleges) • Dominant in American history • Religiously diverse—Protestant beginnings, Catholics and Jews • Ethnic diversity of African American, Hispanic, Asian American, Italian, Irish, German, and Franco American	• Wealthiest part of the United States • Urban—medium to large manufacturing cities; now looking for new economic base • Wide disparities between rich and poor in cities • Major cities—New York, Boston, and others offer financial and governmental services that are not reliant on unskilled labor • Mass transit within and between cities
Midwest States included: Ohio, Indiana, Michigan, Illinois, Wisconsin, Iowa, Kansas, Minnesota, Missouri, Nebraska, North Dakota, and South Dakota	• U.S. Census Bureau regions: East North Central States and West North Central States • Great Lakes and Ohio and Mississippi Rivers • Foothills of the Appalachians and Porcupine Mountains	• Cultural crossroads • European immigrants • German Catholics/ Calvinist/Protestantism— "Bible Belt" • Slavery was not allowed in this area • Land-grant colleges • Rural heritage-pioneer • Strong support for Democratic party	• Chicago largest city • Other cities: Cleveland, Columbus, Indianapolis, Detroit, St. Louis, Kansas City, Minneapolis • Fertile soil—nation's breadbasket—corn, oats, and wheat • Abandonment by many industries of Midwest— "Rust Belt"
South States included: Delaware, Florida, Georgia, Maryland, North Carolina, South Carolina, Virginia, West Virginia, District of Columbia, Alabama, Kentucky, Mississippi, Tennessee, Arkansas, Louisiana, Oklahoma, and Texas	• U.S. Census Bureau Regions: East South Central, South Atlantic, and West South Central • Mississippi River, Chesapeake Bay, Florida Everglades, southern Appalachian Mountains (Blue Ridge and Great Smoky Mountains), and South Carolina's Sea Islands	• European Celtic immigrants • Slavery was allowed • Switch from solidly Democrat to now more Republican • More conservative than the North • "Bible Belt"— Protestantism predominates • Also Jews, Muslims, and Catholics • Southern cuisine, music, and sports	• Houston largest city • Other cities: Dallas/ Fort Worth, Miami, Atlanta, Baltimore, and Tampa • Rural areas • Crops/trees easily grown—oaks, magnolias, dogwoods

(continued)

TABLE 8.2   U.S. Geographic Regions (*continued*)

Four Geographic Regions	Physical Characteristics	Cultural Characteristics	Economic Characteristics
West States included: Alaska, Arizona, California, Colorado, Hawaii, Idaho, Montana, New Mexico, Nevada, Oregon, Utah, Washington, and Wyoming	• U.S. Census Bureau Regions: Mountain and Pacific • Most geographically diverse: Pacific Coast, temperate rainforests of Northwest, Rocky Mountains, Great Plains, and deserts • Missouri, Colorado, Columbia, and Snake Rivers	• Wyoming least-populated state while California is the most-populated • Sparsely settled • Asian, Mexican, and Native American populations • Mormons • Cowboy image and westward expansion • West not unified politically; urban and Pacific coast Democratic, interior states more Republican	• Los Angeles largest city • Other cities: San Diego, San Jose, San Francisco, Seattle, Portland, Denver, Phoenix, Las Vegas, and Salt Lake City • Beef cattle industry • Apples in Washington and potatoes in Idaho • Los Angeles—aerospace industry since World War II

STEP 2: DESCRIBE, COMPARE, AND SEARCH FOR PATTERNS IN A DATA SET

The integrative model allows teachers to level the classroom playing field. All students have the opportunity to engage in the discussion because the data are organized and available to students as the conversation occurs. The teacher begins the lesson by providing background information on the data set and focuses the students' attention by asking them to describe what they notice. Debbie begins using Table 8.2 by asking her students to look at the rows and columns carefully. She calls on students by name to describe how many columns and rows there are and what the columns and rows present. She then asks students to consider the following questions:

- What are the physical characteristics of the West region? How do these characteristics differ from the South or Northeast regions?
- Which region has the greatest physical diversity?
- Which region has the least-populated state and which has the most-populated state? What determines the population of a state?
- What types of businesses support the economies of these four regions? How are these businesses similar to one another? Different? Why do these regions have different economic characteristics?
- What similarities and differences do you notice on this matrix?

Other questions can be generated. Many other similarities and differences could be noticed by either the teacher or the students. Instructional options include directing attention to a particular attribute of the data display, directing students to look for and describe specific similarities and differences, and asking students to identify the comparisons they notice. During this phase of the model, teachers and students control the pace of the discussion, and clear and simple questions are used to facilitate the construction of basic information about the topic.

STEP 3: EXPLAIN THE IDENTIFIED SIMILARITIES AND DIFFERENCES

Once students have identified the rich similarities and differences displayed in the matrix, they should be asked to explain the identified comparisons. Explaining the reasons for similarities and differences engages students in deep analysis of the data set. For example, Debbie might follow up on some of the identified comparisons with the following questions:

- How can you explain the differences in economic characteristics between the Northeast and West?
- Why might you expect to see some similarities between major cities of all four regions of the United States?
- What political similarities and differences did you notice among the regions? Do any of these differences have something to do with immigration patterns to the region?
- What might account for differences in population across regions?

Although some relationships cannot be explained, there will be many relationships in the data set that invite explanation. Because explanation is a higher level of reasoning than description, providing this opportunity helps to increase the complexity of the schemata that students develop about the topic. Explanations tie bits of information together, weaving a variety of threads into developing schemata that will become more intricate as the lesson progresses and more explanations are shared, much as a handwoven rug becomes more colorful and detailed as workers weave in individual threads. The role of the teacher in this phase of the model is to look at the list of identified comparisons and ask for elucidation, making certain that students document their explanations with information from the data source.

STEP 4: HYPOTHESIZE WHAT WOULD HAPPEN UNDER DIFFERENT CONDITIONS

During this stage of the model, students are asked to hypothesize an outcome if conditions change, allowing an opportunity to apply recently acquired knowledge and link it to prior knowledge and skills. Students should be asked to explain their hypotheses and conclusions. Marzano (2001) discusses the use of organized bodies of knowledge, or systems of knowledge, as a method for practicing hypothesis testing and increasing student understanding. Debbie might ask students to imagine what would have happened if the United States had not developed the atom bomb to drop on Hiroshima and Nagasaki, which forced Japan to surrender, or to think about what would happen if there were a major revitalization of "Rust Belt" cities of the Midwest.

Designing experiences that provide students with guidance in testing hypotheses is inherent to the integrative model. In addition, teachers can provide templates for explanations, provide sentence stems to help students articulate their reasoning, develop rubrics that identify and describe the quality of explanations, and set up numerous opportunities for students to share their explanations.

STEP 5: MAKE BROAD GENERALIZATIONS ABOUT THE TOPIC AND THE DISCUSSION

In this phase of the model, students summarize and synthesize the discussion and make broad generalizations about the topic under study. Summarization and synthesis allow students to process new information. Asking students to summarize

STRATEGY ALERT   Summarizing

Teaching summarization skills gives students agency to process and remember new information. Summarization will be a benefit in all of the instructional models in this text, but it is particularly appropriate for the integrative model because of the amount of academic content in play. Students can summarize in any medium, either individually or in groups. Students can learn to follow a series of steps to form a summary: (1) Delete the material that is not important and does not contribute to understanding, (2) remove redundancies, (3) substitute category names for lists of things, (4) identify or supply a topic sentence. Teachers can help students practice summarization through a series of specific questions, through the use of graphic organizers (e.g., Venn diagrams, cause and effect, chronological series), or by using metaphors and analogies. Different kinds of questions are appropriate for different kinds of texts, which indicates that teachers must take the time to discuss the kinds of information found in a text with students. Content area teachers should point out common text structures and graphic representations in their discipline. Other strategies can also be used in the quest for accurate and powerful summarizations, such as memory models and graphic organizers.

frequently helps move new information into long-term memory. Summarization is a benefit in all of the instructional models in this text, but it is particularly appropriate for the integrative model because of the amount of academic content in play. Students can summarize in any medium (written, oral, visual), either individually or in groups. The primary-recency effect (students remember best what they first heard in a lesson and remember second best the last thing they experienced in a lesson) plays a role in this phase (Wormeli, 2004). Teachers can use the integrative model to develop a questioning plan that builds on this effect. In step 5, it is important that students share their synthesis of the lesson—the broad generalizations that help to describe the complexity of the topic.

Generalizing is a sophisticated skill enhanced when good summaries of a discussion are provided. Once they have captured the robust information that was shared, students can synthesize that information and create broad statements to represent the deep understandings that they have developed. Debbie might ask students to summarize the conversations that occurred in class. She might also ask students to make broad statements about some of the relationships discovered between the physical, cultural, and economic characteristics of the regions under study.

SUMMARY OF STEPS IN THE INTEGRATIVE MODEL

Table 8.3 shows examples of literature texts objected to in many communities. The steps of the integrative model are summarized for a lesson based on this table, with examples of specific questions a teacher might ask in each of the steps.

1. *Planning for the integrative model.* Identify the topic. Target generalizations. Prepare a data display such as the matrix on objections to books.

2. *Describe, compare, and search for patterns in a data set.*
   - Describe: What do you notice about the types of objections that were made about *The Catcher in the Rye?*
   - Describe: What types of concerns are expressed in these objections?
   - Compare: How would you characterize the objections to *Huckleberry Finn?* To *1984?*

TABLE 8.3   Objections to Books Commonly Used in School

Title	Objections
The Adventures of Huckleberry Finn	Characterization and language offensive to African Americans; use of word "orgy"; taking name of Lord in vain; promotes discrimination
The Catcher in the Rye	Not proper for teenagers; dirty words; negative impact; too sophisticated; lack of plot; profuse vulgarity; sacrilegious, pornographic; objectionable references to homosexuality; not a positive example for youth; no redeeming social value; hero has loose morals and lack of direction
Deliverance	Unacceptable language; sexual references; sex scenes; antireligious matters; promotes homosexuality
The Good Earth	Content includes sex lives of old men with concubines and prostitutes; killing of children
The Grapes of Wrath	Immoral; obscene; objectionable political ideas; sexual activity; antichurch; depressing story; bad language; demeaning to Southerners
I Know Why the Caged Bird Sings	Sections not suitable for young people; pornographic; demeaning to African Americans; too realistic
The Learning Tree	Adult language; sexually explicit; too mature for teenagers; Christ portrayed as white man who loves only white people; teaches secular humanism
1984	Immoral; depressing; obscene; study of communism; communism portrayed in positive light; disliked treatment of marriage and family; drug-oriented; sordid
To Kill a Mockingbird	Immoral; obscene; indecent; vulgar; includes reference to rapes; racist themes; not suitable for adolescents
The Scarlet Letter	Degrades Christian ministry; vulgarity; immorality; adultery; too frank

Source: Information from Burress, L. (1989). *Battle of the books: Literacy censorship in the public schools, 1950–1985.* Metuchen, NJ: Scarecrow Press.

- Compare: What are the similarities between the objections to *The Grapes of Wrath* and *1984?*
- Search for patterns: What differences do you notice between the objections to *The Scarlet Letter* and the other books?

3. *Explain the identified similarities and differences.*

- What information is provided on this chart to help explain why these books were the most objected to at the end of the 20th century?
- Can you explain why the attempts of groups to have these books taken out of public schools have been successful in some situations and unsuccessful in others?
- What types of books might not receive any objections by parents, teachers, school boards, or community members?

4. *Hypothesize what would happen under different conditions.*

- Suppose a school curriculum included Homer's *The Odyssey*. Do you think any objections would be made regarding this book? Support your answer from the matrix.

- What would you do if a parent came to your class asking that you not teach a particular book to your class? What would you say?

- You are assigned to teach one of these books. Would you make any special preparations?

5. *Make broad generalizations about the topic and the discussion.* Think about the target generalizations you want students to reach about this topic, such as the following:

- Many community members object to sexual references in adolescent novels.

- Community members do not believe children in school should be exposed to adult themes.

- Teachers need to be sensitive to these beliefs and should be prepared for objections.

In this video, a ninth grade classroom is studying the relationship between geography and the economy across regions of the United States. Which parts of the lesson follow the steps of the integrative model presented in this chapter? How did you make this determination? Are students meeting the goals of the integrative model? What else did you notice about this lesson?

The preceding list of steps describes the process of using the integrative model, but there are many nuanced student and teacher behaviors that are embedded in the steps. The integrative model has a high cognitive demand on teachers (who must identify or construct a data set that represents a rich organized body of knowledge) and on the students (who must try to make sense of this display). By examining the potential behaviors of teachers and students working within the integrative framework, you can consider what is needed to master the instructional moves of the model and include the model in your professional toolbox. Table 8.4 will help you consider what student behaviors are needed for successful understanding of the process of looking for relationships in a data set, providing you with a roadmap for molding your teaching behaviors to students.

Evaluating Learning in the Integrative Model

Like most of the models presented in this text, each step of the integrative model can serve as an assessment—process as well as content can be evaluated in this way. After some experience with the integrative approach, an assessment could provide students with a similar data set such as a matrix, map, picture, or other visual organizer. The students would then be asked to follow each or some of the steps of the model: (1) identifying similarities and differences, (2) explaining the reasons for these similarities and differences, (3) hypothesizing as to different outcomes if the data set changes, and (4) making generalizations about the relationships represented in the data set. Evaluation criteria may include the number and quality of the comparison identifications and the logic, knowledge, and quality of explanations. For example, the family picture lesson described earlier in this chapter may have been part of an immigration unit. The integrative process may have been the basis for the quiz in Figure 8.2.

More traditional assessments can also be used with the integrative model. The rich data sets that are the foundation of the model (see Table 8.2) are a source for selected response items. When developing multiple-choice questions, matching items, and essay questions from data sets remember to use best practice guidelines. Multiple-choice questions should be clear, have only one correct or best answer, have similar option lengths, and so forth. A number of assessment texts and websites discuss writing test items (Stiggins, 2008).

TABLE 8.4   Potential Teacher and Student Behaviors in the Integrative Model

Step	Teacher	Student
1. Plan.	• Decides on target generalizations aligned with curriculum • Finds or develops a data set (matrix, photograph, map, etc.) that provides an opportunity to support generalizations • Provides a data set that provides an opportunity to explain relationships • Makes certain that data set is accessible to students	
2. Describe, compare, and search for patterns.	• Provides background information on data set • Focuses student attention and asks students to describe an aspect of data set • Asks students to note similarities and differences within data set • Scaffolds student observations through questioning and graphic organizer • Elicits observable patterns in data set • Notes quality of student observations, descriptions, and patterns	• Constructs clarifying questions about data set • Describes attributes of the organization and content of data set • Notes similarities and differences across various points in the data set • Uses graphic organizer to organize impressions • Reflects on information presented in data set and connects new information to prior knowledge
3: Explain similarities and differences	• Asks students to explain identified similarities and differences • Questions students about cause-and-effect relationships in data set • Provides scaffolding to individual students when necessary • Monitors student reasoning	• Explains identified similarities and differences using information in data display • Searches for cause and effects in data set • Checks personal understanding of shared explanations • Evaluates personal ability to provide explanations
4. Hypothesize outcomes under different conditions.	• Provides a new situation or condition to extend data set • Asks student to hypothesize a new outcome • Provides a variety of opportunities for students to construct and share hypotheses including modeling hypothesis generation • Monitors student understanding of content and process	• Considers new situation and condition • Constructs hypotheses describing possible new outcomes • Links new information to prior knowledge • Reflects on the integrative process and new content
5. Construct. generalizations.	• Defines generalizations • Provides an example of generalization • Asks for generalizations that describe broad relationships • Scaffolds discussion by providing summary and cues to target generalizations • Monitors student reasoning and content knowledge	• Demonstrates understanding of data set and generalization construction • Summarizes and synthesizes discussion • Infers generalization of organized body of information • Supports inferences • Thinks about what was learned in the lesson and what challenges were encountered

FIGURE 8.2   Sample Integrative Assessment for Immigration Unit

> **Immigration Unit**
>
> **Quiz 1**
>
> Directions: On your desk are two pictures, one of the family that we discussed in class and one of a family of recent legal immigrants. Answer the following questions on a separate sheet of paper.
>
> **1.** What do you notice in the new picture? List four things that you see.
> **2.** How do the two pictures compare? List two similarities and two differences.
> **3.** Why do you think the pictures are different? Give two reasons.
> **4.** Think about the family in the second picture moving into your neighborhood. What might happen? Why do you think that would happen?
> **5.** Some of our neighbors don't want legal immigrants coming into our city. What would need to happen to change that attitude?

Meeting Individual Needs with the Integrative Model

The key to an aligned integrative lesson is the data set. Whatever is used to help students learn the target content and thinking skills must be appropriate to the interests, readiness levels, and learning approaches of students. Data sets can come from textbooks, trade books, newspapers, Internet sources, reference books, or from the teacher's or students' thinking. They can be a collection of real-life objects, a piece of art, a map, a table of relevant information, a photograph, or any other item or collection that shows a relationship in information. Thus, data sets can be manipulated to meet the needs of students by varying the type of media for levels of complexity and abstraction and by highlighting specific bits of information to play to student interests.

Teachers can prepare the data set specifically for the objectives of the lesson and the specific students in the class, or adaptations can be made from published materials. Students can be part of developing the data set in small or large groups by putting together matrices or graphs of information that will be explored with the integrative process. The integrative model is useful for the whole class, flexible small groups, and individuals at interest centers—another way to meet specific student needs. The cubing strategy, discussed in the Strategy Alert, can add energy and excitement to a task and engage a wide variety of students.

STRATEGY ALERT   Cubing

As students complete the integrative process by making generalizations, cubing can help to complete and extend the discussion. Cubes have six sides with a different task on each side. Tasks are designed for specific groups of students and can vary on a number of attributes. Students roll the cube to find a task. Tasks can vary on the level of cognitive complexity, student interests, or specific remediation needs. Different groups can have different cubes. Cubes to extend thinking on a specific topic may use the following prompts:

- Describe it: Include all aspects of the topic.
- Compare it: Find similarities and differences.
- Associate it: Tell how it fits with other things we have studied.
- Apply it: Tell how it is used.
- Analyze it: Tell how you can break it into smaller parts.
- Argue it: Argue for or against a position related to the topic.

Questions are also a powerful differentiation tool and become even more powerful with the integrative model. Building on what is known about classrooms and students, questions can be personalized. Although the model has a suggested order of questions, the teacher can make connections for specific students by providing more, or less, background information. For example, in Debbie's geography class, she could highlight the travels of individual students or students' background knowledge or interests. She may provide cues to finding patterns for students having less experience with the model or use other visual clues on the data set to help some students distinguish patterns.

Benefits of the Integrative Model

All of the instructional models in this text help to develop students' critical thinking skills. The integrative model, however, also helps students navigate through organized bodies of information—webs of information that have rich and varied connections about which students must make sense. The integrative model is efficient and congruent with the way we learn. Because a great deal of curriculum content is detailed and layered, having a method by which students can access this information is important. The integrative model also allows students to make connections between what they know and what is being presented by helping them to build personal schemata. These personal schemata also become increasingly intricate because of the steps of the model itself. By participating in the model, students develop generalizations that explore relationships within a specific organized body of knowledge. The questioning helps students move from conclusions to inferences—and beyond the presented information.

In addition, the integrative model extends the power of textbooks and curriculum materials. Many textbooks are not friendly to the needs of students. They are written in unfamiliar language, the organization can be confusing, and the amount of information is astounding. The integrative model provides a structure for making sense of the contents of textbooks. Teachers can use visual materials from texts and provide scaffolding for divergent and higher-level thinking. The integrative model is also congruent with new classroom technologies. Data sets can be projected from computers, brought up on a SmartBoard, or found on a laptop. Most important, the integrative model permits the teacher to control the amount of information presented to students because data sets can be borrowed, constructed by teachers, or developed by students. The complexity of the information and the sophistication of the questions can flex readily to the teacher's instructional decisions.

ELEMENTARY GRADES LESSON

INTEGRATIVE MODEL: Fractions

OBJECTIVES

Common Core State Standards—Mathematics 4NF.A.1

Extend understanding of fraction equivalence and ordering. Explain why a fraction a/b is equivalent to a fraction $(n \times a)/(n \times b)$ by using visual fraction models, with attention to how the number and size of the parts differ even though the two fractions themselves are the same size. Use this principle to recognize and generate equivalent fractions.

Common Core State Standards—Mathematics 4NF.A.2

Compare two fractions with different numerators and different denominators. Recognize that comparisons are valid only when the two fractions refer to the same whole. Record the results of the comparisons with symbols and justify the conclusions.

continued

Students Will Know

- The meaning of numerator and denominator
- How to compare the size of fractions
- Similarities and differences in a set of fractions

Students Will Understand That

- All parts of a set must be equal to one another and total the whole

Students Will Be Able To

- Compare fractions
- Explain the relationships between fractions
- Hypothesize new relationships between fractions
- Summarize the information in the lesson and form a generalization to describe the patterns that were noticed in the class

ASSESSMENT

Students will design a worksheet (with answers) that helps students practice comparing fractions.

PROCEDURES

1. *Describe, compare, and search for patterns.* Ask the following questions:
   - What do you notice?
   - What is this table about?
   - What do the symbols mean?
   - Can you read each box in the matrix?
   - Do you notice any patterns in the boxes?
2. *Explain similarities and differences.* Project the following table.

1/2 > 1/5	1/4 > 1/6	1/8 > 1/10
1/5 < 1/3	1/10 < 1/5	1/10 < 1/3
1/5 > 1/8	1/6 > 1/10	1/5 = 1/5

   Ask questions like the following:
   - "Let's look at the first pair in the top row. It says that 1/2 is larger than 1/5. Explain to me why this is true."
   - "Move down the first column to the next pair. Which is the larger number? How do you know?"
   - (Ask an individual student) "Pick one of the pairs and tell me which is the smaller number and how you know that it is smaller."
   - (Ask an individual student) "Pick one of the pairs and tell me which is the larger number and how you know that it is larger."
3. *Hypothesize outcomes for different conditions.* Ask questions about the table:
   - "What would happen to the first pair if 1/2 were changed to 1/3?"
   - "Is 1/3 larger than 1/5?"
   - "What would happen to the first pair if 1/8 were substituted for 1/2? Would we need to change the symbol?"
4. *Generalize to form broad relationships.*
   - Ask students to summarize the information in the lesson by providing a statement that captures the discussion.
   - Ask students to discuss the patterns that they noticed in the lesson.

It might prove interesting to call attention to the fact that the first syllable of the word *fraction* is a base part with the meaning "break." Students can probably see this base in a word like *fracture* (a break), and you can point out that with a slight change of spelling, words like *fragile* (easy to break) and *fragment* (part broken off) are in the same family as the key word *fraction*. Ask the students to be on the lookout for other words—like one they may have heard or read in the news, *fracking*—that are related to this one.

MIDDLE/SECONDARY GRADES LESSON

INTEGRATIVE MODEL: Societal Changes Affecting Families

OBJECTIVES	**Common Core State Standards—English/Language Arts RH9-10.1** Cite specific textual evidence to support analysis of primary and secondary sources, attending to such feature as the date and origin of the information. **Common Core State Standards—English/Language Arts CCRA.R.7** Integrate and evaluate content presented in diverse formats and media, including visually and quantitatively as well as in words. **Students Will Know** • Generalizations about the changes in clothing, photography, homes, technology, educational opportunities, and attitudes toward women from 1950 to the present **Students Will Understand That** • American society has changed in many ways during the last 70 years and that these changes have had a major impact on American families **Students Will Be Able To** • Make generalizations from an old photograph • Hypothesize changes to family life in the next 70 years
ASSESSMENT	Have students prepare 10 interview questions for someone the same age as one of the people in a 1950s picture; these questions should provide information about the important trends of the last 70 years.
PROCEDURES	1. *Describe, compare, and search for patterns.* Review with students the broad changes in our society over the last 70 years and how these changes might affect families. List these societal changes on the board. Next, share an old family photograph with students and ask the following questions. As the students discuss their thoughts, add any additional information to the board. • "What do you notice about the photograph? Describe what you see." • "How would you compare this photograph to what you would expect a contemporary photograph of [five cousins, a family reunion, etc.] to look like?" • "What societal changes might have affected these people during the last 70 years?" 2. *Explain similarities and differences.* • Explain the similarities and differences noted between this photograph and one taken today. • Explain the similarities and differences between the social issues affecting men and women in the photograph during the last 70 years. 3. *Hypothesize outcomes for different conditions.* • Reflect on the changes of the last 70 years and invent a likely scenario for someone in the picture. • Reflect on the changes in the next 70 years and invent a likely scenario for people in your family. 4. *Generalize to form a broad relationship.* Make statements about the changes in the United States over the last 70 years that might have had an effect on the children in the picture and on their families.

SUMMARY

The purpose of the integrative model is to help students make sense of complex and rich relationships found in most disciplinary knowledge. The integrative model supports critical thinking strategies while helping students learn specific content concepts, facts, and generalizations. Students do not always have the opportunity to examine relationships between the components of disciplinary knowledge. The model allows examination of these relationships by providing guidelines for the types of questions teachers ask, the social structure of the classroom, and the data source of the discussion.

The model begins with careful planning by the teacher to choose a topic and select the essential understandings to be attained by students during the lesson. It is important that these understandings guide both the questioning and construction of the data set. Once the planning is completed, students will describe, compare, and search for patterns in the provided information. They will then explain identified similarities and differences and hypothesize as to what would happen under different conditions. The lesson ends with students making broad generalizations about the topic.

EXTENSIONS

ACTIVITIES

1. Find an organized body of knowledge or a rich set of interrelated concepts, facts, and generalizations in the state standards with which you currently work or will be working. Design a concept map to show the relationships in the information that you will be teaching.

2. Revisit the scenarios at the beginning of the chapter. Do you think the objectives of these lessons were met? What evidence do you have to support your conclusion? List what you see as the best features of the lessons and the features that you think might be changed if you were to try to replicate the lesson.

3. Design or find a data display that could be used in an integrative lesson in your content area or at your grade level. Develop questions related to the data display for each of the steps of the integrative model.

4. Make a two-page handout explaining the integrative model that could be used with in-service teachers in the area you would like to teach. Try to anticipate the questions that teachers would have about the model, and include at least one graphic.

REFLECTIVE QUESTIONS

1. What do you think about textbooks in your field? Will you be relying on textbooks? Why? Why not? With what caveats?

2. What are the most important generalizations in the discipline that you will be teaching? How do you know that these are the important generalizations?

3. What problems do you anticipate as you attempt to implement the integrative model? What aspects of the model will you find beneficial?

9 The Socratic Seminar Model

 Chapter Objectives

You Will Know

- The basis for the Socratic seminar model
- The steps in the Socratic seminar model
- How to evaluate learning in the Socratic seminar model
- How to meet individual needs with the Socratic seminar model
- Benefits of the Socratic seminar model
- What the Socratic seminar model looks like in both elementary and secondary classrooms

You Will Understand That

- Careful analysis of text can increase academic knowledge, cooperative skills, and the ability to think critically
- Discussions of open-ended problems can greatly enhance students' thinking

You Will Be Able To

- Plan lessons that center on multiple reactions to the same text by different readers

In the Elementary Classroom

The second graders in Alyssa Raskind's class are having trouble distinguishing between rights and responsibilities. Her students also need practice in identifying problems and problem solutions in texts. She decides that a seminar on the book *Old Henry*, by Joan Blos, might help her students figure out the differences. The book is about a man who moves into an old, vacant, run-down house and settles in without making the repairs that his neighbors feel should be accomplished. He prefers to read his books, paint his pictures, care for his birds, and live his more leisurely life. Eventually the conflict with his neighbors drives Henry away. But then the neighbors begin to miss Old Henry and his parrot, and, in his new place, Henry begins to miss his old neighbors.

Ms. Raskind spends some time thinking about the questions that will be used in the seminar and how she should remind the students of seminar rules and procedures. She determines that the seminar will have an entry ticket. Students will be asked to complete the following sentence: "A good neighbor is _____." Each student will need the completed sentence to participate in the seminar.

The seminar begins once everyone is seated and has handed in their tickets.

Ms. Raskind: What are the responsibilities that neighbors have to each other?
Alex: They have to be nice to each other.
James: They have to help when your grandma is sick.
Annika: They bring you food when you are hungry.
Ms. Raskind: Neighbors can help you out and that is a nice thing to do, but is it a responsibility of being a neighbor to help out? Can you be a good neighbor

without helping out? Think about what it means to have a responsibility. What kind of responsibilities do people who live in the same neighborhood have?

After some discussion, the class determines that neighbors have a responsibility to make certain that when neighbors have needs, they try to help them and that they have a responsibility to take care of the neighborhood. They also have a responsibility to not bother each other.

Ms. Raskind: Was Henry a good neighbor? Did he have the right to ignore the concerns of his neighbors?

Chloe: He was a good neighbor because he didn't bother anyone.

Sophia: But he wasn't a good neighbor because he didn't keep the neighborhood nice.

Chloe: He doesn't have to do everything his neighbors want him to do.

Ms. Raskind: Were Henry's neighbors good neighbors? Give me some examples of good neighbor behavior that you saw in the book.

The class determines that Henry and his neighbors were not perfect and that each learned something about being a good neighbor during the story.

Ms. Raskind: What is the problem in Henry's old neighborhood? How would you solve the problem?

Travis: Henry and his neighbors wanted different things.

Annika: Henry wanted to be left alone. The other people wanted a pretty neighborhood.

The conversation continues with a discussion of the rights and responsibilities of neighbors. Ms. Raskind reviews the discussion by helping her students summarize the big ideas that they covered.

Ms. Raskind: What did we decide a good neighbor's rights and responsibilities are?

The students reiterate their criteria for being a good neighbor in terms of rights and responsibilities and determine that Henry and his neighbors were all trying hard to be good neighbors. Ms. Raskind then asks the students whether they had been good seminar participants. She calls on Travis and asks him to tell her why he thought he had been a good participant.

Travis: I listened to everybody without interrupting. I asked Chloe a question. And I did not get mad when James kept talking.

Several other students shared their evaluations. ■

In the Middle/Secondary Classroom

The students in the U.S. history class have participated in Socratic seminars before, and they are looking forward to today's lesson because it is a break from trying to memorize information about numerous Civil War battles. Last night, Mr. Gupta asked them to read Mark Twain's *The War Prayer* and "Sullivan Ballou's Letter to His Wife." He also asked them to find three similarities between the texts. This assignment will be used as an entrance ticket. Each student hands in the ticket in order to participate in the seminar.

WEB RESOURCE

The War Prayer and Sullivan Ballou's Letter

The War Prayer is available from several links, including warprayer.org. The Civil War home page contains many artifacts of the conflict, including Sullivan Ballou's letter at civil-war.net.

Mr. Gupta: Thank you for coming to class prepared. We have some difficult topics to discuss today as we continue our study of the Civil War. War has a profound impact on both the winners and the defeated. Today's seminar question examines the losers—What happens to the vanquished? We will begin by pointing out how Mark Twain and Sullivan Ballou describe the victors and the vanquished. Who would like to begin?

Ivy: Well, Twain seems to be really against war and makes a big deal out of the losers suffering. But isn't that what happens and doesn't that make countries work harder at trying to win?

Daniel: Where do you get the idea that Twain is against war?

Ivy: Twain wrote "If you pray for the blessing of rain upon your crop which needs it, by that act you are possibly praying for a curse upon some neighbor's crop which may not need rain and can be injured by it." I think that means that we shouldn't pray to win.

Daniel: So how does that show that Twain is against war?

Several other students join into the discussion and use the text to make the case that Twain was against war in general. Olivia, on the other hand, feels that the stranger wants everyone to know that war can be very bad, but doesn't say that all wars are bad.

Mr. Gupta: How do the concerns of Sullivan Ballou and the stranger in the church compare? Would Sullivan Ballou have wanted Twain's *The War Prayer* to be published? How do you know?

Julio and Nolan jump right into the conversation and Marisa follows. Here is a small part of what they said:

Julio: I don't think that Sullivan would have published *The War Prayer*, because he believed that there were some ideals that were important enough to die for in war.

Nolan: I agree. He says, "And I am willing—perfectly willing—to lay down all my joys in this life, to help maintain this Government." He may have been afraid that if something like *The War Prayer* had been published, some people would not have supported the Union war effort.

Marisa: But haven't there always been people against all wars?

The discussion continues for a number of minutes when Mr. Gupta begins to question students about the Battle of Bull Run, in which Sullivan Ballou was mortally injured.

Mr. Gupta: Do you think it is possible for the perceptions of a warrior to change in the course of battle?

Again, his students are eager to share. They show some consternation when Mr. Gupta interrupts and repeats the seminar question—What is the other side of victory? What happens to the vanquished?

Fatma: I don't know, but I wonder what Sullivan Ballou's family would have thought if their side had lost the war. They wouldn't have had a husband and father, and their side still would have lost the war!

Julio: Yes, but they did win, and they still didn't have a husband and father.

Several students then comment on what the war brought both the Union and the Confederacy. Ten minutes before the end of class, Mr. Gupta asks the students to review the discussion and share some statements about what they had heard during the seminar.

Ivy: War is bad for everyone.

Nolan: There are some things that you have to fight for even if you know that people will suffer.

Annika: Not everyone agrees with that. Some people feel all wars are bad.

Most of the students share a statement or two to summarize the discussion, and the seminar ends with students evaluating their own performance and the quality of the seminar question. ■

The Basis for the Socratic Seminar Model

The idea of a Socratic seminar stems from one of the dialogues of Plato entitled *Meno*. (See socraticmethod.net for a thorough explication of this time-honored instructional technique.)

In this most famous Socratic dialogue, the character Meno asks whether virtue can be taught, and that leads Socrates to suggest that no idea can be taught directly. On the contrary, he suggests, all that we know must be extracted from us through a series of questions and a process of inquiry. This is the foundation of the Socratic seminar. The job of the teacher, according to Socrates, is to help the learner collect his or her thoughts from which to build new understandings from prior knowledge. This may well be the source of the etymology of the verb *educate*, meaning "to lead out." As it has evolved to the present time, the Socratic seminar tends to focus on open-ended or controversial questions (for example, was U.S. isolationism justified in the 1930s?) that have no unequivocal resolution. That is not to say the topic of a seminar could never be a math problem, but, if it were, the problem would have multiple solutions.

The differences between discussion and dialogue are important. Dialogue requires different communication skills from students than does engaging in give-and-take discussion. In this video, you can learn a bit about these differences. wwww.youtube.com/watch?v=e9a6-MZc_ok

The purpose of this chapter is to expound on the instructional value of dialogue and inquiry in classrooms, focusing particularly on Socratic seminars. Discussions play an important role in student learning because students are able to converse with knowledgeable peers and adults. Discussion allows for the acquisition and construction of information, along with the linking of new information to personal prior experiences. Not all classroom talk is discussion oriented, however. There is a great deal of talk in the classroom that is not discussion. For instance, there are fast-paced teacher-to-student recitations that have a teacher question–student response–teacher feedback pattern. Discussions, on the other hand, provide the opportunity for sustained critical inquiry and student-to-student conversation and are an alternative to recitation-style teaching. In the case of the Socratic seminar, the conversation is a specialized discussion—a dialogue. There are several differences between a general discussion and a dialogue. During a discussion, points are argued and rebutted, and there is generally an attempt to make strong arguments for a single position. In a dialogue, participants move beyond a single point and search for larger connections between ideas. Participants use listening skills to gain perspectives and empathy for different ideas.

Planned dialogues support student growth toward sophisticated cognitive, social, and emotional objectives. Socratic seminars boost students' content learning, develop students' cooperative social skills, and help students discover their competence as members of a productive learning community. In addition, the Socratic seminar provides a safe place for the discussion of values associated with the problems under deliberation.

The Socratic seminar model is designed to use the Socratic dialectic—the examination of ideas through a logical progression of questioning to help students reach a deep understanding of a controversial topic after considering a number of perspectives (Fischer, 2008). Socratic seminars are applicable in all content areas and at all grade levels. Every discipline has conflicting viewpoints that can be examined by identifying assumptions and various interpretations and by studying the construction of conclusions. Because Socratic seminars allow students to construct new knowledge by interacting with the ideas and understandings of others, they are congruent with what we know about how students learn and how they "own" and construct their understandings. Students are active learners during a Socratic seminar; they are not simply provided information by either the teacher or the text as in didactic instruction. Dialogical instruction requires that students consider a variety of perspectives. In a Socratic seminar, students are involved in discussions in which contradictory ideas are weighed logically, with a view to the resolution of the inherent contradictions by finding the connections between the ideas. The seminar is student centered rather than teacher centered, with the teacher playing the role of "guide on the side" instead of "sage on the stage." In fact, a visitor to a class where a Socratic seminar was in progress might need to look twice to find the teacher.

VERSIONS OF THE SOCRATIC SEMINAR

There are several current iterations of seminars structured around Socratic questioning. Each relies on a dialogue among students centered on a specific text (written, visual, or auditory) or question. The Socratic seminar model is one that has evolved over time and has been implemented in several ways. Socratic questioning within a conversation that examines complex, rich questions stimulates student thinking. The premise of the Socratic seminar model is that student awareness of important questions plays a large role in intellectual development and that the exploration of a text allows for disciplined conversation—a way to examine ideas logically. The Socratic seminar model asks students to think critically about a text through a cooperative and respectful conversation based on personal reactions to the material. These personal responses reflect prior knowledge and experience. The model does not rely on memorizing discrete pieces of information, and it does not tolerate superficial coverage.

The discussion that constitutes a Socratic seminar should be conducted in a circle instead of rows of desks. Students should be able to look at the speaker to encourage listening. Seminars might be held with the whole class participating in the dialogues or in an inner or outer circle. The size of the class may affect your decision as to whether to use two circles or one. The two-circle approach (inner/outer) can be implemented by having the occupants of the circles change places after a brief time. The main discussion is held by the inner circle; members of the outer circle do not contribute to the dialogue, but they take notes and form questions that they can pose when their turn comes. Another option is to have each student in the inner circle partner with a student in the outer circle. The outer circle partner acts as the inner circle coach—listening carefully to the dialogue and responses, if there are any, and sending notes to the inner circle participant with suggestions for questions and/or comments.

Seminars are congruent with what we know about how people learn and how classroom and school environments can be organized to promote learning. The Socratic seminar model allows for the development of a learner-centered, knowledge-centered, assessment-centered, and community-centered environment. In the words of Bransford, Brown, and Cocking (2000), "If teaching is conceived as constructing a bridge between the subject matter and the student, learner-centered teachers keep a constant eye on both edges of the bridge" (p. 136). Seminars allow students to share insights and knowledge based on their own experiences and cultural lenses, enabling teachers to facilitate explanations, expose assumptions, and recognize misconceptions. In addition, there is a strong diagnostic component to Socratic seminars because thinking and learning are so transparent.

The public nature of these seminars requires a strong community focus in a knowledge-centered classroom. Students must use sophisticated academic skills as they discuss important topics—summarizing, paraphrasing, making explanations and interpretations, analyzing ideas and assumptions—all of which contribute to a milieu that promotes comfort and security in the sharing of important concepts and understandings. Students have the opportunity to become more knowledgeable in a safe environment as they make sense of these shared ideas.

In addition, the Socratic seminar model provides the chance for students to develop metacognitive skills as they receive feedback on their thoughts and the thoughts of their peers. Teachers and students are able to share their prior knowledge and experiences, cultural perspectives, and community orientations, allowing the teacher/facilitator the opportunity to make learner-centered decisions. Seminars are also aligned with what is known about good teaching because of the opportunities for self-evaluation and metacognition. As students participate in the discussion, there are norms against which they can evaluate their performance. And a good seminar develops a community of learners engaged in inquiry—perhaps the most important characteristic of all learning environments.

Interestingly, Socratic seminars have been around for a lot longer than has the research on how people learn. Certainly, dialogues are a natural way of communicating and have been used along with debate since the beginnings of civilization. Unlike debates, however, dialogues are collaborative. Every participant works at making meaning from the text and finding common ground. Dialogues have the potential to change a point of view by examining assumptions, leading to an open-minded approach to problem solving. The respect inherent in a Socratic seminar helps develop an active citizenry in a democracy that is continually engaged in searching many positions for a common solution.

QUESTIONING

The caliber and success of all classroom discussions depends on the kinds of questions that are prepared by the teacher. Questions should help students learn. Good questions are educative—they provide the opportunity for deeper thought. There are several ways to distinguish between the types of questions that teachers can ask and the effect different kinds of questions can have on student learning. For the purposes of this chapter, we will be examining the questions based on Bloom's revised taxonomy and Paul's taxonomy of Socratic questions (Anderson & Krathwohl, 2001; Paul, 1993). Bloom's revised taxonomy of educational objectives is useful for evaluating all of the components of instructional alignment—objectives, instruction, and assessment. Questioning is just one aspect of instruction. By delineating the range of cognitive processes and types of knowledge used in classrooms, the taxonomy provides guidance for planning, implementing, and evaluating instruction.

The revised taxonomy has six cognitive levels at which questions can be asked. Examples of questions at each of the following levels will be provided in the next section:

1. *Remembering questions* ask students to recall information.
2. *Understanding questions* ask students to explain ideas or concepts.
3. *Applying questions* ask students to use information in another familiar situation.
4. *Analyzing questions* ask students to break information into parts in order to explore the relationships between the parts.
5. *Evaluating questions* ask students to justify a decision or a course of action.
6. *Creating questions* ask students to generate new ways of thinking about things.

Richard Paul (1993) has categorized the types of questions that a teacher/ facilitator can use in a Socratic seminar:

- Questions of clarification
- Questions of assumptions
- Questions that probe reasons and evidence
- Questions about viewpoints or perspectives
- Questions that probe implications and consequences
- Questions about the question

Examples of Paul's questions are provided in the discussion of evaluating the Socratic seminar (step 6 of the model) later in this chapter.

EXAMPLES OF QUESTION TYPES

Do you remember the story of "The Ugly Duckling" by Hans Christian Andersen? We will use this story as the text to help illustrate the different kinds of questions that can be used during a Socratic seminar. The story describes a mother duck waiting what seems like a very long time for her eggs to hatch. Finally, all but one egg hatches. While sitting on this large egg, an old duck pays a visit and tells Mother Duck to leave the egg. But Mother Duck waits until the egg hatches, and a very large and very ugly bird emerges. This duck is never accepted by the barnyard, the Queen Duck, or even his mother. After being harassed by his own siblings, the young duckling leaves home to fend for himself, determined to find his place in the world. He wanders away and meets a trio of boisterous wild ducks, an old woman and her pets—a hen and a cat—and some beautiful swans flying south for the winter. Soon after, the pond freezes over, and the duckling becomes trapped in the ice. A kind woodsman rescues him and brings him home. The duckling is teased by the woodsman's children, and he again runs away. Somehow the duckling survives the winter on his own, and in the early spring he comes upon a pond where beautiful white swans are swimming. As he comes closer, the beautiful creatures welcome and accept him. Surprised, the duckling gazes in the water and realizes that he, too, is a swan.

Remembering

Remembering questions ask students to recall, restate, or remember learned information:

- "What advice did the old duck give to Mother Duck as she waited for her large egg to hatch?"
- "Describe what happened to the duckling during the harsh winter."

Understanding

Understanding questions ask students to make sense of the information by interpreting and translating what is learned:

- "How would you explain why the large egg took so long to hatch?"
- "What happened after the duckling left the farmyard?"
- "Can you illustrate the unfair treatment of the duckling?"

Applying

Applying questions asks students to use information in a context different from the one in which it was learned:

- "Can you think of another time when someone was treated poorly because of the way he or she looked?"
- "What would you have told Mother Duck as the duckling hatched?"
- "In the story, the swans left the cold winter for warmer climates. Do you know of any others who leave the cold weather and go to a warmer environment for the winter?"

Analyzing

Analyzing questions ask students to break down the learned information into its parts:

- "Which of the adventures that the duckling had could have been left out of the story?"
- "If the duckling hadn't found the small house with the old woman, what might have happened?"
- "Can you explain what must have happened to the duckling's brothers and sisters?"
- "Can you explain why the animals in the farmyard were mean to the duckling?"
- "What would have happened if the Queen Duck had accepted the duckling?"

Evaluating

Evaluating questions ask students to make decisions based on reflection and assessment:

- "How would you have treated the duckling if you lived in the farmyard?"
- "What do you think of how Mother Duck treated the duckling?"

- "Do you think it was a good idea to let the duckling leave the farmyard?"
- "How would you feel if you were the duckling as he first saw the beautiful swans?"

Creating

Creating questions ask students to develop new ideas and information:

- "Can you figure out what might have had to happen for the duckling to live in the farmyard happily?"
- "What would have happened if there had been two swan eggs in the nest?"
- "Can you tell a story about people who are treated poorly because of the way that they look?"

Bloom's revised taxonomy of educational objectives is helpful in asking students a variety of questions with varying cognitive demands. Socratic seminars, however, also demand an analysis of a different kind of question. Seminars are fast paced and require a number of unscripted follow-up questions as the students examine an issue in conversation with one another, guided by the teacher. These follow-up questions can benefit from Paul's taxonomy of Socratic questions because the perspective provided by the taxonomy reminds teachers to prompt students to clarify, examine assumptions, probe evidence, explain perspectives, and investigate implications and consequences—all to contribute to the dialogue of the seminar (see Table 9.1 later in the chapter).

Steps in the Socratic Seminar Model

STEP 1: CHOOSE THE TEXT—WRITTEN, VISUAL, OR AUDIO

The text you choose should be related to the big ideas that are listed in your state curriculum standards and the *understand* objectives that you have designed for the unit of instruction being planned. The Socratic seminar model is appropriate for objectives that ask students to articulate ideas, use higher-level thinking, and problem solve in a community of learners. The text must be at an appropriate reading level so that students can read or examine it independently. If the text is art, music, or a video clip, age appropriateness is an important consideration. Students should feel comfortable reading and reflecting on the text and should not feel confused and frustrated when they enter the seminar.

The opening seminar question should be broad, abstract, and engaging—something that encapsulates the essence of the text, as in the following examples:

- "How has the American dream changed in the last 100 years?" *(The Great Gatsby)*
- "Is there such a thing as a good war?" (The Declaration of Independence)
- "Can important music sound bad?" (musical excerpt)
- "Does art have to be representational to be good?" (piece of modern art)

Opening questions may transcend the text; that is, the question might be larger than the issues that are obvious in the text and transferable to other works, but the discussion should help students answer the broad question and should engage them in a way that elicits a personal response.

STEP 2: PLAN AND CLUSTER SEVERAL QUESTIONS OF VARYING COGNITIVE DEMAND

Group the questions by topic. Identify basic questions and begin to cluster the questions. A basic question is an "umbrella" question—a higher-level question, fairly broad in scope, that raises an issue. Cluster questions are both lower- and higher-order questions that develop an issue. A cluster, as illustrated in Figure 9.1, consists of one broad question and six to eight focused questions. Having several different clusters affords different entrances to the issue under discussion. This allows students to move beyond initial responses to the "big" question and toward a wide spectrum of information before settling on a personal perspective.

Clustering provides flexibility to the seminar leader as the discussion unfolds. Different clusters can be tapped depending on the answers to previous questions. It must be remembered that basic cluster questions may be answered in several different ways; the strength of supporting data from the text determines the validity of individual answers. If a question points to only one answer, it is not a basic question. The essence of the Socratic seminar is that there are valid justifications for all sides of an issue. The goal of the seminar is to find the connections between all of the sides.

STEP 3: INTRODUCE THE MODEL TO THE STUDENTS

Let students know that a major purpose of the Socratic seminar is to help them learn to think for themselves as they engage in intellectual interaction with others. Seminars are designed to allow teachers and students to practice dialogue with certain characteristics:

- Openness to ideas from the text that disconfirm previously held beliefs
- Suspended judgment while dissecting the text with others

FIGURE 9.1 Sample Cluster on Genghis Khan

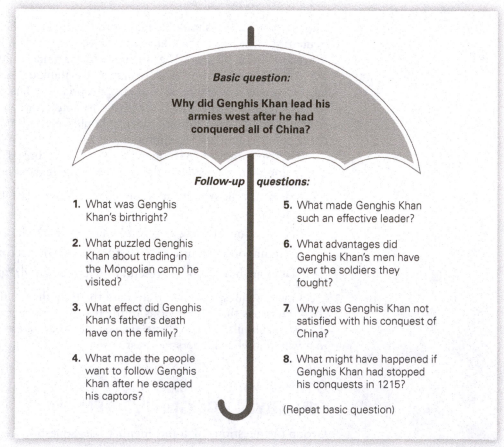

Basic question:

Why did Genghis Khan lead his armies west after he had conquered all of China?

Follow-up questions:

1. What was Genghis Khan's birthright?

2. What puzzled Genghis Khan about trading in the Mongolian camp he visited?

3. What effect did Genghis Khan's father's death have on the family?

4. What made the people want to follow Genghis Khan after he escaped his captors?

5. What made Genghis Khan such an effective leader?

6. What advantages did Genghis Khan's men have over the soldiers they fought?

7. Why was Genghis Khan not satisfied with his conquest of China?

8. What might have happened if Genghis Khan had stopped his conquests in 1215?

(Repeat basic question)

- Lack of defensiveness in communicating beliefs and reasoning with others
- Acceptance of other viewpoints as valid and as a way to discover a common ground
- Finding commonalities among viewpoints through active listening.

These behaviors are critical for citizens in our democracy—an important goal in the United States of America.

With your students, review the criteria for fruitful seminar participation. An excellent seminar member demonstrates respect for the learning of all participants by (1) showing patience with a variety of ideas and contributions, (2) asking for clarification, (3) moving the conversation forward, (4) addressing comments to all or most of the other participants, and (5) not speaking too much. The last characteristic is often the most difficult to get across to students. A number of factors can lead a single or small group of students to dominate a discussion. This is not a norm of Socratic seminars and must be addressed by the group and the group leader. Often, just reminding the offending students of the seminar's purpose is enough to remedy the situation.

Excellent seminar members also demonstrate reasoning skills by waiting to answer a question until evidence can be cited from the text and thoughts can be expressed clearly, thoughtfully, and logically. Outstanding group members make connections between several of the presented ideas and consider the viewpoints of others along with their own.

Figuring out what other people mean is an important part of getting along in the real world. This is not easy, because sometimes people do not want to say what they really mean or they have trouble expressing their thoughts and feelings precisely. People tend to think of the written word as more definitive than conversation. In conversation, body language, facial expression, and tone help communicate meaning. It is not unusual to have to think long and carefully in figuring out what a piece of writing means. Writers strive to say what they mean in clear terms, but there are always gaps between a writer's and reader's personal experiences and the meanings they give to words and phrases. Different people can read the same piece of writing and come up with different ideas about what it means. But if several readers discuss their ideas together, they will all come to a clearer understanding of the text. Socratic seminars are designed to help a community of learners make sense of a text together.

Before the discussion, the classroom should be prepared by putting desks or chairs in a circle so that everyone can see other participants. Each student should have a copy of the text with personal annotations highlighting interesting ideas or questions. Remind students of the ground rules of the seminar—the most important probably being that participants must not talk or contribute until they have been recognized.

STEP 4: CONDUCT THE DIALOGUE

Once students have participated in several Socratic seminars, you may have a student lead the conversation. If the model is new to students, it is recommended that teachers conduct the dialogue. When leading the discussion, frequently ask follow-up questions that force students to reason aloud and air their thoughts. The tone of the probing should be encouraging, as you ask students what they think and whether they can support their ideas.

After asking a question, allow sufficient wait time before eliciting an answer. Wait until many hands are up, and do not always call on the same people or on those whose hands went up first. The students will begin to understand that you prefer them to take time to consider a response. Again, ask for several students' opinions before asking another question. For each idea, ask follow-up questions about why the student thinks that and what evidence he or she can cite in the text to support the thoughts. Others' insights help students develop their own ideas. It is the richness of varying perspectives that makes the insights so penetrating.

If you feel that a student's comment is not valid, ask the student to support it from the text. If, however, the students fail to see that the inference is unsupported, you should not point it out; you should only ask further questions. Most students have very little confidence in their own abilities to solve problems or make decisions. If you step in and provide answers when they are floundering, they may learn more about the specific point you are discussing, but does that knowledge outweigh the imperceptible loss of confidence in themselves? The need for a pattern of supporting evidence for an idea will become clear through repeated discussions.

Remember that the questions you ask should be open-ended questions, not questions to which you have specific answers. Also remember that you must guard against less-stringent probing related to those answers with which you agree. Guard against this by requesting supporting evidence for comments that seem true to you but that have not been adequately supported.

Because the stress in this model is on the process of developing critical thinking skills rather than the achievement of one specific conclusion, there is no closure in the sense of reaching a stated conclusion. The idea that there is no one right conclusion is difficult for students to grasp, but it is good if they come to grips with this concept. It is also good if they see that disagreements can be healthy and can lead to greater insights.

STEP 5: REVIEW AND SUMMARIZE THE SEMINAR

Once the seminar is complete, students need to share what they heard or observed during the session. In a short discussion of how they felt about the process and their own thinking, it is important that students practice metacognition so that the benefits of the seminar are not lost. In the same vein, the facilitator and students should make generalizations about the themes and images discussed, allowing students to continue to process the information and insights that were shared. Without this opportunity, many of the most salient ideas can be left unattached to the essential curriculum content of which the seminar was a part. Students must be reminded that the process of the seminar was important—critical thinking is a useful and important skill, and the ideas that were pursued together are representative of the knowledge for which the class is responsible.

STEP 6: EVALUATE THE SEMINAR WITH THE STUDENTS BASED ON PREVIOUSLY STATED CRITERIA

The Socratic seminar model is an excellent tool for students to use when thinking independently, when solving problems of interpretation, and when thinking in concert with or in opposition to their peers. But how does one evaluate this activity?

To evaluate the leader's performance, review the questions that were asked in the seminar. Did you deviate from your plan? When? Where? Why? How did you return to the questions again? Did you follow the leads of students? Did you feel you missed some opportunities to clarify comments, probe assumptions, ask for specific reasons and evidence, and question viewpoints, implications, and consequences? The six types of Socratic seminar questions identified by Paul and Elder (2006) in their taxonomy (see Figure 9.2) provide a good evaluation checklist for discussion leaders.

FIGURE 9.2   Taxonomy of Socratic Questions

Clarification Questions
- What do you mean by …?
- How does this relate to your first point?
- What exactly are you saying here?
- Can you tell me more about what you are thinking?
- What is an example of this?
- How does this relate to the previous point?

Assumption Questions
- What is your basic assumption?
- You are basing all of your comments on one assumption. Is this what you want?
- What other assumptions could we make?
- Why would someone make this assumption?
- Is that always true?
- How can you justify this assumption?

Reason and Evidence Questions
- How do you know that?
- Can you give us an example?
- Are these reasons enough to make that assumption or to generate that conclusion?
- What are your reasons for saying that?
- How does this apply to this case?
- What would change your mind?
- Why do you think that is true?
- Is there reason to doubt that evidence?

Viewpoint Questions
- What are you implying?
- What do you believe about …?
- How would other types of people respond to this?
- What would someone who disagrees with this idea say?
- What are alternatives to this point of view?
- What effect would that have?

Implication and Consequence Questions
- How can we find out?
- If that happened, what else might happen?
- What effect might that have if this happens first?
- Is it likely that this will happen?
- What are you implying?
- If this is the case, then what else must be true?

Initial Questions
- Why are we examining this question?
- Is the question clear? Do we understand the question?
- To answer the question, what will first have to be answered?
- Is this the same issue as …?
- Is this question easy or hard to answer? Why?
- How could someone settle this question?

Source: Adapted with permission from Paul, R., & Elder, L. (2006). *The art of Socratic questioning.* The Foundation for Critical Thinking. www.criticalthinking.org

Socratic seminars provide an opportunity for students to practice metacognitive thought. During the first few sessions of the seminar, students can use the following questions to evaluate their participation in the discussion:

- Did I speak clearly so everyone could hear?
- Did I cite reasons and evidence for each of my comments?
- Did I use the text as a source of my evidence?
- Did I listen to others respectfully?
- Did I impede the flow of the conversation?
- Did I speak with other discussants besides the leader?
- Did I paraphrase when appropriate?
- Did I ask for help when I was confused?
- Was I supportive of my classmates?
- Did I avoid hostile exchanges?
- Was I prepared for the seminar?

There are several ways of grading student participation in the seminar. A number of websites offer holistic rubrics evaluating overall performance using categories congruent with those discussed here. Students can be evaluated on participation using the following indicators:

- Demonstrates listening skills by paying attention to the details of the discussion
- Utilizes the contributions of others in response
- Keeps up with conversation flow by offering clarifications that extend previously shared ideas
- Politely points out gaps of understanding, evidence, or logic
- Ignores distractions

Students can also be evaluated based on their preparation for the seminar:

- Demonstrates careful reading and thought through familiarity with the text—identifying main ideas, contradictions, and accurate use of vocabulary
- Has annotated personal copy of the text that allows the participant frequently to refer to specific parts of the text

These attributes of participation and preparation can form the basis of an evaluation of all seminar participants. Other assessment possibilities are addressed in the "Evaluating Learning in the Socratic Seminar Model" section.

SUMMARY OF STEPS IN THE SOCRATIC SEMINAR MODEL

1. *Choose the text—written, visual, or audio.* Read the material (or provide access to supporting material if it is in visual or audio form). Relate the text to curriculum standards and choose a basic, powerful, essential question.

2. *Plan and cluster several questions of varying cognitive demand.* Questions should allow students to take a position and also reflect what you know about the students and their readiness and interests.

3. *Introduce the model to the students.* Through a series of questions about what students think they should learn, explain the benefits of the Socratic seminar model.

Reciprocal teaching is sometimes called a *structured dialogue*, the structure coming from the four activities that make it up: predicting, questioning, clarifying, and summarizing. The idea is that, as they read, students should constantly be predicting (and modifying those predictions), asking questions that arise, clarifying any confusion that occurs, and summarizing at successive points in the reading. The teacher and students model these activities by taking turns as a text is read.

Distribute to students a set of index cards, each labeled with one of the activities. Open the textbook or other reading material and ask whether anyone with a "prediction" card would like to venture a guess as to what we might expect to learn from the reading. Write these predictions on the board. Next ask whether anyone with a "question" card can offer a question about the topic we are about to

study. Write these questions on the board also. Now ask that everyone read a page or two of the text, down to a logical breakpoint. Ask those students with "clarify" cards whether they have seen any answers to questions that were raised before. Record these possible answers. Ask also whether any part of the text seemed confusing or unclear, and, if so, whether the "clarify" students can clear anything up. This might mean looking something up in another resource. Next come the "summarizing" cards. What could be said to summarize what we have read thus far? Put brief summaries on the board.

Now have students exchange cards with another person who has a different card. Repeat the process several times as the text is read through, or until you are certain that students are empowered to complete the activities on their own. ■

Next, introduce expectations of student behavior and how behavior during seminars will be assessed. Assign the reading and remind students of how to prepare for the discussion.

4. *Conduct the dialogue.* During the dialogue, try to maintain a nondirective role as much as possible. Encourage interactions among the students. Use your cluster questions and show flexibility as you probe student positions and understandings.

5. *Review and summarize the seminar.* Review the major points made during the discussion or encourage the students to jot down ideas that impressed them. Ask for their contributions. You might also ask whether any students changed their minds during the discussion about the answers to the basic questions. How did their ideas change, and why?

6. *Evaluate the seminar with the students based on previously stated criteria.* The seminar leader and students should evaluate personal behavior during the seminar. Grading should be assigned through the use of rubrics and checklists.

The preceding list describes the process of planning and using the Socratic seminar model, and the preceding text articulates how the seminar fits into classroom instruction. The Socratic seminar model requires careful selection of text, planning, and a high level of trust in students. By examining the potential behaviors of teachers and students working within the seminar framework, you can consider what is needed to master the instructional moves of the model and identify what skills and knowledge you need before you can include the model in your professional toolbox. Table 9.1 will help you consider what the teacher and students need to do to construct a successful and rich seminar experience. This is more than a discussion—the seminar requires sophisticated student behaviors and astute teacher responses.

A case study showing how to use the Socratic seminar in context can be seen in Chapter Fifteen.

TABLE 9.1 Potential Teacher and Student Behaviors in the Socratic Seminar Model

Step	Teacher	Student
1. Choose text.	• Chooses an accessible text (written, visual, or audio) • Relates text to curriculum standards; ensures alignment Constructs a basic power essential question with which to focus seminar	
2. Cluster questions.	• Prepares and groups a series of seminar questions to help students articulate ideas, use higher-level thinking, and problem solve	
3. Introduce the model.	• Explains Socratic seminar process • Reviews behavioral expectations and evaluation process • Introduces and assigns text • Situates text in student past experiences and prior knowledge • Scaffolds student preparation	• Asks clarifying questions about process and text if necessary • Considers prior knowledge related to process and text • Anticipates personal challenges that might arise during instruction • Constructs a plan for preparation
4. Conduct dialogue.	• Asks opening and follow-up questions • Facilitates discussion by asking for supported inferences, strong summaries, and attention to discussion rules • Notes student responses • Attempts to deepen student understanding	• Attends to opening information • Engages in discussion following stated rules • Constructs and supports inferences about text • Notes confusion about particular discussion points
5. Review and summarize seminar.	• Reviews major points of discussion • Asks students to summarize main ideas of discussion • Contributes important ideas that might not have emerged from discussion • Elicits student responses to discussion	• Responds to teacher and peer questions in discussion • Summarizes main points of seminar • Evaluates contribution to identifying main ideas in seminar • Assesses personal understanding of seminar objectives
6. Evaluate seminar.	• Facilitates evaluation of the seminar discussion and student participation • Discusses individual accountability and grading • Monitors student judgments about seminar • Works with student on realistic personal evaluations	• Evaluates peer and personal participation in seminar • Provides the teacher feedback on facilitating seminar • Considers personal challenges in participating in seminar and making generalizations about the discussion

Evaluating Learning in the Socratic Seminar Model

Students can be evaluated both formatively and summatively through the Socratic seminar model. Formative assessment opportunities can occur before, during, and after the seminar. Prior to the seminar, students could be asked to write clarification questions and answers that are directly related to the text. These questions will reflect the students' comprehension level and provide formative information to both the teacher and the students. Student-generated questions may also be evaluated during the seminar (either in a whole class or in an inner/outer circle arrangement). Questions may be evaluated in terms of clarity, complexity, relationship to the text, and seminar objectives. Students may be asked to evaluate the questions that they felt were the most important in the seminar once the dialogue has been completed. Students can then share and discuss this information providing data on what was noticed and learned in the seminar.

This chapter has discussed some of the metacognitive approaches to assessment available to teachers as they implement the Socratic seminar model. These checklists and rubrics may also be used to evaluate students summatively, for a grade. There are several considerations to bear in mind as assessment tools are chosen for this purpose in the classroom:

- Tools (checklists or rubrics) must be clearly aligned with curriculum standards and class objectives.
- Tools must be developmentally appropriate.
- Tools must be clearly written and understood by both the teacher and the students.
- Common tools must be used for all students involved in a particular seminar.
- Clear indicators of which behaviors result in which grades should be made public.

Besides holistic discussion participation, students can be assessed on the content of the seminar through writing assignments, projects, and role plays. Students can also be asked to plan new questions for the seminar in which they just participated or plan a new seminar to demonstrate their understanding of the content and the seminar process. There is probably no better way to ensure their enjoyment and commitment.

Meeting Individual Needs with the Socratic Seminar Model

The Socratic seminar, as do most models, offers a host of possibilities for personalizing instruction. The choice of the text is one critical chance to differentiate. By choosing audio and visual text, on occasion, teachers can meet the learning preferences of a variety of students and provide the chance to build new strengths for others. Texts can also be chosen to respond to students' cultural background and interests.

Planning specific questions offers another chance to personalize instruction. Clusters of questions can be planned to meet the specific learning needs of particular students, to extend cultural understandings, and to pique student interests. All of these goals can be reached while also helping students demonstrate the achievement of standards and objectives.

Students can participate at varying levels during a seminar, especially through the use of the inner/outer circle approach. Assigned opportunities or student choices could include observing a seminar and providing feedback to participants, charting discussions, preparing seminar questions, and keeping track of personal participation. The key is to use the information that you have collected through close observations of your students to make significant instructional decisions that allow individual students to gain the most from the seminar opportunity. Decisions about these options will be based on teacher observations and evidence of student interests, readiness, and learning preferences.

Follow-up products that use the information and skills obtained in the Socratic seminar may also be differentiated. You may provide students a choice of writing a summary of the seminar, constructing a concept web of the ideas presented in the conversation, or writing a short paper showing the connections between the ideas discussed. There are many other options that can be used to allow for student choice in a culminating product—the key is to provide options that match the characteristics of the students with whom you are working.

Benefits of the Socratic Seminar Model

The main argument in favor of the Socratic seminar model is that it is always based on an open-ended question designed to lead students to active dialogue in which multiple ideas can be proposed. The seminar is based not on "right" answers but on "thoughtful engagement" with a question and information related to it. Students in a seminar have the opportunity to make sense of difficult ideas within a supportive learning community. They are asked to support these ideas clearly and with evidence. In addition, students become more comfortable listening to peers and to ideas with which they may disagree. Thoughtful engagement is the seed for critical thinking and for creating new relationships and ideas.

ELEMENTARY GRADES LESSON

SOCRATIC SEMINAR: *Old Henry,* **by Joan W. Blos**

OBJECTIVES	**Common Core State Standards —English/Language Arts RL.3.1** Ask and answer questions to demonstrate understanding of a text, referring explicitly to the text as the basis for the answers. **Common Core State Standards— English/Language Arts RL.4.2** Determine a theme of a story, drama, or poem from details in the text; summarize the text. **Common Core State Standards—English/Language Arts RL.4.3** Describe in depth a character, setting, or event in a story or drama, drawing on specific details in the text (e.g., a character's thoughts, words, or actions). **Students Will Know** • The rights and responsibilities of neighbors • How to identify the main idea, the problem, and a solution in a text **Students Will Understand That** • Citizens have a responsibility to protect the rights of others, and this might cause problems **Students Will Be Able To** • Cooperatively participate in active and thoughtful discussion of the text • Identify the feelings and beliefs of Old Henry and his neighbors and what responsibilities each had to the other • Explain the conflict between Old Henry and his neighbors • Identify how the conflict was resolved and in what additional ways the conflict might have been resolved • Consider and build on a variety of perspectives

SEMINAR TEXT

Old Henry is the story of a man who moves into an old, vacant, run-down house in a neighborhood of houses that are in good shape—lawns are mowed, houses are painted, and repairs are made. But Old Henry likes his house just like it is when he buys it and prefers to read his books, paint his pictures, care for his birds, and live his more leisurely life. The neighbors are astounded that Henry does not sweep his walks or cut his grass or fix things up. No, things suit him just fine. Eventually the conflict with the neighbors drives Henry away. But then the neighbors begin to miss Old Henry and his parrot, and in his new place, Henry begins to miss his previous neighbors.

ASSESSMENT

Students will make a six-frame storyboard of the book *Old Henry* that has a different ending. The storyboard should identify the problem, show how the characters feel, and propose a solution. (The first three steps may take place prior to the lesson.)

PROCEDURES

1. Choose the text. Read the material. Relate the text to curriculum standards and choose a basic, powerful, and essential question. This lesson asks the question, "Does Henry have a right to ignore the concerns of his neighbors?"
2. Develop question clusters similar to the following examples.
   - Cluster 1: What is a neighborhood? How does a neighborhood get made? Do the citizens of a neighborhood have any responsibilities? What are these responsibilities? What responsibilities did the citizens in Old Henry's neighborhood have? Did Old Henry have any responsibilities? How do you know what their responsibilities are? Did either the neighbors or Old Henry have any rights addressing how they could live in the neighborhood? How does the neighbors' behavior tell you about what they see as their rights and responsibilities?
   - Cluster 2: What is the problem in the book? What does Old Henry think the problem is? What do the neighbors think the problem is? What does Old Henry want? What do the neighbors want? What did Old Henry decide to do? Is this a solution to the problem? How did Old Henry and the neighbors feel after Old Henry left? What was the next problem? How did Henry solve the problem? How would you solve the problem? Were the neighbors and Old Henry good citizens? How do you know?
3. Introduce the model to the students. Ask the students what they think they should learn and how they might benefit from the Socratic seminar model. Next, introduce expectations of student behavior and how student behavior will be assessed. Remind students that good seminar participants (1) are patient with the ideas of classmates; (2) ask a question when something is confusing; (3) move the conversation forward, not letting the discussion focus on only one idea; (4) address comments to the teacher and classmates; and (5) make sure everyone has a chance to speak. Read the text to the students.
4. Conduct the discussion.
5. Review and summarize the discussion.
6. Evaluate the discussion with the students. Ask students to consider whether they were good seminar discussants. Did they speak clearly? Give reasons for their answers? Listen respectfully? Use the ideas of other students well? Keep the conversation moving? Offer support and encouragement to their peers?

MIDDLE/SECONDARY GRADES LESSON

SOCRATIC SEMINAR: *The War Prayer* and "Sullivan Ballou's Letter to His Wife"

OBJECTIVES	**Common Core State Standards—English/Language Arts RH.9-10.1**
	Cite specific textual evidence to support analysis of primary and secondary sources, attending to such features as the date and origin of the information.
	Common Core State Standards—English/Language Arts RH.9-10.2
	Determine the central ideas or information of a primary or secondary source; provide an accurate summary of how key events or ideas develop over the course of the text.
	Common Core State Standards—English/Language Arts RH.9-10.3
	Analyze in detail a series of events described in a text; determine whether earlier events caused later ones or simply preceded them.
	Students Will Know
	• The details about the Battle of Bull Run and why it is considered a turning point in the Civil War
	Students Will Understand That
	• The impact of war is beyond the battlefield
	Students Will Be Able To
	• Cooperatively participate in active and thoughtful discussion of the text
	• Identify Twain's and Ballou's assumptions and interpretations of the consequences of war
	• Consider and build on a variety of perspectives
SEMINAR TEXTS	Each of these short pieces is available on the Internet. Suggested links are listed in the Web Resource earlier in this chapter.
ASSESSMENT	Students will write a short essay contrasting Twain's and Ballou's positions on the benefits and costs of war using excerpts from the texts to support their conclusions.
PROCEDURES	The first three steps may take place prior to the lesson.

1. Read the chosen texts. Relate the texts to curriculum standards and choose a basic, powerful, and essential question. This lesson asks the following: "What is the other side of victory? What happens to the vanquished?"
2. Develop question clusters similar to the following possibilities.
    • Cluster 1: How were the concerns of Sullivan Ballou and the stranger in the church different? How were they similar? What concerns about war have you noticed in our country? If Sullivan Ballou had not died of his wounds, would his letter have been as powerful? Would you have published Twain's *The War Prayer*? Would you republish it now? Can you share your beliefs about war in general and the Civil War specifically?
    • Cluster 2: The Battle of Bull Run was considered a pivotal battle of the Civil War because the perceptions of both sides concerning quick victory and the costs of war had to change. What did Sullivan Ballou think would happen in the battle? How might the perceptions of warriors change the course of the battle? What might Mark Twain have written about the Battle of Bull Run? If you could speak with either Twain or Ballou, what would you say? Why?

3. Introduce the model to the students. Ask the students what they think they should learn and how they might benefit from the Socratic seminar model. Next, introduce expectations of student behavior and how student behavior will be assessed. Remind students that good seminar participants (1) exhibit patience with the ideas of others, (2) ask for clarifications, (3) move the conversation forward, (4) address comments to all, and (5) do not monopolize the conversation. Prepare an entry ticket to ensure that students have read or viewed the text. The ticket may be a question or series of questions, a journal entry, a document analysis worksheet, or other work sample.

4. Conduct the discussion. The word *civil* is worth exploring in the context of discussion of civil wars. The teacher and students can use techniques from the vocabulary acquisition model to delve into this short but very important word. They will find that the word is part of a family of words that include *civility, citizen, city, civilization,* and *civics,* a social studies course they may be taking. *Civics* was actually created by adding the final letter *-s,* in kinship with the word *politics.* Thus, there seems to be a conceptual connection between *polite* and *civil,* which we see in use of the word in phrases like "civil behavior." All this suggests that there is nothing really "civil" about "war"—it is merely a label for a war among citizens of the same country who have taken up arms against one another. Actually, America's Civil War cost more lives of its citizens than the combined losses of all the other wars the country has had! Perhaps the students will come to see the idea of "civil war" as a contradiction in terms, an oxymoron.

5. Review and summarize the discussion.

6. Evaluate the discussion with the students. Ask students to consider whether they were prepared for the seminar, spoke clearly, gave reasons from the text for their comments, listened respectfully, paraphrased when appropriate, kept the conversation flowing, asked for help when confused, or offered support for others.

SUMMARY

This chapter examines a specific discussion strategy—Socratic seminars based on conversations about particular texts. The chapter discusses how to prepare for, conduct, and evaluate a Socratic seminar and provides information about classroom questioning that helps to structure both the seminar and other classroom discussions. The Socratic seminar provides opportunities for differentiating content to meet student needs and allows for variations in assessments.

EXTENSIONS

ACTIVITIES

1. Choose a favorite nursery rhyme. Construct a series of questions using all the levels of questions in Bloom's revised taxonomy—remembering, understanding, applying, analyzing, evaluating, and creating.

2. One of the challenges in engaging in a Socratic seminar is that people are inclined to debate rather than to dialogue. What do you think are the differences between these two forms of interaction? Prepare a table with two columns and a number of rows. Label the columns "Dialogue" and "Debate." Label the rows, as a start, with features

such as "interactions," "beliefs," "questions," or "purposes." The goal of this activity is to create a list of features that distinguish these two kinds of verbal give and take.

3. Review the state standards for your grade level and content area and choose two or three standards that would align with the Socratic seminar method. Identify a text that could be used to meet the standard and that is aligned with this model. Using Paul and Elder's questions for a Socratic seminar (Figure 9.2), construct questions that could form the basis for your Socratic seminar.

REFLECTIVE QUESTIONS

1. Students in your class may be accustomed to discussions driven by right answers, and surely there are many settings where this is appropriate. But the Socratic seminar is a context in which multiple answers to open-ended questions compete for dominance, and all may be winners. Do you think this approach will be difficult or easy to adopt? What can you do to ensure that every opinion and perspective is honored in the seminar setting?

2. It is important that at the onset of a Socratic seminar each participant has read the targeted text. What are some ways to ensure this is the case?

3. Aside from deepening skills of reading comprehension, what other skills do you see the seminar as fostering? Might it be a good idea to ask the students to help with this skills list?

10 Cooperative Learning Models

IMPROVING STUDENT LEARNING USING SMALL, COLLABORATIVE GROUPS

 Chapter Objectives

You Will Know

- The basis of cooperative learning models
- The template of the generic cooperative learning model
- Specific cooperative models: the graffiti model, the jigsaw model, the academic controversy model, and the student teams-achievement division (STAD) model
- How to evaluate learning in cooperative learning models
- How to meet individual needs with cooperative learning models
- The benefits of cooperative learning models

You Will Understand That

- Cooperative learning models offer the opportunity to develop social, academic, and cognitive skills effectively and efficiently

You Will Be Able To

- Design, implement, and reflect on cooperative learning models in your planning and teaching
- Explain to students, parents, and peers the value and mechanics of cooperative learning

In the Elementary Classroom

In Ms. Wright's fourth grade science class, the new unit is on clouds and weather. The fourth grade team has been working with their students on basic cooperative skills. Now they move into groups well and speak quietly when they are working, taking turns and listening carefully. Polite behavior has become the norm, although this was not always true at the beginning of the school year. With this progress in mind, Ms. Wright has decided on a jigsaw lesson to begin the new unit.

She introduces the jigsaw model to the students by sharing student-friendly learning objectives for the activity, providing the composition and duties of the learning and expert groups, and explicitly naming the steps of the jigsaw process.

Ms. Wright: Today we are going to work on learning new information about clouds. People have been interested in clouds and their relation to weather as long as there have been people on earth. Why do you think people were interested in clouds?

Cookie: They are always changing.

Larry: Yes, and we can tell what kind of weather is coming if you look at the clouds, so there must be a pattern.

Ms. Wright: We learn a lot about our world by observing it and trying to make sense of what we see—we look for patterns. Watching clouds is one way of trying to figure out some kind of order in our world. Today, we are going to begin a unit on clouds and weather. You will learn about five different kinds of clouds, the ways in which clouds form, and the kind of weather that is associated with specific kinds of clouds. First, we are going to get into our expert groups and together you are going to learn about your assigned cloud type.

Ms. Wright projects the list of expert group members and tells the students they have 60 seconds to settle into their groups and read the directions for the activity.

Ms. Wright: Elizabeth, please remind us of what we will do in our expert jigsaw groups.

Elizabeth: We stay with our group until all work is completed, we follow our class rules, we make certain that everyone in our group understands the material before we ask you for help. The directions say that you are going to assign our cloud types. Can we choose which cloud type we will learn about?

Ms. Wright: You are going to choose your cloud type out of a hat. The questions that you are to answer are on the direction sheet. You can use Internet sources, our class library, and the textbook collection. Remember that before the end of our expert groups today, you will make a brochure that describes your cloud type using six different pieces of information, tells the way that your cloud is formed, and explains the type of weather associated with your cloud. The brochure will be the basis of your presentation to your learning groups tomorrow. Be certain that everyone in your group is ready to present to their learning groups before the end of class. I will make copies of your brochure for you so that there are enough for everyone in the class.

The expert groups get to work and Ms. Wright circulates around the room, helping groups figure out how to divide the task so that they can finish in the allotted time. At the end of the period, all of the groups are ready for the next day's learning groups. ■

In the Middle/Secondary Classroom

Mrs. Bonigiraud's overarching objective is to have her students understand that communication is about sending and receiving messages. Today's lesson will focus on communicating using appropriate formal and informal phrases in different settings. Mrs. Bonigiraud has chosen the graffiti model because of the feedback the model will provide her about student understanding and for the review it will provide the students.

> **Mrs. Bonigiraud:** We are going to do a graffiti exercise today. We've done this once before. Do you remember how to do this poster activity?
>
> **Denis:** Yes, we had too much time to work on our posters and it got too loud!
>
> **Mrs. Bonigiraud:** I remember. Today, we will only have three minutes with each poster, and that should help. Let me remind you of the expectations of this activity.

Mrs. Bonigiraud reviews the process and behavioral expectations for the students. She asks students to explain the process again to make certain that everyone will know what to do.

> **Mrs. Bonigiraud:** I believe that many of you have accounts on Facebook and know about wall posts and commenting on other people's posts, right?
>
> **Marguerite:** Oh, yeah! You can also just click "like it" if you agree with what someone has posted.
>
> **Nicolas:** Some posts are private though, so there's no point in commenting—you just write your own note back. It's just between your wall and theirs.
>
> **Mrs. Bonigiraud:** Right, you are both describing communication. Sometimes, it goes back and forth a little until both people have talked through a whole idea. In either case, the original post should be as clear as possible, if the writer wants to communicate. Today, we will discuss formal and informal language. Clear communication demands that we know when to use formal or informal language.
>
> **Adrien:** Do you mean we talk in one way in one setting and a different way in another setting?
>
> **Mathilde:** Well, I don't use the same words with my grandmother as I do with my friends at the movies.
>
> **Mrs. Bonigiraud:** That is exactly right. Let's see what phrases you would use in the settings described on these posters. I will use this timer to keep us on track.

The group activity begins and continues over the next 15 minutes. Mrs. Bonigiraud circulates, responding to questions, correcting misconceptions and inaccuracies, and offering suggestions. The students are working well together and following the cooperative rules that have been discussed throughout the school year. The timer keeps the students on track throughout the activity. They are enthusiastic when they summarize and share their group findings with the whole class.

> **Mrs. Bonigiraud:** What did all of the presentations have in common? Can we make any broad generalizations from the group presentations?
>
> **Gustave:** There are times and places when it is appropriate to use formal phrases.
>
> **Adrien:** It is easier to come up with formal than informal phrases.
>
> **Mathilde:** I think that's because we used a lot of the phrases from our textbook.
>
> **Mrs. Bonigiraud:** How do people learn informal expressions?
>
> **Adrien:** I think we learn the informal expressions by just living, from hearing, and by using the expressions.

The discussion continues until the bell rings. ■

Basis of Cooperative Learning Models

The age of accountability has many advantages and some disadvantages for teachers—especially novice teachers. Standards provide guidance for the development of objectives (what students need to know, understand, and be able to do), but standards often explicate so much content that, taken at face value, teaching becomes superficial coverage. In addition, there have been continuous calls for different goals in schooling, as some point out that the society and workplaces these students are being prepared for demand more than academic content. Schooling is meant to socialize our children into adult society, demanding attention to character development and social skills. These pressures can make a teacher's daily planning an overwhelming process. The models of instruction presented in this text are designed to help with everyday instructional decisions by organizing the learning environment so that students can reach content goals and have the opportunity to develop higher-level thinking as well. Cooperative learning models also allow pupils the chance to develop personal and social skills.

Cooperative learning models have been used at educational levels from kindergarten through grade 12, and with adult professional development in business, education, law, and medicine. The concept of group learning is not new in education. Reading groups, team sports, group science projects, student drama productions, and school newspapers are a few examples of activities that permeate the American school experience.

People are accustomed to working in groups both in and out of school—some of these groups are cooperative, though some of them are not. It is important to remember that not every group is a cooperative one. Most researchers agree that groups are cooperative when there is a common or closely related set of goals, equal distribution of labor in meeting the goals, and close contact as the goals are being pursued. Face-to-face interaction and individual accountability are additional hallmarks of cooperative learning (Frey, Fisher, & Everlove, 2009).

It is also important to consider that not all school tasks should be completed cooperatively. Cooperative learning models are instructional sequences—a series of processes that structure pupil interactions in order to accomplish a specific (usually teacher-assigned) goal. There is not a single approach to cooperative learning. In fact, there have been several interpretations of how the power of groups can be used to help pupils succeed academically and socially. Specific academic and social skills enhanced by cooperative learning approaches are identified in Figure 10.1. This chapter will examine the support for cooperative learning models and will present a general template of cooperative learning along with four specific cooperative learning models—jigsaw, graffiti, academic controversy, and student teams-achievement division (STAD).

Figure 10.1 lists the cooperative skills, both elementary and advanced, that are necessary for success in the cooperative learning models. Some of the skills are more appropriate for some tasks than for others. These skills must be explicitly taught to our pupils.

Cooperative learning is supported by information processing theories and cognitive theories of learning. Information processing highlights the encoding process of learners—the act of relating new information to the ideas and concepts stored in long-term memory. Encoding strategies can be taught directly, but not everyone benefits from the encoding strategies chosen by a teacher, so more personal and elaborative forms of connection making can be useful. Teaching students to self-question as they integrate new information is helpful, as is listening to other students as they are involved in the same academic task. Learning with others can increase knowledge through modeling and coaching.

Cognitive theories of learning also support the use of cooperative groups in classrooms. According to theorists, activity is the center of human learning, and

FIGURE 10.1   Cooperative Skills

Basic Cooperative Skills: Foundational Skills for Groups to Work in a Classroom Setting

- Moving into groups responsibly
- Speaking quietly
- Taking turns
- Addressing group members by name
- Eliminating put-downs
- Remaining with the group
- Encouraging everyone to participate
- Paying attention to materials
- Looking at the person speaking

Functioning Skills: Managing Group Efforts to Complete the Task and Maintain Productive Relationships

- Being able to restate the assignment limits
- Offering procedural ideas
- Seeking ideas of others
- Paraphrasing contributions of others in the group
- Describing personal feelings when appropriate
- Setting time limits and calling attention to time
- Supporting peers through eye contact
- Asking for or providing help or clarification
- Using humor and enthusiasm to energize

Formulating Skills: Intellectual Skills Needed for Deep Understanding

- Summarizing document or discussion completely without reference to the original document
- Seeking accuracy of processed information
- Seeking elaboration of information by relating it to past knowledge shared by the group
- Developing mnemonics to remember ideas and facts
- Checking for understanding by articulating reasons behind behavior and products
- Providing feedback as to procedures and progress to task completion

Fermenting Skills: Highest Intellectual and Social Skills

- Criticizing ideas, not people
- Integrating a number of different ideas into a single position
- Asking for justification of a peer's position
- Extending another's conclusion by adding further information or implications
- Going beyond first, apparent, or simple answers
- Testing conclusions against reality and group process constraints

Source: Based on information from Johnson, D. W., Johnson, R. T., and Holubec, E. J. (1994). *The new circles of learning: Cooperation in the classroom and school.* Alexandria, VA: Association for Supervision and Curriculum Development.

A description of cooperative learning can be found in this video. What is cooperative learning? Compare the attributes provided in the video and those discussed in this chapter. Do you notice any differences? www.youtube.com/watch?v=7E24c5RkrMw

interactions with peers are a springboard for cognitive development. All learning requires active involvement, and cooperative models provide the opportunity for structured and targeted student talk about concepts and skills (Hattie & Yates, 2014). Cooperative learning models provide carefully structured academic activities in a social environment. Cooperative learning groups allow students to share cultural experiences and examples through academic tasks that provide an opportunity for increased learning by all group members. Because higher-level mental processes frequently occur in a group context, the cooperative group is fertile learning ground. As students act within a group, the group changes and evolves, creating a dynamic and opportunistic learning environment. It is natural that our students learn in a social environment in cooperation with peers.

The Cooperative Learning Model: The Template

All lessons, curricula, and courses can be designed to include cooperative learning by tailoring existing materials to include the five key elements of cooperative learning (Johnson, Johnson, & Holubec, 1994). These skills are critically important in almost all work settings. Their value to students beyond the years of formal schooling can hardly be overestimated:

1. **Positive interdependence** to ensure that work is equally distributed among all participating students and no one takes on a disproportionate share of the work
2. **Individual accountability**, meaning that each student is responsible for his or her own learning
3. **Face-to-face interaction** in which students explain to one another how to solve problems, share information, and connect information to prior knowledge
4. The explicit teaching of **social skills** (see Figure 10.1)
5. **Group processing** during a discussion about whether the activity met cooperative learning goals

In addition, consideration must be given to the curriculum, the physical setting, and a diagnosis of and remediation for problems that pupils might have in working cooperatively. This template model was adapted from guidelines for cooperative learning lessons in science and math (Blosser, 1991) and lists a series of steps that are required in planning for and implementing a cooperative learning lesson. It is a template because it provides guidance to teachers of students at any developmental level in any content area and can be adapted by the teacher from previously existing curriculum materials or lesson activities and units found on the Internet. The teacher is required in the model to design the cooperative structure of the task and setting.

There are many cooperative learning strategies that can be used to support instructional planning with the general template—think-pair-share, find the rule, three-step interview, corners, etc. Information about cooperative learning strategies can be found on the Internet. One example, "numbered heads," is described in the Strategy Alert.

STRATEGY ALERT   Numbered Heads

Numbered heads is a cooperative learning strategy designed to promote individual accountability in group work. Divide students into groups of four and provide them with clear directions for a comprehension or review task. Remind students that each group member will be held accountable for reporting the information being practiced or reviewed. Group members count off, one through four. Once the task is completed and all of the students in each group are ready to report to the large class, use a random number generator or dice to select a number. The student with that number reports to the class. (Other group members can provide aid during the presentation, if necessary.) Group processing can be evaluated at the completion of numbered heads by asking students to explain how the group supported the learning of each group member.

The other models found in this chapter have the key elements of cooperative learning within their organizational structure. The general model requires that teachers build that structure—providing both opportunity and challenge. There are three planning steps and six implementation steps in the cooperative learning model.

PLANNING STEPS

1. *Develop clear instructional goals* in the KUD (know, understand, and able to do) format.

2. *Consider and plan the size and composition of groups.* Try to keep groups to no more than four or five students. Groups should be heterogeneous in ways that are *applicable to the goals of the lesson* (gender, achievement, ethnicity, prior experiences, etc.). For example, if you want students to examine a science problem from a variety of perspectives, you want to vary the groups as much as possible. If, on the other hand, your objective is to provide the opportunity for students to practice new math skills, you want to group students on the same achievement level but with different genders and ethnicities.

3. *Make certain that the cooperative activity has all of the key elements of cooperative learning*—face-to-face communication for positive interaction, materials and roles that support interdependence, necessary social skills, positive goal interdependence, and individual accountability.

IMPLEMENTATION STEPS

1. *Explain the task.* Explain the academic task clearly and succinctly. Remember that clarity is an important need of learners.

2. *Identify the social skills that are critical for the task so that the group will be successful.* Not all cooperative learning skills are applicable to all tasks. Remind students of the attributes of the skills and the criteria employed to determine whether students are using the skills appropriately. Review a T-chart that shows what the skill sounds like and looks like. For example, in a lesson on the Vietnam War, the objective is to identify the positions of the North and South Vietnamese. Your pupils' assignment is to study the position of each of the groups by looking at reprints of newspapers from around the globe. This is a complex task for your students, and you want to remind them of the importance of supporting each other during this difficult task. You can ask students what behaviors they will see when a person is being supportive. Pupils may identify such supportive behaviors as eye contact, praise, leaning forward, and the like. You also want to ask students what supportive behaviors sound like. What do your peers say when they are being supportive of your efforts in completing a difficult task? Specify these desired behaviors and the criteria that will be used to evaluate whether students have been supportive in their groups.

3. *Monitor and provide feedback to individual groups as they are working.* Use the rules of providing good feedback. Make certain that feedback is timely, focused on specific pupil behaviors, descriptive, and related to the cooperative task's instructional goals.

4. *Ask each group to summarize.* Provide closure for the lesson by asking each group to summarize its work. The summarizing role can be assigned at the outset of the lesson or can be determined by asking students in each group to count off (numbered heads), allowing for another individual accountability opportunity.

5. *Evaluate.* Evaluate student work from established criteria. This can be done either during the lesson or soon after. Students should be involved in the evaluation process, helping to create the evaluation rubric or checklist.

6. *Assess group process.* Assess group cooperation by evaluating the way in which the groups performed. Each group member should have the opportunity to comment on the positive and negative aspects of the group process.

SUMMARY OF STEPS IN THE COOPERATIVE LEARNING TEMPLATE MODEL

Planning

1. Develop clear instructional goals.
2. Consider and plan the size and composition of groups.
3. Make certain that the cooperative activity has all of the key elements of cooperative learning.

Implementation

1. Explain the task.
2. Identify the social skills that are critical for the task so that the group will be successful.
3. Monitor and provide feedback to individual groups as they are working.
4. Ask each group to summarize.
5. Evaluate.
6. Assess group process.

> This video segment shows students working in groups in an elementary classroom. See whether you think that this group work can be labeled as cooperative learning. Explain your reasoning.

Specific Cooperative Models

Becoming familiar with specific cooperative models helps teachers and students incorporate the best attributes of cooperative learning into the classroom. The specific cooperative learning models discussed in this chapter are more formal and incorporate all of the essential characteristics of cooperative learning in their structures. The graffiti model, the jigsaw model, the academic controversy model, and student teams-achievement division are instructional arrangements that can be used in any content area and at any grade level. They vary from strategies because they have a blueprint for teacher and student behavior that is much more detailed than teaching strategies, which may be used and adapted in many ways.

THE GRAFFITI MODEL

Graffiti is a cooperative brainstorming process that can be used at any point in a unit of instruction to check for understanding, to evaluate progress toward objectives, and to do an informal needs assessment. Pupils work in groups on previously identified questions or topics and simultaneously record responses on large sheets of paper during a specified period of time. After the time period has elapsed, either groups or sheets of paper move until each group has answered each available question. When a group returns to the original question, they read and summarize all of the class's responses and make several generalizations representing the comments. As in all cooperative models, preparation should begin with the planning steps of the template model—identifying objectives and organizing group size and composition.

The graffiti structure ensures positive interdependence and face-to-face interaction. Group skills should be taught or reviewed prior to the graffiti activity. Individual accountability can be ensured through several means. Students can initial their responses and generalizations. Numbered heads may be used. And, if appropriate, an individual assessment can be administered to students at the end of the lesson.

Step 1: Prepare the Graffiti Questions and Group Number Composition

The teacher prepares a series of questions aligned with the instructional objectives of the lesson. There should be as many questions as groups. Each question should be written on a large sheet of paper. A topic or prompt may also be used. Answers to the questions may be in graphic or bulleted list form. Questions can be diagnostic—asking students to share prior knowledge on a new topic or a review of material previously covered in class.

Step 2: Distribute Materials

Depending on the objectives, students may use text materials as they respond to questions. If it is important to identify which responses are from a particular group, distribute colored markers so that each team has a different color. This will provide an easy way for each team to keep track of its own answers. Students may also initial responses.

Step 3: Groups Answer Questions

Each team receives a sheet of paper with a question or topic, and groups are asked to read the question and spend 30 seconds thinking about a response. (If appropriate, you can give students more time as they examine text to find or solidify an answer.) Cue the students after 30 seconds and give them a set amount of time for writing responses on the sheet of paper. This time period should be delineated at the beginning of the lesson and should be about the same throughout each question-answering phase; as the rounds continue and there is more for students to read on the large sheet, you might extend this time by several seconds. Three- to four-minute periods are usually appropriate.

Step 4: Exchange Questions

At the end of the timed interval, question sheets are exchanged. Or groups can physically move to the next question. The process continues until all of the groups have had the opportunity to respond to the prompts or questions on each sheet.

Step 5: Return to the Original Question, Summarize, and Make Generalizations

Each team returns to its original question. Team members review all of the responses on the graffiti sheet and arrange the responses into categories. Categories are listed on the back of the sheet. Once all of the possible categories have been listed, students produce generalizations that encompass all of the categories.

Step 6: Share Information

Each group has the opportunity to share the information from its graffiti sheet with the full class. To ensure individual accountability, have students number off and call one number to share information. Other individual accountability measures may include a quiz or a short paragraph explaining the generalization. Students can also be given a quiz at the end of the lesson.

Step 7: Evaluate the Group Process

A teacher-led discussion is held in which the robustness and accuracy of generalizations are discussed and the graffiti process itself is evaluated. The relationships among the questions and the big ideas of the unit may also be addressed at this time.

Summary of Steps in the Graffiti Model

1. Prepare the graffiti questions and group number composition.
2. Distribute materials.
3. Groups answer questions.
4. Exchange questions.

5. Return to the original question, summarize, and make generalizations.
6. Share information.
7. Evaluate the group process.

The graffiti model allows for seamless integration of literacy activities into content teaching.

All of the criteria for cooperative learning are embedded in the graffiti model: positive interdependence, individual accountability, face-to-face interaction, social skills instruction, and group processing. A potential flaw of the graffiti model is the facility with which it can be planned by the teacher and implemented by the students. This ease can lead to less attention paid to the specific academic and cooperative content and skill goals. Skating on the surface of the graffiti model (by focusing on the directness and simplicity of implementation) does the model a disservice. By examining the potential behaviors of teachers and students working within the graffiti framework, you can consider what is needed to make certain that the inherent benefits of the model are achieved. Table 10.1 will help you consider what teacher and students need to do to construct a positive graffiti experience, allowing for more than a social activity in the classroom.

THE JIGSAW MODEL

The jigsaw model by Elliot Aronson and colleagues was developed in the early 1970s as a way to help students and teachers successfully navigate newly desegregated schools (Aronson, Blaney, Stephan, Sikes, & Snapes, 1978). Instead of providing each student with all of the necessary materials to study independently, Aronson assigned students to teams and gave each team member one piece of information. To reach all of the lesson's objectives, students were forced to fit their individual pieces together as if they were working on a jigsaw puzzle. The puzzle could not be completed unless each team member shared his or her piece. Three decades of research support this specific cooperative learning model. The version of the model presented in this chapter is based on the original jigsaw as developed by Aronson and his team, with some of the adaptations of later researchers such as Robert Slavin (1996).

In a jigsaw lesson, each member of the class is a member of two different groups, an expert group and a learning group. The members of an expert group all read and study the same materials—they become experts on the assigned topic and prepare an outline or graphic that summarizes the critical information of their unit. As a group, they determine how this information will be shared with their peers. After the expert groups have completed their study, they meet with their learning group, composed of a member of each expert group. Each expert teaches his or her topic to the members of the learning group. Students may be given a quiz, a graphic organizer, or an exit card to complete at the end of the learning group to ensure individual accountability.

Step 1: Introduce the Jigsaw

In the first few encounters with the jigsaw model, students should be carefully supported. With students who have less experience in cooperative learning models, a graphic representation like the one shown in Figure 10.2 may be helpful. Explain the cooperative process by highlighting the following points of the lesson in which students will be involved:

- The learning objectives for this lesson
- The composition and size of each group and the reasons behind these decisions
- The differences between the expert and learning group
- How much time students will have to work in each group

TABLE 10.1   Potential Teacher and Student Behaviors in the Graffiti Model

Step	Teacher	Student
1. Prepare for task.	• Shares student-friendly objectives • Prepares series of questions aligned with objectives and assessments • Constructs questions within students' prior knowledge and experience • Varies cognitive demand of questions	
2. Distribute materials.	• Reiterates objectives and process for task • Distributes appropriate materials to groups • Reminds students of behavioral expectations • Monitors student behavior throughout process	• Asks clarifying questions about process and goals if necessary • Collects all materials • Uses positive social skills in group • Reviews task expectations with group
3. Group answers questions.	• Asks for questions about process • Checks for student difficulties • Scaffolds when necessary • Monitors time and presents time cues	• Follows teacher directions and cues • Reads each question • Thinks about response in relation to what is known • Writes individual response
4. Exchange questions and continue cycle.	• Reminds students of appropriate classroom rules and process guidelines • Monitors exchange • Scaffolds as necessary	• Follows classroom rules • Waits with group for next question
5. Summarize and generalize.	• Monitors group interactions • Clarifies student thinking when necessary • Scaffolds higher-level thinking • Provides corrective feedback when appropriate	• Reads all responses to original question • Works with team to categorize responses, note outliers, and summarize • Constructs generalizations based on categories with group • Determines what will be shared with class
6. Share information.	• Reminds students of behavioral expectations • Facilitates presentations • Encourages presenters • Questions presenters when appropriate • Measures individual accountability	• Follows presentation directions • Actively processes information from presentations • Presents generalizations or supports peer presentation • Shares what was learned with teacher
7. Evaluate the process.	• Encourages discussion of individual and group behaviors during instruction • Asks students to support conclusions • Shares personal impressions with students • Asks students for recommendations for future iterations	• Shares personal experience with process • Reflects on what was learned during the lesson and what facilitated learning • Supports statements with specific examples • Provides recommendations for future iterations

FIGURE 10.2   Jigsaw Expert and Learning Groups

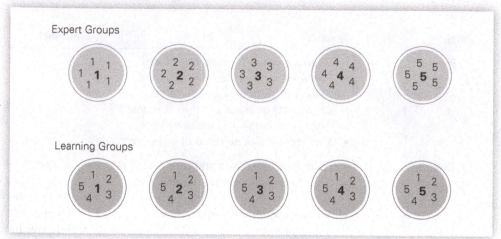

- Access to the required materials
- The expert group task goal
- The learning group task goal
- The method of determining individual accountability

Step 2: Assign Heterogeneously Grouped Students to Expert and Learning Groups

Whenever the lesson objectives and materials warrant, students should be grouped heterogeneously for cooperative lessons. By controlling team assignments, the teacher may ensure that teams are balanced in terms of achievement, motivation, gender, ethnicity, and other factors deemed important. When students are allowed to choose teammates, friendships tend to determine team membership, and many of the advantages of cooperative learning, especially achievement and social skills, are lost. Groups can also be formed randomly by pulling names from a hat, lining up students by height, birth date, number of siblings, or the like, and having students count off. One of the important principles of group composition is that unless you are using semester- or year-long cooperative groups, cooperative learning groups should vary across lessons. And even when base groups are used in classrooms, there should be times when students are assigned to different groups for particular lessons. This alleviates the concern students have about not working with their friends. Students should have the expectation that over time they will have the opportunity to work with all class members.

WEB RESOURCE

Random Number Generator

Random number generators that are available on the Internet can be used to assign groups or to determine a random order in calling on students. One online random number generator is at mathgoodies.com.

Review the rules that will be in effect while groups are working. These rules will be specific to the class and the behavioral norms that have been established; they might include the following:

1. No student may leave his or her team area until all students have completed the assigned work.
2. Each team member is responsible for learning the material and making certain that every member of the team also has learned the material.
3. If an individual group member is having difficulty understanding any part of the assignment, all members of the team respond with attempts to assist before the teacher is asked for help.

Step 3: Explain the Task and Assemble Expert Groups

Students assemble into expert groups. If this is a jigsaw that will be used over a significant number of class periods or with a new group of students, allow pupils to choose a group name, and make certain that they are familiar with each member of the group. This early bonding process can help teams focus and get to the task at hand more quickly. A number of age-appropriate team building activities can be found on the Internet.

WEB RESOURCE

Team Building Activity

Teampedia (teampedia.net) is a collection of team building activities, icebreakers, and resources for group leaders and trainers interested in collaboration.

The teacher introduces the lesson objectives and explains how the jigsaw will help the students reach these objectives. Students are provided the materials they will rely on as they become experts and are given the opportunity to have any procedural questions answered. Sometimes, students can prepare for the jigsaw experience through homework assignments.

The jigsaw task is structured so that a topic is subdivided among the groups. For example, if pupils were expected to understand the interdependence of community, groups may be assigned to become experts on different members of that community. Or if pupils were expected to understand that an ordinary individual can have an impact on history, groups may be assigned to become experts on some of the individuals who have had a profound effect on important events in American history. In a general methods education class, a jigsaw on different models of classroom management can be used.

Step 4: Allow Expert Groups to Process Information

Expert groups should be provided sufficient time to process the new information. Expert team members can assist one another with the reading or viewing material and making sense of the ideas that are being studied. These teams can be given guiding questions to help make connections between new information and background knowledge. Members of expert groups should complete the questions individually before discussing them as a group. Expert group members should then decide on what is most important about their topic and how they will convey this information to their peers in learning groups.

Step 5: Experts Teach in Their Learning Group

When all students master their expert topics, learning teams are assembled, and the experts teach their topics in turn. A time limit should be given for each presentation and the time periods should be monitored. Each expert is responsible for teaching his or her topic, checking for understanding, and assisting teammates in learning the material. A graphic organizer (such as a matrix, Venn diagram, or concept map) can be provided to all learning group members so that the most important ideas can be recorded, retrieved, and compared.

Step 6: Hold Individuals Accountable

Individual students are held accountable for their learning though a quiz, participation checklist, essay, discussion, or other assessment method aligned with the learning objectives for the lesson or unit.

Step 7: Evaluate the Jigsaw Process

Students are asked to debrief the jigsaw process and their own learning in relation to the lesson or unit objectives. This can occur in a full-class discussion, within the expert groups, on an exit card, or in an individual conference with the teacher.

Summary of Steps in the Jigsaw Model

1. Introduce the jigsaw.
2. Assign heterogeneously grouped students to expert and learning groups.
3. Explain the task and assemble expert groups.
4. Allow expert groups to process information.
5. Experts teach in their learning group.
6. Hold individuals accountable.
7. Evaluate the jigsaw process.

The jigsaw model is grounded in cooperative learning theory and has a strong body of empirical evidence supporting it (Aronson & Patnoe, 2011) The jigsaw model is a strong strategy for supporting student learning that also promotes strong face-to-face interaction. By examining the potential behaviors of teachers and students working within the jigsaw framework, you can consider what is needed to master the instructional moves of the model and identify what skills and knowledge you need before you can include the model in your professional toolbox. Table 10.2 will help you consider what the teacher and students need to do to construct a positive jigsaw experience, allowing students to practice important academic and social skills.

Case studies demonstrating how to use the jigsaw model in context can be seen in Chapters Fourteen and Fifteen.

THE STRUCTURED ACADEMIC CONTROVERSY MODEL

A structured academic controversy is a sophisticated cooperative learning model. Designed by Johnson and Johnson (1995) to harness the power of conflicts in classrooms, this approach is based on the belief that intellectual conflict is healthy and that students need to be trained in how to discuss controversial topics.

Johnson and Johnson have proposed a theory to explain how controversies can promote academic learning, productivity, and positive relationships and have used their theory to develop an instructional model. They believe that individuals at first categorize and organize information based on prior experiences and knowledge. As their conclusions are presented to others in the position-building and position-sharing steps of the model, students deepen their understanding and use higher-level thinking strategies. When confronted with different viewpoints and conclusions, conceptual conflict and disequilibrium are aroused. This leads to an active search for more information, more connections, and a path for resolving this uncertainty. Uncertainty is associated with increased attention and higher-level thinking—a strong motivator

TABLE 10.2 Potential Teacher and Student Behaviors in the Jigsaw Model

Step	Teacher	Student
1. Introduce jigsaw.	• Provides lesson's learning objectives and objectives of jigsaw process • Explains group size, composition, time requirements, and individual accountability • Checks for student understanding of process and goals	• Attends to teacher presentation • Asks clarifying questions when necessary • Reflects on past cooperative learning experiences and the objectives for this lesson • Considers possible personal challenges
2. Assign groups.	• Assigns groups and explains basis for assignments • Reviews behavioral expectations • Checks for student understanding of team expectations	• Accepts group assignment or assignments • Reflects on needed social skills to complete group task • Asks clarifying questions if necessary
3. Explain task and assemble expert groups.	• Reiterates purpose of learning task and role of expert groups • Provides and explains necessary materials • Answers procedural questions • Assembles groups	• Asks procedural questions if necessary • Examines materials • Sets tone for group work
4. Expert groups process information.	• Provides sufficient time for groups to complete task • Directs students to guiding questions • Clarifies questions and task when necessary • Scaffolds new information • Supports group efforts in preparing presentation • Monitors student behavior	• Stays on task within time limits • Works on guiding questions individually and with group • Asks content and procedural questions when necessary • Links new information to prior knowledge • Prepares presentation and materials for learning group that build on previous class experiences
5. Experts teach in learning groups.	• Assembles learning groups • Sets and facilitates time limits for expert presentations • Monitors group work, clarifying task when necessary • Looks for comments and behaviors that indicate student learning, confusion, or misinformation • Conveys accurate information when appropriate • Provides assessment review	• Gets into learning group quickly • Sets tone for group work • Presents new information to peers clearly and accurately • Attends to presentations of others • Asks questions when appropriate • Links new information to prior knowledge • Prepares for assessment
6. Hold individuals accountable.	• Assesses individual students in relation to lesson objectives • Shares assessment results with students	• Prepares for individual assessment by revisiting learning objectives and reflecting on what was learned during instruction and what needs to be reviewed and or relearned • Reviews personal assessment results
7. Evaluate the process.	• Encourages discussion of individual and group discussion behaviors • Asks students to support conclusions • Provides generalizations about process to students based on personal observations • Supports student metacognitive thinking	• Shares personal experience with process • Reflects on what was learned during the lesson and what facilitated learning • Supports statements with examples

in classrooms. At the end of the process, students are motivated to accommodate multiple viewpoints.

Before the academic controversy can begin, a topic must be identified and materials supporting each side of the issue gathered. Teachers are responsible for deciding on the topic of the controversy and the materials that will be used to provide background. The topic must be developmentally appropriate for students and should have identifiable pro and con sides. Materials should be organized into pro and con packets and may include primary source documents, summaries, graphic organizers, pictures, and the like. Older students may find their own source materials. Academic controversies can be adapted for younger students by structuring and adapting the information required for understanding each position. These controversies may come from community, school, or classroom experiences: Should cookies be served in the cafeteria? Should there be more time for physical education classes? Should report cards be abolished? Regardless of the elegance of the topic, it is important that students be exposed to the sophisticated process of sorting through positions, ideas, and support. They also should have the opportunity to practice the individual skills before they are used in the academic controversy.

It is not only the ideas and understandings that are complex; the process itself requires some high-level social skills, many of them fermenting or high-level skills (see Figure 10.1). Students should be reminded of what the critical social skills are for this instructional event and have a discussion about what those skills look like and sound like in the classroom.

Teachers are also responsible, as in all cooperative learning, for determining group composition and size. Ideally, there should be four students in a cooperative group—two students assigned to each position. Students are provided with their pro or con packets and given class time to do the readings on their position. The readings could be assigned for homework. Younger students can brainstorm their position with the teacher. Directions for the controversy must be clear and should be provided orally and in writing; they should be clearly related to the publicly stated learning objectives. Once these preparations are made, the academic controversy model begins.

Step 1: Students Prepare Their Positions

Students meet with their same point-of-view partner and review their position materials. Together they determine the theses of their position and arrange the supporting evidence (facts, information, and experiences) to support their claims. Students need to develop a presentation that leads their peers to understand and support their argument.

Step 2: Students Present and Advocate Their Positions

Once the pair has worked out a strong position, they return to the original foursome, and each pair presents its arguments. It is important that both members of the pair are involved in presenting their position. The positions should be organized around several points of evidence that are supported by examples, stories, and personal experiences. As presentations are given, the opposing pair listens so that a list of arguments can be made and each argument can be evaluated as weak or strong. If there are particularly unclear points in the presentation, the opposing group should ask for clarification.

There is no arguing or debating during this step of the model. Students should be learning the opposing position, which they will use to better craft their own position, and be able to share what they have learned on an individual accountability measure.

Step 3: Open Discussion and Rebuttals

Once both positions have been argued, the group of four discusses both presentations by listing the arguments and discussing the strength of each. Pairs continue to advocate for their position and attempt to refute the position of the opposition. Rebuttals should be based on counterarguments, clarifications, and extensions. Students should ask each other for supporting information, clarification, and reasons for the claims. In this phase of the model, uncertainty is building, and students need to be comfortable expressing opinions and being challenged. In turn, they must be comfortable challenging opinions in a polite and reasonable manner.

Step 4: Reverse Positions

Students reverse positions and present each other's perspectives by first discussing the new presentation with their partner. It is important that the new positions are presented forcefully and persuasively; if possible, new facts, information, or evidence should be presented. The pro team gives the argument for the con position, and the con position is presented by the pro team.

Step 5: Synthesize and Integrate the Best Evidence into a Joint Position

Once each member of the team has participated in presenting both sides of the issue, the four group members drop their advocacy and synthesize in order to integrate what is known into a joint position on which both sides can agree. To do this, students will need to step back and revisit the question from a variety of perspectives. Students need to look at the different positions, summarize them, and then create a new unifying position—a synthesis. Taking the best ideas of both positions and making a general statement will require students to use higher-level thinking and social skills.

Step 6: Present the Group Synthesis

Synthesis statements can be shared in a number of ways. Students can present their positions to the class by having a single group member present that position. Students can be asked to describe the new position in a written paragraph or two, or students can be asked to share their new position in an outline or by using presentation software. Individual accountability can also be ensured by giving each student a test on the information that was embedded in each of the position packets.

Step 7: Group Processing of the Controversy and Participation of Members

The class has a discussion about the positive and negative aspects of the experience, what the most successful and least successful aspects of the group experience were, and how the synthesis statements captures the dilemma under study.

Summary of Steps in the Structured Academic Controversy Model

1. Students prepare their positions.
2. Students present and advocate their positions.
3. Open discussion and rebuttals.
4. Reverse positions.
5. Synthesize and integrate the best evidence into a joint position.
6. Present the group synthesis.
7. Group processing of the controversy and participation of members.

The academic controversy model is a sophisticated cooperative learning model that is grounded in what we know about how we learn and social psychology findings. Part of our work is to help students understand their own argument and the arguments of others. Providing an academic structure in which to examine yes and no positions and then synthesize these positions is an invaluable skill and one that requires careful and intentional design by the teacher. By examining the potential behaviors of teachers and students working within the controversy framework, you can consider what is needed to master the instructional moves of the model and identify what skills and knowledge you need before you can include the model in your professional toolbox. Remember that this is an advanced instructional model that will take time to learn. Table 10.3 will help you consider what the teacher and students need to do as you work on making the academic controversy model your own.

THE STUDENT TEAMS-ACHIEVEMENT DIVISION (STAD) MODEL

The student teams-achievement division (STAD) model was developed at Johns Hopkins University in the context of research on cooperative learning. STAD is a model used for meeting well-defined instructional objectives. Students study in four- or five-member learning teams that are representative of the characteristics of the class as a whole and are heterogeneous with respect to students' ability, race, gender, ethnicity, and so on. The team study typically follows a succinct presentation of the basic material and objectives by the teacher, often as a direct instruction lesson. The material to be learned centers on specific information (capitals of the major countries of Europe, data on the major rivers of Africa, spelling and grammar rules, basic mathematics, biological classification, properties of the planets in our solar system—anything in the curriculum grounded in single right answers that must be learned). Students study the material in whatever way makes the best sense to them, using whatever approach to study and learning they choose. They may take turns quizzing each other, discuss problems as a group, check online resources and other texts, and generally use whatever means they wish to master the material. The participants should also be clear that their task is to learn the concepts, not simply to fill out worksheets. The goal of every member of the group is to master the material and do whatever possible to help every member of the team to achieve the same goal.

Step 1: Present a New Concept

STAD is not a model to be used as the basis of all instruction but is designed for meeting well defined, lower-level instructional objectives. Because of the nature of the content for which STAD is appropriate, the presentation and guided practice phases of direct instruction are often used. The teacher plays the role of facilitator and coach—a resource whom the students can call on as needed—and a gradual release of responsibility is followed (see Chapter Three). In the example that follows, the objective is to teach students to apply four rules for the formation of plural nouns. The information may be presented as a mini-lecture, embedded within stories and paragraphs, or through a digital presentation.

1. Most nouns form their plural by simply adding *s* to the singular form:

girl, girls	tiger, tigers	toy, toys
shirt, shirts	angel, angels	willow, willows

2. Some nouns ending in *f* or *fe* form their plural by changing their ending to *ve* before adding *s*.

wife, wives	leaf, leaves
life, lives	self, selves

TABLE 10.3   Potential Teacher and Student Behaviors in the Academic Controversy Model

Step	Teacher	Student
1. Prepare positions.	• Identifies topic and learning objectives aligned with curriculum and standards • Gathers materials supporting yes/no positions that are appropriate for learners • Determines group composition • Reviews process • Scaffolds logical argument making • Monitors quality of student arguments	• Meets with same position partner and follows the process with that partner • Determines position argument • Organizes supporting evidence • Prepares position presentation • Reflects on quality of position statement
2. Present and advocate position.	• Facilitates process • Answers questions about content and process when necessary • Reminds students of purpose and procedures of this step • Monitors student compliance with model	• Presents position to opposing team with partner • Attends to opposing position • Notes similarities and differences with personal position
3. Conduct open discussion and rebuttals.	• Defines and/or reviews definition of rebuttals, counterarguments, clarifications, and extensions • Monitors rebuttals for accuracy and supporting inferences • Monitors student cooperative behaviors	• Advocates for position while noting weaknesses in other arguments • Provides evidence for argument • Refutes opposing argument • Asks opposing team for supporting evidence • Challenges opposing position and accepts opposing challenges respectfully
4. Reverse positions.	• Monitors student groups for content accuracy and cooperative behavior • Answers clarifying questions about content and process	• Discusses and prepares new position with partner, adding new facts and information if possible • Attends to new opposing argument and identifies newly presented information • Evaluates present arguments in terms of logic and supporting evidence
5. Summarize and generalize.	• Reviews synthesis process with students • Scaffolds students toward joint position that is feasible and logical • Provides appropriate feedback about content and behavior	• Summarizes different positions • Identifies the strongest aspects of each argument • Identifies aspects of arguments with which each side can agree • Prepares joint position with group • Evaluates position as to feasibility and logic • Prepares presentation
6. Present synthesis.	• Explains how synthesis statements will be presented (orally, in written form, posted on Internet, etc.) • Determines, shares with students, and administers individual accountability measure	• Attends to teacher explanations and directions • Presents joint position according to directions • Participates in individual accountability
7. Evaluate the process.	• Facilitates discussion of positive and negative aspects of controversy process • Asks students to support opinions with specific examples • Reflects on and shares observations of students during the controversy • Requests suggestions (and reasons for suggestions) for next controversy	• Articulates personal challenges and opportunities within controversy process with specific examples • Evaluates the process in terms of learning objectives and personal learning • Provides suggestions for future controversies

3. Nouns ending in *s*, *sh*, *ch*, or *x* form their plural by adding *es*.

fox, foxes	kiss, kisses
wish, wishes	church, churches

4. Nouns ending in *o* preceded by a vowel usually form their plural by adding *s*, but nouns ending in *o* preceded by a consonant usually form their plural by adding *es*.

radio, radios	rodeo, rodeos
zoo, zoos	zero, zeroes
hero, heroes	tomato, tomatoes
potato, potatoes	memento, mementoes,
ratio, ratios	or mementos

Step 2: Form Teams for Study and Practice

Divide students into heterogeneously grouped study teams. Each team should have one member from the high achievement, high average achievement, low average achievement, and low achievement groups. Teams should also be heterogeneous with respect to characteristics like race and gender. Once the study teams are formed, resources like worksheets and study guides are provided for team study. Participants know that their job is not complete until all team members are convinced that everyone fully understands the material being studied.

Step 3: Test Students on Newly Learned Materials

In the third step, individuals composing the teams are given quizzes to complete independently for individual scoring and team scoring. Individual scores are totaled for the team score, and teams are rewarded for improvement over past performance (for example, on pretests).

Step 4: Recognize Winning Teams

Possible means of student recognition include posting the names of top-scoring team members on the bulletin board, awarding certificates, and sending home notes to parents. Extra recess time, being first in lines, extra time on preferred tasks, or no weekend homework are other ways that academic accomplishments may be rewarded.

Summary of Steps in the Student Teams-Achievement Division Model

1. Present a new concept.
2. Form teams for study and practice.
3. Test students on newly learned materials.
4. Recognize winning teams.

The preceding list describes the process of using the student teams-achievement division model, but the detail in specific teacher and student behaviors is lacking. The competitive nature of the cooperative model makes it important to highlight the underlying cooperative structure so that students can see the strength of practicing with a team. By examining the potential behaviors of teachers and students working within the STAD framework, you can consider what is needed to master the model and include it in your professional toolbox. Table 10.4 is a guide to help you consider what student behaviors are needed for successful understanding of cooperative effort and individual metacognition, providing you with a roadmap for molding your teaching behaviors to students.

TABLE 10.4   Potential Teacher and Student Behaviors in the STAD Model

Step	Teacher	Student
1. Present new information.	• Determines lesson objectives and shares them appropriately with students • Presents new information that is situated within student prior knowledge • Responds to student questions • Monitors student understanding and behaviors during presentation	• Attends to presentation • Links new information to prior knowledge and experiences • Asks clarifying questions if necessary • Identifies personal challenges with new information
2. Form study and practice teams.	• Divides students into heterogeneous teams • Provides study and practice materials • Reminds students of the cooperative instruction criteria—(1) they interact with all group members, (2) they help each other learn materials, (3) they have team members help them learn materials, and (4) they practice pro-social skills • Monitors group practice for both content and on-task behaviors	• Works with assigned group • Reviews and asks clarifying questions about objectives, content, and materials • Uses provided materials appropriately • Asks for and provides help when needed • Identifies and evaluates team's attention to criteria
3. Test students.	• Designs and administers group and individual assessments • Provides feedback on assessments to teams • Scores assessments	• Takes assessments • Reflects on scores and personal learning
4. Recognize winning team.	• Identifies and recognizes winning team • Asks team to reflect on winning strategies • Discusses these strategies and others with class	• Recognizes winning team • Reflects on winning strategies • Thinks about what team did to help personal learning

Evaluating Learning in the Cooperative Learning Models

Groups are powerful and occur naturally in the classroom and in school hallways and playgrounds. In fact, groups are ubiquitous and influential and enhance achievement, relationships, psychological health, and social skills. It makes sense to incorporate group work into classroom instruction. Because instruction and assessments should be aligned and integrated, it makes sense to occasionally use groups to help with evaluation. And because time for providing feedback, grading tests, and developing evaluations is always at a premium, student help with evaluation tasks can be invaluable. Peer review and student grading can take place in cooperative groups and still be reliable and valid. The key is that the groups must be cooperative and adhere to the five basic elements of cooperative learning.

Teachers decide when cooperative learning is to be used, with what content, in what structure, and how the outcomes will be assessed. As the cooperative group works on the teacher-designed instructional task, students can provide immediate remediation and enrichment to each other as they work together. Practice in how to provide neutral feedback (timely, specific, and tied to instructional goals) can be provided to students. Individual accountability is essential for each group product and can be determined through the use of multiple-choice, matching, and essay test items and projects. But the group product should also be evaluated. Of course, evaluation and grading are not the same thing. When grading group projects, grades must be given based on individual student achievement (Brookhart, 2013).

Evaluation of the process can also be done through participation charting (see Richard Lander's Scored Group Discussion Guide, which can be found on the Internet.) Scored discussions allow students to earn points or grades for the demonstration of targeted positive behaviors (providing evidence for a position, listening attentively, etc.) in a discussion. Negative marks can be earned for interrupting, monopolizing the conversation, making personal criticisms (as opposed to criticizing a position), and for being distracting.

WEB RESOURCE

Scored Discussion Guide

Richard Lander's Scored Discussion Guide can be found at curriculum.org.

Rubrics, oral questioning, checkpoints, paper-and-pencil tasks, unit assessments, and papers can all be used to evaluate what students have learned in cooperative tasks. Students can be involved in establishing criteria and building a rubric for group products and for individual learning goals, and they can practice using the rubrics on draft or model products—guiding student behavior as they are developing their own work. The important rule of thumb with both individual and group assessments is that they should be aligned with the identified objectives of the lesson or unit. If the purpose of cooperative work is to assess both learning and process goals, there are other evaluation options—self-reported rubrics, reflections, and teacher observations can all be used.

Meeting Individual Needs with the Cooperative Learning Models

Cooperative group work easily translates into differentiation opportunities if the key elements of cooperative learning are in place. Cooperative learning goals and differentiation are both responsive teaching strategies. Because objectives are the key to all differentiation and cooperative learning decisions, once the *know, understand,* and *able to do* objectives are in place, the teacher can determine how best to help all students reach the goals. Differentiation can be achieved with the content or with the task. Jigsaws, for example, are a natural content-differentiation activity and can be organized by interest or need. Group tasks can also be determined by student learning profiles—different groups can be formed around intelligence preferences (practical, analytic, or creative tasks); student interests; or academic, social, or emotional skill needs. It is important to remember, however, that cooperative learning models have goals that go beyond academic achievement and that learning from others with a different constellation of characteristics is an important cooperative learning attribute. Each individual has a unique set of strengths and weaknesses, and cooperative groups can build on strengths and shore up weaknesses. To do this, teachers must know a great deal about their students.

A unit on the regions of the United States may contain achievement differentiation through questioning and interest differentiation through a jigsaw. Students can have the choice of researching the history of the different regions—Northeast,

Midwest, South, and West—and cooperative groups can be organized around these choices. Within the groups, students can also be assigned roles based on the teacher's understanding of the students. Students who are comfortable with text are assigned the role of summarizer, students who are more analytic may be assigned the role of researcher, creative students may organize the presentation to the jigsaw learning group, and so on. It is helpful to keep careful records so that students are not always assigned to the same role.

Benefits of the Cooperative Learning Models

In traditional classes, most of students' experiences with content are limited to listening and taking notes. In classrooms organized for cooperative learning, students listen, write, tell, paraphrase, read, assist others, and interact—they are actively engaged in promoting their own learning. When students work cooperatively, they process information by discussing subject matter with peers rather than acting as passive recipients of information. Because they are working in small groups, even reticent students tend to enter discussions and ask clarifying questions.

Many studies have shown that when correctly implemented, cooperative learning improves information acquisition and retention, higher-level thinking skills, interpersonal and communication skills, and self-confidence (Johnson, Johnson, & Stanne, 2000). Beyond the classroom, there are as-yet unimagined advantages to learning in groups. Most of the jobs that today's students will need to fill at graduation do not even exist today, and almost all of them will require skills of learning and working with others. Kevin Faughnan, director of IBM's Academic Initiative, has this to say to students in U.S. classrooms today: "Getting smart about your skills today, which must include a balance of deep technical skill and an interdisciplinary approach to business, will help you find that dream job tomorrow" (Faughnan, 2009). Ideas such as these point to the benefits of cooperative learning models. Hattie & Yates (2014) quote Phil Collins "in learning you will teach, and in teaching you will learn" (p. xvii). Our students can learn by helping others along with themselves.

ELEMENTARY GRADES LESSON

COOPERATIVE LEARNING Jigsaw: Clouds

OBJECTIVES	**Science Standard**
	Represent expected weather conditions in a graphical display.

Students Will Know

- The characteristics of five cloud types (stratus, cirrus, cumulus, cumulonimbus, and fog)
- The ways in which clouds form
- The types of weather associated with specific clouds

Students Will Understand That

- Clouds provide pleasure and information

Students Will Be Able To

- Summarize information about clouds
- Work together in a cooperative group
- Design and execute a pamphlet about a type of cloud

continued

ASSESSMENTS	• Students will develop a pamphlet describing an assigned cloud type that includes six pieces of information about the cloud, how the cloud is formed, and the types of weather associated with the cloud type. The pamphlet will be evaluated on whether the information is accurate.
	• Students will complete self-evaluations on their team work on this project, including specific contributions made to the project.
PROCEDURES	1. Introduce the jigsaw model. Tell the students the lesson's objectives, the composition of expert and learning groups, specific directions for the task, the resources available for completing the task, and the method for determining individual accountability.
	2. Assign students to expert and learning groups; review behavioral norms.
	3. Assemble expert groups and review the task.
	4. Give students the time to complete the task. Circulate to provide assistance and support to students.
	5. Remind students that they will be working in learning groups tomorrow, but will have time to review with their expert group at the beginning of the class. Students will take a short quiz about clouds after the learning group presentations and question/answer sessions are complete.

MIDDLE/SECONDARY GRADES LESSON

COOPERATIVE LEARNING Graffiti: Formal and Informal Speech

OBJECTIVES	**Common Core State Standards—English Language Arts L.9-10.3**
	Apply knowledge of language to understand how language functions in different contexts, to make effective choices for meaning or style, and to comprehend more fully when reading or listening.
	Students Will Know
	• When to use formal and informal expressions
	• Forms of formal and informal expressions
	Students Will Understand That
	• How we speak in different settings demonstrates our cultural awareness and language fluency
	Students Will Be Able To
	• Explain the difference between formal and informal speech
	• Distinguish between settings in which formal and informal speech is used
	• List a minimum of five phrases that might be used in an assigned setting
ASSESSMENT	Students will be randomly assigned to pictures and asked to create a brief dialogue (five exchanges) that would be likely in the context of the picture. Students will also write a description or narration of the episode.
PROCEDURES	1. Prepare questions or posters and assign groups.
	2. Introduce the graffiti model. Share the following directions with the class:
	• Once you are in your groups, look at your poster and note the location about which you will write (e.g., home/family, school/friends, shopping/business, hospital/patient, sporting event/friends).

- In your group, think about the setting and with whom you would interact. Are you expected to use formal or informal language when speaking with these people? Why? What kinds of phrases are you likely to use?
- On your poster board, write at least three phrases or expressions that you would commonly say or hear in the setting listed on the poster.
- Posters will be exchanged in a clockwise pattern and you will add three additional phrases.
- When your original poster returns, read all of the phrases and see if you notice patterns or inaccuracies. Is the language appropriate for the setting? What did you notice about the kinds of phrases that were shared? Summarize your findings and make generalizations that will be shared with the class.

3. Distribute posters and markers.
4. Give the groups time to answer questions. Allow three minutes for each poster; then provide five minutes for the final round.
5. Exchange posters in a clockwise pattern.
6. Summarize and make generalizations about the original poster.
7. Share information.
8. Discuss the process.

SUMMARY

The cooperative learning models discussed in this chapter each promote interdependence of learners, individual accountability, positive face-to-face interactions, and social skills that foster group processing. These are the key elements of all successful cooperative learning. The graffiti model allows pupils to work in groups to respond to prepared questions and to share answers that lead to generalizations. The jigsaw model places initial responsibility for learning on individuals in groups that become experts on a topic before splitting into separate groups composed of experts on the various topics. Once in these expert groups, students have the secondary responsibility to teach one another what they have learned as members of the initial groups. The academic controversy model asks students to research and prepare a position on a controversial issue, organize and persuasively present that position, refute the persuasive presentation given by peers on the opposite side of the issue, view the issue from multiple perspectives, and collectively create a position integrating the opposing views. The student teams-achievement division (STAD) model is initiated with a direct instruction lesson on a concept or skill to be studied cooperatively. Following the direct instruction lesson, typically delivered by the teacher, students form heterogeneous study teams for practice. They then test one another on the new material, and rewards are given for high scores, most improved from pretests, and highest group scores total. Winning teams are acknowledged in various ways.

EXTENSIONS

ACTIVITIES

1. Select a chapter from a content area textbook. Choose a specific topic from the chapter. List four or five important subtopics presented and develop expert question sheets for each subtopic. Select an appropriate instructional model that can be combined with jigsaw to provide an introduction to the chapter.
2. Brainstorm with students a list of jobs they might aspire to. Expect these to range from professional sports to military enlistment. Once you have compiled a list of a

dozen or so professions, ask students to list all the ways they might expect a person in that profession to engage in cooperative learning and work.

3. Interview two or three practicing teachers about their use of cooperative learning. Do they use cooperative models? If not, why? If so, what do they see as the benefits of cooperative learning? What problems have they encountered? What recommendations do they have for you as you implement cooperative learning in your classroom?

4. Research cooperative learning structures that can be used in your classroom in concert with many instructional strategies and models. These structures can include think-pair-share, round robin, three-part interviews, numbered heads, and corners. There are many online resources that have team building and academic activities in which students can begin to develop important group skills.

REFLECTIVE QUESTIONS

1. What do you anticipate will be the biggest threat to classroom management as you implement cooperative learning?

2. What long-term benefits do you feel are associated with cooperative learning? On what are you basing your hypothesis?

3. How will you teach the different levels of cooperative skills to your students? In what ways are cooperative skills related to academic skills?

Inquiry Models

TEACHING PROBLEM SOLVING THROUGH DISCOVERY AND QUESTIONING

 Chapter Objectives

You Will Know

- The basis for an inquiry approach to instruction
- The steps of the Suchman inquiry model
- The procedures in the WebQuest model
- The steps of the problem-based inquiry model
- How to evaluate learning in inquiry models
- How to meet individual needs with inquiry models
- Benefits of inquiry models

You Will Understand That

- Inquiry is a life skill

You Will Be Able To

- Identify inquiry models in K–12 classrooms
- Design, implement, and reflect on an inquiry lesson

In the Elementary Classroom

The students in Ms. Levy's fifth grade class are fascinated by butterflies. She decides to capitalize on this interest by asking students to help solve the problem of the declining population of monarch butterflies. She herself had recently enjoyed Barbara Kingsolver's novel *Flight Behavior*, a story woven around this decline, so she came to the lesson with great personal interest.

> **Ms. Levy:** Let's take our science period today to talk about butterflies. Can you remember the stages of the life cycle of a butterfly?
>
> **Micah:** Egg, caterpillar, chrysalis, and butterfly.
>
> **Ms. Levy:** Is there another word for caterpillar?
>
> **Ivy:** Larva.
>
> **Ms. Levy:** Do monarch butterflies have the same life cycle?
>
> **Micah:** Of course, it's a butterfly!

Ms. Levy continues to share information about the monarch butterfly—its migration and why the monarch butterfly population is declining. The presentation also includes ideas about stewardship and the ways in which we can help to protect the earth. She introduces the PBL Inquiry Chart and asks students to work together in small groups to identify questions and hypotheses to solve the monarch butterfly problem.

> **Ms. Levy:** What suggestions do you have for helping monarch butterflies?
>
> **Perla:** We think we should raise money and give it to the Wildlife Center.

> **Alex:** We want to tell the community about the butterflies.
>
> **Madison:** We want to help protect the places that the butterflies live.
>
> **Ms. Levy:** Where would you put these ideas on the inquiry chart?
>
> **Ivy:** We want to build a butterfly garden like they have at the middle school. My brother worked on it and told us all about it.

Ms. Levy writes down all of these ideas on a large inquiry chart at the front of the classroom.

> **Ms. Levy:** Over the next couple of days, you will decide on how we can best help the monarch butterfly. You will work on this problem in your inquiry groups. In the meantime, talk to your family and friends about our plans and see if they have any questions or recommendations. Remember that our goal is to help the monarch butterfly. Our inquiry chart will help keep our efforts organized. Each of you will also keep your own inquiry chart.
>
> **Perla:** I think we are going to need to get money to help the monarch butterfly no matter what we decide.
>
> **Ivy:** How will we get money?
>
> **Ms. Levy:** That will be part of our problem solving. Let's think about that tonight and discuss how we can focus our work tomorrow. ∎

In the Middle/Secondary Classroom

In her environmental science class, Ms. Whitaker introduces the unit on toxins using the inquiry process. She begins by asking the students whether they have heard the expression "mad as a hatter." One girl raises her hand and says that she remembers a character called the Mad Hatter in the movie *Alice in Wonderland*. Another says that the movie was made from a book by Lewis Carroll in which the Mad Hatter had a tea party. Another student recalls having read a book in which someone was described as being mad as a hatter. "I thought it meant the character was really angry about his hat," the student says.

Ms. Whitaker tells the class that she is going to present a problem for which they will try to find an acceptable solution. They will ask her questions that can be answered with a yes or no. She explains the rules for the inquiry procedure, which she has posted at the front of the room, and then assigns the students to small discussion groups. She encourages the students to ask questions as though they were actually doing research. She also gives them examples of the type of questions they might ask her, ranging from simple fact questions to more complex questions, such as "If I did _____, could I expect _____ to happen?" Because she will be the source of the information, she has prepared a fact sheet for her own use (see Table 11.1).

Ms. Whitaker reads aloud the following problem statement:

In England during the 18th and 19th centuries, a very large number of workers who made men's hats went "mad" and behaved as though they were insane. In fact, many of them were committed to the lunatic asylums of that time. Why did this group of people have such a high incidence of insanity, thus giving rise to the saying "mad as a hatter"?

She then asks the students to begin the questioning process.

Student: What about the people who made women's hats—did a lot of them go mad too?

Ms. Whitaker: No.

Student: Did men wear some particular kind of hat in those days?

Ms. Whitaker: Yes. Ask another question.

Student: Was it those stovepipe-looking hats like Abe Lincoln wore?

Ms. Whitaker: Be more specific.

Student: Those black hats with the high tops—they called them top hats, I think.

Ms. Whitaker: Yes, most were like that.

Student: Did it have something to do with what the hats were made of?

Ms. Whitaker: Yes.

Student: Can we discuss in our small groups?

Ms. Whitaker: Yes.

TABLE 11.1   Fact Sheet Used by Teacher in Responding to Questions

1. Working conditions in 19th-century England were bad, and many people developed work-related illnesses without realizing the cause.
2. Workplaces were not well ventilated, and few safety precautions were taken. Workers did not wear protective clothing.
3. Most men's hats were made from felt, which was processed from the underhair of beavers imported from Canada.
4. Mercury was one of the chemicals used in the manufacture of felt hats.
5. As we now know, mercury is highly poisonous and, if allowed to build up in a person's body, can cause an illness resembling insanity.
6. Today, this illness is named Minamata disease after a small factory town in Japan where thousands of people were poisoned after eating fish taken from a bay into which tons of mercury had been dumped by a local industry from 1932 to 1968.

Student: (After the small group discussion.) Didn't they also call those hats "beavers"?

Ms. Whitaker: Yes.

Student: Were they made out of beaver pelts?

Ms. Whitaker: Yes. Ask another question. You may keep asking questions as long as you get a positive response.

Student: If we went into one of those factories, could we see what was making the people go mad?

Ms. Whitaker: Be more specific, please.

Student: Well, could we see the workers being beaten, for instance?

Ms. Whitaker: No. Let's review what you have found already. Pay attention to those facts that you already know. (She points to the board, where a student has been summarizing the responses to their questions.)

Student: Did they have to treat the beaver pelts in some way?

Ms. Whitaker: Yes, they did.

Student: Did they use high heat, which made the people go crazy?

Ms. Whitaker: They may have used heat, but it was not the primary cause of the problem.

Student: Did they use a chemical?

Ms. Whitaker: Yes.

Student: Was it poisonous?

Ms. Whitaker: Yes.

Student: Did they inhale the fumes?

Ms. Whitaker: That might be a part of it. Do you wish to pose a hypothesis?

Student: The hatters were poisoned by handling a toxic substance used in the making of felt for the hats.

Ms. Whitaker: Good. Now, you all can ask questions to test this hypothesis or to make it more complete.

Student: Was it arsenic?

Ms. Whitaker: No.

Student: Is this poison still in use today?

Ms. Whitaker: Yes.

Student: Do they still use it to make hats?

Ms. Whitaker: Not to my knowledge.

Student: Do people know that this substance is poisonous?

Ms. Whitaker: Yes.

Student: Can we discuss in our small groups?

Ms. Whitaker: Certainly. Remember we are now testing the hypothesis that is written on the board.

Student: (After the small group discussions) Was the substance mercury?

Ms. Whitaker: Yes, it was. So now you can restate your hypothesis to make it more complete. (The students add the word *mercury*.)

The teacher asks the class to state some rules they could draw from the hypothesis they postulated. They say that (1) people may be harmed by a substance when they are unaware of its dangers, and (2) when they do not know all the facts, people may ridicule a group for being different.

The students also discuss how they arrived at their hypothesis and what steps were most helpful in deciding. They note that recording the data during the process was helpful. ■

The Basis for an Inquiry Approach to Instruction

Questions are often the driving force behind learning, as the interactions between teacher and students in this video illustrate.

Why are caterpillars fuzzy? What causes snakes to slither and bears to growl? Why do cats always land right side up? What happens to the lightning bug's light during the day? Is a baby fish afraid of the water? Why does the moon change shape every night? Who ever thought up the name *Brussels sprouts,* and why does ketchup stick in the bottle? Was the red color in the leaves hiding under the green? Is my skin brown because I was toasted? Will the rain melt the flowers?

Remember when the world was full of questions to ask rather than answers to learn? Somewhere on the way to adulthood, children inevitably get the idea that becoming a grown-up means leaving the world of questioning for the world of knowing. Schools institutionalize the move from questions to knowing, as success becomes measured by putting the right answer into the blank or circling the correct response. Questions in school seem to have one right answer, and questions for which there are no answers do not often arise. Lemov (2010) responds to this characteristic of school:

> Error followed by correction and instruction is the fundamental process of schooling. You get it wrong, and then you get it right. If getting it wrong and then getting it right is normal, teachers should normalize error and respond to both parts of this sequence as if they were totally and completely normal. After all, they are. (p. 221)

But beyond aid in getting the correct answer, scaffolding or reteaching is how we can help our students become real learners.

True wisdom might better be defined as the realization of how little one knows in contrast to how much one knows. Think of what one knows as encompassed by a circle. Now think of what one does not yet know as everything touching the circumference of that circle. The effect of learning, then, as the circle of knowing expands, is to touch on still more that one might come to know. The real excitement of learning is daring to challenge ignorance with unbridled curiosity. *Homo sapiens,* meaning quite literally "humankind who tastes of wisdom," have aptly named themselves. If knowing how to learn is more important than knowing all the answers (which is the mission of most school districts and state departments of education), then the greatest realization of a person's intellectual life must be that good questions are more important than right answers. Thus, the quality of the questions one can ask, rather than the correctness of the answers one can give, shows one's wisdom. Scientist and philosopher Lewis Thomas has described this intellectual journey:

> Science, especially twentieth-century science, has provided us with a glimpse of something we never really knew before, the revelation of human ignorance. We have been accustomed to the belief, from one century to another, that except for one or two mysteries, we more or less comprehend everything on earth. Every age, not just the eighteenth century, regarded itself as the Age of Reason, and we have never lacked for explanations of the world and its ways. Now, we are being brought up short. We do not understand much of anything, from the episode we rather dismissively (and, I think, defensively) choose to call the "big bang," all the way down to the particles in the atoms of a bacterial cell. We have a wilderness of mystery to make our way through in the centuries ahead. (Thomas, 1982, p. 2)

The idea of inquiry learning is based on the premise that there is indeed a "wilderness of mystery" to be explored in all fields and that every school subject represents a discipline of inquiry in which all students can participate, regardless of their past school achievement.

Too often children are taught in school as though the answers to all the important questions were in their textbooks. In reality, most of the problems faced by individuals have no easy answers. There are no reference books in which one can find the solution to life's perplexing problems. Although it is true that those who succeed in school are often those who can remember the "correct" answer, those who succeed in life are usually those who are willing to ask questions, be flexible, and search for solutions.

In today's world, it is more important to know how to frame questions than it is to have answers to questions one might not have asked.

> Content of disciplines is very important, but as a means to an end, not as an end in itself. The knowledge base for disciplines is constantly expanding and changing. No one can ever learn everything, but everyone can better develop their skills and nurture the inquiring attitudes necessary to continue the generation and examination of knowledge throughout their lives. For modern education, the skills and the ability to continue learning should be the most important outcomes. (Educational Broadcasting Company, 2004)

The inquiry model is grounded in the concept of problem-based learning. In problem-based learning, the teacher serves as subject matter expert, resource guide, and task group consultant, but not as information transmitter or sole source of knowledge. The major role of the teacher is to encourage student participation, provide appropriate information to keep students on track, assume the role of fellow learner, and avoid the all-too-common tendency to negative feedback. In addition, the teacher monitors student participation, inquiry, and learning and maintains the flow of the lesson. In all problem-based learning (PBL), the teacher serves as subject matter expert, resource guide, and task group consultant.

A Chinese proverb provides the most succinct basis for problem-based learning: "Tell me, I forget. Show me, I remember. Involve me, I understand." When students are involved in a search for the solution to an open-ended problem whose solution they are committed to finding, they learn and retain more than if the content were merely given to them in a lecture or text. Pay a visit to thirteen.org for a basic explanation of problem-based teaching and learning.

Here are some generalizations about PBL, points that can serve as guidelines for thinking about issues and approaches to the design of PBL opportunities for students. Although there are many possible formats for presenting PBL units, the following principles remain consistent:

- Hattie and Yates (2014) emphasize "the value of *worked examples* . . . as one effective and easy-to-apply means of providing necessary guidance to beginners." They continue by saying, "In many areas it is possible to show students fully worked examples, but then to introduce examples that are only partially completed" (p. 151). For example, in the study of principles of genetics, students might be shown a completed Punnett square to illustrate how a blue-eyed child might have a brown-eyed mother and a blue-eyed father. (You can review your understanding of the basics of genetics at scienceprimer.com. The blue-eyed child's mother with brown eyes must have had a recessive gene for blue eyes!) Following this, students can be given other problems of inheritance that they can solve together in groups. An Internet search for the topic of "Punnett square" will yield many examples to begin this problem-solving exercise. By beginning with a completed problem as an example, students can be asked to solve more complex inheritance puzzles together.

- In a PBL unit, the focus is often on ill-structured problems presented first and serving as the organizing center and context for learning.

Teaching from questions in the PBL approach gives the instruction more refined dimension and gives the students increased commitment to the outcome of their learning, as you can see in this video of a high school social studies class.

- The problem on which learning centers
  - Is ill-structured in nature
  - Is met as a messy situation
  - Often changes with the addition of new information
  - Is not solved easily or formulaically
  - Does not always result in a right answer
- In PBL lessons, students assume the role of problem solvers; teachers assume the role of tutors and coaches.
- In the teaching and learning process, information is shared, but knowledge is a personal construction of the learner.
- Thinking is fully articulated and held to strict benchmarks.
- Assessment is an authentic companion to the problem and process.
- The PBL unit is not necessarily interdisciplinary in nature, but it is always integrative. Ideas and skills from other disciplines may be used.

The idea of anchoring instruction in authentic problems is not especially new. It formed the basis of much of what John Dewey advocated at the beginning of the 20th century. It has been used in medical education for many years. Jerome Bruner described four benefits to be gained from the experience of learning through the process of discovering answers to problems (Bruner, 1961).

1. *An increase in intellectual potency.* Bruner hypothesizes that in the process of discovery, the learner learns how to problem solve and learns the fundamentals of "the task of learning." He suggests that learners who engage in discovering possible answers for themselves learn to recognize constraints in hypothesizing solutions, which reduces what he calls "potshotting," or stringing out random hypotheses, one after the other. These learners also learn to connect previously obtained information to new information and to develop persistence in sticking to a problem until it is satisfactorily resolved—an important noncognitive skill.

2. *The shift from extrinsic to intrinsic rewards.* Rather than striving for rewards gained primarily from giving back the right answer, students achieve rewards from solving problems. The learner develops an ability to delay gratification in seeking the solution to a problem rather than depending on the immediate reward of giving back to the teacher what was expected.

3. *Learning the heuristics of discovery.* Bruner points out that the process of inquiry involves learning how to pose a problem in such a form that it can be worked on and solved. He believes that only by practice and by being involved in the process of inquiry can one learn how best to go about solving problems. The more experienced the learner, the more the inquiry process can be generalized to other tasks and problems to be solved.

4. *Aid to memory processing.* The primary problem in the memory process is the retrieval of what is to be remembered, according to Bruner. He believes that material that is figured out by the learner is more readily available to memory than is information transmitted more directly to the learner. In addition, the learner who is a good problem solver also discovers techniques for remembering information. Hattie and Yates (2014) offer this insight in regard to teaching and learning:

> One of the major principles of learning is that a learner needs to make an *active response* to the source of learning. This idea runs through all theories of learning. . . . There is no such thing as passive learning, unless this term applies to learning to do nothing, in a manner akin to learned helplessness. (p. 47)

In the inquiry model, strategies used by scientists for solving problems are presented as a systematic mode for processing data and for learning to approach

Inquiry leads to understanding and ideally motivates action on the part of learners, as illustrated by this video of Darren Gutierrez, middle school science teacher, and his class.

puzzling situations in all fields of study. In teaching with any variety of the inquiry model, be aware that there are both convergent and divergent ways of conducting the process. Confronted with ill-structured and open-ended problems, students practice a heuristic process in learning to solve problems and deal with ambiguity such as that presented in everyday world problems.

Inquiry Model 1: The Suchman Inquiry Model

Richard Suchman, who believed that the intellectual strategies used by scientists could be taught to young learners, developed one widely accepted approach to inquiry-based instruction. The natural curiosity of children and adolescents can be trained and disciplined in procedures of inquiry. When students ask *why* out of genuine interest, they are likely to grasp the information and to retain it as their own understanding when they are provided with the tools to answer the question. They will also come to understand the value of working within a discipline—that is, of participating in the way of knowing and thinking that is at the core of every discipline (Suchman, 1962).

STEP 1: SELECT A PROBLEM AND CONDUCT RESEARCH

The Suchman model begins with the teacher's selecting a puzzling situation or problem that is genuinely interesting and stimulating to the learner—a discrepant event. It may be a scientific problem, such as why moisture sometimes accumulates on the outside of a glass or why sugar disappears in water. It may be a puzzling event, such as the mystery of the Lost Colony or of the Bermuda Triangle. It may be a scene from a play or a story that requires the students to formulate an outcome. It may be a problem requiring mathematical skills, a problem in health, or a situation to be resolved in the athletic program. Here are some examples of potential problems for students to begin the inquiry process. The answers are not provided. Most of the problems have several possible answers:

1. In 1692, there was a surge in the number of witches put to death, marking the worst outbreak of the persecution of witches in America. Strangely, this outbreak occurred 47 years following a previous epidemic of witch persecution. No one has been able to prove why this happened in 1692 in Essex County, Massachusetts, and Fairfield County, Connecticut, and not in other counties; however, there are several alternative explanations of this phenomenon, and one in particular that seems very plausible.
2. Jefferson Davis, the president of the Confederacy, was considered to be an outstanding leader and more capable than Abraham Lincoln at the beginning of the Civil War. Yet, by the end of the war, Davis was totally ineffectual. What might account for a leader becoming ineffectual?
3. Two plants growing in the classroom receive the same amount of water and are planted in the same soil, yet one of the plants is much larger than the other. The plants were replanted from seedlings that were exactly the same size. What might cause this difference in plant growth?
4. The slate formations found in some areas of the eastern United States are very similar to the slate found on the western side of Africa. What might account for such an unexpected similarity?

Any subject lends itself to inquiry. All that is required is a puzzling situation for which the students can search for a logical and reasonable solution. For many students, especially those accustomed to the process of inquiry, the best and most realistic problem situations are those for which there may be more than one answer or for which no final answers have been determined. Once a problem has been selected, the teacher completes the necessary research on the problem and prepares a data sheet for quick reference during the questioning periods. (See Table 11.1 for an example.) The teacher also determines how much information should be provided to the students at the beginning of the inquiry process and what additional information could be supplied if the class has difficulty.

STEP 2: INTRODUCE THE PROCESS AND PRESENT THE PROBLEM

Before beginning the inquiry lesson, the teacher explains the process to the class: In the Suchman model, the entire class can participate—both as a whole group and in small discussion groups. The teacher is the main source of data and will respond only to questions that can be answered with a yes or a no, thus placing the burden of framing the question on the learner. The teacher may choose to add additional information or guide the questioning, but the responsibility for hypothesizing must remain with the students; the teacher is in control of the process but not in control of the outcome or of student thinking. The students are presented with the following rules:

1. A student may ask a question only when called on.
2. Students may talk with one another only during times designated for small-group discussion and cooperative work.
3. Questions must be phrased so that the teacher can answer with a yes or no response. (The teacher may choose to give additional information if needed.)
4. A student may continue to ask questions as long as the questions are receiving a yes response from the teacher.

The teacher reads the problem aloud or distributes problem statement sheets to the class. If the students are nonreaders, the teacher provides them with the problem orally and uses pictures to illustrate the problem if possible. Students are encouraged to ask for explanations if a term is unclear.

STEP 3: GATHER DATA

In most classrooms, students ask questions that require the teacher to do the thinking. In this step of the model, each question must be asked as a tentative hypothesis that allows for the gathering of data. The student cannot ask, "What makes the plant lean toward the sun?" because that would require the teacher to give the information. Rather, the question must be phrased so that the teacher can respond with a yes or no answer: "Does the plant lean toward the sun because of a magnetic force?"

The teacher may decide to add information or expand on the problem at any time; it is important, however, to let students experience some frustration as they question. There is a temptation for the teacher to rephrase the question and say, "Is this what you mean?" It is better to say, "Can you restate that question?" or "Can you state the question more clearly?" or "Can you state the question so that I can answer it either yes or no?" A teacher might also say "Yes, that is a part of the answer, but why don't you consider (this additional piece of information) in light of what you already have discovered?" The data gathered through the questioning process should be recorded on the board or on data sheets kept by each student.

STEP 4: DEVELOP A HYPOTHESIS AND TEST IT

When a student poses a hypothetical question that seems to be an answer to the problem, the question is stated as a hypothesis and is written on the board in a special area reserved for this purpose. After a hypothesis has been identified, all data gathering relates directly to testing this one statement. In the problem regarding the different rates of plant growth, once the students have posed a hypothesis that the amount of light received by plants affected the rate of growth, all questions are now focused on either accepting or rejecting this idea.

Students may ask to meet in small groups to discuss the information and frame hypothetical questions they will ask the teacher. (Some teachers assign small discussion groups and leaders prior to instruction, thus saving time and reducing confusion.) Depending on the nature of the problem, the teacher directs the students to other sources of information or to actual laboratory experiments. Students are encouraged to ask hypothetical questions at this point, such as, "If both plants are positioned in the same part of the room, will their growth be the same?" As before, the teacher's response is either yes or no.

If the students reach a point where the hypothesis they have posed seems to be justified, then the class accepts the hypothesis as a solution and moves to the next step of the model. If the hypothesis is not acceptable and does not satisfy the class as plausible, it is rejected and the general data gathering begins again. Small-group discussions may be allowed at any point, but only with the teacher's permission. If students have difficulty converging on a hypothesis, support should be continued through the provision of additional information.

STEP 5: EXPLAIN THE HYPOTHESIS AND STATE THE RULES ASSOCIATED WITH IT

In this step, students are asked to explain the hypothesis accepted as a tentative solution and state the rules associated with it. In addition, they must determine how the hypothesis could be tested to see whether the rules can be generalized to other situations. Students will sometimes discover essential flaws in their hypothesis at this stage, forcing them to return to data gathering and experimentation.

In terms of the problem of plant growth and sunlight, for instance, the teacher would have the students, in their own words, state the rule based on their idea that the sun was the factor, such as, "Plants need sunlight to grow strong and healthy." The class would then discuss whether all plants need the same amount of sun and decide how to test for that generalization.

STEP 6: ANALYZE THE PROCESS

Students are asked to review the process they have just used to arrive at acceptance of the hypothesis. At this step, it is important that the students consider how they could have expedited the process. Students should analyze the types of questions they asked to see how they could have formed more effective questioning techniques. As students become more efficient in using the steps of inquiry, the teacher may relinquish some control and allow the students to set up their own inquiry processes.

STEP 7: EVALUATE

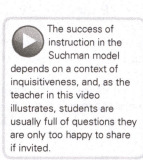

The success of instruction in the Suchman model depends on a context of inquisitiveness, and, as the teacher in this video illustrates, students are usually full of questions they are only too happy to share if invited.

Ask the students to locate and research their own puzzling situations. Conduct a survey of the class to select the most interesting problems. Test to determine whether the students understand the hypothesis and whether they can generalize the rules related to their explanation to other situations. For a hypothesis that has no "right" answer, ask the students to identify another viable hypothesis. The two contrasting hypotheses can then be the basis for a debate in the class.

SUMMARY OF STEPS IN THE SUCHMAN INQUIRY MODEL

1. *Select a problem and conduct research.* Choose a puzzling situation or an event that will entice the students to discover the answer, and then research the problem for possible solutions.

2. *Introduce the process and present the problem.* Carefully explain and post the rules that the students will follow for the inquiry. Present the puzzling situation to the students in writing and provide them with a means for recording data.

3. *Gather data.* Respond to questions posed by the students for the purpose of gathering and verifying data. Guide the students to ask questions more clearly or more completely, but avoid restating the questions for them. Encourage the students to call for a small-group discussion when they need to talk with one another, but do not permit students to talk to each other during the questioning periods. Reinforce the idea that this is a group process requiring the attention and participation of the entire class.

4. *Develop a hypothesis and test it.* When a student poses a hypothesis, stop the questioning and write the hypothesis on the board. The class decides to accept or reject it. Emphasize that at this stage the questioning is directed toward experimenting with one particular hypothesis. If other hypotheses are posed, write them on the board and tell the class that they will be explored later if the hypothesis under examination does not prove adequate. Encourage the students to consider all possible types of questions. For example, if they are focusing on an event, encourage them to consider conditions that might cause it. Questions are valuable tools at this point in the model. Students may be encouraged to do further research or to experiment in the laboratory as they try to accept, modify, or reject a particular hypothesis. The Suchman model can be used over a variety of time frames. In the case of gathering data from sources outside of the teacher, the model may be used over a number of classroom periods.

5. *Explain the hypothesis and state the rules associated with it.* Once a hypothesis or a possible answer has been verified by the students, lead them into an explanation and application of their hypothesis. Discuss the rules or effects of the hypothesis as well as the predictive value the explication may have for other events.

6. *Analyze the process.* Finally, discuss the inquiry process with the class. Examine how they arrived at an acceptable explanation of the problem and determine how the process could be improved. As the class gains confidence, they may assume more responsibility for the process.

7. *Evaluate.* Test to determine whether the students have understood the hypothesis derived from the process and determine whether they are able to generalize the rules to other situations. Also, encourage the students to look for other puzzling situations and to develop a habit of asking questions and looking for answers. Because this model is based on a scientific method, determine whether the students are solving problems more effectively with this technique.

The Suchman inquiry model, like many advanced instructional models, appears to be a simple application for classroom use; in actuality, the model supports very sophisticated teacher preparation and student thinking. The key to the success of this model is the selection of an engaging and appropriate problem with which students can grapple. By examining the potential behaviors of the teacher and students working within the model's framework, you can consider what is needed to identify a robust and intriguing problem that will support student interest through the steps of the model. A classroom climate of respect and belief in student learning is also required for successful implementation. Remember that this model will take time to master. Table 11.2 will help you consider the ways in which you can plan and implement a successful Suchman inquiry model for your students.

TABLE 11.2   Potential Teacher and Student Behaviors in the Suchman Inquiry Model

Step	Teacher	Student
1. Select problem and conduct research.	• Selects engaging problem aligned with standards and curriculum • Chooses problem with several possible answers • Prepares data sheet for quick reference during questioning period • Prepares scaffolds to be used in lesson	
2. Introduce process and present problem.	• Explains process to class • Highlights students' responsibilities for framing questions • Shares questioning rules • Assigns discussion groups • Provides data sheet	• Attends to process explanation • Asks clarifying questions about process if necessary • Makes sense of data sheet • Reflects on personal knowledge of data sheet information
3. Gather data.	• Manages information about problem in response to student questions • Responds to student questions only; does not rephrase • Records information uncovered by questioning	• Constructs yes/no questions that focus on tentative hypothesis • Works with peers to gather information from teacher through questioning • Records gathered information on data sheet • Reflects on what is known and what information still needs to be gathered
4. Develop and test hypotheses.	• Records student hypothesis • Focuses student questions on hypothesis • Directs students to additional information sources • Encourages increasingly sophisticated questions • Scaffolds students toward acceptable hypothesis through additional information and use of small-group discussions	• States hypothesis when ready • Constructs questions to test hypothesis • Considers what is know about problem • Attends to peers' questioning and extends and refines peer thinking • Asks to meet in small groups to caucus on problem solution • Continues to question teacher • Reaches consensus on hypothesis
5. Explain hypothesis and state associated rules.	• Asks for explanation of hypothesis • Challenges students to explain rules or principles that support the hypothesis • Prompts students to consider whether explanations can be generalized to other situations	• Provides explanations for hypothesis • Identifies rules/principles that support the hypothesis • Evaluates generalizability of hypothesis • Returns to data gathering if necessary • Reflects on personal difficulties with process
6. Analyze the process.	• Facilitates discussion of the Suchman process • Encourages reflection on process and hypothesis generation	• Reflects on student questions asked during process and how questions could be improved • Discusses process in small groups • Reflects on personal growth during process
7. Evaluate the process.	• Assigns and provides feedback on individual accountability measure • Encourages the use of questioning to solve problems • Surveys class for problems that arose in the process	• Takes accountability measure • Reflects on personal challenges during process • Responds to teacher feedback • Shares process challenges

An example of the Suchman approach is illustrated by the middle and secondary scenario at the beginning of this chapter.

Inquiry Model 2: The WebQuest Model

Once students are familiar with the basic steps of the inquiry model, they may be ready for a more adventurous, less teacher-directed experience. The WebQuest model is a special form of inquiry teaching that takes advantage of the Internet as a primary source of information. There is a wealth of resources related to this model, as a search of the Web on the topic of WebQuests will reveal. You do not need to be a webmaster yourself to design a unit in this format. Someone who has good technology skills—another teacher, administrator, or technology coordinator can help you.

WEB RESOURCE

Creating WebQuests

There is, fortunately, one great website that is built for beginners in WebQuest design. Bernie Dodge, inventor of the strategy, and his colleagues at San Diego State University are the major contributors to the site webquest.org, a treasure trove of resources and links to all the tools one could need in getting started with this approach.

Originated by Bernie Dodge of San Diego State University in 1995, WebQuests are thematic units that incorporate information available on the Internet with a variety of other resources. The WebQuest is presented to students as a web page built by the teacher, but sources for study include much more than the Web and incorporate textbook reading, supplemental reading and study in other sources (news sources, video, etc.), and independent activities related to the topic of the unit. In addition, the resources and activities embedded in a WebQuest include interviewing and reporting, observation and note taking, survey research, and many other real-life experiences that students may consider and write about.

WebQuests are focused on problems that students are to solve. The problem is generated from the topic under study in the classroom. The distinguishing feature of a WebQuest lies in the instructional approach it requires. WebQuests create open-ended learning opportunities for students and teachers. The underlying purpose of a WebQuest is to pose a problem for students to solve with the resources put at their disposal to help them learn the content required in the curriculum. The teacher is responsible for developing and arranging the materials and experiences. Thus, Web-Quests provide an organizational scheme for student-centered, teacher-facilitated learning.

STEP 1: THE TEACHER SELECTS A PROBLEM AND CONDUCTS PRELIMINARY RESEARCH

The WebQuest model begins with an open-ended problem or a puzzling situation that the students are to explore with websites and other resources put at their disposal. The problem is based in the content of the state standards and district curriculum, but its solution is based in the quest that the students will undertake. For example, if the curricular area is ecology, the problem might concern the reintroduction of wolves into Yellowstone Park. If the curricular area centers on basic operations in mathematics, the problem might concern when, where, how, and why humans invented numbers, including the question of whether the base-ten system is ideal. If the curricular area is Columbus's "discovery" of America, the issue of the WebQuest might be whether Europeans were justified in claiming the Western Hemisphere as their own.

The first step in creating the quest is for the teacher to search for appropriate web pages and other sources that address the issue or problem. Much of what is on the Internet may not be accessible for English language learners, young readers, or students with less prior knowledge or experience with the topic, so the bulk of the work for the teacher will be to find links that will be the most helpful to the students for whom the WebQuest is being created.

For the purpose of illustrating how a WebQuest is built, consider the topic *weather*. Weather is in the state standards and district curriculum at several grade levels, and it certainly encompasses many open-ended problems. We will look at the question, "What causes the weather to change, and would we want to change it if we could?"

The teacher's research is straightforward. Can a local meteorologist pay a visit and talk to the class? Does the school library have books on the topic of weather? What does the students' science textbook have to say on the topic? Is there any mention of weather in the students' other textbooks, such as the geography text? And, of course, what websites contain helpful information related to weather?

Answering the last question requires the use of a good search engine. The key is to word the search topic in a way that keeps the number of hits reasonable. Because even the narrowest search may yield a thousand or more sites, your job is to sift and sort them, listing in the completed WebQuest only those that will be the most useful to your students. Most search engines use ranking criteria that cause the most relevant sites to appear at the top of the list, typically based on the number of times the words in the search topic match words on a web page. Because the engines differ somewhat in the criteria they use to choose and list their findings, using at least two search engines is usually worth the time and effort.

STEP 2: PRESENT THE PROBLEM IN THE WEBQUEST UNIT

Templates are available that can be used to create and present a WebQuest to students. Go to the address WebQuest.org to view the many choices available to you, most of them free of charge. There are several online authoring systems that are available for designing WebQuests, as you will find. Any computer server in your school would be a good place to store and access your web page. Your school technical resources person or librarian can probably help you with this. Storing your web page on such a server will make your web page available to students from any computer at school or at home.

STEP 3: STUDENTS GATHER DATA AND INFORMATION TO SOLVE THE PROBLEM

In the WebQuest form of inquiry, the students, not the teacher, gather the information and solve the problem. It is the students' inquiry that drives the learning. Through the structure of the WebQuest, all the resources, online and otherwise, are listed in the context of an open-ended problem that the students must solve by working alone or in groups. The teacher's role is to answer technical and other questions and to guide the students to the tools they will need to create a unique and reasonable product. The variety of these products is practically limitless, as a quick survey of WebQuest examples will illustrate.

STEP 4: STUDENTS DEVELOP AND VERIFY THEIR SOLUTIONS

Responsibility for developing, testing, and verifying solutions to the problem rests with the students. As they present the products of their work to the rest of the class or to other groups, they will test their findings. Because a problem posed by a WebQuest is open ended, there is never a single solution, and every solution is subject to revision. The greatest value of WebQuests, as for other forms of inquiry, rests in their potential for teaching students that the nature of true scholarship lies in the search for plausible answers to the complex questions that humankind faces. WebQuests help students realize that researchers often do not understand much that must be learned, but they have the courage to face the "wilderness of mystery" that constitutes every discipline. Inquiry learning invites students to participate in this great adventure.

SUMMARY OF STEPS IN THE WEBQUEST MODEL OF INQUIRY

1. *The teacher selects a problem and conducts preliminary research.* In this first step, the teacher narrows the problem to ensure that the solutions students arrive at are grounded in online resources at an appropriate level of difficulty.

2. *Present the problem in the WebQuest unit.* The structure of this format, organized into sections that logically reflect the steps of problem solution, makes it easy for students to see what they are to do in attacking a particular problem.

3. *Students gather data and information to solve the problem.* Now the students work on their own as much as possible, with the teacher serving as technical adviser and answering questions related to the mechanics of the WebQuest. The result will be a product that lays out a logical solution.

4. *Students develop and verify their solutions.* By sharing the product of their WebQuest with other students and adults, students get feedback that helps them refine their answers to the complex questions surrounding the problem. There are likely many solutions to the problems posed by a WebQuest, and the final step of the process is to test the plausibility of the solution students have decided on.

The WebQuest inquiry model utilizes technology in supporting student inquiry skills. Teachers must be well versed in the use of technology to apply this model in the classroom. Planning for the model, as in most good instruction, takes time. By examining the potential behaviors of teachers and students working within the WebQuest framework, you can consider what is needed to make certain that the inherent benefits of the model are achieved. The technology is used in support of inquiry—not as an end in itself. Table 11.3 will help you consider what the teacher and students need to do to construct a positive WebQuest experience. The attention to authentic problem solving can be achieved in many ways in the classroom—mastering the intricacies of the WebQuest model is one of these approaches.

Inquiry Model 3: The Problem-Based Inquiry Model

In one sense, all three problem-centered inquiry models (Suchman inquiry, WebQuest, and problem-based inquiry) might be labeled "problem-based learning." The steps of the problem-based inquiry model and the use of a PBL inquiry chart set this particular model apart, however, as a distinct model of instruction.

TABLE 11.3   Potential Teacher and Student Behaviors in the WebQuest Model

Step	Teacher	Student
1. Select problem and conduct preliminary research.	• Identifies puzzling situation aligned with standards and curriculum • Evaluates the school's technological support for student web-based research • Searches for appropriate and aligned web pages for WebQuest and evaluates each page for student access • Identifies additional resources to support student knowledge • Builds class WebQuest page infrastructure	
2. Present the problem.	• Chooses a WebQuest template that shows problem-solving steps • Shows students how to access web pages • Reviews WebQuest process, including when partners or groups are appropriate • Answers students' questions about process and content	• Attends to teacher review of process • Asks content and process questions when necessary • Reflects on personal technology access and skills • Links prior knowledge and experiences to WebQuest demands
3. Gather data.	• Supports student data gathering • Answers student questions about content and process • Guides students to appropriate sources and tools • Monitors student activities and group behaviors	• Engages in WebQuest problem-solving process • Reflects on personal understanding of problem and process • Asks necessary questions about process and content • Works appropriately with peers to solve problem
4. Develop and verify solution.	• Facilitates sharing of WebQuests • Serves as resource guide • Requires that students test feasibility of solution • Provides feedback on content and process • Encourages accurate and substantive feedback from peers • Summarizes and synthesizes new information generated by WebQuest • Facilitates discussion of what was learned and how it was learned	• Develops, tests, and verifies problem solution • Presents solution to class • Receives and acts on feedback from teacher and peers • Revises solution, if necessary • Reflects on process and what was learned

The problem-based inquiry model will be described through the 5E Learning Cycle Model (Bybee, 2009). This instructional model has been used successfully in science classrooms for several decades and can readily be adapted to other content areas. The 5E is an instructional model for both units and individual lesson plans. The E's are *engagement, exploration, explanation, elaboration,* and *evaluation.*

STEP 1: ENGAGE WITH A PROBLEM

Every problem must be anchored in the prior knowledge of the student so that the links between what is known and what needs to be found become explicit. This phase should pique student curiosity through a single activity or series of short activities, presentations, or discussions prepared by the teacher. Teachers present an open-ended and researchable problem to students. Together students and the teacher explicate the problem and write questions to be answered in the PBL inquiry chart (Figure 11.1). The PBL inquiry chart organizes the data and provides a framework from which students can work in solving the problem under study. Students can use the chart to track hypotheses, data collection, and problem solutions.

Problem-based learning does not happen in a curricular vacuum. Look at the curriculum you have to teach and ask yourself what problem or problems are embedded in the objectives of the curriculum. One way to do this is to look at the standards to which you are teaching or the test you will hold students accountable to, asking yourself what problem this information solves. Try to define that problem in a way that ensures students will become engaged with the issues.

In teaching about the Constitution of the United States, the Bill of Rights is always a good source of problems to explore. Amendment One to the Constitution states, "Congress shall make no law respecting an establishment of religion, or prohibiting the free exercise thereof; or abridging the freedom of speech, or of the press, or the right of the people peaceably to assemble, and to petition the Government for a redress of grievances." This simple statement has given rise to countless problem questions! For example, does freedom of speech include the right to speak out against one's supervisors in the workplace or government, as did Edward Snowden in revealing National Security Agency strategies? Does the right to assembly mean that any group of students on school property can assemble for worship before or after classes are in session if they are not required to be elsewhere? How far can schools go in prohibiting student access to the Internet in the interest of protecting them from harm? One does not have to look far to see how many issues citizens face every day that relate to the 45 words of the simple statement that is the First Amendment.

Table 11.4 demonstrates the flexibility of the problem-based inquiry approach across discipline areas. The table lists several content areas, topics, and possible

FIGURE 11.1   PBL Inquiry Chart

Problem Statement	Question	Question	Question	New Question
Hypotheses				
Common Knowledge Sources				
Expert Knowledge Sources				
Observations				
Problem Solution				

STRATEGY ALERT   GENERATING AND TESTING HYPOTHESES

Generating and testing hypotheses are consistently used in inductive learning. Students should be provided opportunities to practice how to generate and test hypotheses about new knowledge. Hypothesis generation and testing create a powerful and engaging learning experience. Opportunities for students to generate and test hypotheses can be provided through specific instructional approaches such as concept attainment, cause-and-effect, and problem-centered models. Teachers can also support the explicit use of hypothesis generation by focusing on the different ways that students can provide support for a conclusion— through what they already know, from what experts can tell us, by looking at raw data or evidence, and through factual evidence gathered in reading and discussions. Generating and testing hypotheses have been shown to increase student metacognition and learning. ■

TABLE 11.4   Problem-Based Inquiry Model Problem Topics across the Curriculum

Content Area	Problem Area	Possible Question
Mathematics	Congruence and similarity	How do transformations affect a geometric shape?
Reading	Text structure	What text structure would best make a case for global warming to be presented in Congress?
Art	Representation	Did Vermeer use a mechanical device to achieve the photolike quality of his paintings?
Social studies	Government	How can organized groups of citizens encourage immigration reform?
Science	Environment	How can the world become less dependent on fossil fuels?

inquiry questions. Of course, teachers will need to determine the questions for an inquiry project based on the needs of the students in the class, the required curriculum, the available resources, and their own background knowledge. It is also possible to develop interdisciplinary problem-based units. Examples of problem-based inquiry units and lesson plans are readily available on the Internet.

STEP 2: EXPLORE THE PROBLEM WITH THE PBL INQUIRY CHART

The PBL inquiry chart (see Figure 11.1) is a way to scaffold the 5E instructional model by supporting the exploration of the problem under study. The chart asks students to identify a problem and to analyze the problem in terms of a series of sub-questions that can be purposefully explored. These sub-questions can be determined by the whole class or small groups by brainstorming exercises with teacher guidance.

Next, students draw on their prior knowledge to create hypotheses that might provide answers to the questions they have posed. At this point, the teacher provides activities for students that utilize the important concepts embedded in the problem statement. The teacher prompts students, makes suggestions, provides feedback and resources, and assesses understanding. The goal is to make certain that the important concepts and ideas are understood by the class. The students explore, design and plan data collection approaches, and reflect and evaluate. Students may conduct a preliminary investigation. The PBL inquiry chart helps keep track of the relevant information and the sources used as the problem is being researched.

STEP 3: EXPLAIN AND SHARE THE INFORMATION

Students can begin to formulate potential solutions to the problem. These are drawn in part from the chart, answers that are based on different resources. An important idea is to emphasize the fact that different resources may provide different answers to the same question. If several resources confirm one another in their answers, the student can be all the more certain that he or she is on the track of a justifiable solution to the problem. This is what constitutes critical inquiry and is the basis on which problem-based study rests.

Teachers can ask questions that require students to use the chart for explanations. The chart can also support student discussion as data collection and solutions are shared. Explanations must include specific references to sources, and the PBL inquiry chart allows students to track this information.

STEP 4: ELABORATE AND TAKE ACTION

During this step, students challenge each other to apply and elaborate their researched solutions to the real-world problem through the extension of knowledge and skills. It is in this step in the problem-based inquiry model that actions are decided. Depending on how local the problem is, students may decide on poster sessions they can hold in public places. A panel of experts in the problem may be invited to hear the solutions the students have conceived. Letters to the editor of the local or national press may be appropriate. A spot on a television station's community service timeslot or a presentation to a local governing authority may be the perfect venue for sharing. If the problem that students have spent so much time investigating and solving is real to them, they will want to take appropriate action with what they have created as solution to the problem.

In order to take action, students must apply new knowledge, make decisions, and resolve conflicts as the new project is designed and implemented. The teacher continues to ask questions, provide feedback, make suggestions, and evaluate the action that students present. The possibilities for this are limited only by the imagination, and students who are committed to solving real-world problems are usually very creative in deciding what actions to take.

STEP 5: EVALUATE THE PROCESS

Students assess the inquiry process, problem solutions, and their own knowledge and skills. The teacher may provide activities that evaluate mastery of subject knowledge reasoning and collaborative skills. This assessment can be administered in large groups, small groups, or individually. Students and teachers should also evaluate the inquiry process itself through group and individual debriefings, discussions, and surveys.

SUMMARY OF STEPS IN THE PROBLEM-BASED INQUIRY MODEL

1. *Engage with a problem.* Virtually every part of the curriculum provides an answer to some problem or another. Science and history in particular are composed of answers to problems, and there is always a problem at the core of literature.

The history of mathematics is replete with problems that demanded solutions. World languages present opportunities for the study of problems of communication and culture. Survey the standards that you are teaching to, asking yourself, "To what problem is this information the solution?"

2. *Explore the problem with the PBL inquiry chart.* This chart maps the questions surrounding the problem to sources that students can use in finding answers to the questions. The chart is an organizing tool to help students in their pursuit of problem identification, data collection, and problem solutions; it can be developed individually and in groups.

3. *Explain and share the information.* Different sources may provide at least slightly different answers to the questions or solutions to the problem. The PBL inquiry chart allows students to map different perspectives on the same questions.

4. *Elaborate and take action.* Students elaborate on the solutions through clarifying terms and conclusions and by justifying the problem solution that was identified. The solutions to the real-world problem at the heart of the inquiry can now be put into action—through letters to the editor, communication with state or Congressional representatives, presentations to relevant boards, or by whatever means the students' imaginations can conjure. The point is to take learning seriously enough to lead to action of some kind.

5. *Evaluate the process.* Student learning must be assessed. Were the objectives of the unit met? Was the PBL inquiry model helpful to students as they progressed toward the clearly stated objectives? The PBL inquiry model must be evaluated by attending to the specific content and processes students have learned.

The problem-based inquiry model highlights five E's—engagement, exploration, explanation, elaboration, and evaluation. These processes are key to students using an inquiry approach to learning important information and critical thinking and metacognitive skills. PBL inquiry charts are the foundation for this model. By examining the potential behaviors of teachers and students working within the model's framework, you can consider what is needed to master the instructional moves and include the problem-based inquiry model in your professional toolbox. Although an inquiry approach can be difficult to execute in the classroom, Table 11.5 allows you to consider what the teacher does and says and what we hope students will do and say while involved in worthwhile problem solving activities.

Evaluating Learning in the Inquiry Models

In some schools, there is enough technological support to allow each student to design a WebQuest as a culminating assessment. This assessment would allow students to follow their own interests in a structured and detailed manner. WebQuests can be designed by groups, individuals, or teachers. Teacher-designed WebQuests can serve as both instruction and assessments. WebQuests would need to be carefully evaluated with a rubric or checklist. The rubric or checklist should consider the visual appeal and ease of navigation of the quest; the efficacy, accuracy, and clarity of the task; and the quality of the resources.

Traditional paper-and-pencil tasks can also be incorporated in inquiry methods to help students and teachers see progress toward clearly stated objectives. Essays can be used to hold students individually accountable for their part in a group inquiry project. Multiple-choice and short-answer items can demonstrate foundational knowledge and scaffold students to higher-level thinking. For example, if students are working on an inquiry about swine flu, it would be a good idea to make certain that they understand the mechanisms of influenza and something about the transmission of the disease before attempting to solve the problem of the spread of this feared disease.

TABLE 11.5   Potential Teacher and Student Behaviors in the Problem-Based Inquiry Model

Step	Teacher	Student
1. Engage with problem.	• Prepares series of activities and presentation to capture student interest in problem • Presents open-ended, researchable problem aligned with standards and curriculum • Evaluates student interest in problem and makes adjustments if needed • Introduces PBL inquiry chart	• Attends to teacher presentations and assesses personal interest in problem • Shares interests and concerns with class • Asks content and procedural questions when necessary • Links prior knowledge and experiences to PBL task
2. Explore problem with PBL inquiry chart.	• Discusses problem and process highlighting role of PBL inquiry chart • Scaffolds process of developing problem analysis questions • Reminds students of hypothesis generation process • Designs, organizes, and implements instruction on integral concepts • Provides content resources and feedback • Monitors PBL inquiry chart development through observation and feedback • Checks on student understanding of content and process	• Clarifies researchable problem based on presentations and teacher input • Develops (with teacher and peers) problem analysis questions • Links the problem statement to prior knowledge and experiences • Creates hypotheses that might solve problem • Explores, designs, and plans data collection approaches • Reflects and evaluates problem exploration through inquiry chart
3. Explain and share information.	• Reminds students of role of resources and confirmatory and contradictory information and points of view • Facilitates discussion of data collection and possible solutions, requiring support from specific resources • Scaffolds student use of PBL inquiry chart • Requests that students note and share difficulties with content and process	• Formulates possible problem solutions through the PBL chart • Shares and supports data collection options and possible solutions • Makes specific references to PBL chart • Reflects on personal challenges with chart and the process of generating solutions
4. Elaborate and take action.	• Poses questions to students about decision making and action plans • Provides feedback and suggestions on logic and feasibility of plans • Supports student evaluation of action plan • Monitors student activities and understanding	• Applies and elaborates possible solutions • Supports solutions with gathered information and prior knowledge and experiences • Develops and evaluates action plans to help solve the problem • Resolves potential conflicts related to decisions about action plan
5. Evaluate the process.	• Designs and administers formative and summative assessments on content and process • Facilitates discussion of inquiry process • Requests ideas for improving the process in the future • Considers students' ideas	• Assesses process and action plans • Links new information and interests with prior knowledge and experiences • Participates in teacher-led assessments • Reflects on inquiry process and individual challenges and new learning • Provides suggestions for future PBL activities

Performance assessment can also be part of the inquiry instruction. Teachers can determine student success by looking at the number of and accuracy of questions and answers that are being explored and used to build understanding. Longer inquiry projects are performance tasks and can have a number of time checks so that the teacher can assess the probable success of the process and whether misconceptions are being constructed. Inquiry models offer a wealth of opportunity for assessment.

Meeting Individual Needs with the Inquiry Models

Inquiry is built on asking questions and finding solutions. Teachers who use inquiry instructional models have a great opportunity for responsive teaching by varying the content, process, and product of the tasks provided to students (Tomlinson & Imbeau, 2010). Questions and research topics can be based on individual interests and skills, allowing for personal discovery. These individual searches are motivating for students of all ages. Teachers can help students link personal searches and quests to prior knowledge and clearly stated objectives so that students are readily able to incorporate new information and skills. This guided teaching allows students to become more metacognitive and self-regulatory.

Teacher-selected problems for group inquiry allow for process variation and can also represent student interests and cultural background. And, when appropriate, individual students can be challenged to inquire about unfamiliar problems that help to extend and enrich their current knowledge. By guiding them to new resources and information individually and in groups, teachers can extend and enrich the knowledge that students bring to an important question. By understanding individual student needs, teachers will be able to make certain that there is a "good fit" between the kinds of inquiry used with students and the instructional goals.

Each inquiry requires data collection, and the data collection process allows for several differentiation approaches. For students who enjoy working with and talking to people, interviews and focus groups can be used. Library research will work well for those students who enjoy analytic tasks. Other students might prefer getting out into the real world to collect information and data that can be used to answer the questions being pursued. The important connection between differentiation and inquiry methods provides a multitude of differentiation opportunities. The key is to find ways to personalize the approach while helping all students learn.

Product differentiation—alternative tasks from which students might choose—also works well with inquiry models. Students can be given the opportunity to write a report or present a report orally or digitally. In some cases, students may be able to choose how the results of their inquiry will be presented.

Benefits of Inquiry Models

Inquiry models have many benefits; the most obvious is that the focus of learning is on questions rather than answers—on problems rather than solutions—which allows students to be actively engaged in learning. Too often, instruction is about answers to questions that the learner is not even aware of, let alone curious about or interested in. Inquiry models, by contrast, are organized to generate the interest that provides a place for solutions and answers, giving ownership of the learning to the learner and increasing metacognitive knowledge. Problems can also be identified that link to students' learning needs, interests, and readiness levels, scaffolding student understanding and developing all of the cognitive processes described in Bloom's taxonomy (Anderson & Krathwohl, 2001)—understanding, remembering, applying, analyzing, evaluating, and creating.

Inquiry models allow for the development of group skills as students work together to learn how to solve problems and learn new knowledge and skills. During these group pursuits, students learn to work with others, respect the contributions of others, and negotiate the steps in the problem-solving process.

Students may study different aspects of a problem, allowing for the differentiation of skills and knowledge. A major benefit of problem-centered inquiry is the flexibility afforded to teachers in adapting the curriculum to the needs of the students with whom they are working, fostering knowledge of how to learn.

Connections between Models

It is often possible to make interesting connections between models. One of the *know* objectives for the Elementary Grades Lesson is centered on the concept of stewardship. The word means "to watch over, to keep, or to guard." A *ward* in a hospital is a place where patients admitted for similar care are kept and watched over—for example, the "maternity ward." In modern usage, a steward is one who takes responsibility for the care of something entrusted to him. The stewards on an airplane take care of and are responsible for the passengers on board. The final syllable of the word *stewardship* now vaguely relates to a large floating vessel of a certain "shape." Things kept neat and orderly, cared for carefully are said to be "shipshape." But you can encourage students to think of various *-ship* words, all of which refer to a state of being, a condition, a quality: *friendship, companionship, fellowship, championship, ownership,* and *dealership* are but a few examples. Students will likely come up with a different list, all of which illustrate how *stewardship* bears its meaning.

You might also find it easy to meld the inquiry approach with elements of the more basic cause-and-effect model. The cause-and-effect relationships of toxicity in various environmental tragedies can be usefully analyzed with steps in the model. You can review one disastrous example, the infamous Love Canal tragedy, at the Environmental Protection Agency (EPA) website epa.gov. As you and your students fold the data you find here into the cause-and-effect steps, the connection to problem-centered thinking will become even clearer. Both the inquiry approach and the cause-and-effect model provide practice in critical thinking. Taken together, they illustrate any number of critical reading skills.

ELEMENTARY GRADES LESSON

PROBLEM-BASED INQUIRY: Monarch Butterflies and Stewardship

OBJECTIVES

Science Standard
Organisms survive and adapt in particular environments.

Common Core State Standards—English/Language Arts SL.5.1
Engage effectively in a range of collaborative discussions (one-on-one, in groups, and teacher-led) with diverse partners on *grade 5 topics and texts*, building on others' ideas and expressing their own clearly.

Students Will Know
- The definition of the word *stewardship*
- The reasons for the decline in the population of monarch butterflies
- Places and conditions in which monarch butterflies thrive
- How to use a PBL Inquiry Chart

continued

Students Will Understand That

- We are all responsible for protecting the earth

Students Will Be Able To

- Explore the question "How can we help the monarch butterfly repopulate?" and generate responses
- Translate responses into researchable questions
- Make a plan for collecting information and resources

ASSESSMENT

Students will complete an individual inquiry chart and participate in a discussion that explains and defends their proposed actions to help save the monarch butterfly.

PROCEDURES

1. Review the life cycle of a butterfly studied earlier.
2. Share information about the monarch butterfly, the long migration of the butterflies, and why the numbers of monarch butterflies are falling.
3. Use the PBL inquiry chart to organize the problem of the monarch butterfly with the students. Help students determine questions that need to be answered, resources to answer the questions, and possible hypotheses to help solve the problem.
4. Have students work in groups to design and plan data collection based on the PBL inquiry chart.
5. Students collect data and formulate potential solutions.
6. The teacher leads a discussion in which students explain and defend their findings and solutions.
7. Students share their possible solutions and a solution is agreed upon by the class as a whole. Students plan and implement the action that is designed to help solve the monarch butterfly problem.
8. Students evaluate the impact of the solution.

MIDDLE/SECONDARY GRADES LESSON

SUCHMAN INQUIRY: Toxins

OBJECTIVES

Science Standard
Analyze and present evidence to demonstrate cause and effect relationships in an ecosystem.

Common Core State Standards—English/Language Arts SL.1
Prepare for and participate effectively in a range of conversations and collaborations with diverse partners, building on others' ideas and expressing their own clearly and persuasively.

Students Will Know

- The definition of *toxin*
- Working conditions in 18th- and 19th-century England
- The puzzle of the mad hatters
- How felt hats were made

Students Will Understand That

- A structured inquiry approach can solve puzzling situations

Students Will Be Able To

- Work with the class to construct a reasonable hypothesis that explains why so many hatters behaved as though they were insane
- Write an essay to explain the puzzle of the mad hatters, the solution to the problem, and how this makes a difference in today's world

ASSESSMENT	Students will write an essay that includes (1) an explanation of the puzzle of the mad hatters, (2) the conclusions that were reached in the class discussion about this puzzle, and (3) how this puzzling situation can be related to something in the world today.
PROCEDURES	1. Review the information surrounding the case of the mad hatters in 18th- and 19th-century England. 2. Remind students of the Suchman inquiry model. Explain the roles of students and teacher. Review the rules:

2. (continued)
- Students may only ask a question when called on.
- Students may talk to each other only during small-group discussion times.
- Questions must be those that require only a yes/no answer.
- A student can continue to ask questions as long as a positive response is received from the teacher.

3. Students gather data by asking questions. Data should be recorded.
4. Students may ask to meet in small groups for discussion.
5. Students pose a hypothesis; the class determines the validity of the hypothesis.
6. Once the class accepts a hypothesis, students are asked to explain it and the rules associated with it.
7. Analyze the Suchman inquiry process with the class.

SUMMARY

The first inquiry model presented in this chapter is primarily based on the work of Richard Suchman. The model uses the steps employed in scientific inquiry to approach problems in general. The second inquiry model utilizes the Internet as a primary source of information as students solve problems through their own investigation. Problem-based learning characterizes all the models in this chapter, but the problem-based inquiry model itself is built around a structure called the PBL inquiry chart. The problem-based inquiry model, the third such model reviewed here, thus provides a structure for authentic student-generated questions. The inquiry approach in general is appropriate whenever the learning that is to take place requires students to be actively involved with information while challenging and questioning solutions to determine whether they are acceptable. Used in conjunction with other models in a design process, an inquiry model provides a stimulating option for solving problems and teaching thinking skills.

EXTENSIONS

ACTIVITIES

1. Look through a current textbook. Are there any inquiry opportunities for students in the text? Can any of the lessons suggested by the text or in your district's pacing guides be adapted for an inquiry lesson? Make a list of at least five possible inquiry lessons.

2. Explore the webquest.org website. There are sample WebQuests and information about setting up WebQuests. Complete one WebQuest and find two pre-made ones that might be useful in your classroom.

3. Read the local newspaper for a week and keep track of all of the possible problems that your students may be able to address in a Suchman inquiry lesson.

REFLECTIVE QUESTIONS

1. Which of the following would be appropriate problems for an inquiry lesson?
   a. What is the answer to 3×8?
   b. Who was president of the United States during the Civil War? Who was president of the Confederate States?
   c. The changes of the tides on earth seem to be related to earth's position relative to the moon. What factors might explain this relationship?
   d. We have learned how plants make food through photosynthesis. Here are pictures of certain plants that can grow in the dark. How are these plants able to survive?
   e. Shakespeare did not leave even a shred of paper that can be verified as his own writing, aside from a possible signature. Did he himself write all those plays and sonnets, or is it possible that someone else did the work and put Shakespeare's name on it to preserve his or her anonymity? Explore the Shakespeare mystery and search for clues others may have found to one of literature's most enduring questions.

12 The Synectics Model

DEVELOPING CREATIVE THINKING AND PROBLEM SOLVING

 Chapter Objectives

You Will Know

- The basis of the synectics model
- How to make the familiar strange
- How to make the strange familiar
- How to problem solve with the synectics excursion
- How to evaluate learning in the synectics model
- How to meet individual needs with the synectics model
- The benefits of the synectics model

You Will Understand That

- Metaphorical thinking supports student academic learning, problem solving, and creative thinking

You Will Be Able To

- Identify, design, and implement a synectics model lesson
- Explain how the synectics model can enhance the school curriculum across all disciplines

In the Elementary Classroom

In his fifth grade social studies class, Mr. Broome is about to begin a Making the Strange Familiar lesson. This variation of the synectics process involves leading students through the use of analogies to see relationships between new and unfamiliar material and information they already know. The class has been studying the Civil War for the last few days. Mr. Broome reads the picture book, *Cecil's Story* by George Ella Lyon, about the departure and return of a father during war, to the class. When he finishes reading the book, Mr. Broome asks the students to think about the similarities between the Civil War and an earthquake. He provides the following comparisons:

- In an earthquake, the land often splits apart. The North and South were one country, and then they split apart.
- In an earthquake, many people are killed by strong forces. In war, this is also true.
- Before an earthquake, there are warning tremors. Before the Civil War, there were some warning signs that trouble was coming.
- After an earthquake, there are usually aftershocks; following the Civil War there were many aftershocks.

Mr. Broome asks the students to identify any of the aftershocks from yesterday's discussion, and they contribute "Lincoln's assassination," "increase of racial prejudice," and "cotton became a less important crop."

Mr. Broome asks the students to imagine what it feels like to be an earthquake. He writes on the chalkboard each of the feelings the students mention. Mr. Broome also asks students to explain why an earthquake would feel these things. Students share the following list:

powerful	angry	like a leader
natural	predictable	strong
noisy	stressed	embarrassed
forceful	frightening	sad
omnipotent	energetic	violent
ashamed	apologetic	unstoppable

Mr. Broome continues and asks the students to find words on the list that fight with each other or don't fit well together—compressed conflicts. The compressed conflicts are also listed on the board: *angry* and *natural, sad* and *energetic, stressed* and *powerful, predictable* and *powerful,* and *omnipotent* and *ashamed.*

The class then discusses how the Civil War was both powerful and predictable or how the participants might feel both omnipotent and ashamed. Students may role play some of these ideas, write about the ideas, or find specific examples of the ideas in the readings or work they have done in class. After examining the ways that the Civil War was similar to an earthquake, Mr. Broome asks the class to consider how the Civil War and earthquakes differ. Daniel responds, "Earthquakes don't last as long."

Matt explains, "War is not a natural event the way an earthquake is." Other ideas that students share include that wars are caused by people and earthquakes are caused by shifting plates. Wars can be prevented; earthquakes cannot be prevented. When earthquakes are over, the government goes back to what it was. After a war, there are big changes, especially for those who lost.

Mr. Broome is pleased with the good thinking of his fifth grade class and asks the students to write a paragraph about the Civil War using some of the words and images discussed in class. This paragraph is a good formative assessment for Mr. Broome as he is refining the rest of the unit's lessons, but he still wants students to use metaphorical thinking to help them understand the reasons for and consequences of the Civil War. He asks the students to create their own analogies. "To what can you compare the Civil War that would help us learn about its impact? I would like you to think of as many things as you can to which you might compare the Civil War. Tomorrow, I'll ask you each to share your list with us all." ■

In the Middle/Secondary Classroom

Ms. Amato's seventh grade students have been studying the early colonists in New England, and they are about to begin a unit on the Salem witch trials. Ms. Amato asks the class to write a paragraph describing witches, a subject that they seem to know a lot about from a variety of media. Ms. Amato writes *Witches* on the board.

Ms. Amato: What words or phrases did you use to describe witches in your paragraph?

Rob: They are spooky.

Ms. Amato: Why do you think they are spooky?

Rob: Well, you never know what they are going to do, and people are afraid of them.

Ms. Amato: Would you say that they are unpredictable?

Rob: I suppose.

Jeremy: I think they are powerful because they can cast spells and make things change without our permission.

Emily: Some people believe that witches are evil and do the work of the devil.

Isabella: There are good witches too. Remember in *The Wizard of Oz,* it was a good witch who saved Dorothy. Witches are like people, some good, some bad.

Shenice: I wrote that witches are not real. They are based on superstition and ignorance.

Ayla: When I was little, I dressed up like a witch for Halloween. I wore a long, black dress and a pointed hat.

Jennell: Me too. I put a big wart on my nose with clay and used an old mop to make stringy hair.

Deven: And they fly around on broomsticks.

The class continues to share and Ms. Amato writes the words on the board.

spooky	unpredictable
powerful	cast spells
some good/some bad	imaginary
based on superstition	based on ignorance
wear funny clothes	fly on brooms
make brew	can disappear

Ms. Amato: This is quite a list of descriptors. Look at the list closely for a few minutes and then tell me what plant comes into your mind when you look at some of these words. I'll list the plants on the board.

Cindy: I think of a Venus flytrap because they can be beautiful but they trap insects.

Rob: How about an old oak tree in a swamp with moss hanging from the branches? I saw one like that on a trip, and it made me feel really spooky.

Isabella: How about a dead tree standing all alone in the field?

Emily: I think of those trees in the swamps with the big roots that grow down to the water.

Jeremy: Are you thinking of a cypress tree?

Emily: Yes. They seem to be powerful, but they are frightening, too. They aren't really evil, but they make me feel uncomfortable not knowing what is down below those roots.

Jennell: It makes me think of a weeping willow blowing in the wind. They always seem to be flying, and they make me feel sorry for them.

Deven: Well, I think of a potato. They usually have warts on them, and they have rough, ugly skin.

Ms. Amato: Look at the list and vote on which of the images you would like the class to pursue.

Venus flytrap plant	old oak tree with moss
weeping willow tree	cypress tree in swamp
potato	witch

A vote is taken.

Ms. Amato: It looks like the oak tree with moss has been selected. Close your eyes and imagine what it would be like to be a tree like this.

Matthew: It feels lonely. There aren't any other trees around that are like me. I am old and different.

Rob: It feels like I am being used, with all this moss hanging on me. I can't get away, and this moss is taking advantage of me.

Isabella: I feel strong and powerful. I am bigger than everyone else, and this moss needs me.

Jennell: I feel peaceful. It is very quiet here, and the wind is stirring in my branches.

Deven: I feel trapped because I can't get away. I just have to stay in this place forever.

Paul: I feel independent. There is no one around and I am free.

lonely	needed
old	trapped
powerful	independent
different	used
taken advantage of	strong
peaceful	free

Ms. Amato: Look at the list and pick out pairs of words that seem to fight each other and have very different meanings.

The students come up with a list of compressed conflicts.

powerful and trapped	lonely and peaceful
trapped and free	powerful and taken advantage of
needed and taken advantage of	trapped and independent [class choice]

Ms. Amato: Let's try an animal for the direct analogy step. What animal seems to be both trapped and independent?

Deven: A horse in a corral. It is trapped, but is still very independent in the way it moves around in the corral.

Shenice: It reminds me of an animal—a leopard—in one of those zoos where the animals seem to be free but they really can't get away.

Jennell: I've been at a zoo like that. You just walk around, and there aren't any cages or bars. The animals seem to be free, but you hope they really can't get away. There is always something that is stopping them. There was this beautiful big parrot that couldn't get away because its wings had been clipped.

Isabella: My grandmother has a parrot, and that bird is so independent. She won't talk or do anything unless she wants to, but she is still in that cage.

Paul: I saw a film about trapping otters. The animals caught in the trap always seemed to be independent and fierce, even when they were bleeding and in pain.

Emily: My cat is like that. Even though she has to stay in the apartment and she can only sit in the window and look out, she is still independent.

Ms. Amato: Let's select one of these that seems to be the best example of something that is both independent and trapped. [A vote is taken.] It will be the otter caught in the trap that we will examine further. Now, here is the question. Suppose you lived back in the day when witches were condemned and put to death. How is a person who has been condemned as a witch like an otter who is caught in a trap?

Isabella: They would probably be fighting for their lives and would try anything to escape.

Rob: Trapping animals is illegal in most places now because it is so cruel to the animals. We don't believe that people should be called witches anymore either.

Cindy: But there are people who want to be called witches today.

Paul: Sometimes people hunt and trap animals because they are beautiful. Sometimes people were jealous of the witches because they were different and people wanted to destroy them.

Shenice: People used to trap animals because they didn't know any better, and that was the way it was with witches. They just didn't know how wrong it was.

There are still people today that think that it is OK to trap animals just like there are still people who believe in witchcraft.

Ms. Amato: We have discussed lots of images of witches. Now, think of a new description of witchcraft and think about how some of these images might have angered the people of Salem. Write a paragraph explaining why the people of Salem might have been afraid of the accused witches. ∎

Basis for the Synectics Model

William Gordon (1961) is credited with the development of the process called *synectics,* which is derived from the Greek word *synecticos,* meaning "understanding together that which is apparently different." Synectics uses group interaction to create new insights through an "understanding together" process. As an instructional model, synectics is specifically designed to enhance creativity in problem solving by having students consciously develop analogies that allow for an emotional as well as a rational approach to solutions. Experts have a more refined conceptual framework than do novices. To help our students develop more expertise in a content area, we need to provide students opportunities to make their thinking public and to develop more intricate webs of knowledge and skills (National Research Council, 2000). Synectics allows students to share their prior knowledge and extend their understandings of the organized network of a specific discipline.

Synectics includes elements that have been highly associated with student achievement. Working with a group cooperatively allows for deeper understanding of the ideas and skills being studied. As students apply, listen, and explain new learning, they establish strong connections between new and prior knowledge. Working with peers can also engage students in learning activities. Group interaction increases pro-social behaviors that can help establish a positive classroom environment. But it is not only the group aspect of synectics that is important. The use of metaphors and analogies in this model provides a spotlight on identifying similarities and differences (Dean, Hubbell, Pitler, & Stone, 2012) between the elements under study. Metaphors help make direct connections between new and prior knowledge, and analogies help us to see commonalities among elements that seem quite dissimilar (Prince, 1970). Connection making is the key to learning; by explicitly identifying similarities and differences, we help students develop more sophisticated neural networks allowing for new and timely associations.

Most of the models in this text focus on the acquisition of academic content and skills. Synectics skills include the process of creative problem solving—useful in all disciplines. Creativity and problem solving have been listed as critically important skills for the 21st century (Trilling & Fadel, 2012). In fact, critical thinking, communication, collaboration, and creativity have been identified as important student outcomes. All of these skills are fostered with the synectics model.

Synectics has evolved over the years and has been used in both business and education. Synectics uses specific techniques that foster creative thinking and collaboration in all curriculum areas. The synectics process has led to inventions, innovations, and increased learning because of the structure it offers to teams and individual learners (Gordon, 1961). Through the use of comparisons, connections develop or grow stronger. Detached observation and analysis are essential to solving problems in all academic disciplines, but the ability to use empathy, imagination, and feelings is equally essential (Hilton, 2014). The flashes of insight and creativity that come from our nonrational thinking create unique and extraordinary images and solutions. It is this irrational part of our thinking that synectics is designed to enhance in order to deepen our learning (Dean et. al, 2012).

The synectics process works most effectively when the objective is for students to look at reality in a different way and experiment with possibilities. Inductive thinking, as well as seeing wholes in relation to parts, requires that students juxtapose seemingly disparate facts or occurrences. Because students seldom know how to do this, synectics instruction that helps them recognize relationships is very important. In fact, synectics is the ideal means to this end. Originally, synectics was used in developing new products for industry by having groups play with metaphors in solving problems. In making the familiar strange, our minds expand and accept creative insights and solutions. In making the strange familiar, the mind connects that which is already known to the unknown, thus facilitating the new learning.

Contrary to the common belief that creativity is an isolated activity that cannot really be understood or taught, Gordon (1961) maintains that it can be taught and that learners can understand how to use the process in solving problems or in developing more insight into descriptions and analyses. Using synectics in a group can actually enhance the creative process for many individuals. It provides an important kind of interaction: the sparking of ideas from one person to another.

Synectics also encourages interdisciplinary relationships. The act of combining seemingly unlike entities causes both students and teachers to search for relationships. How are volcanic eruptions and civil wars alike? Frost's poetry and Euclid's geometry? Paragraphs and biological classification? Grammar and diplomatic protocol? Maps and story plots? This ability to hold two very different concepts together in the mind has been described as Janusian thinking, after the Roman god with two faces, Janus. Janusian thinking consists of actively conceiving two or more opposite or antithetical concepts, ideas, or images simultaneously: as existing side by side, as equally operative or equally true, or as both. In apparent defiance of logic or matters of physical impossibility, the creative person joins two or more opposites or antitheses—a formulation that leads to interrelated concepts, images, and creations (Rothenberg, 1979).

The ultimate goal of synectics is to find practical and realistic solutions to problems and more effective and powerful ways of communicating ideas. Yet the means used to achieve these goals is unique to the process. By insisting on the involvement of the irrational and emotional part of the brain before engaging the rational and the analytical, synectics seeks to open new dimensions of thought and new possibilities for problem solving.

There are three versions of synectics presented in this chapter. The first helps students see new patterns and relationships from previously learned knowledge and understandings. The second helps make new knowledge more meaningful by bridging new and familiar information. And the third approach to synectics uses analogies and metaphors to solve problems.

Making the Familiar Strange

In this version of the model, students are encouraged to see the ordinary and the familiar in a new and different way. Through this process, they can often see unexpected possibilities in what they may have thought to be routine and predictable. This is a good model for helping students look at familiar content in a new way so that information can be extended and new conceptual schema built.

STEP 1: DESCRIBE THE TOPIC

The teacher begins by asking students to describe a topic with which they are familiar (e.g., a character of fiction, a concept, or an object), either in small-group discussions or by individually writing a paragraph. In the case of young children or students who cannot write, discuss the subject with them and write down their descriptive words and phrases. Or have them draw a picture or act out their interpretation of the subject. Use this step to frame an initial description of the topic.

When the students have completed their writing or discussion, ask them to share the words they have used to describe the topic. Write them on the board or on large sheets of paper. List the words or phrases without evaluating them; all student contributions are welcome.

STEP 2: CREATE DIRECT ANALOGIES

In the second phase, the students form a direct analogy between the descriptive words on the board from step 1 and words from an apparently unrelated category—helping to make the familiar strange. For instance, the teacher may ask them to examine the list and name a machine that reminds them of as many of those words as possible. Plants, foods, flowers, and animals are other possible categories.

Direct analogies are direct comparisons between two objects, ideas, or concepts. For instance, how is a classroom like an anthill? How are the veins of our bodies like a plumbing system? With practice, students can increase the strangeness or abstraction of their similes.

Add each student's contribution to the board and encourage each person to explain why he or she chose a particular analogy. When the teacher feels that everyone has had an opportunity to participate and the class is ready, the students vote on one particular analogy that they would like to pursue in the next step of the synectics model.

In one class, students produced the following initial list of descriptive words while exploring the word *math*:

difficult	obscure
sometimes hard, sometimes easy	necessary
frightening	a key
rewarding	a mystery

When asked to name a machine that these words reminded them of, they listed the following:

- Cars, because they are necessary, but they are also frightening
- Pianos, because they have keys but they can be obscure and difficult
- A dentist's drill, because it is frightening but necessary

STEP 3: DESCRIBE PERSONAL ANALOGIES

In the third phase, learners are asked to view reality from the perspective of the metaphorical object that they just selected. After giving students a short time to think, ask them to tell you how it feels to be this object. List their reactions on the board. Encourage each person to explain why he or she had a particular feeling. It takes older learners more time to accept this step in the model, but once they do, the response can be exhilarating. For the preceding list of machines, a teacher may ask, "What does it feel like to be a piano?"

A group of teachers participating in a synectics lesson used student behavior in the lunchroom as their subject. The teachers compared the children to a swarm of bees; when asked to consider what it would feel like to be a bee inside a swarm, they expressed the following perceptions:

- *Helpless.* "I have to do what the others are doing."
- *Powerful.* "I am the queen and I can make the others follow me."
- *Frightened.* "I don't know what will happen next."

- *Secure*. "I don't have to make decisions for myself."
- *Dangerous*. "I can harm people with my stinger."
- *Carefree*. "I can fly, and I don't have to make decisions."
- *Armed*. "I have my stinger."
- *Imprisoned*. "I have to follow the swarm, and I am inside, and I can't escape."
- *Vulnerable*. "I can be swatted if I get away from the group."
- *Independent*. "I can fly away from trouble."

A group of third grade students described how it felt to be a rose blooming on a fence:

- "It feels like I'm safe because I have thorns all around me."
- "I feel fragile because I can't bloom very long and the heat makes me wilted."
- "I am beautiful and admired: People come by and see how nice I look."

STEP 4: IDENTIFY COMPRESSED CONFLICTS

The fourth step is the most exciting and important step in this version of the model. Ask the students to examine the list of descriptive feelings they created in the previous step and to put together pairs of words that seem to fight each other—compressed conflicts. For instance, our example of the teachers comparing the children to a swarm of bees might produce the following list:

- Frightened and secure
- Helpless and powerful
- Armed and vulnerable
- Carefree and frightened
- Independent and imprisoned
- Armed and carefree

These are all combinations of words that seem to be in conflict, yet each pair is in metaphoric tension. The conflict between such juxtaposed words causes a tension that is felt as each pair of disparate ideas is considered. This incompatibility invites the student to ignore the literal meaning of each word and to attend more closely to the abstract or figurative connections between the pair. Take all suggestions, and encourage the students to explain why they think the words fight each other. Then have the students vote once again on which combination of words contains the best compressed conflict.

STEP 5: CREATE A NEW DIRECT ANALOGY

Using the compressed conflict chosen by the class, ask the students to create another direct analogy. For instance, if the combination chosen were *independent and imprisoned*, ask the students to describe an animal that is both independent and imprisoned. Some possible analogies would be:

- A tiger in a cage
- A human being in society
- A powerful dog on a leash
- An astronaut in a space shuttle

Then, once again, have the students vote on the best direct analogy.

Another category for the compressed conflict could be that of food: Hot sauce in a bottle or seeds inside an orange are foods that are both independent and imprisoned.

The more experience teachers and students have with the model, the more categories they will be able to use with confidence.

STEP 6: REEXAMINE THE ORIGINAL TOPIC

In this step, return to the last direct analogy chosen by the class and compare it to the original topic. For instance, if the last analogy chosen were "a dog on a leash" and you had begun the process with a character in a novel, you would ask the class to describe the characteristics of the leashed animal and then to consider the character in terms of those descriptors.

No mention is made of the original subject until this step. The purpose is to get away from the original topic, step by step, and then to return with all the rich imagery that has been developed during the process. An important part of this step is that each student hears the thoughts and relationships expressed by the others.

Asking the students to describe the original topic in writing again gives them the opportunity to use any of the images that were generated during the exercise, not just those of the last analogy. This works particularly well with older learners and with students who are experienced in working with this model. The list of analogies provides the students with a rich resource of words and images.

SUMMARY OF STEPS IN MAKING THE FAMILIAR STRANGE

1. *Describe the topic.* Select a subject to explore with the class. It can be from any discipline: a character from a novel that has been read; a concept such as freedom or justice; a problem, such as behavior on the school bus; or a technique, such as diving. Ask students to describe the topic. The descriptive words or phrases are written on the board.

2. *Create direct analogies.* Select a category, such as machine, plant, or food. Ask the students to examine the list of words generated in step 1 and describe how those words are like an item in the chosen category. Ask the students to explain the reasons for their choices.

3. *Describe personal analogies.* Have the students select one of the direct analogies and create personal analogies. Ask the students to become the object and describe how it feels and works. Write down the words used by the students to describe their feelings.

4. *Identify compressed conflicts.* Direct the students in creating a series of compressed conflicts using the words from the personal analogy stage. Ask the class to pair words that seem to conflict or fight with each other and that seem charged with tension.

5. *Create a new direct analogy.* For one of the pairs of words from the compressed conflict step, ask the students to create another direct analogy by selecting an object (animal, machine, fruit, or the like) that is described by the paired words.

6. *Reexamine the original topic.* Return to the original idea or task so that the students may produce a product or description that uses the ideas generated. They may concentrate on the final analogy or they may use ideas from the total experience.

The synectics models are complex and intricate and place heavy cognitive demands on both the teacher and students. These models also allow for creative thinking and problem solving and support new ways to engage students' efforts and critical thinking. The first variation of the synectic model, Making the Familiar Strange, is the least complicated to execute in the classroom, but it requires the teacher to have a good facility with creating and engaging students to create different kinds of analogies. Table 12.1 details the possible implementation steps and associated student responses

TABLE 12.1   Potential Teacher and Student Behaviors in Making the Familiar Strange

Step	Teacher	Student
1. Describe the topic.	• Defines *synectics* and describes process of making the familiar strange • Elicits descriptions of topic from students (individually or in groups) • Lists words from shared descriptions by students	• Asks clarifying questions about process if necessary • Constructs descriptions of assigned topic • Shares words from descriptions with class
2. Create direct analogies.	• Reviews definition of *direct analogy* • Provides a category as basis for direct analogy • Lists all direct analogies shared by students • Conducts vote for analogy to be pursued	• Reviews understanding of direct analogy • Constructs one or more analogies by choosing a word from the projected list and making a comparison to the assigned category • Attends to the contribution of peers • Participates in vote
3. Describe personal analogies.	• Focuses student attention on winning analogy • Asks students to share how it feels to be the object in the analogy—to "become" the analogy • Lists student-generated reactions • Asks students to explain shared reactions	• Considers winning analogy • Constructs personal analogies and shares analogies with class • Shares reasons for personal analogies
4. Identify compressed conflicts.	• Asks students to consider list from step 3 • Shares definition of *compressed conflicts* • Asks students to find compressed conflicts in list and share with class • Asks students to explain reasoning behind shared compressed conflict • Conducts vote to determine the conflict to be pursued	• Reviews list from step 3 • Asks clarifying questions if necessary • Creates compressed conflicts • Shares compressed conflicts with class • Explains reasoning behind the compressed conflict • Participates in vote to identify the conflict to be pursued
5. Create new analogy.	• Asks students to create a new direct analogy using the winning compressed conflict and an assigned category • Requests student explanations for the shared direct analogy • Conducts vote for the analogy to be pursued	• Constructs new direct analogy following teacher specifications • Asks process questions if necessary • Shares reasoning behind shared direct analogies with class • Participates in vote
6. Reexamine original topic.	• Directs students to "winning" analogy in step 5 • Engages students in comparing the direct analogy to the topic that began the synectics process • Asks students to make comparisons in writing, suggesting they refer to words and images from previous steps in the process	• Considers the "winning" direct analogy from previous step • Constructs new direct analogy following teacher specifications • Uses words and images from previous steps in making comparisons and new analogies

during this variation of a synectics lesson. By examining the potential behaviors of teachers and students working within the synectics framework, you can consider what is needed to master the instructional moves of the model and identify what skills and knowledge you need before you can include the model in your professional toolbox. Remember that this is an advanced instructional model that will take time to learn. This should not stop you from trying out this model with your students and reflecting on the challenges and opportunities it provides in your classroom.

Making the Strange Familiar

In this variation of the synectics model, the teacher leads the students through the use of analogies to see relationships between new and unfamiliar material and information they already know.

STEP 1: PROVIDE INFORMATION

The teacher selects the new material to be learned, perhaps the study of reptiles, adjectives, fractions, or the periodic table. The teacher provides factual information for the topic.

STEP 2: PRESENT THE ANALOGY

If the new subject is multiplication, the teacher might present the analogy by listing the similarities between multiplication and a factory.

- In a factory, the same objects are made over and over again. In multiplication, the same number is added over and over again.
- In a factory, it is important to keep track of the numbers of things that are made. In multiplication, it is important to keep track of how many times you add a number.
- In a factory, there are machines to help the people make things. In multiplication, we can use manipulatives to help us find the answer to multiplication problems.
- In a factory, there is a boss who tells the workers what to do. In multiplication, the teacher tells us what problems to do.

STEP 3: USE PERSONAL ANALOGIES TO CREATE COMPRESSED CONFLICTS

The teacher asks the students to imagine what it feels like to be a factory. The teacher writes these feelings on the board, and the students are asked to pair these words to create compressed conflicts. One pair is selected for further exploration. For instance, the students might select *busy* and *lonely* or *productive* and *tired* as their compressed conflict.

STEP 4: COMPARE THE COMPRESSED CONFLICT WITH THE SUBJECT

The class then discusses how multiplication is both productive and tired or busy and lonely. The teacher can ask students to explain how they feel on each side of the conflict.

STEP 5: IDENTIFY DIFFERENCES

Students explain where the analogy does not fit. The students might recognize that factories are buildings and multiplication is something we do. Factories are filled with people, and multiplication is filled with numbers. They may also notice that factories can close, but multiplication will always be around.

It will be useful at this point in the lesson to interject a mini-lesson on the word *multiply*. Drawing on the vocabulary acquisition model, the teacher can ask the students to break the word into its meaningful parts and think of other words that contain one of these parts. Consulting a good dictionary projected onto a SmartBoard or screen, the teacher and students can examine the word in some detail. They will find that the *multi* part of the word bears the meaning "many, or more than one," as in *multimillionaire* or *multilevel*. The *ply* part of the word means "fold" or "layer," as in *plywood* or *pliable*, meaning "easily bent or folded." Interestingly, this family of words includes *pliers*, the everyday tool made of two parts. This brief discussion should lead students to an understanding of *multiply* as meaning "to increase in number by multiples." Weeds *multiply* in every garden, as do stray cats in every city.

STEP 6: REEXAMINE THE ORIGINAL SUBJECT

The teacher asks students to discuss or write about the original subject (e.g., multiplication) using images and ideas that were discussed in the lesson.

STEP 7: CREATE NEW DIRECT ANALOGIES

The students are encouraged to create their own analogies for the original subject. The teacher instructs them to select analogies that are as far removed as possible from the subject. For instance, the idea of a calculator is quite close to multiplication. However, a track race seems very dissimilar and might therefore create some interesting comparisons.

SUMMARY OF STEPS IN MAKING THE STRANGE FAMILIAR

1. *Provide information.* Students must understand basic facts and information related to the subject to be explored.

2. *Present the analogy.* Have a prepared analogy involving a subject that will be familiar to the students.

3. *Use personal analogies to create compressed conflicts.* Have students describe how it feels to become the subject; then have them create compressed conflicts.

4. *Compare the compressed conflict with the subject.* The students select one compressed conflict and then compare it to the original subject.

5. *Identify differences.* Students discuss the differences between the original subject and the compressed conflict.

6. *Reexamine the original subject.* Ask the students to write about or to discuss the original subject using the ideas, words, and images in the exercise.

7. *Create new direct analogies.* Encourage the students to create new analogies different from the initial one.

The Making the Strange Familiar version of the synectics model helps students take some new ideas and connect them with previously held ideas. The model's steps help students move away from the topic and the teacher's presented direct analogies through the creation of personal analogies and the identification of compressed conflicts. Playing with these ideas through analogies supports students in making sense of new ideas through creative connections. Table 12.2 will support your efforts in comprehending the purpose and implementation of this variation of the model.

TABLE 12.2 Potential Teacher and Student Behaviors in Making the Strange Familiar

Step	Teacher	Student
1. Provide information.	• Defines *synectics* and discusses process of making the strange familiar • Selects topic aligned with standards and objectives • Provides factual information on topic	• Connects previous experiences and prior knowledge to assigned topic • Attends to teacher presentations
2. Present the analogy.	• Constructs and presents direct analogy between topic and pre-decided category	• Follows and engages in teacher presentation • Asks clarifying questions about content and process when necessary
3. Use personal analogy to create compressed conflicts.	• Defines and provides an example of personal analogy • Elicits personal analogies from students about topic explored in previous step • Lists feelings shared by students • Asks students to explain shared feelings • Asks students to create compressed conflicts from list of shared feelings	• Restates definition of personal analogy • Constructs personal analogies on provided topic • Explains feelings shared in personal analogies • Creates compressed conflicts and shares with peers • Notes any difficulties with process
4. Compare the compressed conflict with the topic or subject.	• Asks students to choose one compressed conflict and compare it to original subject • Clarifies and summarizes process • Monitors student understanding of content and process • Scaffolds comparison making	• Asks clarifying questions if necessary • Chooses one compressed conflict • Links process to what is known about topic with which the class is working • Compares compressed conflict with subject under study • Notes difficulties with task
5. Identify differences.	• Models the identification of differences between the compressed conflict and the original topic • Monitors student understanding of content and process • Continues scaffolding process	• Asks clarifying questions if necessary • Links process to what is known about original topic • Identifies differences between the compressed conflict and the original topic
6. Reexamine original topic.	• Constructs and facilitates discussion or writing task about the original topic • Encourages students to use images and ideas discussed in previous steps	• Reflects on original topic in discussion or writing task • Uses images and ideas from previous parts of lesson to complete the task
7. Create new direct analogies.	• Encourages students to create a personal direct analogy for the original subject • Asks students to make comparisons that are far removed from original subject and use different ideas and images than have been presented • Scaffolds students' efforts	• Considers original topic and previous steps • Creates new direct analogies • Reflects on difficulties and/or ease in creating new analogies • Thinks about what new analogies indicate about personal understanding of subject

It details the possible implementation steps and associated student responses. The potential behaviors of teachers and students working within the synectics framework gives you what is needed to master the instructional moves of the model. You can also anticipate and manipulate student behaviors to make certain you reach your instructional goals. This is an advanced instructional model that will take time to learn and will be used in your classroom somewhat infrequently. This should not stop you from experimenting with the model so that your students can stretch their creative wings.

The Synectics Excursion

The synectics excursion process uses all three forms of analogy—direct, personal, and symbolic—to solve a problem. Ask students to design a particular product, such as a better mousetrap or a new app. Students may be asked to solve a problem that has surfaced in the school or community. Or ask them to develop procedures to accomplish a task more effectively, such as running a marathon or translating an ancient map to locate a buried treasure (Weaver & Prince, 1990; Wilson, Greer, & Johnson, 1963). They may even discuss issues of national and international importance!

STEP 1: PRESENT THE PROBLEM

The problem should be one that will excite the interest and the enthusiasm of the participants. It should be stated in general terms by the teacher. For example, one problem is how to design a more efficient process for leaf removal.

STEP 2: PROVIDE EXPERT INFORMATION

Information about the situation and as much expert advice as possible are provided to the class. For instance, a catalog containing various rakes and leaf removal machines could be presented. A group of students could report on the current techniques for removing leaves, the problems faced by landfills, and the air pollution from burning leaves. A person from the city garbage collection department could be invited to discuss the problems of removing leaves and dealing with leaves once they arrive at a landfill.

STEP 3: QUESTION OBVIOUS SOLUTIONS AND PURGE

The teacher encourages the students to brainstorm obvious solutions to the problem and the relative merits of these. Solutions identified by the group as unworkable are purged from consideration. The problem can be solved in this step if everyone in the class agrees to a particular solution; usually, however, the answers that come most readily are the least effective. The teacher should be prepared to assist the students in identifying the flaws. For instance, a student might suggest that the leaves be burned. The teacher might, in turn, question the problem of burning in relation to air pollution.

STEP 4: GENERATE INDIVIDUAL PROBLEM STATEMENTS

The students are asked to write and restate the problem individually as each understands it. They are instructed to break the problem down into the component parts and state one of these in their own words. For instance, one student might focus on the problem of overcrowded landfills. Another student might focus on the problem and the fire hazard of piles of leaves on the streets awaiting removal.

STEP 5: CHOOSE ONE PROBLEM STATEMENT FOR FOCUS

The students read their descriptions of the problem to the class, and the class selects one to pursue further. For instance, one student may have focused on developing a new technique for reducing leaves at the landfill, whereas another student may have focused on treating the leaves as a valuable natural resource. The class must choose to explore one possible approach to the problem.

STEP 6: QUESTION THROUGH THE USE OF ANALOGIES

At this point, the teacher presents the students with a number of analogies. They can be direct analogies, personal analogies, symbolic analogies, or fantasy analogies.

Direct Analogies

1. A leaf on the ground is like what animal?
2. How is a leaf like an elderly person?
3. What do leaves and garbage have in common? How are they different?
4. How is a leaf like an orphan?

Personal Analogies

1. What would it feel like to be a leaf?
2. What does it feel like to be a machine that collects leaves?
3. What does it feel like to be abandoned?
4. What does it feel like to be a load of leaves in a landfill?

Symbolic Analogies (Using Compressed Conflicts)

1. How can a leaf be both free and doomed?
2. How would you describe something that is both essential and a nuisance?
3. How would *useful* and *nuisance* apply to this problem? *Helpful* and *destructive?*

Fantasy Analogies

1. If you could suspend the laws of gravity, how could you prevent the leaves from falling off the tree?
2. If you could control the tree, how could you prevent the leaves from falling?
3. Create an animal that could help solve the problem.

STEP 7: FORCE ANALOGIES TO FIT THE PROBLEM

The students are asked to return to the problem of designing a better system for leaf removal and to apply the analogies directly to this subject. For instance, the teacher might ask questions about the analogies.

1. If leaves are essential to life, why do we consider them a nuisance?
2. If leaves are like orphans, how can we provide more effective homes for them?
3. If allowing the leaves to remain where they fall is like allowing the elderly to remain productive, how can the leaves continue to be productive?

STEP 8: DETERMINE A SOLUTION FROM A NEW VIEWPOINT

Using one or more of the analogies, the teacher assists the group in looking at the problem from a new viewpoint. From this viewpoint, the group determines whether they have discovered a solution to the problem. For instance, they may have decided that a special type of worm could be genetically engineered that would live in residential mulch piles and reduce the leaves to mulch or that a mechanical "worm" could be designed to reduce leaves to mulch. If students decide that there are still some situations in which leaves must be removed, the class can continue the cycle of exploring analogies leading to additional solutions.

Elements of the cause-and-effect model can be integrated with this synectics lesson. The falling leaves may cover the grass in yards, with the effect of killing or retarding growth of the lawn. Students can explore the causes and subsequent effects as they decide on which problem they wish to focus on, the leaves or the lawn.

SUMMARY OF STEPS IN THE SYNECTICS EXCURSION

1. *Present the problem.* Select and then present to the class an interesting and challenging problem.

2. *Provide expert information.* Provide the class with as much expert information as possible.

3. *Question obvious solutions and purge.* Lead the class in an exploration of the most obvious solutions and have the students purge those that are not feasible.

4. *Generate individual problem statements.* Have each student write a statement regarding the problem, giving his or her interpretation or focus.

5. *Choose one problem statement for focus.* The problem statements are read aloud, and one is selected by the class for focus.

6. *Question through the use of analogies.* Present analogies to the class stated in the form of evocative questions.

7. *Force analogies to fit the problem.* Return to the original problem and ask the students to force the analogies to fit the problem.

8. *Determine a solution from a new viewpoint.* Ask students to determine a solution by looking at the problem from a new viewpoint.

For the synectics excursion to be successful in the classroom, the teacher and student must have strong problem-solving skills and some experience with using analogies to create new viewpoints, ideas, and products. This is the most advanced model presented in this text, but even a novice teacher can master this with time and practice. The synectics excursion helps open students to creative solutions to a persistent problem by asking them to use a variety of analogies modeled and used by the teacher as questions. Table 12.3 will support your efforts in figuring out the implementation of synectics excursion. It details the possible implementation steps and associated student responses. Again, this is an advanced instructional model that will take time to learn and will be used in your classroom somewhat infrequently. And, as in the other synectics approaches, this model will allow students to stretch their creative juices.

Evaluating Learning in the Synectics Model

Synectics requires students to construct analogies and to use the analogies to help find innovative solutions to problems, to deepen connections between new and prior knowledge, and to practice creative connections. The model itself offers the opportunity for formative assessments. Teachers can monitor individual contributions to the discussion of personal and direct analogies and compressed conflicts during the implementation of the synectics process and during the subsequent discussion. Analogies can be assessed as to their construction and quality. Although every contribution to the discussion is accepted, the teacher can evaluate contributions by taking notice of the construction of the analogies and how prior knowledge is extended with the analogies. A debriefing after the lesson about the quality and construction

TABLE 12.3   Potential Teacher and Student Behaviors in the Synectics Excursion

Step	Teacher	Student
1. Present the problem.	• Defines *synectics* and discusses the process of the synectics excursion • Reviews the purpose and steps of the synectics excursion • Selects an engaging problem to be solved aligned with standards and curriculum • Asks students to assign a product or process to solve the presented problem	• Asks clarifying questions about problem and process if necessary • Surveys personal knowledge of problem • Links prior knowledge and experiences with new problem and the synectic excursion process
2. Provide expert information.	• Shares expert information about the problem in a variety of ways • Provides outside experts to share knowledge and experiences • May provide additional information through videos, games, mini-lectures, and organized activities	• Asks questions to aid in understanding the problem under discussion • Works with peers to gather information if applicable • Attends to presentations of teacher and peers • Participates in activities • Links new information to prior knowledge and experiences
3. Question solutions and purge.	• Facilitates brainstorming on problem solutions • Asks students to evaluate the merits of the solutions based on feasibility and logic • Helps students purge solutions deemed unworkable • Scaffolds students evaluations by providing additional information when necessary	• Brainstorms possible solutions to problem with peers • Evaluates merits of solutions with class and support of teacher • Explains why some solutions are not worthwhile • Asks clarifying questions of teacher and peers when necessary
4. Generate individual problem statements.	• Provides directions for problem statements • Asks students to restate and analyze problem, choosing one component of the problem to pursue • Scaffolds task completion	• Asks procedural questions if necessary • Shares understanding of the problem and focus component • Adjusts problem statement with feedback from teacher and/or peers
5. Choose focal statement.	• Organizes and facilitates sharing of problem statements • Helps class select one statement to pursue • Reminds students of purpose of lesson	• Shares problem statement with class • Participates in the selection of one problem statement to pursue in the next steps of the model
6. Questions with analogies.	• Reminds students of types of analogies • Presents direct, personal, symbolic, and fantasy analogies (as questions) to class as questions about the problem and the product/solution • Encourages students to deepen understanding of problem and possible solutions	• Asks clarifying questions if necessary • Responds to analogy questions • Expands focus of problem product/solution with analogy questions • Links questions and peer responses to problem statements and possible solutions/products.

continued

TABLE 12.3   Potential Teacher and Student Behaviors in the Synectics Excursion (*continued*)

Step	Teacher	Student
7. Force analogies to fit problems.	• Helps students use analogies to consider the problem by asking questions that force consideration of analogies • Supports students in solving problems	• Responds to teacher questions by using analogies discussed previously • Focuses on how analogies are related to potential solutions/products
8. Determine new viewpoint.	• Scaffolds students to look for new viewpoint of problem based on previous exercises • Supports evaluation of possible solutions/products	• Organizes information and previous knowledge and experiences to provide a problem solution • Evaluates solution together with class

of analogies can occur, providing information to students that can be used to sharpen the comparison process.

A summative assessment might require a constructed response that examines the quality of the novel solution to the problem being examined and the accuracy of the concepts that have been used in analogies. For example, if students participated in a synectics lesson on homework, they may be asked to write an essay to share what they learned about homework and how teachers and students can find a way to use homework to everyone's advantage. Students may also be asked to generate additional analogies and metaphors that are associated with the topics or problems under discussion. Rubrics can be developed to provide structure for feedback and student performance.

The synectics process itself can serve as an assessment. Asking students to develop direct analogies, personal analogies, and compressed conflicts can demonstrate student understanding of academic content and the skill of identifying similarities and differences. The steps of Making the Strange Familiar and Making the Familiar Strange can be used as the basis for a paper-and-pencil or web-based assignment. In this case, student work can be evaluated by the number and quality of the metaphors and the writing that accompanies the last step of the model.

Meeting Individual Needs with the Synectics Model

Providing support for students to learn specific skills, processes, and information results in increased student learning (Good & Brophy, 2003). When this support is also stretched to meet the needs of a variety of students, teachers differentiate. Scaffolding students through the different synectics processes allows a variety of opportunities for supporting student learning. In synectics, the goal is to help students develop a conscious creative process to find solutions to problems by examining relationships between new and unfamiliar things, finding patterns, and identifying similarities and differences between elements. Teachers can provide practice in constructing metaphors and analogies by using stretching exercises and graphic organizers. For example, at the beginning of the academic day or period, teachers could provide some analogies for students to grapple with as they get their creative and academic juices going.

Marzano (2001) defines creating metaphors as identifying a general pattern in one topic and finding another element that appears to be very different but follows

Graphic organizers are visual displays that show relationships between ideas and words. They come in a variety of forms, and graphic templates are readily available on the Internet. Graphic organizers play a powerful role in student learning by providing support for the development of new skills, including generating analogies. A graphic organizer can help students see the connections between the two elements of an analogy. The organizers facilitate learning and teaching by making relationships explicit to students. To differentiate, teachers can include more or less information on the organizer or ask students to develop their own graphic to demonstrate the comparisons.

the same abstract pattern. Teachers can use student interests as the foundation for building metaphors. Analogies identify relationships between pairs of concepts. Stretching exercises that ask students to develop direct and personal analogies and compressed conflicts before the complete instructional model is used can be helpful to students who are not comfortable with these comparisons or with students who need the opportunity to choose comparisons from an unlimited universe. The range of stretching exercises might extend from teachers providing the first element of the analogy and defining the abstract relationship, to providing the abstract relationship alone, to simply providing a broad topic in which analogies can be constructed. Differentiated prompts can be provided to the class. For example, students may be asked to compare a hurricane to food served at a restaurant, or to compare weather to food, or to make comparisons that include things that affect us with things that we need to survive. The following are some examples of sentence stretchers:

- How is a cat like a motorcycle?
- In what ways is taking a nap like taking a trip?
- How is bird migration like making dinner?
- What does it feel like to be a computer?
- How are maps like chocolate bars?
- What does it feel like to be the Declaration of Independence?

In addition to differentiated stretching exercises, graphic organizers can help students practice building analogies. Having students make connections between words, fill in linked boxes, or construct Venn diagrams can provide the opportunity for students to identify similarities and differences.

Benefits of the Synectics Model

Creativity is important in our everyday life. We need to be creative when we solve problems, express our feelings, demonstrate empathy, or move toward deep understanding of complex concepts. Synectics helps students find fresh ways of thinking about ideas and problems. Because creativity is a learned behavior and the creative process is similar across all grades and curriculum subjects, synectics is a meaningful addition to your instructional toolbox, and it is an adaptable and rewarding process. Remember that metaphors are the language of creativity and that creativity allows for the development of new conceptual structures, so synectics can play an important role in academic achievement and in the development of problem-solving and social skills. The use of direct and personal analogies and compressed conflicts invites all students to join into the discussion. And the model is very amenable to both differentiation and alternative assessment options.

ELEMENTARY GRADES LESSON

SYNECTICS MODEL: The Civil War

OBJECTIVES

Common Core State Standards—English/Language Arts L.4-6
Demonstrate understanding of figurative language, word relationships, and nuances in word meanings.

Common Core State Standards—English/Language Arts W.2
Write informative/explanatory texts to examine a topic and convey ideas and information clearly.

Students Will Know

- The short- and long-term effects of the Civil War
- The definitions and use of metaphors and analogies

Students Will Understand That

- The effects of war are long lasting

Students Will Be Able To

- Explore analogies and metaphors of the Civil War

ASSESSMENT

Ask students to construct a different analogy that can be compared to the Civil War. Have them explain why they chose the analogy and how it helps to understand the effects of war.

PROCEDURES

1. *Provide information.* Review figurative language and analogies. Read *Cecil's War* to the students.
2. *Present the analogy.* Present the analogy by listing the similarities between the Civil War and an earthquake and then discussing these similarities with the class.
   - In an earthquake, the land often splits. The North and South were one country, and then they split apart violently.
   - In an earthquake, many people are killed by strong forces. In war, the same thing happens.
   - Before an earthquake there are warning tremors. Before the Civil War there were warning signs that trouble was coming.
   - After an earthquake, there are usually aftershocks; following the Civil War there were many aftershocks.
3. *Use personal analogies to create compressed conflicts.* Ask students what it feels like to be an earthquake and why they feel that way. Record the feelings that are shared by the students. Ask the students to look over the list and find words that don't fit together—ideas that fight (compressed conflicts). You may need to provide an example. Once there is a list of compressed conflicts, ask the students to choose one to pursue.
4. *Compare the compressed conflict with the subject.* Ask the class to discuss how the Civil War is like the chosen analogy. (You can ask the students to write about their feelings on each side of the conflict—the North and the South.)
5. *Identify differences.* Ask the students to consider how the war and an earthquake are different.
6. *Reexamine the original subject.* Students reflect on the discussion and on what they know about the reasons for and consequences of the Civil War. Ask the students to identify their own analogies to help demonstrate their understanding.

MIDDLE/SECONDARY GRADES LESSON

SYNECTICS MODEL: Witches

OBJECTIVES	**Common Core State Standards—English/Language Arts RI.8.4** Determine the meaning of words and phrases as they are used in a text, including figurative, connotative, and technical meanings; analyze the impact of specific word choices on meaning and tone, including analogies or allusions to other texts. **Common Core State Standards—English/Language Arts W.6.2.D** Use precise language and domain-specific vocabulary to inform about or explain the topic. **Students Will Know** • The images associated with witches **Students Will Understand That** • The political, religious, economic, and social stresses of life can lead to mob behavior **Students Will Be Able To** • Explore analogies and metaphors about witches and make connections between their ideas and those of the Salem, Massachusetts, community
ASSESSMENT	In a written paragraph, students will use the analogies discussed in class to explain why the people of Salem might have feared the witches.
PROCEDURES	1. *Describe the topic.* Ask each student to write a short paragraph about witches in 10 minutes. Once all students have completed writing, have them share some of their descriptive words. Write all contributions on the board. 2. *Create direct analogies.* Ask the students to use the words in the list and name a plant that reminds them of as many of the words as possible. As students share their contributions, write them on the board. Encourage students to explain why they chose a particular analogy. When everyone has had an opportunity to participate and the class is ready, have the students vote on one particular analogy that will be pursued during the next steps. 3. *Describe personal analogies.* Ask the students to "become" the analogy they selected in step 2. How does it feel to be this thing? Ask students to explain why they feel this way. Record all contributions on the board. 4. *Identify compressed conflicts.* Have the students examine the list from step 3 and put together pairs of words that seem to fight or contradict each other. List all contributions, and have students vote on the best compressed conflict. 5. *Create a new direct analogy.* Using the compressed conflict voted on in step 4, have students create another direct analogy comparing the compressed conflict to an animal. Have the class vote to choose their favorite direct analogy. 6. *Reexamine the original topic.* Return to the direct analogy identified in the previous step. Compare this direct analogy to witches. Have students share their observations. Make connections to Salem, Massachusetts.

SUMMARY

Synectics is an advanced instructional model that can provide novelty and variety to a classroom while helping students develop important communication, collaboration, critical thinking, and creativity skills (Trilling & Fadel, 2012). The synectics process allows students to put some distance between the problem that needs to be solved, the learning that needs to be incorporated, and the project that needs to be completed, allowing for a creative process to improve the solution, acquisition, and product. Three different synectics approaches were presented. Making the Familiar Strange takes what students know and finds direct, personal, and symbolic analogies (compressed conflicts) to make connections with new information and skills. Making the Strange Familiar presents new content to students and uses the three types of analogies to link to familiar knowledge and skills. In both cases, students identify similarities and differences between new and prior knowledge helping to build more sophisticated neural networks. The synectics excursion provides steps for creative problem solving. The benefits of synectics were discussed, as were possible evaluation and differentiation occasions.

A case study showing how to use the synectics model in context can be seen in Chapter Fifteen.

EXTENSIONS

ACTIVITIES

1. The following words were developed by a class to describe the character of Tom Sawyer. What vehicle do the words in this list make you think of?

clever	naughty	young
headstrong	old-fashioned	original
brave	funny	smart

2. Select a topic and follow the steps of the Making the Familiar Strange model on your own. Then repeat the experience with several friends. Compare the richness of the images created both individually and when in a group.

3. Create an analogy to use with each of the following subjects: fractions, nutrition, bridges, nouns, Declaration of Independence, and poetry.

4. Select a problem about which you are concerned, and go through the steps of the synectics excursion on your own. Determine whether approaching the problem in this manner helps you explore possible solutions effectively. Then repeat the activity with a group of adults and see whether the results are different.

5. Think about how you might use the synectics model in the knowledge and skills that you teach. List the problems you anticipate in implementing the synectics model in your classroom.

REFLECTIVE QUESTIONS

1. How well do you need to know your content to develop analogies and guide your pupils in developing successful analogies?

2. What could a teacher do to help students who have difficulty working with synectics models?

3. In what ways can the synectics process improve your own teaching and learning?

4. Identify the responses your students might have to their first synectics experience. How might they respond to the synectics model after several synectics lessons?

RESOURCES

1. Jane McAuliffe and Laura Stoskin developed the synectics model into workbook form for elementary teachers and students in *What Color Is Saturday? Using Analogies to Enhance Creative Thinking in the Classroom,* published by Zephyr Press in 1993. You may need to check online sources to purchase the book.
2. An Internet search on the uses of analogies and metaphors in classrooms will provide you subject specific information that can be used in the design of synectics lessons.
3. Check YouTube for additional videos on synectics instruction in classrooms.

PART THREE SUMMARY

In Part Three, five advanced instructional models were presented. The integrative model provides a structure for helping students make sense of an organized body of knowledge through specified steps leading to the identification of relationships and the construction of broad generalizations. The Socratic seminar model supports the critical analysis of text (written, auditory, and visual) with clearly established roles for students and the teacher, allowing for the aligned evaluation of student understanding. Cooperative learning was discussed in Chapter Ten, beginning with a cooperative learning template that described the general architecture of cooperative learning exercises. Four variations of cooperative learning were looked at: graffiti, jigsaw, academic controversy, and student teams-achievement models. These models all work on the development of important cooperative social and academic skills, along with a range of academic objectives—from recall through creation. Chapter Eleven examined three models that use the inquiry approach—the Suchman inquiry model, the WebQuest model, and the problem-based inquiry model. Each of these inquiry models presents students with an ill-structured, complex problem and provides scaffolding for problem solutions. Teacher cognitive demand is high during the planning phase of these models, and student cognitive demand is high during the implementation of the models. The final chapter in Part Three described the creative problem-solving process of the synectics model through three different versions: Making the Familiar Strange, Making the Strange Familiar, and the synectics excursion. These approaches are the farthest from traditional instruction and require creativity in planning and in presentation in the classroom. Students will need support in understanding the content and the process of these models. Taken together, Part Three offers many intricate instructional models that challenge both teachers and students and that will be a foundation for sophisticated thinking in the classroom.

Putting It All Together

Effective teachers design good instruction. This design task requires the identification of objectives, assessments, and instructional models and strategies. The first part of this text discussed how to create robust objectives from state standards in the *know, understand,* and *do* format. The second and third parts of this text offered instructional models that can increase instructional variety and student engagement in the classroom while supporting students as they reach academic goals and practice higher-level thinking skills.

In Part Four, we describe the integration of planning, instruction, assessment, and management that takes place in an effective classroom environment. These activities are interrelated, and each must be taken into consideration with each decision that is made. Every teacher, however, must develop his or her own way of achieving this integration. There is no one way to approach the process of putting it all together in the classroom. Classroom decisions are dependent on the individual school content. But every good teacher attends to certain essential components of this process: (1) planning, (2) instruction, (3) assessment, and (4) classroom management.

In this part, we describe how teachers in classrooms use the ideas presented earlier and give some general suggestions for managing the classroom. There are four chapters in Part Four—three case studies and a concluding chapter that looks at important practices for teachers to implement in the classroom (because good instruction alone will not be enough). There are also other teacher behaviors that allow for the critical development of positive student–teacher relationships—necessary components of student learning (Hattie & Yates, 2014).

The first case study, Chapter Thirteen, looks at a fourth grade elementary math unit studying angles. The teacher in this case (as in all of the others) employs backward design. She exemplifies understanding that the instructional models she has chosen to use increase the power of her planning and help her meet the needs of a variety of learners in her classroom. By choosing to use a particular instructional model, a teacher knows exactly what the instructional moves and needs will be in the classroom, limiting some of the on-the-fly decisions about what is needed. The variety in models supports an array of student preferences and needs. Novice teachers can share in Mrs. Evans' reflections and note the preliminary steps in designing a unit. The vocabulary acquisition model, concept attainment, and direct instruction are used in this case.

Chapter Fourteen is a case study of a middle school interdisciplinary unit prepared by a team of teachers. The common concept is perspective, and each teacher prepares a unit in his or her content area that meshes with the units that the other teachers have prepared. There are common objectives, assessments, and experiences. Evident in this chapter (as in all of the cases) are individual approaches to instructional planning, which use some of the processes and strategies described in the earlier chapters. For example, these middle school teachers use a variety of instructional models that were specifically chosen to meet targeted Common Core State Standards. These models include concept attainment, concept development, jigsaw, direct instruction, Suchman inquiry, and vocabulary acquisition. As you read the case, you will be able to offer conjecture as to why the teachers chose to use these models and how the structure of the models will help students reach unit objectives.

In the high school case study in Chapter Fifteen, a department chair designs a challenging unit about Shakespeare's *Macbeth* for a general-level senior English classroom. In this case, the teacher sought out the challenge of using backward design and instructional models to engage students in the rigors of making sense of a serious and much loved play. Various models were used to reach clearly articulated objectives—concept attainment, direct instruction, concept development, jigsaw, synectics, Socratic seminar, inquiry, and cause and effect.

There are several models that were used across all of the cases, and some were used in only one or not at all. Why might that be? What limited the use of models in the cases? What opportunities were provided to use a variety of models? The teachers in these examples do not arrive at their plans by the same route, nor do they incorporate exactly the same instructional steps in their individual plans. All the teachers do, however, attend to the needs of their students, and they systematically determine objectives and match those objectives to instruction and assessment.

The final chapter in this part, Chapter Sixteen, is titled "The Wisdom of Practice"; it contains a broad view of effective teaching. Although the purpose of this text is to provide you with information about instructional planning and specific instructional models, the development of a repertoire of instructional models is only one of the many practices necessary for good teaching. This chapter describes techniques for dealing with classroom management and the relationships between students and teachers that are required for student learning to occur. Most of the material presented in this last chapter is drawn from our personal experience; we have attempted, however, to connect this experience with research regarding effective classroom practice.

We would argue that the most important teacher behavior is monitoring student learning, and thus the instructional models presented in this text provide opportunities for learning about students using different instructional contexts and moves. These differences provide an opportunity for deep reflection about pedagogy, providing feedback to students and to yourself and making deeper and more specific connections to student prior knowledge.

It is our belief that teachers are essentially instructional experts, not therapists or counselors. Like all good managers, they must have very keen interpersonal skills and be able to think quickly on their feet. Anyone responsible for managing groups of people and for the welfare of individuals under their direction should have the personality and skills to manage the group and to give direction. But we should not ask of teachers what we do not ask of other professionals. Teachers should not be expected to prescribe and treat seriously challenged individuals without help from other professionals, such as psychologists, social workers, and guidance counselors, nor should they be expected to teach in life-threatening situations.

Having said this, it is our belief that many students who are considered to be serious discipline problems and are sent out of the classroom, often labeled as hyperactive or emotionally disturbed, are in fact suffering because of the way they are being taught. Youngsters who are bored, whose learning preference is different from the teaching style, or who are asked to learn material that is too difficult or too easy can become management issues. Too often, teachers diagnose instructional problems as emotional, physical, or mental problems, thus failing to meet the challenge of finding an instructional solution. In this part of the text we reemphasize the need for careful instructional planning and design and for creating a classroom environment in which all students can and will learn (Noguera, 2008).

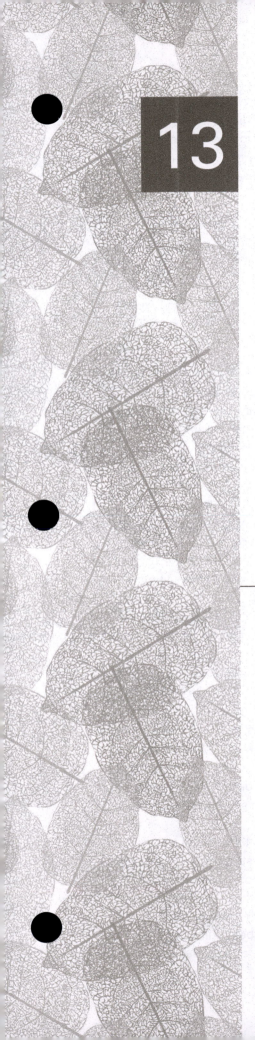

13

A Fourth Grade Case Study

ANGLES

 Chapter Objectives

You Will Know

- The opportunities for using diverse instructional models in an elementary classroom
- The planning components needed to implement an elementary unit
- The relationship between desired objectives and instructional models
- The role of student achievement, experiences, and interests in choosing academic content and instruction

You Will Understand That

- Effective instruction requires careful planning and strong pedagogical knowledge
- Planning involves the application of diverse instructional models

You Will Be Able To

- Reflect and comment on the instructional planning of an elementary teacher
- Consider how you would develop a detailed plan for a lesson or unit you might teach
- Determine whether the teacher described in this chapter used the principles of backward design

Veronica Evans, a fourth grade science and mathematics teacher at Wilson Elementary School, relaxed one weekend before the fall semester began. She was reminiscing about why she had become a teacher. The answer was clear and had been so from the beginning of her teacher preparation—she wanted to be the kind of teacher who made the basic STEM concepts of science, technology, engineering, and math familiar to young students. Lately, she had modified her thinking to give particular consideration to the girls in her class. Studies had been repeatedly reporting that girls in school come quickly to believe that the sciences and mathematics are not for them. Like many folks, Mrs. Evans believed that the nation needed more females in these fields of study and work. Her views were reinforced by various organizations devoted to reversing the anomaly—groups like GEMS, Girls Excelling in Math and Science.

WEB RESOURCE

Girl Power

Visit gemsclub.org or drop a note to info@gemsclub.org for more information about Girls Excelling in Math and Science. Worth a look also is a particular comic strip featuring Hispanic characters and one very ambitious young female. Don't miss the cartoon ahead of the article entitled "Girl Power: The STEM Issue Branches Out to the Funny Pages."

But how to make the basic concepts of math and science appealing to all her students, girls and boys alike—that was the question Mrs. Evans faced with each new crop of young minds that came before her. Her answer was to teach the concepts of math and science in ways potentially appealing because they could be seen as ways of thinking about relationships of all kinds. In her introductory lessons in math, she decided to focus on a particular Common Core State Standard, the mathematic standard for grade four geometric measurements: understand concepts of angle and measure angles.

WEB RESOURCE

Math Standards

Visit the Common Core State Standards website (corestandards.org) and explore the math standards either by grade level (K–12) or domain (including geometry).

The standard seemed to lend itself nicely to both a logical and an aesthetic way of viewing the world, features that had potential to appeal to girls and boys alike if presented in a way that had more appeal than formulas. Lines and points are universals in the experiences of everyone. There are yard marker lines on playing fields, lines on basketball courts, lines on the floors and ceilings of buildings—all of which demark edges and boundaries. Though they often do define boundaries, lines also represent infinity. On sailing vessels, one never refers to *ropes*: everyone knows those are *lines*. Every family tree is drawn with lines that track the family's *lineage*. Straight lines can be assembled to represent figures of three or more sides, and the straight lines at their intersections, called *vertices*, form angles—sometimes *right angles*, sometimes *acute angles*, sometimes *obtuse angles.* The meanings of those words, aside from their special use in mathematics, would no doubt make for interesting discussion and exploration.

As she continued to think, Mrs. Evans considered how the two ends of a line can be brought around curvilineally to form a circle. The circumference and the diameter of a circle are represented by lines of different kinds, curved and straight, and the famous number π is the relationship of the two. The fact that the ratio of the circumference to the diameter of a circle is constant but an indefinite number has been known for so long that it is quite untraceable. What we do know is that it has fascinated mathematicians and other thinkers for centuries, dating back at least 4,000 years ago to Egypt, and is even mentioned in the Bible (1 Kings 7:23) and in popular culture—in the title of a movie, π, in a novel by Carl Sagan in which it is suggested that the creator of the universe buried a secret within the digits of π, in the lyrics of a song, "Pi" included in the album *Ariel*, by Kate Bush. No single number has held more fascination for humankind.

The question for Mrs. Evans and for all teachers of mathematics is whether the topics of mathematics can be taught in ways that provide students with glimpses of such fascination. This day she smiled to herself as she realized that her own enthusiasm could cause her to go off in many directions at once. There was always a limit to what could be included in one unit and how much students could absorb. "Keep in mind how many times the same concept has to be experienced before it can be owned," she reminded himself. The time had come to order her own thoughts in developing the unit on lines and angles.

Mrs. Evans' Plan

Typically, Mrs. Evans planned her units of instruction to last two to three weeks, depending on the content to be covered. Still, every journey begins with small steps, and this plan was no different. Working from the appropriate Common Core mathematics standard, and using this as the basis of designing backwards from the expected outcomes, she specified the general objectives for the first few lessons of the unit:

Students Will Know

- How to draw and identify lines and angles and how to classify shapes by properties of their lines and angles
- How to draw points, lines, line segments, rays, angles (right, acute, obtuse), and perpendicular and parallel lines

Students Will Understand That

- Lines are the foundation of shapes

Students Will Be Able To

- Identify linear features of two-dimensional figures
- Classify two-dimensional figures based on the presence or absence of parallel or perpendicular lines, or the presence or absence of angles of a specified size
- Recognize right angles as a category and identify right triangles
- Recognize a line of symmetry for a two-dimensional figure as a line across the figure, such that the figure can be folded along the line into matching parts
- Identify line-symmetric figures and draw lines of symmetry

The following lessons are based on the standards and the proposed unit objectives.

Lesson One: Words We Use to Talk about Angles

Instructional Model

Vocabulary acquisition

Estimated Time

Thirty minutes

Rationale for Choice of Model

Mrs. Evans believes that words are the basis of concepts, and she wants to make certain that the students understand the basic ideas that will be discussed in the unit. In addition, the words we use to label and discuss concepts often have interesting histories and reflect how we understand phenomena. Vocabulary allows learners to engage in accurate descriptions of concepts and to understand what they hear and read about the concepts they are studying.

The first of three lessons Mrs. Evans planned on the topic of angles is aimed at an understanding of the vocabulary used in talking about angles. She starts with a brief pretest of the words *point, line, ray, segment, angle,* and *degree*. The pretest is a matching exercise in which students are shown drawings of each of the words and are asked to pick the word that would label each and would form the basis of the following discussion:

Mrs. Evans: These words and their drawings are the basics we will need to talk about the idea of angles. Let's review them together. What can you say about a *point*?

Robert: It doesn't go anywhere, it just sits there.

Mrs. Evans: That's right. We say that a point does not have length or width or depth. It actually doesn't have as much dimension as the drawing we use to represent it. It is more like a place we can only imagine and mark with a dot so we'll know where it is. We might say, "At what point did you remember the answer?"

Notice that when we say that, we are using the word figuratively. There is no actual *point*, is there? Still, we need to *point* to it by naming it.

Now, what can you say about a line? It contrasts nicely with a point, we might say. But how does it differ from a point?

Margie: Does this have anything to do with the way you have drawn it?

Mrs. Evans: Yes. You're on the right track.

Margie: Does a line actually go off in both directions? Like the directions of the arrows you have drawn on each end? As if there really were no ends?

Mrs. Evans: That's exactly right, Marge. A line really goes in two directions without ending in either direction. Like to infinity. But like a point, this is what we imagine, since we can really only imagine infinity. Just think of a line like Margie thinks of it—it has no end we can mark.

Mrs. Evans continues with the word *ray* and reminds students that a ray has a specific beginning, but no identified end. She compares that with the definition of a segment. When discussing the line segment, the conversation continues.

Marie: Looks like it maybe has two points rather than arrows, one on each end, and doesn't go farther than the points in either direction. No arrows on the ends.

Mrs. Evans: Very good, Marie. Most of the time when we talk about a line, like a "line" of students at the lunch bar or customers at the checkout in a store or cars at a stoplight, we really mean a "line segment." I know it may sometimes feel that way, but it really doesn't go on forever in either direction, does it? Let's look now at the prefix *seg-*. Like a lot of English, this came to us from Latin and it means "cut." A *segment* is a part that is "cut."

Mrs. Evans draws a line, arrows on both ends, and then marks off a segment with two separate hash marks. She mentions that the verb *hash* actually means "to chop into pieces."

Mrs Evans: What we've done here is to chop a segment out of the line. Let's think about our *angle* words. What strikes you about the word itself, *angle*?

Marcus: It looks like *ankle*.

Mrs. Evans: Well, to my amazement, the word *angle* comes from a Latin word meaning "corner" or "bend." What do you notice about your ankle?

Cheri: Your ankle is a bend between your leg and your foot. Is that where it gets its name?

Mrs. Evans: Yep, that's exactly where we get the name. Matter of fact, *angle* is related to a Greek word that means "elbow." When we think of angles, we might think of these angles in our arms and legs. Angles are bends, aren't they? We measure these bends by *degrees*. What else can you think of that is measured by degrees?

Ronald: How about the temperature? Like when the thermometer says it's cold outside, like 30 degrees. Or when we get a fever, we say how many degrees it is.

Mrs. Evans: Right again. And a degree is a step, or a grade. Each mark on a thermometer is a "step" or "grade." Those steps differ on two different thermometers—the Fahrenheit and the Celsius, or centigrade—scales. The centigrade thermometer is divided into hundredths, each division thought of as 1/100 of a degree between the freezing and boiling points of water. The prefix *centi-* means "hundred," as you may know.

Now, when we come to measuring angles, I'll explain how each angle is measured in degrees up to, but not as high as, 360. You may be wondering about where we get that number, 360. For now, I'll tell you that the way we measure them, angles will always be less than 360 degrees. There is a geometric figure that does measure 360 degrees, but I'll leave that for you to think about for now. We'll get back to our discussion of angles tomorrow, when all these words will take on better meanings for you as we use them in talking about angles.

Assessment

Following this lesson, a variety of common objects related to one or more terms taught in this unit will be placed on a table. These will include things such as a string with knots on each end, a small carpenter's square, a hammer with a nail pull, a small rod, a hinge, a round coaster for a glass, a hand-operated juicer, a pair of eyeglasses, a boot or high-top shoe, a pair of scissors, a book, a kite, a dollhouse-shaped straight-backed chair, or any fairly small object that can be defined in shape or use with reference to angles. Students will be asked to pick one of the objects and be prepared to "show and tell" how the shape or the use of the object relates to what they know about angles.

Lesson Two: Exploring Angles

Instructional Model

Concept attainment

Estimated Time

One hour

Objective

Students will be able to identify the essential characteristics of three common types of angles.

Rationale for Choice of Model

A concept is a general idea derived from encounters with specific instances. Before this lesson (and the lessons and units that will build on it) can proceed, it is crucial that students have a working definition of angles. As we said in Chapter Four, all concepts have (1) a name and definition, (2) examples of items that are included in the concept class, and (3) critical attributes that define the concept. There will be many opportunities for students to refine their concept of angle in the lessons and learning activities to follow. These and many other very sophisticated concepts will be built on the initial understanding of what an angle is and is not.

The second lesson on angles is aimed at understanding what an angle is—identifying the essential attributes and the different types of angles, by examining examples of items that have angular shapes. This is a variation of the concept attainment model. Mrs. Evans projects clip-art pictures on the screen (she could also have opted to draw the pictures on the board) like the following:

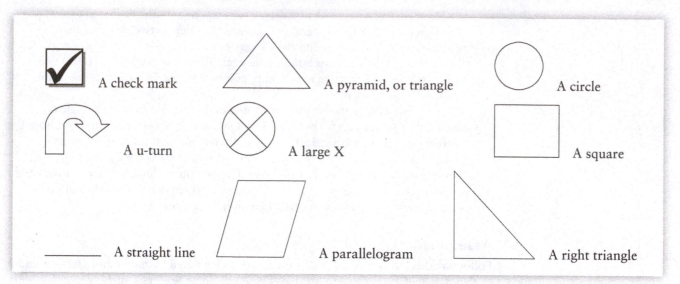

Mrs. Evans: So, looking at each of these pictures, which would you say are examples of angles? Notice that some pictures have more than one angle.

Maria: That check mark is one angle, isn't it?

Ralph: The circle is not an angle, I think, but the X inside the circle seems to be.

Mrs. Evans: Correct, Ralph. And how many angles do you see in the X?

The discussion proceeds until all the examples are classified as angles or not angles, remembering that an angle is a bend. Students count the angles in the illustrations that included more than one angle: the X, the square, the right triangle, the parallelogram, and the triangular pyramid.

Next, Mrs. Evans draws three different angles for students to examine: an acute angle, a 90° angle, and an obtuse angle. She leads the students to see that these three differ in type, related to the idea of 90 degrees.

Mrs. Evans: An acute angle is so called because it is sharp, like the angle of a knife's blade. We refer to excellent vision as *acute* eyesight, meaning "sharp" eyesight. We might call an angle of less than 90 degrees a *sharp* angle. By contrast, *obtuse* means "dull" or "not sharp." A leaf that has a rounded end is called an *obtuse leaf.* What do you think a leaf with a sharp end would be called?

As an extension of the concept attainment exercise, Mrs. Evans explains the idea that the four 90° angles in the square add up to 360 degrees.

Mrs. Evans: So, you see, all the way around is 360 degrees. That is true whether we're talking about a square or a circle or this globe (pointing to the classroom globe of the earth). The lines of longitude, which you might call the "up and down" lines, are numbered from zero to 180 to get exactly halfway around. All the way around would be twice 180, or 360.

Mrs. Evans shows this on the globe and follows with explanation of how the lines of longitude intersect at 90 degrees at the equator, a special line of latitude. She mentions that the "equator" is a line dividing the globe (and earth) into two "equal" parts.

Mrs. Evans: Lines of longitude are also measured in degrees, as are the lines of latitude.

This sidebar discussion is a deliberate attempt to set the students up for the next lesson, concerning how to measure angles with a protractor.

Assessment

The assessment of angle recognition is conducted with a matching exercise. The task is to classify a number of pictures of angular objects as acute, right, or obtuse. The pictures are of common objects like a rectangular tabletop, a straight-backed chair, a utility pole, a television antenna, a fishing rod and line, and a drafting T-square.

Lesson Three: Measuring Angles

Instructional Models

Direct instruction and vocabulary acquisition

Estimated Time

One hour

Objective

Students will be able to measure angles with the use of a protractor and to draw arcs and circles with the use of a compass.

Rationale for Choices of Model

By the time of this lesson, the students should be familiar with the basic vocabulary and concept of angles. The new words in this lesson will be *protractor* and *compass,* tools that have use in drawing and measuring angles. The goal now is that they become more sophisticated in their understanding of the concept of an angle, including how angles are measured. The direct instruction model is ideal for teaching skills and understandings such as these. The model is grounded in what Hattie and Yates (2014) refer to as "ostension," the act of showing, pointing out, or exhibiting. Direct instruction is characterized by ostensible teaching, or teaching and learning by showing and then having students practice the new learning together and independently. As we defined the model in Chapter Three, the process can be expressed as "I do, we do, and you do." We might also add that ostension is more than showing by the teacher. Direct instruction must involve learners, in part by letting them become doers rather than merely receivers.

Mrs. Evan's presentation begins when she draws a large X on the board to create four angles that share the same vertex at the center, reminding the students of the previous lesson in which they looked at X as a drawing of four angles. Next, she explains that the students will learn how to measure angles with tools made for the purpose. She holds up a large compass and a protractor, explaining that *compass* means "to go around" or "to *encompass* with a perimeter, a border or circumference that goes all the way around an area." She draws a large circle on the board, using the large compass. She then illustrates another meaning of *compass* by projecting from her electronic tablet an image of a compass showing direction in degrees from magnetic north.

> Mrs. Evans: This compass shows all directions: north, east, south, and west. Using north as zero, it tells how many degrees from north it is pointing. Can you guess what the total degrees on the compass are?

This reinforces and establishes the idea of 360 degrees as the total of a circle.

She next uses the large protractor to show how the size of the angle she has drawn can be measured by placing the midpoint mark on the vertex, aligning the zero line of the protractor on one of the angle's rays, and reading the degrees on the protractor where the opposite ray intersects.

> Mrs. Evans: This is much easier to show than to explain. In a minute I'm going to let you practice it yourself. If you have any difficulty, just ask for help.

By noting each of the four angles' measure, she then adds them together to get the total of 360 degrees. She reminds the class that the 360 degrees was what they found yesterday by adding together four 90° angles. She also reminds them what they just saw on the magnetic compass. That sum is also the total of degrees in the circumference of any circle. What the students are actually measuring in degrees is the degrees of arc of the circle cut by the angle's rays. Using the large compass, Mrs. Evans can draw the arc, the part of the circle, on the angles she measured before.

Next, the lesson turns to guided practice. Each student has paper and a small ruler for a straight edge, a handheld compass, and a small protractor. Working in small groups, the students practice by drawing two intersecting lines on their paper, creating the four angles of an X. They then measure the degrees of each angle with the protractor; when the four numbers are added together, they total 360, allowing for small error in measurement.

When students run into any difficulty, Mrs. Evans is available to provide feedback and suggestions for correction. Once Mrs. Evans believes that students are progressing toward automaticity, she asks them to work on a similar task independently as she monitors the class.

Assessment

The day following the direct instruction, the students are given three angles on a sheet of paper and asked to measure them with their protractors. One of the angles is acute (less than 90 degrees), a second one is a right angle (exactly 90 degrees), and the third is obtuse (more than 90 degrees.) They are deliberately constructed so that the total of degrees measurement in the acute and the obtuse angles is 180 degrees. This leads to a discussion of how the measure of the third would, by inference, lead to the measure of the first, and vice-versa.

Epilogue

The next lesson centers on the topic of supplementary angles, angles whose sum is the measure of a straight line of 180 degrees. This will be found true of each pair of adjoining angles formed by the X the students have seen in each previous lesson. This concept will lead directly to the fourth grade Common Core standard related to recognition of angle measurement as additive. This aligns well with the concept development model. Mrs. Evans also uses a graffiti activity to review the unit's *know* objectives.

In general, Mrs. Evans is pleased with the unit. One of the motivating factors for her was to teach the unit in such a way that the girls in her class would find the material engaging and would develop more confidence and interest in learning math skills. She has not, however, made any explicit efforts in this area. None of the activities or mini-lectures was specifically aimed at girls, and she did not reference any women mathematicians. Now that she has taught the unit, Mrs. Evans will make a concerted effort to make certain that all students can relate to the material she is teaching. In fact, she is thinking about the relationship between success in science and mathematics and social justice issues. That might be a hook that engages all students—across genders, social class, and ethnicities.

WEB RESOURCE

Khan Academy

The design of this particular set of lessons was based in part on brief lessons related to "Angles and Intersecting Lines," available from Khan Academy: khanacademy.org.

Check out the resources available at Kahn, a treasure trove of ideas for teaching many of the subjects and topics in the curriculum. All Khan Academy content is available for free at khanacademy.org.

Also, check out possible data sources to use in mathematics lessons at Corps Watch: corpwatch.org. There are articles, cartoons, and data sets about issues that your students might find engaging.

SUMMARY

This case study took place in a fourth grade classroom during a math unit on angles. Mrs. Evans, the teacher in the class, has designed a unit with a variety of instructional models—all aligned with the unit's objectives. The unit began with vocabulary acquisition and included direct instruction, concept attainment, concept development, and a graffiti review. Mrs. Evans felt comfortable with these models and worked hard at being able to implement them successfully. These models are only some of what Mrs. Evans has in her instructional toolkit, but they were chosen for their alignment with the objectives and assessments that were sketched out in the unit.

Using a variety of instructional models in any classroom can be difficult. As Mrs. Evans discovered, it takes some time to master these models, and she felt more comfortable with some than with others. However, she was surprised by how well her young students were engaged by the variety of instruction, and she was grateful for the classroom management procedures she had in place in order to support her students' success.

EXTENSIONS

ACTIVITIES

1. You might have noticed that Mrs. Evan's lesson plans do not have lesson specific learning objectives. Choose one of the lesson plans and write learning objectives that are aligned with both the assessment and learning experiences of the lesson and the provided unit objectives.
2. Think about a unit you have taught or will be teaching. What are the concepts—the vocabulary—you want students to master during the unit? List the words and think about an appropriate instructional model that will help your students learn these concepts.
3. List the steps you would take in planning a lesson in a unit. What would you do first, second, and so on that would still keep you true to backward design.
4. Draw a flow chart for the decisions that Mrs. Evans made as she planned this unit.
5. Script the directions for a graffiti activity that could be used as a review for the fourth grade unit described in this chapter.

REFLECTIVE QUESTIONS

1. Think about the reasons why young girls might turn away from math, science, engineering, and technology in late elementary and middle school. What can you find out about why this happens, and what recommendations can you find that might turn this tide?
2. Skill and knowledge in mathematics can make or break a student's academic career. Why is this? What is it about algebra, for example, that helps those who are successful in algebra graduate from high school?
3. What problems are inherent in using instructional models in the classroom? What difficulties or opportunities might elementary students have as they participate in some of the instructional models presented in this text?
4. How should Mrs. Evans prepare her students for the routines and procedures associated with the different models she is using in the classroom?
5. How would you evaluate the use of backward design by Mrs. Evans? Was it used? How? Was it used appropriately? How do you know?

14 A Middle School Case Study

INTERDISCIPLINARY TEACHING

 Chapter Objectives

You Will Know

- The opportunities for using diverse instructional models in a middle school classroom.
- How a common theme can be used to connect disparate pieces of content
- The planning components in implementing a middle school interdisciplinary unit
- The relationships between desired objectives and instructional models
- The role of student achievement, experiences, and interests in choosing academic content and instruction

You Will Understand That

- Effective instruction requires careful planning and strong pedagogical knowledge
- Planning involves the application of knowledge of instructional models

You Will Be Able To

- Reflect and comment on the instructional planning of a group of middle school teachers
- Consider how you would develop a detailed plan for one lesson in a unit you might teach
- Determine whether the teachers described in this chapter used the principles of backward design

The interdisciplinary teaching team for the seventh grade at Mumford Middle School had a problem. Some of the teachers on the team—which covered the subjects of math, social studies, language arts, and science—were concerned that the students were fixed in their opinions. As Alice Brown, the science teacher, said one morning in frustration, "Narrow-minded, that's what they are! These kids just won't entertain a new thought about a fact or idea in the courses they take or about each other. Sometimes teaching them feels more like plowing rock than like planting seeds."

So began a conversation that would extend over several days and result in one of the most exciting teaching experiences any of these teachers had known. Like many teachers, the team had fallen into a rut, but they were about to find a way out of it.

Sam Lopez, the math teacher, who was a native of the small Midwestern farming community in which the school was located, came to the defense of the local community. "This may not be cosmopolitan Madison Avenue, Alice, but in place of sophistication, there is good, solid common sense in this community and in these kids. Their behavior is generally very good, and you know it is. They do what they are told and what their parents expect them to do."

"Yes," replied Alice, "but they also think the way they are told, and they can be cruel to those who are different in any way. In science, it is very important to be willing to look at ideas with an open and inquiring mind about issues like climate change."

Mary Teague, the social studies teacher, took her usual role of conciliator. "I appreciate that they are dependable and that they are motivated to do well. I, too, however, am concerned that we should be challenging their intellects and encouraging them to play with ideas instead of being so concerned with grades. The world gets more complicated with each day, and we need to provide knowledge and skills to these students so that they can navigate beyond getting a good grade."

Henry Martin, the English/language arts teacher and the usual bemused observer, said, "If we decide to challenge their intellects, we'd better be sure that the school board doesn't decide to challenge us. Those board members may not be very enthusiastic about the kids playing around with ideas."

"I'm not thinking of turning them into radical revolutionaries," said Alice. "I just want them to have some perspective, a point of view broader than that shared by many members of this community."

"Sounds radical enough to me," Henry rejoined. "Oh, well, it might break the boredom for a while."

Alice ignored the cynicism. "It just so happens that lately I've been thinking of a unit of study based on the concept of *perspective.* My hope is that I can get our students to consider the various ways in which a problem may be approached, whether it is a problem in science or any other subject."

"It's funny you should mention the word *perspective* this morning, Alice," said Sam. "I have been working on a unit in geometry, where perspective is all-important. My thought was that because the kids are fascinated with the design capabilities of computers, I might introduce them to linear perspective in a way that would teach them both about a new design program we have and about lines in three-dimensional space."

Alice responded with renewed enthusiasm, momentarily forgetting her frustration with the students. "You know, understanding the use of perspective marked the Renaissance. It literally changed forever the way we would describe and know the universe. I have always wanted to know more about the mathematical principles involved in the great paradigm shift of the Renaissance. I'd also like to teach the impact of perspective on our understanding of the physical world, particularly in regard to mapmaking. Could we plan this unit together?" she asked Sam.

"The concept of perspective certainly fits into the unit I am preparing to teach on the westward movement," Mary interjected. "I've been trying to think how to get across the idea that historians have their own perspectives that influence the way in which they recount events. No doubt, any historical perspective differs from that of the people who were involved in the events of history. Think how much difference it makes if one looks at the westward movement from the perspective of a settler or from the perspective of a Native American. I've heard it said that those who win the wars win the right to write the histories."

"You know, we haven't taught an interdisciplinary unit in a long time. Why don't we design a unit with a focus on the concept of *perspective?*" said Alice, her excitement evident to all.

Henry abandoned his role of detached observer and enthusiastically joined in. "I have been planning a unit in literature on point of view, but perspective is really the basis for understanding the meaning of point of view. As I recall, the viewpoint—or point of view—is the point where parallel lines converge in a painting to convey a sense of depth." Turning to Alice, he said, "It was the Renaissance painters who rediscovered this technique from the Greeks and who were able to create perspective in their painting, just as the mapmakers learned to do. Perspective is a much better concept to use for the focus of my unit. And I can choose material that will fit into your time frame of the westward movement," he continued, as he turned toward Mary. "That way we can look at historical perspective through the eyes of fictional characters as well as those of the historian. And each of the connections to perspective that we have discussed is addressed in our state standards."

As usual, the other team members were astonished at the wealth of information Henry could bring to a discussion. Everyone was ready, without actually putting the matter to any sort of vote, to try an interdisciplinary unit based on the concept of *perspective*.

The four team members shared a common planning time and were able to schedule the students for blocks of time each day. The rooms in which they taught were traditional classrooms except for one movable wall that allowed them to create a larger classroom for special purposes. In the past, their attempts at team teaching had been only partially successful, but this time they seemed at least to have ignited one another's interest.

At the next team meeting, Mary suggested that they brainstorm objectives for the unit based on the required standards. "For instance," she said, "I want the students to compare and contrast the perspectives of various groups regarding the westward movement. I want them to evaluate the perspective of the historian who is writing as well as to identify other possible perspectives of those who were involved in the events."

"I am concerned that they be able to define the term *perspective* in a general sense and then to see how perspective relates to writing," said Henry. "In their writing, I want them to use various perspectives to describe an event as well as to develop more dynamic ways to describe how others feel and act."

"I want them to be able to accept the possibility that there are various ways to look at the same phenomenon," said Alice, "and I want them to recognize and value the importance of looking beyond and questioning what appears to be obvious. I also want them to use the scientific approach in solving problems that require inquiry, particularly problems in which perspective affects how we interpret the physical world."

"I want them to use parallel lines and viewpoint to create perspective in simple designs with the use of the computer," said Sam. "Some of these kids are way ahead of me already on the computer, and I am really going to have to do my homework to keep up. That's part of the great fun we have teaching in a field that is developing faster than any of us can imagine, let alone keep up with. But in all the excitement of computers, I want the students to develop respect for the capabilities of this tool in describing three-dimensional phenomena on a two-dimensional screen."

Henry rolled his eyes as he sensed just how enthusiastic everyone was becoming, but he did so very slightly, not wishing to offend as much as to poke a little fun. But Alice wasn't going to let the seriousness of the moment pass. "And all of us are concerned that the students develop more understanding for others and increase their willingness to consider another point of view in solving problems in human relations," she said.

"We have our objectives for the unit right in front of us," said Mary. "There is *so much* content that we could incorporate into this unit! I think we should each bring to our next meeting an outline of the most important concepts that need to be covered in each discipline. The standards can help with this, and we can develop a common big idea."

TABLE 14.1 Standards Related to a Seventh Grade Multidisciplinary Unit on Perspectives

Standard Source	Standard
Common Core State Standards— English/Language Arts RH.6-8.2	Determine the central ideas or information of a primary or secondary source; provide an accurate summary of the source distinct from prior knowledge or opinions.
Common Core State Standards— English/Language Arts RH.6-8.6	Identify aspects of a text that reveal an author's point of view or purpose.
Common Core State Standards— English/Language Arts RH.6-8.8	Distinguish among fact, opinion, and reasoned judgment in a text.
Common Core State Standards— English/Language Arts W.7.3	Write narratives to develop real or imagined experiences or events using effective technique, relevant descriptive details, and well-structured event sequences.
Common Core State Standards— Math 7.GA.2	Draw (with the help of technology) geometric shapes with given conditions and describe the relationships between them.
State Science Standard	Evidence is the basis of scientific knowledge. Technology helps us collect evidence, but it is limited by many factors and may vary from place to place.

Table 14.1 contains Common Core English/Language Arts Literacy and Common Core Math Geometry standards as well as state history standards and Next Generation Science standards that are associated with this interdisciplinary unit on perspectives. When the teachers met again, each of them had diagrammed the main concepts that they thought should be included in the unit on *perspective* based on their understanding of the content and the requirements of the identified standards (see Table 14.2).

It was obvious that *viewpoint,* so important in creating perspective, had become an essential concept as it applied to understanding events and ideas relating to perspective. The teachers then realized that the meaning of *viewpoint* was one that the art teacher, Mrs. Fisk, could best explain to the students. She agreed that a

TABLE 14.2 Interdisciplinary Unit on Perspectives: Concepts and Skills

Students will understand that the study of perspective—how we look at things—allows for rich connections among a variety of topics.	
Geometry	point, line, plane, parallel, convergent, design, linear perspective
Science	exploration, mapmaking, scientific inquiry, nature of science
Literature	point of view, characters, plot, narrator
History	point of view, participants, events, document analysis, historiography
Art	viewpoint, convergence, parallel, lines, illusion

discussion on the point at which parallel lines converge in a painting, or in a design, to create the illusion of space would serve as an excellent advance organizer for the study of perspective. It was exciting to think that a fundamental concept of the art curriculum would be the focal point for study in many different disciplines simultaneously. This single concept would bring everything together, just as it had during the Renaissance! After their discussion with Mrs. Fisk, she agreed to do the keynote lesson twice—each time in the double classroom with two of the teachers and their classes present.

WEB RESOURCE

Integrating Art into Teaching

Infusing art into lesson plans in all disciplinary areas can increase student interest, engagement, and understanding. An article on opencolleges.edu.au named "50 Ways to Integrate Art into Any Lesson" provides a number of activities that can be used with instructional models.

The Mumford Plan

As they were designing their unit, the team members at Mumford Middle School decided to emphasize the geometry and earth science portions during the first part of the unit, followed by the literature and history sections. The art teacher's introductory lesson would extend across two days, at which time the main concepts related to perspective would be introduced. *Viewpoint,* or physical point of view, would be tied to visual perspective and to ideas and attitudes.

Mrs. Fisk decided to teach the definition of *viewpoint* by using the concept attainment model (examples and nonexamples were relatively easy to obtain). The definition of *viewpoint* then would serve as an organizer and point of reference for all members of the team throughout the unit. Her idea was to spend one day helping the students to capture elementary perspective in their own drawings. The next day she would bring in prints of pre-Renaissance and Renaissance art to use as positive and negative examples of perspective in art. A collection of M. C. Escher's pen-and-ink drawings, in which the mathematician/artist plays with perspective in a variety of ways, would serve as material for a culminating reinforcement activity. She would close with a brief lesson on how the students could achieve such play and deliberate ambiguity in their own drawings.

Following this lesson, all the teachers would explain their plans for the unit as it pertained to their classes. Each teacher planned to provide an outline of assignments, assessments, and activities and answer any questions the students might have about the unit. A diagnostic, or formative, test of the students' understanding of the content to be covered, to provide valuable information to the teachers regarding any changes or modification that might need to be made in the unit's design, would be given at this point. The test was particularly important to Sam in setting up the teams for instruction in computer skills. Each teacher had prepared a unit to support the broad unit transfer goal—"students will demonstrate willingness to consider different points of views in solving problems." Units also included unit objectives, lesson objectives, formative and summative assessments, daily lesson plans, and assignments and activities.

The geometry and science lessons would be taught for approximately three weeks. After the students had a basic introduction to computer-aided design (CAD), they would learn to create simple three-dimensional designs with the use of the computer. Sam decided that a form of the jigsaw model used in conjunction with the direct instruction model, using a gradual release of responsibility, would be an excellent way to teach the principles of CAD. Students would first work through a tutorial on the basics of computer design individually. Then, pairs of students would be given elementary problems to solve, getting immediate feedback on their success.

Next, teams of students with a range of achievement related to the computer would be formed, making it possible for students with more advanced computer skills to work with those having less skill. Each team would be charged with solving a different problem set while acquiring a different set of computer skills associated with computer-aided design. Individual team members would be expert in a particular aspect of design, and they would have the responsibility of teaching other students in their study group.

Following the computer lessons, the science teacher would introduce the relationship of perspective to an understanding of the physical world, particularly in recording what is observed through the design of maps. Alice would present puzzling but relatively common problem situations involving perspective. The students would solve these problems with an inquiry approach using the Suchman model (see Chapter Eleven). For instance, one problem would be to describe the appearance of a ship on the horizon and explain why it seems to grow larger as it draws near. Another problem would be to explain why the moon seems to be very large on the horizon but appears to grow smaller as it rises in the sky. The third and most difficult problem the students would be asked to solve by inquiry would be that of how to transfer the surface of a sphere (like a globe of Earth) onto a flat surface without distorting the relative sizes of land masses.

With these introductions to the concept of *perspective* as a foundation, Mary and Henry would work with the students toward an understanding of the way in which individuals interpret events in literature and in history, stressing that interpretation often depends on the individual's point of view. They decided that concept development, direct instruction, and jigsaw models would be effective in meeting their objectives. (This part of the unit is described in more detail in the next section.)

To illustrate how the models approach to teaching would work in this unit, we present the detailed lesson design from the portion that focused on the concept of *perspective* in history and literature, which is described in Table 14.3.

TABLE 14.3   Perspectives in History and Literature: Middle School Plan

Lesson	Time	Objectives	Models and Activities
1. Point of view (4 days)	4 hours	1. Students will know that a variety of points of view can exist on a given subject.	Concept development
		2. Students will understand that personal attitudes and beliefs have an impact on the meaning of *point of view* and *perspective* in art, science, and mathematics.	
		3. Students will know the meanings of *bias* and *preconception*.	Vocabulary acquisition
2. Perceptions (3 days)	3 hours	Students will be able to describe how preconceptions and experience can sometimes override perceptions.	Direct instruction Role play
3. Relating perceptions to perspective (3 days)	3 hours	1. Students will understand that the way individuals perceive events is related to the concept of *perspective* in literature and history.	Jigsaw
		2. Students will be able to identify various perspectives in writing.	Classroom discussion

Unit: Perspective—It All Depends on Where You Were When

Teaching Time

Two weeks

Objectives

Students Will Know

- The definition of perspective as it is defined in literature and history

Students Will Understand That

- Perspective cuts across disciplinary boundaries

Students Will Be Able To

- Relate the concept *perspective* to literature and history by recognizing how individuals perceive both real and fictional events
- Identify various perspectives in a situation, represent the point of view of each participant, and explain how the point of view determines the perspective
- Describe, in writing, how previous experiences and preconceptions affect the perception of events
- Describe a perspective other than their own in relation to a situation

Advance Organizer

Relate the meaning of *viewpoint* as it has been discussed in art, geometry, and science to the application of the term in literature, history, and human relations. Introduce the idea that the point of view determines perspective.

LESSON ONE: TOWARD A PERSPECTIVE ON POINT OF VIEW

Instructional Models

Concept development and vocabulary acquisition

Estimated Time

Two hours

Objectives

Students Will Know

- The meanings of *bias* and *preconception* and will be able to relate these terms to their own experience

Students Will Understand That

- A variety of points of view can exist on a single subject

Students Will Be Able To

- Relate attitudes and beliefs to the meanings of *point of view* and *perspective* in art, science, and math

Rationale for Choices of Models

It has been said that there are three kinds of thinkers: those who believe that what they think is the only way to think, those who consider others who think like they do to be the best thinkers, and those who can think in several ways about the same thing. The psychologist Jean Piaget termed the first thinker *egocentric,* the second thinker *concrete,* and the final (and best) thinker *formal.* But Piaget's great contribution to psychology was in proving that the child learns from experience by constructing a model of how the world is (Piaget, 1954). Concept development will provide students the opportunity to see that different points of view (of possibly equal validity) can be held by reasonable thinkers on the same topic. As they have the chance to discriminate between different points of view on a similar topic, they will see that each thinker is at once a concrete thinker, who sees the world through one set of eyes, and a formal thinker, who can recognize the reasonableness of alternative views of the same facts and ideas. Vocabulary acquisition will provide a definition for the terms *bias* and *preconception.*

Application of the Models

After the students have clearly identified the terms, they will be given a series of quotations representing points of view that are both alike and different in various ways. For instance, some will represent the same bias, some will be about the same event, and some will be spoken by the same person. The students will be asked to group and categorize these quotations and then to explain the reason for their decisions. The students will work in pairs and then come together as a large group to discuss their decisions and the reasons for their decisions.

Assessment

At the conclusion of this lesson, the students will discuss what they learned earlier in the unit during the math and science portions and how that material relates to the new learning of this lesson. Students will be asked to make two explicit connections on a card to be given to the teacher as they exit the class. This discussion will also serve as a midpoint evaluation of the students' progress (see Chapter Ten).

LESSON TWO: PERCEPTION—IT DEPENDS ON WHERE YOU ARE COMING FROM

Instructional Models

Direct instruction and Suchman inquiry model

Estimated Time

Three hours

Objectives

Students Will Know

- The definition of perspective as it is defined in literature and history

Students Will Understand That

- Perspective cuts across disciplinary boundaries

Students Will Be Able To

- Describe how preconceptions and experience affect the perception of an event

Rationale for Choices of Models

Instruction will be both indirect and direct as the teachers will set up a circumstance that gives rise to questions to be answered by direct instruction, followed by a Suchman inquiry discussion. (As this example demonstrates, direct instruction does not equal passive learning.) The questions the teachers will pose and the activities in which the students will engage center on the issue of perception: what one is predisposed to see versus what one sees. But predisposition is always governed by three factors, and those factors are the point of this instruction. By setting up a series of experiences for the students whereby they see that the relation between where they are (figuratively and literally) and what they are observing determines what they see, the stage is set for presenting the three factors that define "where the observer is coming from."

Application of the Models

The lesson will begin with the reading of a description of a house. The description includes the setting of the house; the number of windows, doors, and rooms; the present furnishings and decorations; where the occupants keep their valuables; and so on. Half the class will be asked to read the account as if they were a professional burglar, and the other half will read the account as if they were a prospective buyer of the house. (Because directions to the students will be written, rather than given orally, each half of the class will be unaware of the alternative perspective taken by the other half.) Following a silent reading of the passage, students will retell what they recall. This initial experience will provide dramatic proof that the same experience for different people is a different experience. When perception is different, experience is different.

Next the teachers will ask the two groups to consider each of the following questions: (1) You are in desperate need of money for your family and decide to burglarize this home. What do you need to know and be able to do to accomplish this burglary successfully? (2) Your neighborhood has experienced a number of burglaries. What do you need to know and be able to do to protect your family and home? Students will follow the Suchman inquiry process as they work in two separate groups. At the end of their work, the two groups will share and compare their findings.

Building from this activity, the teachers will present a direct instruction lesson on the three factors that influence the perspective of those who witness events:

1. The viewpoint of the perceiver
2. Previous experiences of the observer
3. Preconceptions

After these have been explained, with many examples, students will be questioned and will be asked to give examples themselves to check for understanding. More guided practice will occur when students view a video of an accident and then identify the various perspectives of the witnesses as these relate to point of view, possible previous experiences, and preconceptions. For independent practice, the students will be given an assignment to describe an event depicted on a television sitcom from the point of view, previous experience, and preconceptions of the different characters involved. They will then be asked to retell the event using another point of view, experience, and preconception.

Assessment

Students will be given a worksheet to take home that will ask them to answer specific questions relating to the television program. Those students who choose to write their own essay may do so, but those who have more difficulty in writing may follow the format of the worksheet. These worksheets and essays will be evaluated to determine whether the class understood the assignment.

LESSON THREE: RELATING PERCEPTION AND PERSPECTIVE

Instructional Model

Jigsaw

Estimated Time

Three hours class time plus outside work in preparation

Objectives

Students Will Know

- The definition of perspective as it is defined in literature and history

Students Will Understand That

- Perspective cuts across disciplinary boundaries

Students Will Be Able To

- Relate the concept of perspective to literature and history by identifying how individuals, both real and fictional, perceive events from their particular points of view
- Identify various perspectives in selections of writing, and explain the point of view of each author
- Explain how perception determines perspective

Rationale for Choice of Model

Jigsaw is both an instructional model and an instructional activity, with the great attributes of accommodating a wide range of student achievement in a single classroom and allowing for great efficiency of effort on the part of the group. In this instance, the students can collectively read many selections and thus encounter many historical and fictional perspectives and points of view. By cooperating in their learning and sharing in their understandings, they will cover much ground quickly, reading literally hundreds of pages of material and experiencing the same ideas through many different eyes. Jigsaw thus allows each learner to come to the insights of many different learners merely by sharing his or her own insights.

Application of the Model

The students will be assigned to teams of four, with a range of achievement in each group. Each individual in the team will be given a reading assignment related to the westward movement; assignments will be selected to match the reading readiness of different team members. The teams will be given different sets of readings: some short stories, some selections from novels, some from original source documents, and some from textbook chapters on the westward expansion. The students have three days to study the material and will be directed to discuss their selections with members of a study group who have been assigned readings similar to their own. They are to identify the perspective of the author and of the major characters or persons in the story or essay and then to explain this perspective to the other members of their team. Following team discussions, the class as a whole will discuss the selections and the various perspectives presented in the material using the classroom discussion model.

Assessment

Students will be provided a short excerpt about a family making the trip west. They will write an essay that demonstrates their attainment of the lesson's objectives.

Epilogue

At the end of the actual unit of study, the interdisciplinary teaching team is having dinner together to discuss and evaluate their experience in teaching the unit. Although some activities were unsuccessful, everyone wholeheartedly agrees that the unit has been a success. The assessments of how well the students met the cognitive objectives indicated a high rate of achievement, and attitudinal surveys, designed to ensure anonymity, indicated that most of the students had enjoyed the unit and had an increased awareness of different perspectives.

The team remembers the final discussions with particular pleasure. The students had been presented with a situation that involved a person from another country with an entirely different culture enrolling at the school. The discussion centered on the various problems the student would encounter and how that individual's perspective would differ from that of others. The teachers had taped and compared the various discussions. All agree that the students gained insights into how others might feel about a particular situation. The teachers have also learned that these young people have the capacity to deal with complicated ideas and to respond to material that challenges their preconceptions. "My perception is that these really are a great bunch of kids," says Henry. And to that, there is agreement all around.

SUMMARY

This chapter examined the cooperative efforts of a seventh grade team to plan a multidisciplinary unit on perspective. Cooperative planning by teachers across disciplines can provide a rewarding professional experience. In addition, such cooperation enriches the learning experience for students, particularly young adolescents, who enjoy seeing the way in which a concept threads meaning through a variety of disciplines, increasing the understanding of each.

Interdisciplinary study provides the opportunity to scaffold student learning. Comprehension is increased when students can contrast many examples within and across disciplinary areas that provide a deep comparison pool (Willingham, 2009). In addition, student interest and motivation in one area may spill over to another.

It takes time to organize and prepare interdisciplinary units, and teachers must be willing to take the time to plan cooperatively. The rewards for both teachers and students are high and the use of instructional models can help to support the effort.

WEB RESOURCE

Strategies for Interdisciplinary Teaching

Project Zero at the Harvard University Graduate School of Education conducted an interesting interdisciplinary studies project. An essay by Svetlana Nikitinia, titled "Three Strategies for Interdisciplinary Teaching," posits that there are different strategies for different content areas, namely contextualizing, conceptualizing, and problem solving. You will find the essay at old-pz.gse.harvard.edu. This interesting proposition can have an effect on the success of cooperative planning ventures.

EXTENSIONS

ACTIVITIES

1. Discuss interdisciplinary teaching with a group of teachers. What do they see as the costs and benefits? Do the same with a group of students at the age level in which you are teaching or hope to teach. What are the difficulties and benefits they identify?

2. Think about the big ideas, concepts, and skills that you teach or will be teaching. Can you identify skills or ideas that would be a good fit for an interdisciplinary approach? Develop an overarching understanding and some disciplinary concepts and skills that can be linked together and molded into an interdisciplinary unit.

3. Write a detailed lesson plan for one of the lessons described in the chapter. Include KUD objectives, formative assessments, and instructional procedures.

4. What problems are inherent in using instructional models in the classroom? What difficulties or opportunities might middle school students have as they participate in some of the instructional models presented in this text?

REFLECTIVE QUESTIONS

1. What are the arguments against asking first-year teachers to participate in interdisciplinary work? What are the arguments for first-year teachers participating in such an effort?

2. How would you evaluate the role of the art teacher in the unit on perspective described in this chapter? Would you have increased her involvement? How? Why? Why not?

3. How would you evaluate the use of backward design by the teachers in this chapter? Was it used? How? How might backward design support interdisciplinary efforts?

15 A High School Case Study
AMBITION AND THE POWER OF SUGGESTION

 Chapter Objectives

You Will Know

- The opportunities for using diverse instructional models in a high school classroom
- The planning components in implementing a secondary unit
- The relationship between desired objectives and instructional models
- The role of student achievement, experiences, and interests in choosing academic content and instruction

You Will Understand That

- Effective instruction requires careful planning and strong pedagogical knowledge
- Planning involves the application of knowledge of instructional models

You Will Be Able To

- Reflect and comment on the instructional planning of a high school English teacher
- Consider how you would develop a detailed plan for one lesson in a unit you might teach
- Determine whether the teacher described in this chapter used the principles of backward design

---

As the pungent scent of Rudy's Dry Cleaners greeted Jake Samuels, an unfamiliar voice said, "Hi, Mr. Samuels."

"Hi," responded Mr. Samuels, trying to place the friendly face.

"I'm Chris Pezzoli. I go to Madison High School. May I help you?"

"My cleaning, please," Mr. Samuels answered, as he handed Chris the laundry ticket, still curious about where he had seen this young man. He was just a face in a sea of faces in the halls at Madison.

"Yes, sir. Coming right up." Chris started the line of clothes moving around. When Mr. Samuels's suit appeared, Chris handed it to him, saying, "I always wanted to have you for English, but I'm in a general class. I've heard what a good teacher you are, but you teach only the advanced classes." He hesitated, feeling a little embarrassed at his own boldness.

"Thanks for the vote of confidence. I'm sorry I'm not teaching you, Chris. I'd like to."

"So long." Chris shrugged and smiled with a good-bye, "See you around."

As he left the cleaners, Mr. Samuels thought about Chris. He thought about his own schedule. Now that he was chairperson of the department, he taught only three classes. And Chris was right: They were all top-track classes. The encounter reminded him, though, that he missed the general classes he used to teach. Those students struck a special chord for him, possibly because his was the last English class they might take. He remembered how he always wanted to give it all to them—everything he loved about English—served up on a silver platter so invitingly that they would surely seek more.

He began to think aloud. "Instead we water it down, trying to make it more palatable. But there's a contradiction in that. Shouldn't it be just the reverse? Shouldn't we enrich the content of classes for general students?"

As he turned onto Madison Avenue, he was deep in thought. Sure, there had been problems when he taught general education and remedial classes. His teaching style of lecture and discussion did not work for students who had difficulty taking notes or paying attention for long periods. But he had learned so much in the past few years as department chairperson, observing other teachers and attending workshops and in-service sessions on instructional strategies. And these experiences helped him learn more about what we know about learning and how to support the learning that students need to accomplish in the classroom. He had learned to use a variety of instructional models in his advanced classes, and he was certain that these would work well with all students. The idea he was contemplating would give him an opportunity to put his theory to the test. He wanted to try it.

At 4 o'clock the following Monday afternoon, Mr. Samuels poked his head into the classroom next to his. His colleague, Ms. O'Brien, was correcting papers.

"Liz, do you have a minute?"

"Sure, come on in. I'm always too drained to get anything accomplished this time of day. Good to see you, Jake. How do you manage to look so chipper at the end of a long day?"

"Thanks, I don't always feel chipper. It's just a facade I put on. I need to talk to you, though. I met a student of yours the other day, Chris Pezzoli. Tell me about him."

"Well, Chris is a very nice young man, imaginative and hard working, very likable. He's in my fourth-period class. I see his parents around town now and again. His dad was laid off when the woolen mill closed. He does odd jobs—forced self-employment, he calls it—but he hasn't been able to pick up anything steady. Chris's mother works, but they really need what Chris brings in from his job at the dry cleaner's. I know he's going to work there full time after graduation. I'm trying to talk him into taking community college courses at night, but I think it's futile. Of course, if his dad does find something steady. . . ." Her words trailed off without much hope in her voice.

Mr. Samuels interrupted, "I've been thinking about these kids in the general classes and about how much I miss teaching them. I had an idea. How would you like to try switching classes fourth period for about four weeks as a kind of experiment? I have some ideas I'd like to try with the kids. I thought I'd try to teach them *Macbeth*. The play fits into the standards we follow, and there are some instructional strategies I would like to try. " After a pause, he grinned. "Think I'm crazy? You'd be teaching the poetry of the romantics, not one of my favorite units, but just your cup of tea, I know."

Ms. O'Brien looked at him for a minute as his suggestion took shape in her mind. "Do I think you're crazy? Yes. Do I think it's a good idea? It just might be an excellent idea. I'd love to see how they will respond . . . and I'd love to have a crack at your kids. Nineteenth-century poetry is my first love."

Mr. Samuels's Plan

That night Mr. Samuels put aside the papers he was planning to grade. He thought about Chris and the large, probably slightly jaded group he would face. But the challenge of it was energizing; he was more excited than he had been for some time. He began making notes on what he wanted to accomplish and how the required standards fit in.

First, he wanted them to enjoy the play. This would guide everything he did those four weeks. But wanting students to enjoy his favorite play was not enough. He knew he needed to carefully define his learning objectives. For example, he wanted students to know how shrewd Shakespeare was and how relevant his thinking remains today, so he would need to design objectives, assessments, and learning experiences targeted to this goal.

Mr. Samuels wanted the students to examine the concept *ambition* and how it can be a constructive force in moderation and a dangerous force in excess. To do this, they must understand the complexity of the characters of Macbeth and Lady Macbeth. If these characters were seen as all bad, the students would miss a great deal of the play's wisdom. He wanted them to grasp the power of suggestion and of what it could mean to plant an idea in an all-too-fertile mind. And he wanted them to be stirred by the beauty, subtlety, and bawdiness of the language. He hoped to draw them into this Elizabethan world, much as Shakespeare had drawn his audiences into his stories.

Where did these goals come from? Mr. Samuels was an expert teacher with years of experience, and because of that he was willing to rely intuitively on his judgment as a teacher, his expertise in *Macbeth*, his convictions about students' needs, and his knowledge of the standards to which he is accountable. The Common Core State Standards for English/Language Arts for reading literature in grades 11–12 map to Mr. Samuels's plan fairly well. Thus, with some confidence, he translated his vaguely defined goals into a specific list.

WEB RESOURCE

Teaching Shakespeare in K–12 Classrooms

A number of websites are devoted to teaching Shakespeare in K–12 classrooms. Two of the richest depositories are Teaching *Macbeth*, a resource from Folger Education (an arm of the Folger Shakespeare Library) at folger.edu and *Macbeth* Educator's Guide from Great Performances (seen on PBS), which can be found at pbs.org. Both of these sites have lesson plans, primary sources, curriculum guides, and so on—a great way to begin planning a unit!

Students Will Know

- The poetic rhythm of iambic pentameter
- The major distinguishing characteristics of Elizabethan England
- The meaning of the phrase *power of suggestion*
- The complex qualities of the major characters in *Macbeth*
- *Macbeth* is a play that often evokes strong feelings in readers—many readers love the play and believe it is the best play ever written in English literature
- The themes in the story of *Macbeth* are as powerful and relevant as when it was first written

Students Will Understand That

- Ambition is constructive in moderation and harmful in excess

Students Will Be Able To

- Master difficult material and as a consequence gain confidence in their own intellect

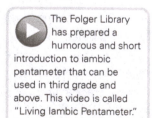
The Folger Library has prepared a humorous and short introduction to iambic pentameter that can be used in third grade and above. This video is called "Living Iambic Pentameter." www.youtube.com/watch?v=9H2htG2bv20

In the not-so-distant past, Mr. Samuels might have stopped his general planning at this point and begun to think in terms of daily lessons. He had recently realized, however, that he needed to be far more precise in his planning—by beginning with what he wanted students to accomplish by the end of the unit (backward design). This meant listing specific student needs after researching the students' backgrounds. It meant selecting specific objectives and models that would help him reach those objectives. It also meant devising means of evaluating how well he had achieved those objectives. It sounded complicated, but it was becoming second nature and saved time and effort in the end. Most of all, it increased his and his students' sense of engagement and satisfaction.

During the next week he gathered a lot of data: He talked to Ms. O'Brien; he reviewed records and test scores; he casually and unobtrusively observed the class he was to teach; and he carefully reread the play, outlining the content for essential understandings. He remembered Chris's shrug. It had been eloquent; it had said, "I guess we get only what we deserve."

Mr. Samuels believed that the students needed to be given challenging material, and implicit in his choice of *Macbeth* was the statement, "You can do it; I will not teach down to you." But that, in turn, implied a commitment to give the students the support they needed to become independent. Although the thought seemed almost contradictory, it implied that he must not fail them or allow them to fail themselves. He would provide the necessary supports through aligned instruction and timely and specific feedback. If the unit were to build their confidence and expand their interests, they would first have to commit themselves to the challenge, to like what they were doing well enough not to fail in it. He listed what the students would need:

1. To be presented with challenging material that is connected to what they already know
2. To know that someone thought they could grasp difficult material and would provide supports for reaching specific goals as a student
3. To be taken seriously and have their opinions sought and valued
4. To gain skills and knowledge that can be useful in school and life and will increase self-efficacy
5. To talk about important issues and real feelings
6. To demonstrate how we get smarter and more competent with each successful learning experience (growth mindset)

Based on the combination of goals and needs that he had listed, Mr. Samuels wrote general objectives for the unit on *Macbeth* and considered how he might evaluate the unit's success. After all, if he could not demonstrate to himself that the students had learned and profited from this unit, then he should stay with the advanced classes. Mr. Samuels wrote his objectives, including methods to evaluate each objective:

1. Students will understand that *Macbeth* is a compelling piece of literature and be interested in learning more about it. This will be evaluated by using pre- and post-unit surveys in which students can react to items without fear of being identified.

2. Students will be able to relate themes in *Macbeth* to their daily lives. This will be evaluated through the scripts that students design to place scenes from *Macbeth* into contemporary settings.

3. Students will understand how the sound of words can augment meaning and humor. They will know the poetic rhythm of iambic pentameter. This will be evaluated by having them present a piece of their favorite music and explain how beat and lyrics work together.

4. Students will be able to analyze the main characters and identify the elements in those characters that create complexity. This objective can be evaluated through words, images, or both: Pictures can be drawn or a collage constructed or an essay written about one or more of the characters and their varied and conflicting characteristics. (Mr. Samuels knew that not all students are successful in communicating their knowledge through words. The students could, however, sometimes express concepts through a different medium. Although there are a number of written assignments in the unit, he also wanted to be sure that he measured what he was teaching and not just the students' reading and writing skills.)

5. Students will know the major distinguishing characteristics of Elizabethan England, and they will convey their knowledge by teaching some aspect of Elizabethan society to a small group of peers. Evaluation will be based on student preparation, knowledge, and performance in teaching the material.

6. Students will know the meaning of the phrase *power of suggestion* and the idea of self-fulfilling prophecy. Students will be asked to give examples of each from their everyday life. Examples will be evaluated based on relevance and quality.

With these objectives in mind, Mr. Samuels contemplated the possible models he would use to achieve them, in what sequence he would use them, and how much time he would allot for each part of the unit plan:

1. He would start with a concept attainment lesson on classics . . . no, he would use the term *best sellers,* because that had more drawing power and was much more appropriate. Shakespeare, after all, was very conscious of box-office appeal. (Later, they would talk about the distinction between a classic and a best seller and about how some works of art are both.) He would use positive examples of best sellers, such as the Bible, *The Avengers* (the movie and comic book), and hip-hop music. His negative examples would consist of a lesser-known short story from their text, a poem he had written, a record called *Comin' Home* that a friend had cut, and a favorite painting by a little-known artist from his hometown. Once they could define the concept of best seller, he would ask what elements they would include if they were trying to write a play that would be a best seller. He would make a list of their ideas (he predicted that they would mention things like suspense, violence, and a little romance), and then as a group they would try to derive a set of standards of excellence from this list.

Later they would apply their standards to *Macbeth,* considered in the time of its first appearance in the Globe Theatre. How many of the same standards did Shakespeare seem to apply? What standards did he employ that they did not? What ingredients did they think of that Shakespeare did not cover (for example, the medium of delivery)? How would the passage of 400 years alter the standards of literature? These questions and others that arose would cast a new light on the play for these adolescent readers.

2. Next, he would use direct instruction with mini-lectures, monologues, videos, and artwork to give them background information on Shakespeare's life and times. He would emphasize the tricks Shakespeare used to capture the attention of the audience in the opening scenes. He would show the ghost in the opening scene of *Hamlet* and the fight in the opening scene of *Romeo and Juliet* and would make the students guess what ploy would be used to open *Macbeth*. Thus, students might accept a gradual release of responsibility as they applied the direct instruction lesson to guided and independent practice.

3. He would also use a cooperative learning model, jigsaw, for background information. He would divide the class into five groups. The groups would do research in preparation for teaching one another, in a variety of ways, about Elizabethan daily life (food, fashion, sports, sanitation, and so on), government, art and architecture, social class structure, education, and agriculture and industry.

4. He would open the play with the movie version of the first two acts of *Macbeth,* allowing the students to track the play in their books as they watched it. With a basic understanding of the plot firmly established, they would read the third act together, dramatizing various scenes and speeches and closely examining words, connotations, and concepts.

5. If the reading of Act 3 went well, they would read Act 4 together rather than view the film. He would use cooperative learning again for Act 5. In groups, they would role play various possible scenarios to present to the class.

6. He would have the students perform the concept development model on the word *ambition*. Students would list and organize all of the words they can think of associated with ambition and then make generalizations from their groupings.

7. While they were working on their scenes, he would interject a lesson on Lady Macbeth, using the synectics model. This would be a powerful and effective tool for showing them the contradictions and opposing forces within a character.

8. When they had finished the play, he would conduct a Socratic seminar. To gain a more sympathetic view of the main characters, they would examine the text through the eyes of specific characters and try to hypothesize particular feelings and motivations.

9. Finally, he would build on these insights by using an inquiry model to explore how the tragedy came about. At the beginning of the play, Macbeth is not such a villain. He had many good qualities, but in a very brief time he had caused the downfall of most of his country's leadership. How had this happened? Was so much violence plausible? This was the puzzle he hoped to get them to consider. He suspected that they would see the cause of the tragedy purely in terms of too much ambition, and he wanted them to look further, to delve into other causes. To understand the answer to the questions posed, they would have to go outside the play and inquire about conditions in 11th-century Scotland. What about the isolation of life then, near the height of the Middle Ages? Perhaps it is easier to plot against someone you seldom see. It was a violent time, with frequent attacks from unknown sources, and a street-gang mentality had developed in response to the constant threat against the territory. Macbeth had gained his reputation by warring successfully. Mr. Samuels wanted the students to search for these explanations themselves; he did not want to spoon-feed them.

Mr. Samuels charted the sequence of lessons within the unit that he had developed (see Table 15.1). He felt that one detailed lesson—using concept development and classroom discussion—held an important key for understanding the play. Initially, he had focused solely in this lesson on the concept *ambition,* but the more he thought about this, the more he felt two primary concepts—*ambition* and the *power of suggestion* — were inextricably woven in the play. This lesson is described in the next section.

TABLE 15.1   *Macbeth:* A Study in Ambition Turned to Avarice

The Stage of Anticipation (before the Play)	The Stage of Realization (during the Play)	The Stage of Contemplation (after the Play)
Concept attainment on best sellers	Synectics on Lady Macbeth	Socratic seminar days
Direct instruction on background	Concept development and cause and effect on ambition/power of suggestion	Inquiry
Jigsaw—research and student presentations on background	Translating scenes to contemporary life	

Unit: *Macbeth*—A Study in Ambition Turned to Avarice

Instructional Models

Concept development and cause and effect

Teaching Time

Six to eight days, on approximately the following schedule:

Monday and Tuesday   Concept development lesson on the witches, culminating with a paragraph by each student on one group of items in the concept development lesson. The group's label will be the topic sentence, and the categorized items will be the supporting evidence.

Wednesday   Cause-and-effect lesson on the dual concepts of ambition and power of suggestion in *Macbeth*.

Thursday   Classroom discussion to continue, with emphasis on contemporary examples and how these concepts are connected in time and behaviors.

Friday   Students to find expression (such as a formal paper, collage, audio recording, drawing, or dialogue) for the single idea from the discussion that they found most interesting.

Monday   Students share their work in groups of three to get feedback, reactions, and suggestions.

Tuesday   Students share their final products with the class.

Objectives

Students Will Know

- The definitions of *ambition* and *power of suggestion*
- The development of and problems associated with too much of any trait, especially ambition
- How to generate hypotheses from text and discussion

Students Will Understand That

- Shakespeare's work represents common themes in contemporary life
- Ambition is constructive in moderation and destructive in excess
- The power of suggestion influences behavior

Students Will Be Able To

- Express in one of several artistic media their comprehension of the meaning of the word *ambition* in its best sense
- State orally their understanding of the danger of a trait possessed in excess
- Demonstrate in writing how the concept of ambition relates to their daily lives
- Infer, from discussions of events in the play, the causes of Macbeth's and Lady Macbeth's excessive ambition
- Describe in writing the power of suggestion by using examples from their daily lives
- Give examples of connections between the power of suggestion and ambition
- Generate hypotheses about the form witches might take in contemporary life

Rationale for Choices of Model

The students in this class will be likely to see things in rather concrete terms and to cast things in black and white. By verbalizing all the impressions they have of the witches in this play, they should see collectively what they may not see individually—namely, that the witches are symbolic of the fate that plays in every person's life. The students also need to see that the witches are Shakespeare's ploy for speaking directly to his audience about what is going on in Macbeth's mind and how strong the power of suggestion is. The cause-and-effect model will extend the ideas generated by the class in the concept development activity by looking at the relationship of the actions of a number of characters.

Application of the Concept Development Model

In effect, these two sophisticated concepts, the power of suggestion leading to unbridled ambition, will be approached through the witches. Specific learning activities will have the students do the following:

1. List everything they remember about the witches (including inferences about their purpose)
2. Group these details
3. Label these groups, showing their understanding and agreement on the reason for connecting the items
4. Rethink these connections and new ones by forming new groups
5. Demonstrate their grasp of the witches' role by synthesizing the items and forming generalizations

The following are some of the questions that will direct this concept development lesson. The parenthetical instructions are reminders Mr. Samuels made to himself:

1. What specific things does the word *witches* bring to mind in the play *Macbeth*? Or name everything you can think of that is connected with the witches. (Do not stop until you have a comprehensive list.)
2. Look carefully at this list. Are there items that belong together or that are alike in some way?
3. Why do you think *cauldron* and *smoke* go together? (Do not label the items until the students have agreed on the reason for the grouping.)
4. Look at the original list again. Are there other groups we could put together? (Move slowly here. Give them time to rethink. List groups.)
5. Looking over the entire chalkboard, what can we say in general about witches?

Assessment for the Concept Development Lesson

The students will express their enriched understanding of the witches' role by developing one of the groups into a paragraph in which the label becomes the topic sentence and the items become supporting evidence.

Application of the Cause-and-Effect Model

A follow-up discussion to the concept development activity.

Estimated Time

Two days

Stated Problem 1: Duncan's Murder

1. Discuss the problem—Duncan's murder.
2. Discuss causes and support. Ask the students to discuss the reasons for King Duncan's murder, giving specific supporting examples.

3. Discuss effects and support. What are some of the effects of Duncan's murder? How do you know that these are effects?
4. Discuss prior causes and support. What caused Macbeth to believe the prophecies of the witches? What makes you think so?
5. Discuss subsequent effects and support. What were the effects of Macbeth's killing spree? Explain why you believe these effects were important.
6. What conclusions can you draw about Macbeth and Duncan's murder?
7. What general statements can you make about our discussion?

Stated Problem 2: The Power of Suggestion and Ambition

1. Discuss the problem—the power of suggestion and ambition.
2. Discuss causes and support. What caused or contributed to Macbeth's ambition to become king? What makes you say so?
3. Discuss effects and support. What effect did this ambition have? Based on what evidence?
4. Discuss prior causes and support. What caused Macbeth and his wife to plot and murder? Explain your answers.
5. Discuss subsequent effects and support. What were the effects of Macbeth believing the prophecies? How do you know that the connections between the prophecies and your beliefs about subsequent effects are reasonable?
6. What conclusions can you make about ambition and the power of suggestion?
7. What general statements can you make about our discussion?

Assessment for the Cause-and-Effect Lesson

The discussions would give Mr. Samuels an excellent idea of how well the students were grasping these concepts. But their knowledge would be taken one step further. They needed practice in writing, because this was a weak area, and it was necessary to know how well each student had grasped these understandings. He would ask them to do one of the following:

1. Choose one of the concepts (ambition or power of suggestion) and, in a one-page paper, give an example of how that concept has affected you in your daily life.
2. Write a one- to two-page paper on your goals in life and what forces have shaped them.
3. Write about the most ambitious person you know. Compare that person with King and Lady Macbeth.

The students were to write a first draft of their papers, share it with small groups of students to get *positive* suggestions, and then write a final draft.

Epilogue

When the four weeks ended, Mr. Samuels was pleased with the outcome of his experiment. By and large, the students had responded to his vote of confidence in their ability. As he had suspected, they had been capable of talking about far more sophisticated ideas than they had been able to get on paper. He was disappointed that they had not been able to read more of the text together. As he had anticipated, it had been very difficult for them, and they had become discouraged and a bit defensive. The reading would perhaps have gone much better if they had seen the entire movie version first so that they would have known what to expect.

The instructional models had allowed the students to be active participants in the learning process. As a result, they had been much more engaged in learning. One highlight of the unit had been the synectics lesson. The following is an abbreviated description of that lesson.

Step 1

Students worked in groups of three to discuss Lady Macbeth and to brainstorm ideas and impressions of her. As a follow up, each student wrote a short paragraph about her. From these paragraphs, the students compiled a list of their strongest specific descriptive words: *shrill, shrew, iceberg, obsessed, conspirator, vixen, acid-tongued, murderous, two-faced, treacherous, sly, wily, conniving.*

Step 2

The students were asked to look at what they had written, to see whether those words suggested an animal or a machine. Here are some examples of their answers:

- Tiger (stalks its prey secretly)
- Spider (lures its prey within its clutches)
- Stiletto (looks delicate, is deadly)

Step 3

Next, the students were asked to pick one item from the list, to pretend they were that object, and to describe how that object felt. They picked the stiletto. Here are some of the feelings individual students described:

- "I feel *dainty:* I am slender, small, tapering, fancy, swift (and deadly)."
- "I feel *proud:* I am slim and fancy and quite beautiful."
- "I feel *sly:* I can be easily hidden, and I fly quickly, silently."
- "I feel *powerful:* I can hurt enemies before they even know it."
- "I feel *sneaky:* I can be concealed and used on someone unsuspecting."
- "I feel *lonely:* I have no friends; I sit alone in my case."
- "I feel *imprisoned:* I am kept covered and hidden."
- "I feel *helpless:* I have no control over when and how I am used."
- "I feel *deadly:* I am small and quiet but razor sharp."

Step 4

The students were then asked to look at their list of feelings and pick out words that seemed to contradict or fight with each other. They picked the following:

- *Proud* and *sneaky*
- *Dainty* and *powerful*
- *Imprisoned* and *powerful*
- *Dainty* and *deadly*

Step 5

The class chose *imprisoned* and *powerful* to pursue. They were asked to name things that are both imprisoned and powerful. They named the following:

- Nuclear power
- A submarine captain
- A boxer against the ropes
- A wounded bear
- A gladiator performing for an emperor
- A tiger in a cage

Step 6

Returning to the subject of Lady Macbeth, Mr. Samuels asked the students to choose one of these images and compare it to her. Most chose "a gladiator performing for an emperor." They described her as powerful and deadly but a puppet of her ambition, just as a gladiator is a puppet of his emperor.

SUMMARY

This chapter examined a rigorous and instructionally diverse unit on Shakespeare's Macbeth, taught to a general-level group of seniors who did not have a deep knowledge of Shakespeare or the tools to analyze Shakespeare's work. Mr. Samuels, who planned this unit, believes in a "growth mindset," believing students can rise to our high expectations and be successful on challenging tasks when they are given good instruction and support. He used a number of instructional models in this unit, continuously engaging his students as they learned about his favorite play.

EXTENSIONS

ACTIVITIES

1. Visit a high school classroom that has been designated a lower-track class. Ask the students what they are learning and what they wish they were learning. Listen carefully to what the students are saying about school and the curriculum. Once your conversations are over, think about what the school can do to help each student have the opportunity to interact with challenging content.
2. Construct a unit blueprint or outline in your content area that would expose lower-achieving students to challenging content. What issues influence your instructional decisions? What role does background knowledge play? Must students be able to demonstrate all prerequisite skills to interact with this content?
3. Draw a graphic organizer for the instructional decisions made in this chapter's unit or for a unit that you will be teaching. Was the process of organizing the information graphically helpful? In what ways?

REFLECTIVE QUESTIONS

1. The chapter case study focused on *Macbeth*. What challenging content might you teach in your content area to a group of students who have not had the opportunity for rich content and varied instruction? Why? How would you make the case to your peers that this content is reasonable for lower-achieving students?
2. Mr. Samuels used a variety of instructional models. Were they used appropriately? How might you determine the answer to this question? Were there other models that would have been effective in this unit? Which models? Why?
3. What elements of backward design were obvious in Mr. Samuels's planning? Which elements were missing?
4. What problems are inherent in using instructional models in a high school classroom? What difficulties or opportunities might secondary students have as they participate in some of the instructional models presented in this text?

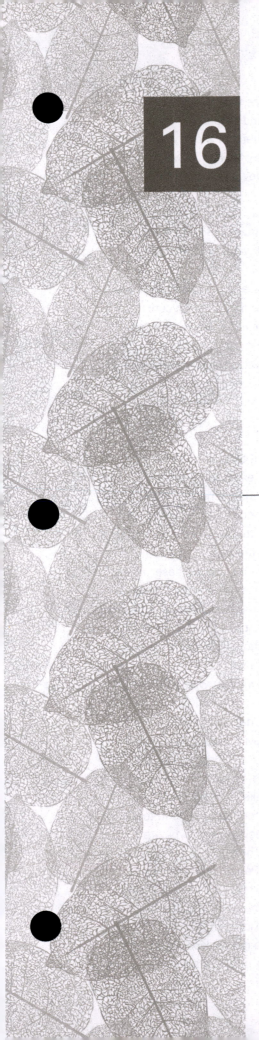

16

The Wisdom of Practice
CREATING A POSITIVE LEARNING ENVIRONMENT

Chapter Objectives

You Will Know

- The characteristics and practices of good teachers
- Evidence-based teacher behaviors that lead to a positive learning community in the classroom

You Will Understand That

- Novice teachers can successfully swim in a pool of knowledge about teaching

You Will Be Able To

- Apply new information to the context in which you find yourself
- Analyze the context and reflect upon best evidence practices to use in your own classroom

The difference between the expert and the novice in any profession is something more than years of service. The word *expert* is from the Latin *experiri,* meaning "to try." It is related to words in the family with the meanings "attempt" and "peril." People who are good at what they do are not afraid to try new ideas, even at some risk. But what are the differences between ordinary and expert teachers? Are gifted teachers born with their gifts, or can those gifts be learned? By examining the nature of expertise, the first question can be answered. It will then be apparent that the second question is moot: These gifts are not really gifts at all. What are seen as gifts in others are actually the result of deliberative, reflective efforts to become expert. The expert will always relish the challenge and delight in the work of confronting a new circumstance or problem, armed with knowledge gained from previous experience. Furthermore, there are remarkable differences to be seen in the achievement of students resulting from expert teaching. It is estimated that at least 20 to 30 percent of the differences in student achievement is attributable to expertise of the teacher (Hattie & Yates, 2014, p. 103).

But how does expertise in teaching come to be? Gladwell (2008) summarizes research in support of "the 10,000 hour rule." The rule posits that it takes about 10,000 hours of practice to become an expert in anything. Of course, this practice cannot be mindless—it must be accurate, purposeful, and intentional and include specific feedback so that skills can be honed. Expert teachers do not teach the same way to every group of students, even if they spend 10,000 hours doing so. We become expert by practicing specific behaviors (Goleman, 2013). Thus, gifted teachers attend to the nuances and lessons of classroom experience. They accumulate hours and hours of reflective professional practice.

One big difference between the expert and the novice teacher is that "expert teachers understand their subject matter and they also understand the students they are teaching" (Findell, 2009, p. 23). The expert teachers, or those who are called gifted, are the ones who most often beat the odds of failure. How does this happen? What, precisely, does the expert teacher know that all good teachers should know?

Before we try to answer that question, remember that there is no formula for becoming a good teacher. For example, models of instruction are not formulas such as "one part oxygen plus two parts hydrogen equals water." Rather, models of instruction are more akin to recipes that have to be adapted to the needs and tastes of the cook, to those who will partake, and to the available ingredients. Teaching, like cooking, is a purposeful activity in the sense that, through conscious reflection or deliberation, the process can always be improved. Even when teachers have not had the opportunity to learn about models of instruction, they can become excellent teachers. What models do is package evidence-based strategies for use in particular settings. Teaching quality and outcome always depended in large part on the judgment of the teacher. Part of that judgment centers on the students and their changing needs, part centers on the process of teaching, and yet another part is determined by the context in which the teaching occurs.

To say that there is no formula for good teaching is not to deny that an accumulated wisdom about the practice of teaching does exist. Judgments are always grounded in knowledge, and the expert knows things the novice does not. Fortunately, there is a large body of recorded experience and research on effective schools and instructional practices that provides the basis for many generalizations about teaching, as you can prove to yourself by searching the Internet for entries on the topic "expertise in teaching." In this chapter, we share some of those generalizations. The basis of these generalizations lies in a large corpus of research and in the knowledge, skills, and experience of countless teachers whom we have asked, "What makes you a good teacher?" But research and the experience of others are never quite enough to define someone else's choices. To prove what we say, you will have to test each generalization in your own practice.

As Hattie and Yates (2014) put it, "expert teachers are vigilant when it comes to monitoring student learning and attention" (p. 105). It was of particular interest to us to note that when we asked a group of teachers "What makes you a good teacher?" responses included 25 characteristics and behaviors, but only one teacher mentioned knowledge of subject matter. That gave us pause at first; certainly teachers must be expert in the content they wish to teach. When we stopped to reflect, though, we realized that good teachers likely take knowledge of their subject matter as a given, a necessary but not sufficient condition for good teaching. In other words, most teachers would probably say that knowing what you are trying to teach is essential to good teaching, but knowing how to teach it is what distinguishes good teachers from mere content experts. Perhaps the real hallmark of expertise in teaching lies in understanding how to blend two different domains of knowledge—knowledge of what to teach and knowledge of how to teach—in a way that compromises neither domain but does allow flexibility in deciding how to teach specific students in a specific context. Teaching, like many skilled behaviors, is highly contextual. We have condensed that understanding into 11 insights that good teachers have.

Good Teachers Are the Leaders of Their Classrooms

We have asked students of elementary and high school age the same question: "What changes would you make in the instruction you have received thus far in school?" We prefaced the question by explaining that the administration had asked us to make recommendations on how to improve instruction in the school, but that we did not feel capable of framing those recommendations without trying to see the present instructional program from the eyes of those learners who had experienced it.

In general, the learners had only three things to say, although they said them in many different ways. Notice that in every case, their proposed changes were under the teacher's control.

- "I'd like teachers to stick to the point and help us learn."
- "I'd like a classroom in which kids don't get away with fooling around. Teachers shouldn't let some kids get picked on."
- "I'd like to know that that I have a chance to be successful on the test because we practiced the stuff in class."

Whether teaching 6-year-old or 60-year-old students, the teacher is the person in charge of the classroom, and everyone will feel better if that is clearly established from the start. The teacher is not a friend, but neither is the teacher a warden or a tyrant. The teacher is the professional responsible for keeping the class focused on what is being taught; for developing a learning community; for maintaining discipline in a fair and consistent manner; and for ensuring the alignment, reliability, and validity of evaluation (Weinstein & Novodvorsky, 2011). Most importantly, the teacher is responsible for providing students the opportunity to be successful. Although much of that responsibility can and should be shared with learners, the teacher must retain the right of ultimate authority in the interest of the safety and physical, emotional, personal, and intellectual well-being of the students.

The teacher's bearing, voice, appearance, and approach to the class should emphasize professionalism and careful preparation for the job. We all are reassured when we feel that persons responsible in controlled situations know what they are doing and will do it responsibly and respectfully. Students of all ages depend on their teachers for that reassurance.

There is a fine line between being controlling and nurturing, and all teachers need to be watchful of that line. Walker (2009) parses the dilemma into when to lighten up and when to tighten up. Expert teachers walk that fine line with an authoritative teaching style. This style is defined as the "use of positive instructional practices within a highly controlling and nurturing context" (p. 126). The warm/strict technique promoted by Lemov (2010) addresses the same balance—being caring, funny, concerned, and nurturing while being firm, unrelenting, clear, and consistent. Often, teachers need to be both warm and strict at the same time. Expert teachers have high expectations for student behavior and demand compliance and self-regulation toward transparent, relevant, and fair goals. At the same time, these teachers are nurturing and build a community in which the norm is positive emotional connections (Pianta, Hamre, Haynes, Mintz, & LaParo, 2007; Walker, 2009).

"Crisp," "businesslike," and "to the point" describe a classroom under a teacher's direction. Research on classroom management quite clearly shows that good teachers establish a system of management as soon as possible in organizing each new class of students. Expert teachers agree that the first few days of school are critical in establishing and practicing instructional and managerial routines for the smooth operation of the classroom. A substantial line of research supports this insight (Lemov, 2010; Weinstein & Novodvorksy, 2011). To make these routines automatic, good teachers tell their students what they expect, they demonstrate it for the students, they guide the students in practicing expected moves, and they accept no less than mastery execution of the routines necessary for successful learning and instruction.

This video looks at how a middle school teacher sets up routines and procedures during the first days of school. What do you notice? With which routines and procedures do you feel comfortable? What would you change in your own classroom?

It is important to note that demonstration and guidance aimed at correct routine are more effective than later correction of errors in routine. "An ounce of prevention" is critical in classroom management.

Good Teachers Create a Productive Environment for Learning

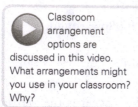

Classroom arrangement options are discussed in this video. What arrangements might you use in your classroom? Why?

Schools vary in many ways, including the physical environment. Some classrooms have natural light, numerous resources, furniture in good shape, and other attributes that make the classroom a pleasant place to be. Classrooms in schools with few economic resources are less pleasant and may send a negative message to children. Regardless of the condition of the classroom, it is imperative that we try to make the physical space in which children are learning as pleasant and productive as possible. A good learning environment is enhanced by good facilities, but good facilities do not guarantee the development of a strong learning community. A strong learning community can be developed in even poor facilities, but this requires creativity, time, and effort in schools that already have difficult demands.

RELATIONSHIP TO STUDENT LEARNING

The physical environment of the classroom has an influence on student learning and teacher satisfaction (Brophy, 2006). It matters that a teacher mediates the space so that students can work productively in the classroom. Teachers must ensure that the physical environment allows students to feel safe and secure—worrying about whether the ceiling is going to fall on you is not conducive to working hard at learning. Students are also more productive in rooms that allow for interactions with other students and with teachers. Comfort is more than physical; psychological comfort is associated with learning. The classroom should be pleasant and aesthetically pleasing while still providing intellectual stimulation (Weinstein & Novodvorsky, 2011).

FURNITURE ARRANGEMENT/SEATING

Ideally, classroom arrangements should be flexible so that the furniture arrangement will not impede student success. It is difficult to work cooperatively in rows, and tables of four can leave some students unable to see a presentation. The need for personal physical space is critical for both instructional and management success. Chairs, tables, or desks should not be too close together. There should be clear paths for unimpeded student movement—a routine can be established for what to do with full backpacks, for example.

Seating arrangements can do a great deal to enhance the success of instruction, and it is essential to plan for the orderly rearrangement of seating as the class activities change. Rows can be used in crowded or difficult-to-manage classrooms or when all students need to be looking forward; however, they are not appropriate for all instruction. Circles and semicircles are generally more effective for sharing information and discussion. Clusters of two, three, or four desks create a setting for small-group cooperative work.

Students need instruction in how to change seating patterns in the classroom efficiently. For instance, if after a presentation the students are to work in small groups, it is necessary to explain carefully in advance how the seats will be arranged and where each group is to be located. Classrooms can also be set up in such a way that individual and group work can go on at the same time. Plan in advance for the type of seating arrangement you will need so that sound and sight disturbances can be minimized. Procedures for furniture arrangement should be routine so that students can be provided a signal and efficiently make changes. Of course, these routines will need to be practiced over time.

CLIMATE CONTROL

It is essential to attend to lighting, air, and temperature. Many excellent lessons have been ruined because the temperature in the classroom was too hot or too cold for students to concentrate.

If the room in which you teach is too crowded, if it is too hot or too cold, or if the air is stale, try to find another space. Talk with the principal about the physical conditions that are creating a problem. As an instructional specialist, you will be the person most aware of the effects of the physical environment on the learners. Pay attention to how the students are responding to environmental conditions, discuss the reasons for any discomfort, and help them find solutions.

EQUIPMENT AND DISPLAYS

Classrooms are cluttered places—there are books, papers, writing tools, computers, display devices, a large desk for the teacher, tables or desks, chairs, plants, pictures, and many small items that are used to personalize the space. Insofar as possible, the classroom should be an attractive, organized, and inviting place to be. Classrooms also need to be safe places—students need to be able to walk around the room without tripping on backpacks and other items. Students with physical challenges need appropriate accommodations, and teachers and students need to be able quickly to find and retrieve the materials and equipment used in lessons. Materials and tools should be in working order and stored in an accessible area. Too much transition time takes away from the momentum of the lesson and provides too great an opportunity for distractions and disruptions.

Displays can consist of student work, motivational and informational posters or bulletin boards, and artifacts. Displays can be used to reinforce the essential concepts of the lesson or unit under study. Put students' work up for all to see, in a manner that reinforces all the students and just not a few. Be certain to ask the students for their permission before you display their work. Pictures of class members and examples of student hobbies or collections can make the classroom reflect positively on individual students and groups and help both the students and teacher feel attachment to the space in which they work.

Good Teachers Manage Human Relations Effectively

Teaching is very complex, and classroom management is one of the more intricate of a teacher's responsibilities. There is no lack of advice about the best methods for managing classrooms and student behavior. By demonstrating respect for students and their learning, and by organizing the classroom and instruction for successful academic encounters, many behavior management problems can be avoided. Creating classroom learning communities means that classroom norms encourage intellectual development within a caring and supportive environment (Weinstein & Novodvorsky, 2011).

Steven Wolk (2002) offers several management suggestions:

1. Get to know your students—their achievements, potential, interests, cultural background, and learning preferences.
2. Manage the class schedule to enhance student engagement.
3. Give students responsibility for helping the classroom run smoothly.
4. Use the physical environment of the room to promote your instructional objectives.
5. Keep the classroom organized, free of clutter, and responsive to the developmental needs of students.
6. Develop a reasonable set of rules and explicitly teach students the rules.
7. First, do no harm. Monitor student behavior. Ignore trivial, annoying behaviors. Try to diffuse disciplinary problems by using proximity, humor, or a private discussion with a student.

8. Identify and work with students with chronic behavior problems.
9. Use good instructional strategies to keep students engaged and academically motivated.
10. Provide clear expectations and directions and an avenue for students to seek help if they are confused.
11. Help students develop self-assessment skills.
12. Be cognizant of cultural influences on learning and behavior.
13. Always be respectful to students. Be just. Provide specific, positive feedback concerning behavior and academic skills.
14. Don't use schoolwork as punishment.

Remember the close connection between instruction and behavior management in classrooms. Thomas Lasley (1981) has suggested four generalizations about classroom and behavior management that have held up over the decades regardless of the classroom context. According to his extensive review of the literature on the issue of classroom management, the effective teacher does the following:

1. Develops and implements a workable set of classroom rules
2. Structures and monitors the classroom in a manner that minimizes disruptive behavior
3. Clearly defines and quickly and consistently responds to inappropriate behavior
4. Couches the response to inappropriate behavior in a tone that does not denigrate the students to whom the response is directed—students are always respected

Good Teachers Engage Learners in Their Own Learning

Eleanor Duckworth (2006) believes we must always put learners in as direct contact as possible with whatever we want them to learn. There are many ways that students can be given direct contact with their learning. They can model the formation and movements of the solar system. They can keep diaries of their observations of animals that they see in the area. They can construct models, engage in mock and simulated experiences, and conduct interviews.

Second—and this is related to the first principle—Duckworth advises that we provide frequent opportunities for learners to explain what they understand, both to the teacher and to other students. Anytime teachers are tempted to tell students something they want them to know, they should start by asking the students to explain what they already know. John Hattie puts it this way: "The more the student becomes the teacher and the more the teacher becomes the learner, then the more successful are the outcomes" (Hattie, 2012, p. 17).

We agree that these guidelines are critical to a beginning teacher's instructional effectiveness. We know that learners will learn more in proportion to how engaged they are with what they are trying to learn. This is the *law of meaningful engagement*, and although it is a law often violated, it implies that everyone in the room—students and teachers alike—must be deeply engaged if learning is to be successful for anyone.

Students learn best when they believe they can learn and are challenged. A competent, interested learner is more likely to be successful. This relaxed alertness allows students to become immersed in complex experiences that use their senses, make connections between prior and new information, and allow them to apply new skills and knowledge. Along with relaxed alertness and immersion in complex experiences, learners need active processing in which there is continuous reflection about what is being learned and constructed (Caine, Caine, McClintic, & Klimek, 2008). These three ingredients of successful learning experiences are similar to what we have referred to as *meaningful engagement*.

The learner's understanding and insight must be the goal of instruction. Metacognition—the ability to monitor one's learning so that further progress can be made—is a necessary component of student understanding. Teachers must develop

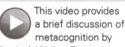

This video provides a brief discussion of metacognition by Dr. Josh Walker. Think about the questions you have about the role of metacognition in the classroom. www.youtube.com/watch?v=mVE21QhY-lI

activities so that students can receive authentic feedback about their progress toward established goals. One of the great paradoxes of education, which every good teacher will sooner or later discover, is that understanding cannot be given to the learner directly any more than a parent can teach a child to tie her shoes by merely telling her how. Give her a shoe to practice on (or, better, let her practice on her own shoe), and have her explain to you or to another person what she is doing as she practices. If that advice is good for learning to tie shoes, how much better is it for learning all the complicated things students are expected to know in school?

Good Teachers Teach Up

In Greek mythology, Pygmalion was the sculptor from Cyprus who carved and then fell in love with a statue of a woman, to whom the goddess Aphrodite later gave life. The Pygmalion theme repeats itself often in Western literature, movies, and verse. George Bernard Shaw immortalized the characters of Henry Higgins, an aristocrat whose hobby is phonetics, and Eliza Doolittle, the Cockney flower seller whose speaking ability he transforms. Hollywood loves this romantic, fairy tale theme, centered on the power of education (particularly language) to elevate one's social class.

Maybe love does not conquer all, but it is a powerful ingredient in education, or so the Pygmalion story would imply. It is best not to forget, too, that in each version of the story, the sculptor has much to learn from his creation. That important lesson is expressed by Eliza near the end of Shaw's play, when she is trying to explain to her friend and benefactor Colonel Pickering how she was transformed from flower girl to lady of refinement. Eliza explains that the difference between a flower girl and a lady is not how she behaves, but how she is treated.

From that speech, we get the term *Pygmalion effect*. The Pygmalion effect in schools was made famous by Rosenthal and Jacobson (1968). Essentially, their research asserts that a teacher's expectation that the student *will* do well can have a positive effect on the academic success of that student. The opposite of the Pygmalion effect in schools, that teachers treat high- and low-achieving students differently to the detriment of the low-achieving student, has also been brought to light by research (Weinstein, 2002). Thomas Good (1981) lists several ways in which teachers most often discriminate in their treatment of the high and low achievers.

- By seating low-achieving students farther away from the teacher than other students
- By paying less attention to low-achieving students than to other students
- By calling on low-achieving students less frequently than other students to answer questions
- By giving low-achieving students less time to answer questions when they are called on than other students
- By not providing cues or asking follow-up questions to help low-achieving students answer questions
- By criticizing low-achieving students more frequently than other students for incorrect answers
- By giving low-achieving students less praise than other students for correct or marginal responses
- By giving low-achieving students less feedback and less detail in the feedback they are given than other students
- By interrupting the performance of low-achieving students more often than that of the high-achieving students
- By demanding less effort and less work from low-achieving students than from high-achieving students

Many teachers may not even be aware of these behaviors, thus demonstrating the need for reflective thinking about daily practices. Rhona Weinstein (2002), after an exhaustive study of the power of expectations in schools, drew the following conclusions:

- Students know that teachers have different expectations for different students.
- How children are treated in schools and classrooms matters. For instance, if school policies are structured on the belief that intelligence is fixed (Dweck, 2007), the opportunities available to some students will be limited.
- Expectations become part of the fabric of the institution, and the processes by which expectations are communicated are similar at all levels of schooling.
- When teachers have low expectations for students and treat students differently because of those expectations, achievement gaps persist and grow.
- Low expectations compound other factors that may put a student at risk for school difficulties—race, culture, language, socioeconomic status, gender, learning preferences, and prior knowledge.

"By our overemphasis on appraising achievement and sorting children, we fail to create conditions in classrooms and schools that substantially develop ability. We fail to meet all learners with a challenging curriculum accompanied by differentially appropriate, nonstigmatizing, and flexible educational supports" (Weinstein, 2002, pp. 291–292).

CAPITALIZING ON WHAT STUDENTS KNOW

What students know about the content determines how well they will learn new information. Teachers should find something in what students already know to establish a basis for new understandings. Students often feel as if they know nothing of what is taught in school, and they could not care less because it all seems so irrelevant. But good teachers help learners see that they already know much about what they are trying to learn, and they impress on students that *what they already know is the single most important factor influencing what they will learn*. Learners are crucially important to their own learning, and teaching should make them feel that way. Recall the story of Anna that opened Chapter One. Once Anna got the idea that what she was being taught was entirely relevant to what she wanted to do with her life, there was virtually no limit to what she could learn.

CELEBRATING DIFFERENCES BETWEEN STUDENTS

An old adage says "None of us is as smart as all of us." That statement is also true in a classroom. If teachers make it clear that what each one knows or learns is of value to everyone, then they make it safe for everyone to share whatever they know and thus to value their own understanding. Half of this concept is polite behavior—respect—and the other half is intellectual honesty: No one knows everything about anything—not even the teacher or the most academically advanced students—and that is acceptable. Every student has much to learn, and every student brings a trove of knowledge to the learning table.

REALIZING THAT THERE IS MORE THAN ONE RIGHT ANSWER

Every teacher's manual includes suggestions about what to say to students and what to expect them to say in return. The manuals for teaching reading to elementary school students often go as far as to put what the teacher is to say in one color print and what

Feedback should provide more than judgment of "right" or "wrong"; it should give students information, facts, and suggestions. You will see an example in this video of a high school art teacher whose comments leave the learner free to weigh options and choose what action might be appropriate.

the students are to say in another color print. But a lesson script can only be an approximation. In fact, the one certain truth found in all teacher's manuals is that answers will vary. Part of the art of teaching lies in knowing how to take advantage of variance.

PROVIDING APPROPRIATE, QUALITY FEEDBACK

Remember learning to drive a car? If you were lucky, the person teaching you kept affirming that you could do it and praising you for all you were doing right. When difficulties arose, your instructor concentrated on helping you focus on what to do rather than berating you for your shortcomings. But if you were unlucky, the person teaching you continually harped on everything you were doing wrong. The effect of this was to shake your confidence, even though that was not the intent. Feedback that is related to learning is neutral, timely, and focused on the task.

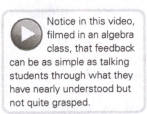

Notice in this video, filmed in an algebra class, that feedback can be as simple as talking students through what they have nearly understood but not quite grasped.

A productive learning environment involves consistent and focused feedback, including attention to as many strengths of students as weaknesses. These practices encourage a safe and effective learning environment in which students can grow and learn (Brookhart, 2008).

Good Teachers Are Good Learners

We are tempted to say that the teacher should be the best learner in the class, but we would not want to imply a competition. In any case, the teacher must be an eager learner and be willing to share the process of learning with other learners in the class. Good teachers learn from their own study and share that study with their students. Frequently, even daily, they bring a new idea to class from something they have read or seen. They are scholars, and they share the process and the product of their scholarship. Teachers learn from their students, both about teaching and about the content they are studying together. Having the chance to teach someone else is one of the best ways to learn, and it is always a favor to both the learner and the teacher to reverse their roles from time to time. Teachers learn from teaching—not just about their teaching, but also about their students and what they are studying (Huebner, 2009). The five core propositions put forth by the National Board for Professional Teaching Standards embody the idea that good teachers are good learners.

It is a serious mistake for any teacher to project the image of the person who knows it all and is here to tell everyone. First, such an attitude conveys an erroneous impression of the nature of knowledge, as if it were a once-and-for-all matter. The knowledge humans possess is expanding so rapidly that the infrastructure of knowledge has to be continually adapted to accommodate new insights and understandings. Thus teachers, like their students, are faced with needing to learn constantly just to keep abreast. The exciting result for the teacher who realizes this is that there is always a ready audience with whom to share new insights and understandings. By contrast, a know-all, tell-all attitude treats knowledge as a fixed entity, excluding learners from the process of learning and dooming them to focus on the acquisition of information that may be obsolete even before their school days have passed. The more appropriate image of teacher as learner invites students to join with others (the teacher included) in the joy and thrill of coming to know. The long-term effect is that students will learn well, learn more, and be learners for life.

RECOGNIZING THE IMPORTANCE OF PROFESSIONAL KNOWLEDGE

There are professional organizations for every branch and subject of teaching and for the field of education in general. A major function of these groups is to provide a comprehensive literature to assist teachers and administrators in their mission to educate. This literature consists mainly of professional journals, books, audio and video recordings, and research and technical reports. Each professional organization also hosts regional, state, national, and international meetings and forums in which teachers share and discuss common problems and ideas. Taken together, these sources form the basis of postgraduate professional study in education.

Disciplinary knowledge increases and changes quickly. It is not only in the sciences that new theories are constructed and tested; all academic fields have benefited from the proliferation of technological tools and communication channels. We have the tools to understand more about our world, and we have the tools to share these discoveries rapidly. As new understandings are combined with prior learning, even more knowledge is generated. The cycle moves quickly.

For classroom teachers, there is a need to keep abreast of rich and tested theories of how we learn and what impact policies have on student development and achievement, along with advances in the content areas and in ways that content can be communicated to students.

A review of the literature identifies the following characteristics of effective professional development (Darling-Hammond & Richardson, 2009):

- A focus on enriching the teacher's content knowledge and how to teach this content to students
- Attention to how students learn specific content
- Opportunities for teachers to process their new learning
- Application and reflection of new knowledge
- Collaborative and collegial development that occurs within the teaching context
- Development that is sustained over time

ACTING AS RESEARCHERS

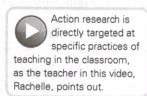

Action research is directly targeted at specific practices of teaching in the classroom, as the teacher in this video, Rachelle, points out.

In addition to attempting to keep abreast of the professional literature (as any professional must), teachers are in a position to be their own directors of research and development. Action research allows teachers to study their own practices alone or with others. John Hattie (2012, p. 17) makes this point frequently in statements like "those teachers who are students of their own impact are the teachers who are the most influential in raising students' achievement." A teacher who wants to learn more about what is happening in his or her own classroom may use action research procedures, as may a group of teachers who collaborate to understand more about what is happening beyond a specific classroom (Brighton, 2009). Table 16.1 details the steps commonly used in action research.

Good Teachers Develop Instructional Objectives with Learners

The quality of instruction in a classroom will be determined largely by whether the students have a vested interest in the instruction and in their own learning. In other words, they have to care about what happens in the class and be willing to cooperate to reach shared objectives. Instructional objectives, from the point of view of the learners, are learning objectives. Whether the objectives are achieved will depend on the learners' willingness to adopt the teacher's instructional objectives as their own learning objectives.

TABLE 16.1   Steps in Action Research

Step 1	Identify a problem.	Choose an area or focus that concerns you in your professional practice. Read about this area of teaching. Formulate a specific question(s) to be answered.
Step 2	Develop a plan.	Decide how you will collect data to answer the question, what data will be collected and why, what you will do to support data collection, how you will analyze the information you collect, and what you will do with your conclusions.
Step 3	Collect data.	Use a variety of data sources and data collection techniques—personal reflections, interviews, student work, audio and video, and so on.
Step 4	Analyze data.	Use appropriate data analysis techniques. Collaborate with knowledgeable others to find patterns in the data that help you to answer your questions.
Step 5	Reflect on and share the results.	Reflect on your findings and how they will affect your professional practice. Share the findings with other professionals.

We are not advocating that teachers plan their instruction based on what students are willing to say they want to learn, even though that can often be taken into account. We do advocate that teachers share the process of their own planning for instruction with their students. One way to do this is to initiate a unit of study with an exploration of what the students have already studied on the topic, followed by a listing of what else they think they want to know. Many studies of effective instructional practices make clear that teaching that builds on what learners already know leads to higher achievement.

Good Teachers Find Out Why a Plan Is Not Working

L. W. Anderson (1982) has summarized the major conclusions to be drawn from the vast body of literature on effective teaching. His review was conducted many years ago, but new research continues to support his conclusions. Effective teachers, he suggests,

- Know their students
- Assign appropriate tasks to their students
- Orient their students to the learning task

- Monitor the learning progress of their students
- Relate teaching and testing by testing what they teach
- Promote student involvement and engagement in the learning process
- Provide continuity for their students so that learning tasks and objectives build on one another
- Correct student errors and misunderstandings

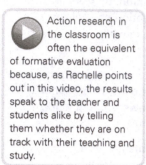

Action research in the classroom is often the equivalent of formative evaluation because, as Rachelle points out in this video, the results speak to the teacher and students alike by telling them whether they are on track with their teaching and study.

If these effective teaching behaviors are to be a reality, it is important that the teacher be aware of options. If one approach or technique is not working with a class, analyze the problem and redesign the instructional plan. For instance, some classes are not ready for group work. Many times, teachers will attempt a group activity and, when chaos develops, decide that they will never try it again. Students must be prepared for group activities, and the procedures for setting up those activities must be carefully planned and directed. The models described in Chapter Ten are only a few of many effective group-process models. With some instructional models, the students may need more preparation time. Perhaps certain steps in the model have not been adequately explained. Or sometimes the instructional plan is too ambitious, the content to be covered is too extensive, or the students do not have the necessary readiness and predisposition for learning. Evaluate the situation and consider what options you have to correct the difficulty. Treat problems as challenges rather than frustrations.

Good Teachers Strive to Make Their Teaching Engaging

The relationship between interest and curiosity is no accident; learners are interested in learning those things about which they feel the greatest curiosity. Therefore, if teachers can pique the curiosity of learners, they will make what they teach interesting to learners. Students are motivated to learn when they are engaged. Student engagement goes beyond interest. A National Research Council (2004) study on secondary school engagement found that when course structure and instruction reflect students' prior knowledge, interests, culture, and real-life experience and when it is varied and challenging, students are more motivated to persist in important tasks. We know that ongoing diagnostic and formative assessments contribute to making school more relevant and reflective of a student's outside-of-school life.

Interestingly, there is also evidence that high expectations for all students help keep students interested in schoolwork. These high expectations and the types of instruction that result help students feel respected and valued. A challenging curriculum, varied tasks that are representative of past experience, and opportunities for scaffolded experiences contribute to student engagement. Student motivation and interest are also predicated on respect. As teachers communicate their respect to students through challenging and interesting classroom experiences, high expectations, engaging materials and tools, and a caring and helpful environment, schools will be filled with motivated and successful students.

Good Teachers Give Learners Access to Information and Opportunity to Practice

Research on effective schools unequivocally supports the idea that learning is likely to occur when learners have access to information and the opportunity to practice using that information. But what kind of information and practice are appropriate? Most obviously, students need whatever information is necessary to accomplish the learning objective at hand: accurate information presented in a palatable form. And students need practice in applying or recalling the new information as a means of solving problems. In the case of a learning objective that called for students to compare and contrast the causes of the French and Indian War with the causes of the War of 1812, the students would need information about these two wars and guidance and feedback on their attempts to make appropriate comparisons and contrasts.

The information needed by students is more than facts, data, and algorithms, however. Paraphrasing from a research report by Robert Yinger (1987), we can identify these other kinds of information as (1) knowledge of what to do with information gained and how to use it in practice, (2) knowledge of when the information will apply and how to apply it, and (3) knowledge of whether the uses of the information have been successful.

Likewise, the practice students need is not solely of those behaviors implicit in the specific learning objective they have been given. In addition to learners applying or recalling information, D. N. Perkins and Gabriel Salomon (1988) state that learners need practice in "low-road" and "high-road" transfer.

When teachers introduce a literary classic with reference to the related experiences of their students, they are creating conditions for low-road transfer. When teachers point out parallels between the elements of content, such as the points of comparison between the civil rights movement in the United States and the breakdown of apartheid in South Africa, they are facilitating high-road transfer.

Low-road transfer is direct application of information to contexts like those in which the information is encountered. For example, students might practice applying the Pythagorean theorem by calculating the diagonals of their classroom and of a football field. High-road transfer is indirect application of information to contexts and problems unlike those in which the information was first encountered. For example, students might compare the events and political alignments of the French and Indian War with the alignments of loyalties in the play *Romeo and Juliet*. It is always important to keep in mind that long-term, meaningful learning depends on the access students have to good information and the opportunity to transfer and apply that information in ways that make it both meaningful and memorable.

Good Teachers Teach for Two Kinds of Knowledge

It is impossible for students to learn in school all they would ever need to know in their lives. They must, therefore, learn how to learn. In every course of study in school, students are given access to a portion of the accumulated knowledge and wisdom of humankind: the facts, ideas, algorithms, events, and implications of history, literature, science, math, health, and so on. But such a set of informational knowledge ("knowing that") will not stand the learner in good stead in the future if he or she does not also acquire a complementary kind of knowledge: the skills of reading, writing, study, and thinking necessary for continued growth and lifelong scholarship ("knowing how").

Thus, teaching in the classroom should give students access to information to be learned and to a conscious knowledge of how to learn it. In this classroom, the teacher would create an environment in which students are responsible for knowing and for knowing how they know—for taking control of the processes of their own learning and thinking. The intended result is an improvement of the learning and thinking necessary for participation in the discipline under study. We would want teachers at all grade levels and in all content areas to believe that the most important thing they have to teach students is the process of learning. Through modeling and think-alouds, teachers show students how to learn. This reminds us of the old expression "Give a man a fish, and he'll eat for a day; teach a man to fish, and he'll eat for a lifetime." Consider the analogy: "Teach students only the information you want them to have, and they'll pass the test tomorrow; teach students how to learn, and they'll pass the test for the rest of their lives."

SUMMARY

There is more to managing a classroom of learners than just containing the students. In fact, the need for most of that kind of management is preempted when the teacher takes control of the learning in the classroom and, in effect, turns the responsibility for learning over to the learners. Good teachers manage their instruction with that objective in mind. They are able to do so because they operate out of a knowledge base and because intuition feeds their good judgment. In this chapter and throughout this text, we have shared the idea that there are always options the good teacher can consider, even though most of the time good teaching, like any skilled performance, looks completely spontaneous. We hope that our suggestions will become part of your instructional repertoire.

EXTENSIONS

ACTIVITIES

1. Discuss professional development with some practicing teachers. What do they think of the professional development experiences they have had? What makes professional development good, helpful, or a waste of time? What do they suggest you do to get the most out of professional development?
2. Ask a group of students of the age that you teach or will be teaching what makes a good classroom environment. Probe to find out what teachers and students can do to make an effective learning community.
3. Review the policies of your district (or a district in which you might work) with an eye toward high expectations for students. Which policies promote high expectations for students? Which policies assume that students will be low achievers? Ask teachers and administrators whether these policies affect responses to student behavior in a particular school.
4. Discuss the ideas about mindset with your peers, your students, and their parents (Dweck, 2007). Explore the differences between a growth mindset and a fixed mindset in many areas of human pursuit—sports, business, and education, for example. Think about your view of intelligence and how it affects your teaching.

REFLECTIVE QUESTIONS

1. What do you still want to know about teaching? How will you find out what you want to know?
2. What do you believe about students and their capacity for learning? How will these beliefs affect your behaviors in the classroom?
3. Many people believe that teaching is sharing content expertise. How would you respond to this idea so that you convey the complexity of teaching?
4. What will the role of students be in your classroom? How will you design your classroom to enhance student opportunities in this role?

PART FOUR SUMMARY

The final part of this text provided three cases (elementary, middle, and high school) that demonstrated the ways in which specific instructional models can be combined to meet clearly articulated learning objectives. In particular, the following ideas were discussed:

1. Instructional models can make planning easier because they provide a road map for setting up the routines and procedures necessary for the instruction to be successful—reducing the ongoing planning load.

2. The teachers described in Part Four are all individuals with different backgrounds, interests, and teaching experiences. Like those of you reading this text, they have a variety of concerns, and they approach instruction in different ways. They all share, however, a respect for their profession and a desire to improve, to find better ways to reach students, and to be successful in the classroom. They are all seeking answers.

3. None of these professionals is willing to follow prescriptive formulas in a mindless fashion, but all attend to essential concerns in their planning. The focus of these teachers is on the learners. They give careful thought to the outcome of instruction and assume the responsibility of evaluating to determine whether what was taught was also learned.

4. A strong repertoire of instructional strategies can help teachers (1) engage a variety of students in academic content and social skills; (2) learn more about individual students as they participate in a range of activities and challenges; and (3) provide for deep reflection on general pedagogical knowledge.

5. Backward design can be used to construct a unit across all grade levels and content areas.

6. The backward design planning process demonstrates the connection between state standards and unit development.

7. The middle school case study demonstrates collaborative planning across content areas and teacher preferences.

8. All of the cases demonstrate teacher planning that has high expectations for students. The instructional models support student academic learning and the development of important critical thinking skills regardless of class organization or school expectations.

Instruction occurs in a context, and the context includes a number of important teacher practices that support student and teacher learning. The use of instructional models is one part of a package of effective practices, skills, and understandings.

Accountability—The idea that teachers and schools are responsible for measurable student achievement (standardized tests, graduation rates, student work samples, etc.), and schools and teachers should either be rewarded or sanctioned, depending on whether the identified standards were met.

Advance organizer—A tool and/or strategy that intentionally links prior school knowledge and specific lesson objectives by introducing the new topic and/or skills in general terms so that students can begin to make connections between their personal knowledge and what is to be learned. Advance organizers are at a high level of abstraction, are implemented prior to the lesson, and can be expository or comparative.

Aligned curriculum—A curriculum in which all curriculum components (state and local standards, assessments, and instruction) work in parallel to meet specified and public targets.

Assessment types—Types of evaluation and testing instruments, such as standardized tests, aptitude tests, performance tasks, paper-and-pencil tasks, and observation instruments.

Backward design—The purposeful planning of curriculum (objectives, assessment, and instruction) that begins with what students should be able to know, understand, and be able to do as a result of instruction.

Behavioral objectives—Objectives that identify specific student behaviors to determine whether the objective has been met. Educators vary in how small these should be and how specific behaviors should be described in objectives.

Benchmarks—Checkpoints to make certain that standards are being followed. The benchmarks are the components of the standards (knowledge and skills) that are measured on state achievement tests.

Best practices—Research-backed educational methods that are agreed upon by most educational scholars. Best practices may vary by context and by individuals who are implementing the practices.

Big ideas—Ideas that help us make sense of a wide expanse of knowledge and experiences. Big ideas represent generalizations that are central to a specific discipline; they are broad, abstract, and useful in providing a structure with which to organize prior knowledge and prepare for new learning.

Bloom's taxonomy/revised taxonomy—Benjamin Bloom's effort to organize educational objectives in the cognitive, psychomotor, and affective domains in the 1950s, and the revision developed under the leadership of Lorin Anderson and David Krathwohl in 2001, which revised and reworked the cognitive domain to reflect current information about learning. The taxonomy is used frequently by classroom teachers as a planning and instructional tool.

Brainstorming—The rapid, noncritical, noncensored listing of any and all ideas or associations on a given topic that focuses student attention and encourages sharing.

Chunking—The act of organizing what is to be learned during instruction into manageable units. Chunking is dependent upon the context of instruction (age of students, resources, specific knowledge, and skills).

Cold calls—Calling on students regardless of whether they have their hands raised. If a teacher uses cold calls, all students are at risk of being called on; the teacher usually announces this.

Collaborative teacher—A teacher who works with the classroom teacher to meet the needs of a particular subset of students (students with special needs, English language learners, gifted students, etc.)

Common Core State Standards—A set of academic standards in mathematics and English/language arts. These learning goals outline what a student should know and be able to do at the end of each grade.

Concept map—A graphic representation of the relationships between two or more concepts.

Concepts—The ideas or abstractions that are formed as a result of categorizing data from a number of observations. To make sense of all the various stimuli in the world, learners of all ages form concepts and give them names.

Constructivist learning theory—A learning theory that espouses we learn by constructing our own knowledge. Constructivists believe that we learn through an active process of discovery.

Deductive approach—An approach that moves from the general to the specific. Lessons using a deductive approach begin with the presentation of a rule or principle; specific examples and facts that support the generalization are then provided. In moving from the general to the specific, students are encouraged to draw inferences and make predictions based on the examples.

Diagnostic assessment—An assessment used to identify persistent learning problems so that these problems can be remediated. There are commercially available diagnostic assessments, but most classroom teachers rely on observation, student work analyses, and judgment to make these diagnostic decisions.

Facets of understanding—Six ways that we can demonstrate understanding according to Wiggins and McTighe

(2005). These include explanation, interpretation, application, perspective taking, empathic response, and metacognition.

Feedback—Response that typically flows from the teacher to the student and is focused on student work. Good feedback is timely, specific, and geared toward the students' developmental level.

Flexible grouping—The grouping and regrouping of students based on instructional needs rather than student categorization. Grouping decisions are made based on a variety of student needs and classroom context and may change frequently.

Formative assessments—Assessments designed to take place during instruction in order to provide information to teachers and to students about student performance in relation to specified instructional objectives. These assessments offer insight so that adaptations can be made to improve student outcomes.

Generalizations—Statements that link two or more concepts. Generalizations are more abstract than facts and concepts and can represent the basic ideas of a discipline.

Graphic organizers—Tools that help students organize their thinking and planning relevant to academic content. These tools can be word webs, timelines, concept maps, tree diagrams, matrices, comparison charts, cause-and-effect charts, Venn diagrams, and different kinds of graphs.

Guided practice—A step in the direct instruction model that allows students to practice targeted skills while receiving teacher feedback on the implementation of these skills.

Heuristic process—A way of solving a problem or figuring out what to do next without applying an established algorithm. A heuristic process involves trial and error using experience as a basis for decision making.

High-stakes testing—Standardized tests that are used for making high-stakes decisions such as high school graduation, promotions, and entrance into special programs. High-stakes tests usually reward those who have high scores and punish those with low scores.

Hypothesis generation and testing—The generation and testing of speculative statements that are derived from a variety of sources. The generation of hypotheses can occur individually or with groups. Hypothesis testing is the systematic evaluation of hypotheses. Many of the instructional models presented in this text provide a structure for hypothesis generation and testing.

Independent practice—Student practice that follows guided practice in the direct instruction model. It is in the independent practice step that students attempt to use new knowledge and skills without immediate teacher feedback.

Individual education plan (IEP)—A federally mandated educational plan for any student identified as qualifying for special education services. The plan lists the educational objectives for the child and identifies how the school intends to help children reach these goals within the least restrictive environment.

Inductive approach—An approach that begins with specific data facts; through the process of investigating and reasoning, generalizations, rules, and concept definitions are gradually created.

Inquiry—The process by which we make sense of the world. The process is open-ended and moves beyond specific facts and the recall of information. Inquiry is supported in several of the models presented in this text.

Instructional alignment—The agreement between instructional objectives, the assessments that will determine what students learned during instruction, and instruction. Alignment means that objectives, assessment, and instruction are all working toward the same end.

Instructional model—A step-by-step procedure that leads to specific learning outcomes.

Interdisciplinary curriculum—A curriculum that cuts across disciplinary lines by using a common concept or theme to plan objectives, assessment, and instruction. The middle school case study in Chapter Fourteen uses an interdisciplinary curriculum.

Invented/inventive spelling—Spelling based on an educated guess and individual knowledge of phonetics. This is a natural process that we all go through as we learn to write.

Knowledge types—The four categories of knowledge according to Bloom's revised taxonomy. They are factual, conceptual, procedural, and metacognitive.

KUDs—Learning objectives that follow backward design. The objectives identify what students will know, what they will understand, and what they will be able to do at the end of an instructional event.

KWL—An instructional strategy that uses a graphic organizer to help students recognize what they know about a subject, what they want to know about a subject, and what they have learned about the subject.

Learning trajectories or progressions—The order in which knowledge and skills should be presented to students to help them learn about a topic or content area. Each of the lessons should build upon the previous one so that students have the opportunity to develop the skills and knowledge necessary to be successful in school.

Mastery learning—An instructional approach that assumes that all students can learn if they have reasonable support and time. Learning is broken into chunks that students master before they move on to the next level.

Metacognition/metacognitive knowledge—Thinking about your own thinking—about how you learn. Metacognitive knowledge includes the knowledge of the reasons for your successes and challenges as you are learning.

Mnemonics—Learning strategies that help students retain information and skills that can be performed with automaticity.

Pacing guides—Guides that outline the academic content for which students and teachers are accountable by providing the order and time frame to be used by all teachers in a district as they instruct their students.

Pedagogy—The study of educational practice. General pedagogy examines the use of instructional methods across all ages and content areas. Content pedagogy is the study of teaching a specific discipline to students.

Performance assessment—A test that asks students to complete a task rather than simply choose a response from a list. Performance assessments involve performances such as demonstrating a skill or sharing information under specified conditions. Performance assessments might include portfolios and tasks that require students to apply what was learned in school—designing a budget, planning healthy meals, or arguing a case in front of city council, for example.

Pygmalion effect—The theory that students will perform according to a teacher's expectations. If a teacher has high expectations for the student, the student will be successful.

Reciprocal teaching—An instructional strategy that uses predicting, questioning, clarifying, and summarizing to help students comprehend written text.

Rubrics—A set of criteria that are used to evaluate student work. These scoring guides are designed to share expectations for demonstrated excellence of a specified task. Rubrics tell students what successful performance looks like.

Scaffolding—An instructional approach that supports students during the learning process. Teachers provide this support to individual students or small groups of students so that they will successfully attain learning goals. There are many supports that teachers can use to help students. These can include modeling, coaching, providing graphic organizers, peer tutoring, and reteaching.

Schemata—The organized patterns we use to make sense of the world. Schemata can direct our attention if new information fits into one of our organized patterns. Schemata organize our thinking and prepare us to learn new information.

Think-alouds—A strategy used by teachers and students to share their thinking as they solve a problem or interpret a text or argument. Teachers use this strategy to model successful thinking, whereas students share their thinking to receive feedback as they work toward learning goals.

Think-pair-share—A cooperative learning strategy that provides structure and time for individual student thinking while acknowledging that we all learn from others. Students begin by thinking about a teacher-presented topic or problem; they then share their thinking with a partner and later discuss these ideas with the entire class.

Units of instruction—A series of lessons designed to meet specific objectives for what students should know, understand, and be able to do at the end of the instruction. Units may be planned around a theme or topic or may encompass a particular set of skills. The unit plan provides students and teachers with an instructional roadmap.

Wait time—The amount of time between when a teacher poses a question and when students or a student are pressed for a response. There is some evidence that a longer wait time results in more expansive and deeper student comments.

References

Airasian, P. W. (2005). *Classroom assessment: Concepts and applications* (5th ed.). Boston, MA: McGraw-Hill.

Anderson, L. W. (1982). *Teachers, teaching, and educational effectiveness.* Columbia: University of South Carolina, College of Education.

Anderson, L. W., & Krathwohl, D. (Eds.). (2001). *A taxonomy for learning, teaching and assessing: A revision of Bloom's taxonomy of educational objectives.* New York, NY: Longman.

Archer, A. L., & Hughes, C. A. (2011). *Explicit instruction: Effective and efficient teaching.* New York, NY: Guilford.

Aronson, E., Blaney, N., Stephan, C., Sikes, J., & Snapes, M. (1978). *The jigsaw classroom.* Beverly Hills, CA: Sage.

Aronson, E., & Patnoe, S. (2011). *Cooperation in the classroom: The jigsaw model.* London, UK: Pinter & Martin.

Ausubel, D. (1960). The use of advance organizers in the learning and retention of meaningful verbal material. *Journal of Educational Psychology, 51,* 267–272.

Ausubel, D. (1968). *The psychology of meaningful verbal learning: An introduction to school learning.* New York, NY: Grune & Stratton.

Ausubel, P. D., Novak, J. D., & Hanesian, H. (1968). *Educational psychology: A cognitive view.* New York, NY: Holt, Rinehart, and Winston.

Ballou, S. (1861). Sullivan Ballou's letter to his wife. Retrieved March 3, 2014, from www.civil-war.net/pages/sullivan_ballou.asp

Bios, J. W. (1990). *Old Henry.* New York, NY: Harper Collins.

Black, P., Harrison, C., Lee, C., Marshall, B., & William, D. (2003). *Assessment for learning: Putting it into practice.* Maidenhead, UK: Open University.

Black, P. J., & Wiliam, D. (2009). Developing a theory of formative assessment. *Educational Assessment, Evaluation, and Accountability, 21*(1), 5–31.

Bloom, B. S. (Ed.). (1956). *Taxonomy of educational objectives: The classification of educational goals by a committee of college and university examiners.* New York, NY: Longmans, Green.

Bloom, B. S. (1983). *Human characteristics and school learning.* New York, NY: McGraw-Hill.

Blos, J. (1990) *Old henry.* NY; Harper Collins.

Blosser, P. E. (1991). Using cooperative learning in science education. *ERIC Clearinghouse for Science, Mathematics, and Environmental Education Bulletin.* Retrieved January 30, 2006, from www.stemworks.org/Bulletins/SEB92-1.html

Bransford, J. D., Brown, A. L., & Cocking, R. R. (2000). *How people learn: Brain, mind, experience, and school.* Washington, DC: The National Academies. (Available online free of charge from www.nap.edu)

Brighton, C. M. (2009). Embarking on action research. *Educational Leadership, 66*(5), 40–44.

Bronfenbrenner, U. (1979). *The ecology of human development: Experiments by nature and design.* Cambridge, MA: Harvard University.

Brookhart, S. M. (2008). *How to give effective feedback to your students.* Alexandria, VA: Association for Supervision and Curriculum Development.

Brookhart, S. M. (2013). *How to create and use rubrics for formative assessment and grading.* Alexandria, VA: ASCD.

Brophy, J. (2006). History of research on classroom management. In C. M. Evertson & C. S. Simon (Eds.), *Handbook of classroom management: Research, practice, and contemporary issues.* Mahwah, NJ: Erlbaum.

Bruner, J. S. (1961). Act of discovery. *Harvard Educational Review, 31*(1), 21–32.

Bruner, J. S., Goodnow, J. J., & Austin, G. A. (1986). *A study of thinking.* New Brunswick, NJ: Transaction.

Burress, L. (1989) *Battle of the books: Literary censorship in the public schools, 1950–1985.* Metuchen, NJ: Scarecrow.

Bybee, R. W. (2009). The BSCE 5E Instructional Model and 21st Century Skills. National Academy Board on Science Education. Retrieved May 1, 2014, from http://itsisu.concord.org/share/Bybee_21st_Century_Paper.pdf

Bybee, R., Taylor, J. A., Gardner, A., Van Scotter, P., Carlson, J., Westbrook, A., & Landes, N. (2006). *The BSCS 5E instructional model: Origins, effectiveness, and applications.* Colorado Springs, CO: BSCS.

Caine, R. N., & Caine, G. (1994). *Making connections: Teaching and the human brain.* Menlo Park, CA: Addison-Wesley.

Caine, R. N., Caine, G., McClintic, C., & Klimek, K. (2009). *12 brain/mind learning principles in action* (2nd ed.). Thousand Oaks, CA: Corwin.

Cohen, S. A. (1987). Instructional alignment: Searching for a magic bullet. *Educational Researcher, 16*(8), 16–20.

Darling-Hammond, L., & Richardson, N. (2009). Teacher learning. *Educational Leadership, 66*(5), 46–52.

Dean, C. B., Hubbell, E. R., Pitler, H., & Stone, B. J. (2012). *Classroom instruction that works: Research based strategies for increasing student achievement* (2nd ed.). Alexandria, VA: Association for Supervision and Curriculum Development.

Dinsmore, D. L., Alexander, P. A., & Loughlin, S. M. (2008). Focusing the conceptual lens on metacognition, self-regulation, and self-regulated learning. *Educational Psychology Review, 20,* 391–409.

Donovan, M. S., & Bransford, J. D. (Eds.). (2005). *How students learn history, mathematics, and science in the classroom.* Washington, DC: The National Academies.

Duckworth, E. (2006). *The having of wonderful ideas: And other essays on teaching and learning.* New York, NY: Teachers College.

Dweck, C. (2007). *Mindset; The new psychology of success.* New York, NY: Ballantine.

Educational Broadcasting Company. (2004). Workshop: Inquiry-based learning. Retrieved February 17, 2014, from www.thirteen.org/edonline/concept2class/inquiry

Eggen, P., & Kauchak, D. (2012). *Strategies and models for teachers: Teaching content and thinking skills.* Boston, MA: Pearson.

Elias, M. J. (2005). *Social decision making/social problem solving for middle school students: Skills and activities for academic, social, and emotional success.* Champaign, IL: Research.

Erickson, H. L., & Lanning, L.A. (2014). *Transitioning to concept-based curriculum and instruction: How to bring content and process together.* Thousand Oaks, CA: Corwin.

Erickson, L. H. (2007). *Stirring the head, heart, and soul: Redefining curriculum, instruction, and concept based learning* (3rd ed.). Thousand Oaks, CA: Corwin.

Faughnan, K. (2009). Get smart about skills for tomorrow's jobs. ZDNet News and Blogs. Retrieved January 12, 2010, from www.zdnet.com/2100-9595_22-258867.html

Findell, C. R. (2009). What differentiates expert teachers from others? *Journal of Education,* 11–23. Retrieved March 3, 2014, from www.bu.edu/journalofeducation/files/2011/06/BUJOE-188.2Findell.pdf

Fischer, C. (2008). *The Socratic method.* Great Neck, NY: Great Neck.

Fisher, D., & Frey, N. (2008). *Better learning through structured teaching: A framework for the gradual release of responsibility.* Alexandria, VA: Association for Supervision and Curriculum Development.

Frey, N., Fisher, D., & Everlove, S. (2009). *Productive group work: How to engage students, build teamwork and promote understanding.* Alexandria, VA: Association for Supervision and Curriculum Development.

Fulghum, R. (1989). *It was on fire when I lay down on it.* New York, NY: Villard Books.

Gallaher, S. (2013). *Concept development: A Hilda Taba teaching strategy.* Unionville, NY: Royal Fireworks.

Gardner, H. (2006). *Multiple intelligences: New horizons in theory and practice.* New York, NY: Basic Books.

Gladwell, M. (2008). *Outliers: The story of success.* New York, NY: Little, Brown.

Goleman, D. (2013). *Focus: The hidden driver of excellence.* New York, NY: HarperCollins.

Gonzalez-Barrera, A., & Lopez, M. H. (2013, August 13). Spanish is the most spoken non-English language in U.S. homes, even among non-Hispanics; Retrieved February 17, 2014, from www.pewresearch.org/fact-tank/2013/08/13/spanish-is-the-most-spoken-non-english-language-in-u-s-homes-even-among-non-hispanics

Good, T. L. (1981). Teacher expectations and student perceptions: A decade of research. *Educational Leadership, 38,* 415–422.

Good, T. L., & Brophy, J. E. (2007). *Looking in classrooms* (10th ed.). Reading, MA: Addison-Wesley.

Gordon, W. J. J. (1961). *Synectics: The development of creative capacity.* New York, NY: Harper & Brothers.

Gove, P. B. (Ed.). (2002). *Webster's third international dictionary* (unabridged ed.). Springfield, MA: Merriam-Webster.

Gronlund, N. E., & Brookhart, S. M. (2008). *Gronlund's writing instructional objectives* (8th ed.). Upper Saddle River, NJ: Prentice Hall.

Hattie, J. (2012). *Visible learning for teachers: Maximizing impact on learning.* New York, NY: Routledge.

Hattie, J., & Yates, G. C. R. (2014). *Visible learning and the science of how we learn.* New York, NY: Routledge.

Haviland, S. E., & Clark, H. H. (1974). What's new? Acquiring new information as a process in comprehension. *Journal of Verbal Learning and Verbal Behavior, 13,* 512–521.

Hilton, M. (2014, March). How social-emotional learning and development of 21st century competencies support academic achievement. *The State Education Standard,* 49–53.

Huebner, T. (2009). What research says about the continuum of teacher learning. *Educational Leadership, 66*(5), 88–91.

Johnson, D. W., & Johnson, R. T. (1995). *Creative controversy: Intellectual challenge in the classroom.* Edina, MN: Interaction Book.

Johnson, D. W., Johnson, R. T., & Holubec, E. J. (1994). *The new circles of learning: Cooperation in the classroom and school.* Alexandria, VA: Association for Supervision and Curriculum Development.

Johnson, D. W., Johnson, R. T., & Stanne, M. B. (2000). *Cooperative learning methods: A meta-analysis.* Retrieved May 5, 2014, from www.lcps.org/cms/lib4/VA01000195/Centricity/Domain/124/Cooperative%20Learning%20Methods%20A%20Meta-Analysis.pdf

Joyce, B., Calhoun, E, & Hopkins, D. (2009). *Models of learning: Tools for teaching.* New York, NY: Open University.

Joyce, B., Weil, M., & Calhoun, E. (2009). *Models of teaching* (8th ed.). Boston, MA: Pearson.

Kendall, J. S., & Marzano, R. J. (1997). *Content knowledge: A compendium of state standards and benchmarks for K–12 education* (2nd ed.). Aurora, CO: McRel.

Kingsolver, B. (2012). *Flight behavior.* New York, NY: Harper Collins.

Klausmeier, H. J. (1990). Conceptualizing. In B. F. Jones & L. Idol (Eds.), *Dimensions of thinking and cognitive instruction: Implications for educational reform* (pp. 93–138). Mahwah, NJ: Erlbaum.

Knowles, J. (1960). *A separate peace.* New York, NY: Macmillan.

Lasley, T. J. (1981). Research perspectives on classroom management. *Journal of Teacher Education, 32*(2), 14–17.

Lemov, D. (2010) *Teach like a champion: 49 techniques that put students on the path to college.* San Francisco, CA: Jossey-Bass.

Lorayne, H., & Lucas, J. (1986). *The memory book: The classic guide to improving your memory at work, at school, and at play.* New York, NY: Ballantine Books.

Lyman, F. (1981). The Responsive Classroom Discussion: The Inclusion of All Students. *Mainstreaming Digest.* University of Maryland, College Park, MD.

Lyon, G. E. *Cecil's story.* NY: Scholastic Books.

Marzano, R. J. (2001). *A handbook for classroom instruction that works.* Alexandria, VA: Association for Supervision and Curriculum Development.

Marzano, R. J. (2003). *What works in schools? Translating research into action.* Alexandria, VA: Association for Supervision and Curriculum Development.

Marzano, R. J. (2004). *Building background knowledge for academic achievement.* Alexandria, VA: Association for Supervision and Curriculum Development.

Marzano, R. J. (2007). *The art and science of teaching: A comprehensive framework for effective instruction.* Alexandria, VA: Association for Supervision and Curriculum Development.

Marzano, R.J. (2009). *Designing and teaching learning goals and objectives: Classroom strategies that work.* Bloomington, IN: Marzano Research Laboratory.

Marzano, R. J., & Pickering, D. J. (2005). *Building academic vocabulary: Teacher's manual.* Alexandria, VA: Association for Supervision and Curriculum Development.

Marzano, R. J., Pickering, D. J., & Pollock, J. E. (2001). *Classroom instruction that works: Research based strategies for increasing student achievement.* Alexandria, VA: Association for Supervision and Curriculum Development.

Maxwell, C. J., Jr. (n.d.) Introduction to the Socratic method and its effect on critical thinking; Retrieved March 3, 2014, from www.socraticmethod.net

McAuliffe, J. & Stoskin, L. (1993). *What color is saturday?: Using analogies to enhance creative thinking in the classroom.* Boston: Zepher Press.

Middendorf, J., & Kalish, A. (1996). The "change up" in lectures. *National Teaching and Learning Forum, 5*(2), 1–5.

National Board for Professional Teaching Standards. (n.d.). The five core propositions. Retrieved March 31, 2014, from www.nbpts.org/five-core-propositions

National Research Council. (2004). *Engaging schools: Fostering high school students' motivation to learn.* Washington, DC: The National Academies.

Noguera, P. A. (2008). *The trouble with black boys: . . . And other reflections on race, equity, and the future of public education.* San Francisco, CA: Jossey-Bass.

Ogle, D. M. (1986). K-W-L: A teaching model that develops active reading of expository text. *The Reading Teacher, 39,* 564–570.

Paul, R. (1993). *Critical thinking: How to prepare students for a rapidly changing world.* Santa Rosa, CA: Foundation for Critical Thinking.

Paul, R., & Elder, L. (2006). *The art of Socratic questioning.* Dillon Beach, CA: The Foundation for Critical Thinking.

Perkins, D. N., & Salomon, G. (1988). Teaching for transfer. *Educational Leadership, 46,* 22–31.

Piaget, J. (1954). *The construction of reality in the child.* New York, NY: Basic Books.

Pianta, R. C., Hamre, B. K., Haynes, N. J., Mintz, S. L., & LaParo, K. M. (2007). *CLASS: Classroom assessment scoring system manual, pilot.* Unpublished manuscript.

Pinker, S. (1994). *The language instinct: How the mind creates language.* New York, NY: HarperCollins.

Piper, W. (1930/1984). *The little engine that could.* New York, NY: Putnam.

Plato. (2000). *Meno* (B. Jowett, Trans.). (Original work written about 400 BCE). Retrieved July 3, 2009, from www.classicallibrary.org/plato/dialogues/10_meno.htm

Prince, G. M. (1970). *The practice of creativity: A manual for dynamic group problem solving.* New York, NY: Harper & Row.

Rosenshine, B. (1986). Synthesis of research on explicit teaching. *Educational Leadership, 43,* 60–69.

Rosenthal, R., & Jacobson, L. (1968). *Pygmalion in the classroom: Teacher expectation and pupils' intellectual development.* New York, NY: Holt, Rinehart & Winston.

Rothenberg, A. (1979). Einstein's creative thinking and the general theory of relativity: A documented report. *American Journal of Psychiatry, 136,* 39–40.

Schunk, D. H. (2004). *Learning theories: An educational perspective* (4th ed.). Upper Saddle River, NJ: Pearson Education.

Silver, H. F., Dewing, R. T., & Perini, M. J. (2012). *Inference: Teaching students to develop hypotheses, evaluate evidence, and draw logical conclusions.* Alexandria, VA: Association for Supervision and Curriculum Development.

Slavin, R. (1996). *Education for all.* Exton, PA: Swets & Zeitlinger.

Slavin, R. E. (2000). *Educational psychology: Theory and practice* (6th ed.). Boston, MA: Allyn & Bacon.

Sternberg, R. J., & Grigorenko, E. L. (2004). Successful intelligence in the classroom. *Theory into Practice, 43,* 274–280.

Stiggins, R. J. (2005). *Student-involved assessment for learning* (4th ed.). Upper Saddle River, NJ: Pearson/Merrill/Prentice Hall.

Stiggins, R. J. (2008). *An introduction to student-involved assessment for learning.* Upper Saddle River, NJ: Pearson.

Suchman, J. R. (1962). *The elementary school training program in scientific inquiry.* Report to the U.S. Office of Education, Project Title VII. Urbana: University of Illinois.

Taba, H. (1962). *Curriculum development: Theory and practice.* New York, NY: Harcourt College Publications.

Taba, H., Durkin, M. C., Fraenkel, J. R., & McNaughton, A. H. (1971). *Teachers' handbook to elementary social studies* (2nd ed.). Reading, MA: Addison-Wesley.

Thomas, L. (1982, March 14). The art of teaching science. Retrieved from www.nytimes.com/1982/03/14/magazine/the-art-of-teaching-science.html

Tomlinson, C. A. (2003). *Fulfilling the promise of the differentiated classroom: Strategies and tools for responsive teaching.* Alexandria, VA: Association for Supervision and Curriculum Development.

Tomlinson, C. A., & Edison, C. C. (2003). *Differentiation in practice: A resource guide for differentiating curriculum, grades 5–9.* Alexandria, VA: Association for Supervision and Curriculum Development.

Tomlinson, C. A., & Imbeau, M.B. (2010). *Leading and managing a differentiated classroom.* Alexandria, VA: Association for Supervision and Curriculum Development.

Tomlinson, C. A., & Javius, E. L. (2012, February). Teach up for excellence. *Educational Leadership, 28–33.*

Tough, P. (2012). *How children succeed: Grit, curiosity, and the hidden power of character.* Boston, MA: Houghton Mifflin Harcourt.

Trilling, B. & Fadel, C. (2012). *21st century skills: Learning for life in our times.* San Francisco, CA: Jossey-Bass.

Twain, M. (2001). *The war prayer.* New York, NY: Harper Collins. (Available online at http://warprayer.org)

Walker, J. (2009). Authoritative classroom management: How control and nurturance work together. *Theory into Practice, 48,* 122–129.

Weaver, W. T., & Prince, G. M. (1990). Synectics: Its potential for education. *Phi Delta Kappan, 72,* 378–388.

Webb, N. L. (2011). Identifying content for student achievement tests. In S. Lane, M. Raymond, T. M. Haladyna, & S. M. Downing (Eds.), *Handbook of Test Development* (pp. 156–180). New York, NY: Routledge.

Weinstein, C. S., & Novodvorsky, I. (2011). *Middle and secondary classroom management: Lessons from research and practice* (4th ed.). New York, NY: McGraw-Hill.

Weinstein, R. S. (2002). *Reaching higher: The power of expectations in schooling.* Cambridge, MA: Harvard University.

Wiggins, G., & McTighe, J. (2005). *Understanding by design* (expanded 2nd ed.). Alexandria, VA: Association for Supervision and Curriculum Development.

Wilder, L. I. (1940). *The long winter.* New York, NY: Harper Collins.

Willingham, D. T. (2009). *Why don't students like school? A cognitive scientist answers questions about how the mind works and what it means for the classroom.* San Francisco, CA: Jossey-Bass.

Wilson, D., & Conyers, M. (2013). *Five big ideas for effective teaching: Connecting mind, brain, and education research to classroom practice.* New York, NY: Teachers College.

Wilson, S. H., Greer, J. F., & Johnson, R. M. (1963). Synectics: A creative problem-solving technique for the gifted. *Gifted Child Quarterly, 17,* 260–266.

Wolk, S. (2002). *Being good: Rethinking classroom management and student discipline.* Portsmouth, NH: Heinemann.

Wormeli, R. (2004). *Summarization in any subject: 50 techniques to improve student learning.* Alexandria, VA: Association for Supervision and Curriculum Development.

Yinger, R. J. (1987). Learning the language of practice. *Curriculum Inquiry, 17,* 293–318.

Index

Academic controversy model, 179, 186, 192–197
Achievement
  academic, 3, 5, 26
  direct instruction model and, 65, 77–78
  student achievement, 11, 20, 32, 43, 54, 67–68, 200, 235, 275, 289
  student teams-achievement model and, 182, 186, 196–198, 203, 253
  synectics model and, 166
Active processing, 332
Advance organizers, 35
Airasian, P. W., 26
Alignment,
  assessment, 5, 291
  instructional, 3m 5m 17, 20, 29–31, 35, 163
Analogies, 136, 143, 148, 231–232, 235–253
Analyzing questions, 163–164
Anderson, L. W., 3, 21, 26–28, 163
Applying questions, 163–164
Aronson, E., 188, 192
Assessment, 9, 17, 19, 31–33, 44, 51–52, 104, 119, 150, 173, 200, 248
Assumption questions, 169
Austin, G. A., 62, 82
Ausubel, D., 5, 10, 45
Automaticity, 49–52, 57, 263

Backward design, 9, 17–19, 31, 37, 255–256, 281, 303
Black, P., 32
Bloom's taxonomy, 27–28, 226
  revised, 27–28, 54, 163, 165
Blosser, P. E., 184
Bransford, J. D., 6–7, 18, 100, 143, 162
Brainstorming 23, 86, 89–92, 186
Brookhart, S. M., 21, 200, 297
Bruner, J. S., 62, 82–84, 211

Caine, G., 7, 116, 294
Caine, R. N., 7, 116, 294
Calhoun, E., 62, 72, 82
Case studies
  high school, 278–288
  middle school, 266–277

Cause-and-effect model, 39, 95–110, 227, 246, 285
Chunking 8, 11, 14
Clark, H. H., 10
Clustering, 166
Cognitive behavior, 28
Cognitive skills, 26, 84
Common Core State Standards (CCSS), 8, 13, 28, 39, 100, 256, 258
Competition, 71, 297
Computer-aided design (CAD), 270–271
Concept attainment model, 39, 59–77, 83, 261, 270
Concept development model, 38–39, 78–94, 124, 133, 256, 264, 271, 283–285
Concept hierarchies, 64–65
Concepts, 6, 9, 12, 14, 18, 21–23, 25, 39, 62–65, 68–72, 75, 82–86, 89, 91, 93, 100, 116, 118–119, 123–124, 125, 129, 132, 142, 163, 183, 236–237, 261, 269, 283, 285
Conceptual knowledge, 6, 22, 23, 71
Conyers, M., 5
Cooperative learning models, 121, 135–136, 144, 179–204, 253, 282
Creating questions, 163, 165
Creativity, 235–236, 249, 252–253
Cubing, 152
Curriculum, 8–12, 17, 21, 29, 64, 84, 118, 123, 130, 143–144, 153, 168, 196, 217–218, 300

Debates, 162
Deductive instruction, 38, 46, 54, 63
Demonstrations, 23, 46
Diagnostic assessment, 44, 119
Dialogues, 160–162
Differentiation of instruction, 53, 71, 91, 105, 144, 153, 200, 226
Direct analogies, 237, 239, 242, 245–246, 248
Direct instruction model, 39, 40–58, 63, 263, 270
Discovery, 32, 205, 211
Discussions, 44, 99, 105, 135, 161, 163, 168, 173, 200–201, 214, 276

Donovan, M. S., 6
Duckworth, E., 294

Eggen, P. D., 142–144
Elder, L., 168–169, 178
Elias, M. J., 26
Erickson, L. H., 24–25
Essential attributes, of concepts, 39, 62–63, 65, 68–70, 72, 75, 261
Evaluating questions, 163–164
Expectations, 38, 171, 288, 291, 294, 296, 300, 303

Facts, 6, 10–11, 21–26, 62, 99, 123, 130, 142, 144, 242, 301
Fantasy analogies, in synectics model, 245
Faughnan, K., 201
Feedback, 7, 14, 20, 32, 43, 46–51, 54, 57, 100, 161–162, 173, 185–186, 199, 210, 219, 223, 248, 256, 263, 270, 281, 289, 294–295, 297
Flexible grouping, 53, 105
Flow charts, 102, 104
Focus, 11–12, 21, 23, 245–246
Formative assessment, 7, 14–15, 31–33, 51, 69–70, 173, 246, 300
Fulghum, R., 7

Gallagher, S., 83–84, 86
Gardner, H., 4
Generalizations , 6, 10, 21–25, 28, 35, 37–39, 62–63, 84–91, 99–100, 103, 105, 110, 135, 142–144, 147–148, 150, 153, 187, 203, 253
Generating and testing hypotheses, 39, 66–67, 72, 121, 222
Gladwell, M., 289
Gonzalez-Barrera, A., 8
Good, T. L., 248
Goodnow, J. J., 62, 82
Gradual release of responsibility, 38, 39, 47, 196, 270, 282
Graffiti model, 179, 181–182, 186–189, 203, 264
Graphic organizers, 23, 45, 51, 71, 102, 104–105, 122, 148, 188, 192, 248–249
Grigorenko, E. L., 105